GOLDEN AGE OF MARVEL® Originally published in magazine form. Published by MARVEL COMICS; 387 PARK AVENUE SOUTH, NEW YORK, N.Y. 10016. Copyright © 1939, 1940, 1941, 1942, 1943, 1944, 1951, 1952, 1953, 1954, 1955, 1957, 1997 Marvel Characters, Inc. All rights reserved. All prominent characters featured in this issue and the distinctive likenesses thereof are trademarks of MARVEL CHARACTERS, INC. No part of this book may be printed or reproduced in any manner without the written permission of the publisher. Printed in the U.S.A. First Printing, October, 1997. ISBN #0-7851-0564-6. GST #R127032852.

10 9 8 7 6 5 4 3 2 1

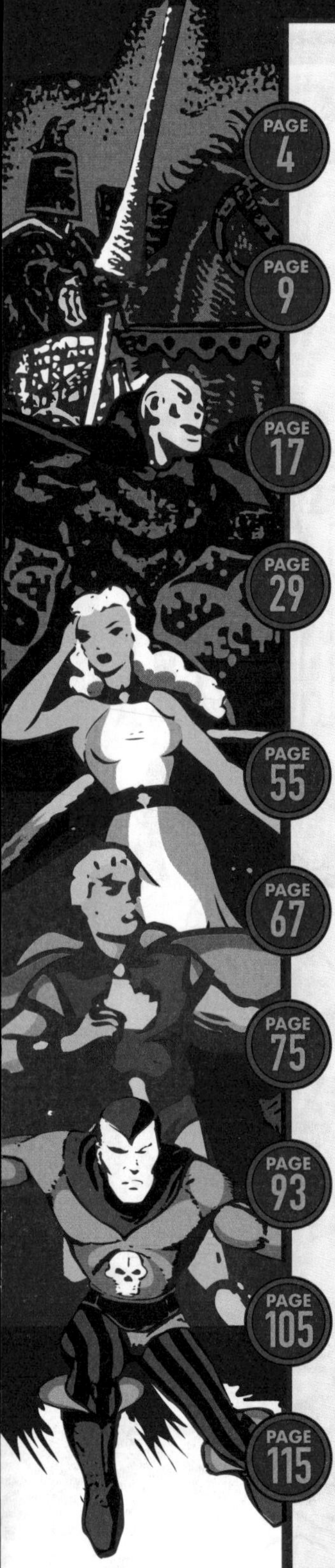

☆ ☆ ☆ **TABLE of**

Consultants
ROY THOMAS
GIL KANE
JOHN ROMITA

Art Reconstruction
DARREN AUCK & MIKE HIGGINS

Color Reconstruction
STEVE MATTSSON

Cover Painting
RAY LAGO

CONTENTS ☆ ☆ ☆

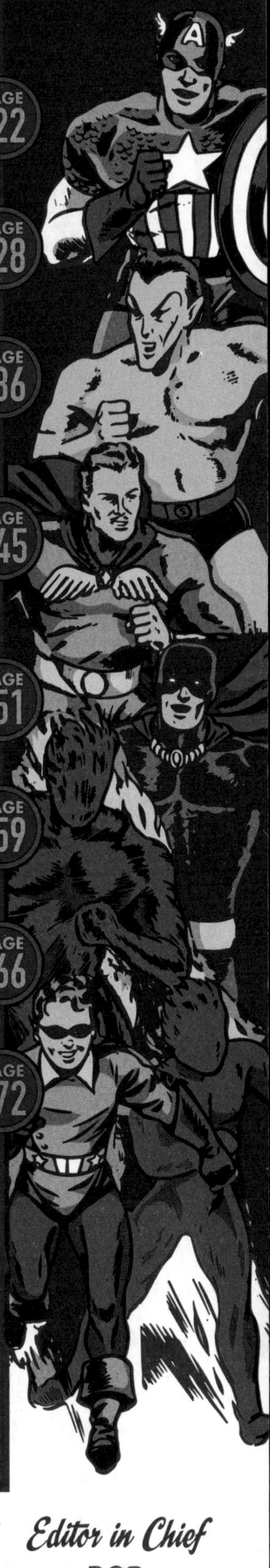

Note: AS IT WAS NOT CUSTOMARY DURING THE GOLDEN AGE OF COMICS TO LIST FULL CREDITS, THE CREATORS LISTED ABOVE IN MANY CASES REPRESENT A BEST GUESS, BASED ON THE EMPIRICAL EVIDENCE.

Book Design COMICRAFT'S JOHN ROSHELL
Editor TOM BREVOORT
Assistant Editor GLENN GREENBERG
Editorial Assistants PETE FRANCO & SARA RAINWATER
Editor in Chief BOB HARRAS

of MARVEL COMICS ☆ ☆ ☆

"MARVEL'S MOST TIMELY HEROES"

By ROY THOMAS

BEFORE MARVEL was Marvel— it was Timely.

Martin Goodman's comic book empire was founded in mid-1939, even as Nazi Germany was poised to make a stab at a European empire of a far more sinister kind— and only a year after Superman had leaped his first tall building, ushering in what is often called the Golden Age of Comics.

THE FIRST COMIC BOOK Goodman published was MARVEL COMICS #1, and it featured not one super-powered hero, but two— Carl Burgos' Human Torch and Bill Everett's Sub-Mariner. Not only that— it was partly a reprint!

The first eight pages of Prince Namor's origin had seen print earlier that year in a black-and-white movie theatre giveaway called *Motion Picture Funnies Weekly* #1. This promotional comic was packaged by Funnies, Inc., whose founder Lloyd Jacquet had persuaded Everett and Burgos to join him after brief stints writing and drawing for the Centaur Comics Group.

10¢
MARVEL
OCT.
COMICS
This Month
"THE HUMAN TORCH"
"THE ANGEL"
"SUBMARINER"
"MASKED RAIDER"
ACTION MYSTERY ADVENTURE

Funnies, Inc. supplied Goodman with the entire contents for a first issue, including cowboy and jungle strips; a pulp-magazine type hero called The Angel (shades of Leslie Charteris' The Saint!); Everett's Sub-Mariner (with four new pages tacked onto the original eight); and Burgos' torch-powered android, who really wasn't "human" at all. (The four extra Namor pages can be seen in the 1990 hardcover reprint of MARVEL COMICS #1; this volume reproduces the 8-page version, first printed in color in THE INVADERS #20 in 1977.)

Since Goodman had been publishing a pulp magazine called MARVEL SCIENCE STORIES since '38, his first comic book was christened MARVEL COMICS. (With #2 the title was changed to MARVEL MYSTERY COMICS, with "MYSTERY" typeset very small, for reasons no one has ever ventured to guess.)

MARVEL #1 contained the germ of a natural fire-and-water rivalry which soon catapulted Timely to prominence in the brave new world of comic books. By MARVEL MYSTERY #8 (June 1940),

Everett and Burgos— perhaps on their own, perhaps spurred by Goodman or his new in-house editor, writer/artist Joe Simon—ratcheted that rivalry up a notch by having the Torch and Sub-Mariner meet—and fight, since Namor was as much a villain as a hero in those days. Their pair of stories in #8 related basically the same events, each from its own hero's point of view, with Everett doing the Namor figures in the Torch story, and Burgos drawing the Torch in the Sub-Mariner tale. (This volume includes the Torch episode; Namor's version of things was reprinted in MARVEL SUPER-HEROES #1 in 1966, in case you want to check it out in back issues.)

The few panels of fire-vs.-water battle in #8 made everyone concerned realize they had a good thing going, so MARVEL MYSTERY #9 was devoted to a 22-page Torch/Namor slugfest—with a special one-page wrap-up that even carried over into #10!

BEFORE LONG, EACH OF OUR flame-and-fathom duo had his own quarterly title—with the Torch acquiring a teenage sidekick named Toro in HUMAN TORCH COMICS #1, and the Sub-Mariner forced to share his own mag with The Angel in a two-stories-to-one ratio. The most famous Torch/Namor bout was the classic HUMAN TORCH COMICS #5, an entire 64-page issue devoted

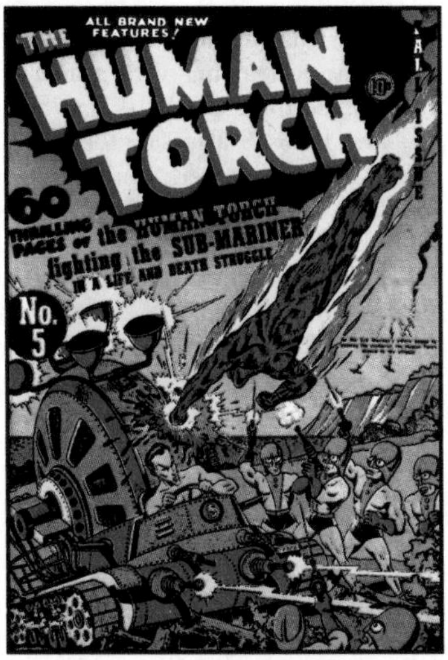
ALL BRAND NEW FEATURES!
THE HUMAN TORCH
10¢
60 THRILLING PAGES of the HUMAN TORCH fighting the SUB-MARINER IN A LIFE AND DEATH STRUGGLE
No. 5

to a deluded Sub-Mariner trying to destroy the surface world, with the Torch and several lesser heroes allied to stop him.

But, as a real World War loomed ever nearer to America's shores, Timely's two greatest stars were inevitably drawn together to combat a common enemy— the Axis powers. Their first team-up occurred in MARVEL MYSTERY #17. (Most of that March 1941 epic was showcased in THE INVADERS #24 in 1978; but its full 26 pages are reprinted here for the first time ever.)

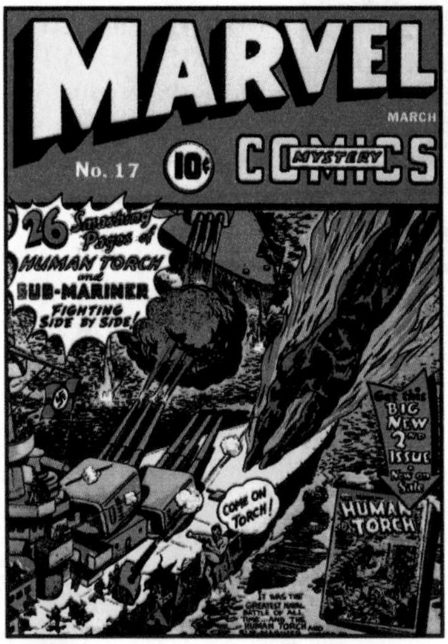
MARVEL
MARCH
No. 17
10¢
MYSTERY COMICS
26 Smashing Pages of HUMAN TORCH and SUB-MARINER FIGHTING SIDE BY SIDE!
COME ON TORCH!
HUMAN TORCH

STILL, DESPITE THEIR HEAD start, Namor and the Torch weren't destined to be the most popular Timely super heroes of the 1940s. That honor belonged to Captain America, conceived by Joe Simon and Jack Kirby. Though he wasn't quite the first stalwart in a red-white-and-blue costume to embody America's need for a living symbol, the monthly CAPTAIN AMERICA COMICS, debuting with a March '41 cover date, quickly left all competitors in its wake. (One Simon-and-Kirby classic, "Horror Plays the Scales," from #7 [Oct. 1941], appears herein, but the entire ten-issue S&K run was beautifully reproduced in the early 90s in a hardcover edition which no Golden Age fan should be without.)

Actually, Namor appeared in more stories in the '40s and '50s than any other Timely hero (292, to

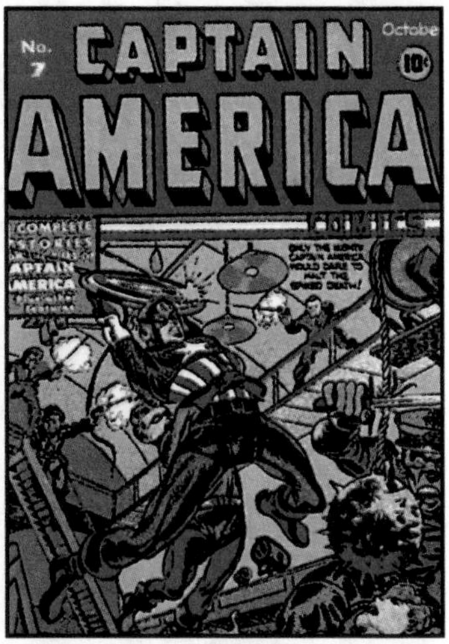
No. 7
CAPTAIN AMERICA
October
10¢

be exact), and even the Torch (with 280 outings) starred in three more vintage tales than Cap did. Yet beyond a doubt Captain America was the company's pacesetter, spawning more imitators than any hero but Superman himself. Timely itself introduced such Cap clones as The Patriot, The Defender, Major Liberty, American Avenger, Miss America, and others in titles like USA COMICS, MYSTIC COMICS, and DARING MYSTERY COMICS, but none of them could touch Cap's appeal. Nor did such Timely heroes as The Challenger, Black Marvel, The Fin, or Blazing Skull ever quite catch fire.

By the time Joe and Jack departed Timely for greener pastures in late '41, they left behind a couple of other legacies, as well—YOUNG ALLIES, co-starring Toro and Cap's young friend Bucky—and The Vision.

The Vision, a.k.a. Aarkus, Destroyer of Evil, debuted in MARVEL MYSTERY #13 (Nov. 1941) as an eerie, green-skinned alien who needs only a puff of smoke to cross from his dimension to ours. (This volume features Simon and Kirby's Vision story from #25, first reprinted in MARVEL SUPER-HEROES #13, 1968.)

WITH SIMON AND KIRBY'S departure, the editorship fell to 18-year-old Stan Lee, who'd started at Timely a year before as a general gofer. Stan inherited the mantle not long before Japan's attack on Pearl Harbor on December 7, 1941.

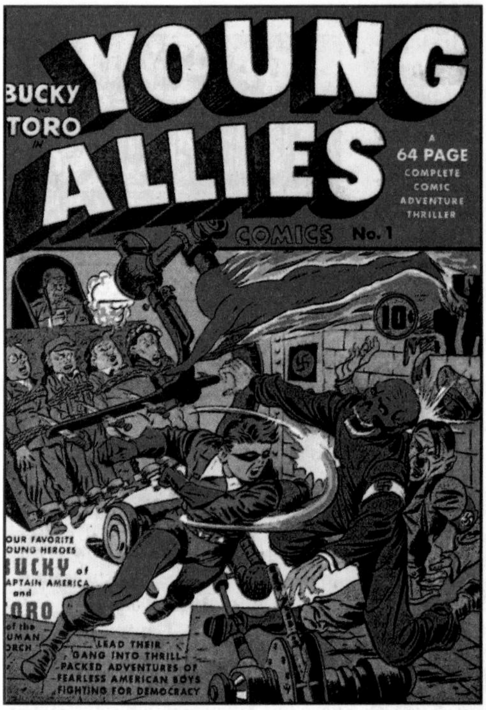

BUCKY AND TORO IN
YOUNG ALLIES
A 64 PAGE COMPLETE COMIC ADVENTURE THRILLER
COMICS No. 1
10¢
LEAD THEIR GANG INTO THRILL-PACKED ADVENTURES OF FEARLESS AMERICAN BOYS FIGHTING FOR DEMOCRACY

Actually, most Timely heroes had been fighting the Nazis since 1940, but now the gloves were off, and Cap, Torch, and Namor were the triple spearhead of some of the most virulently anti-Axis comics of the War period. If the Japanese, and even the Germans, were caricatured in a stereotyped fashion in some of these stories, it's lamentable, but these tales reflected, for better or worse, the American public's reaction to the horrors of war in general and to known Japanese atrocities in particular. To censor or pretty-up these stories for a later generation would be to falsify the past, something there's already been far too much of, so they've been reprinted just as they originally appeared.

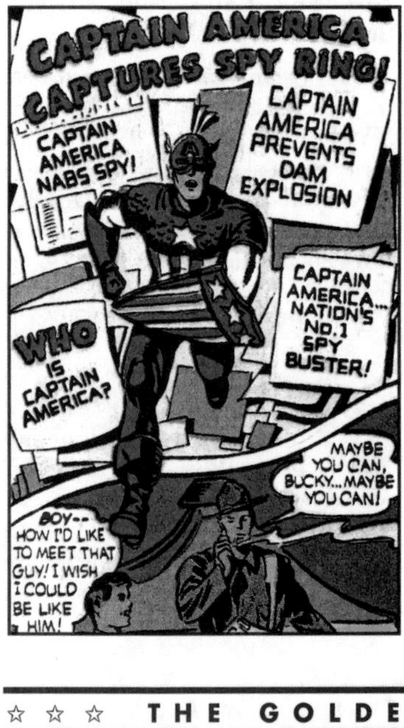

CAPTAIN AMERICA CAPTURES SPY RING!
CAPTAIN AMERICA NABS SPY!
CAPTAIN AMERICA PREVENTS DAM EXPLOSION
CAPTAIN AMERICA... NATION'S NO.1 SPY BUSTER!
WHO IS CAPTAIN AMERICA?
MAYBE YOU CAN, BUCKY... MAYBE YOU CAN!
BOY-- HOW I'D LIKE TO MEET THAT GUY! I WISH I COULD BE LIKE HIM!

First Al Avison, then Syd Shores became the primary post-Simon-and-Kirby artists of Captain America, who soon appeared also in ALL-WINNERS COMICS and ALL-SELECT COMICS (in both of which he shared cover space with Namor and the Torch) and in USA COMICS. This volume reprints a vintage Shores-drawn tale, "The Cobra Ring of Death," from CAPTAIN AMERICA COMICS #22 (Jan. '43). Alas, because few stories in those days carried credits, we can rarely be 100% certain who drew (let alone wrote) 1940s Timelys. It's often stated that many war-era stories were scripted by Mickey Spillane, who would go on to postwar superstardom as the creator of Mike Hammer, but we can rarely be sure who wrote what.

When Bill Everett joined the army in 1942, his major successor as Sub-Mariner artist was Carl Pfeufer. Pfeufer soon evolved Namor's musculature and vaguely triangular head to almost grotesque proportions, but basically filled Bill's shoes admirably. (This book spotlights "Terror of the Boiling Seas" from MARVEL MYSTERY #42, April 1943.)

The Angel, after a strong start, had sunk to lesser status by the time "Quarantine for Murder" appeared in that same 42nd issue of MARVEL MYSTERY. Oddly, this story features a credit "by Garn and Schrotter"— writer Ron Garn and artist Gustav (Gus) Schrotter—one of the few instances in which a writer besides Stan Lee signed a story.

Speaking of Stan, he'd been creating minor heroes since mid-41: Father Time in CAPTAIN AMERICA, Jack Frost in USA COMICS, and (just maybe) even the infamous Whizzer, he of the super-speed gained by an infusion of mongoose blood. Stan's most popular super hero creation before the Fantastic Four was The Destroyer, debuting in MYSTIC COMICS #6 (Oct. 1941). But by '44 Stan was in the army writing training films, so it's unlikely he wrote the Destroyer story included in this collection, "The Beachhead Blitz," from ALL-WINNERS #12, Spring '44 (first reprinted in 1967's MARVEL SUPER-HEROES #12.)

By the time this adventure appeared, the long-delayed European Second Front it predicts was only weeks away. On June 6, 1944, American and British forces landed in France, and though nearly a year of hard fighting still lay ahead, World War Two entered its final phase in Europe, while the war with Japan was ended in a mushroom cloud in August 1945.

The Golden Age of Timely Comics (which briefly went by the name Marvel Comics circa 1947) was slowly winding down as well, as super hero titles began to drop by the wayside. Not even two sterling 1946-47 issues of ALL-WINNERS (#19 and #21) featuring an All-Winners Squad in imitation of DC's popular *Justice Society of America* could keep the readers' interest.

Other types of comics were gaining favor. Funny animals predominated first, starting with Timely's fence-straddling SUPER RABBIT in '44. 1945-48 also saw the emergence of girl-oriented titles such as PATSY WALKER and MILLIE THE MODEL—crime comics such as JUSTICE—westerns such as KID COLT and TWO-GUN KID—war comics such as WAR COMICS (what else?)—love comics such as MY ROMANCE and a zillion others.

In a further effort to woo female readers as a captive audience of young males was mustered out of the armed services, Timely introduced three short-lived titles starring super-women: SUN GIRL (the Torch's gal pal), NAMORA

(Subby's cousin, created by Bill Everett after his army discharge), and MISS AMERICA (which actually changed into a long-running teenage humor title with #2).

The first phase of Timely's Golden Age came to an end in 1949, when MARVEL MYSTERY COMICS metamorphosed into a horror title, MARVEL TALES, and Cap, Namor, and the Torch all vanished into temporary oblivion.

EVEN SO, THE VERY NEXT YEAR, Timely inaugurated a new, science-fictional super-hero in MARVEL BOY #1 (Dec. 1950), with art by Russ Heath. Bob Grayson was an American youth who acquired super-powers on the planet Uranus. After two issues the mag's name was changed to ASTONISHING, but Marvel Boy stuck around for four more increasingly horror-oriented issues, with art and story by Bill Everett, who combined alien invaders and communists in a truly odd melange. Still, the climate wasn't right for super heroes of any stripe, so this volume's "The Deadly Decision," from ASTONISHING #5, was Marvel Boy's next-to-last appearance.

MARVEL BOY
10¢
DEC.
HERE HE IS... THE NEWEST, MOST AMAZING CHARACTER IN COMICS! MARVEL BOY... THE BOY FROM ANOTHER PLANET AT LAST IN HIS OWN MAGAZINE!
MARVEL BOY TRIES TO SAVE EARTH FROM THE MENACE OF THE LOST WORLD!

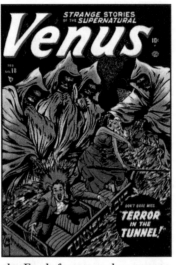

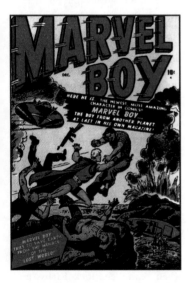

Not that of the ubiquitous Everett, though. He'd also taken over a romance-and-fantasy entry called VENUS which had debuted in '48. Under his aegis it evolved into a horror comic, with the Roman goddess of love doing double duty as a freelance guardian of

STRANGE STORIES OF THE SUPERNATURAL
Venus
10¢
FEB.
NO. 18
DON'T DARE MISS
TERROR IN THE TUNNEL!

the Earth from nameless terrors. This volume re-presents "Tidal Wave of Fear," from VENUS #18 (Feb. '52).

AT THIS POINT TELEVISION, OF all things, came to the rescue of floundering Timely, now better known as Atlas—actually the name of its self-owned distribution company. With *The Adventures of Superman* a smash hit on the small screen, Goodman decided perhaps it was time to revive his Big Three of the 1940s.

Thus, the 24th issue of a lackluster war-and-hot-rods comic called YOUNG MEN (Dec. 1953) cover-featured a Carl Burgos-drawn Human Torch hurling his patented fireballs, above insert illustrations of the "Submariner" [sic] and of Captain America and Bucky. YOUNG MEN #24 is an indisputably wonderful comic, so editor Tom Brevoort elected to reprint it in its entirety; it was earlier re-presented in MARVEL SUPER-HEROES #20 in 1969.

With exquisite artwork by Russ Heath (except for an inexplicable but fine splash panel drawn by Burgos), "The Return of the Human Torch" is a Cold War masterwork, explaining where the Torches have been for the preceding four years, even working in the war just ended in Korea. Its writer is undeservedly anonymous, but may well have been Stan Lee.

"Back from the Dead" turns Cap and Bucky likewise into "commie-smashers"—and the Red Skull, that ultimate Nazi, into a Russian spy! This story is even more likely to have been written by Stan, and was illustrated by a young John Romita in a style combining Jack Kirby and Milt ("Terry and the Pirates") Caniff—except for a splash page by Mort Lawrence, who, John believes, was originally intended to be the artist.

And writer/artist Bill Everett (who else?) brought Prince Namor back from the Antarctic to combat an invasion by robots from the planet (not the goddess) Venus.

Timely's rejuvenated heroes went on to appear in four more issues of YOUNG MEN, in MEN'S ADVENTURES #27-28, and in three issues each of HUMAN TORCH and CAPTAIN AMERICA. In YM #26 (March '54,

THE HUMAN TORCH RETURNS
YOUNG MEN
DEC.
10¢
NO. 24
ALL NEW STORIES!
LOOK! HE'S BACK FROM THE DEAD! IT'S THE HUMAN TORCH!
SUBMARINER AND CAPTAIN AMERICA ALSO IN THIS ISSUE
SUBMARINER
CAPTAIN AMERICA AND BUCKY

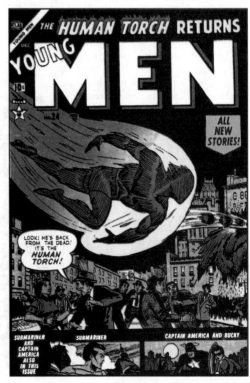

reprinted herein), Namor and the Torch even turned up in a Cap story, probably by Stan, who (artist Romita says) always had a special fondness for the future Star-Spangled Avenger.

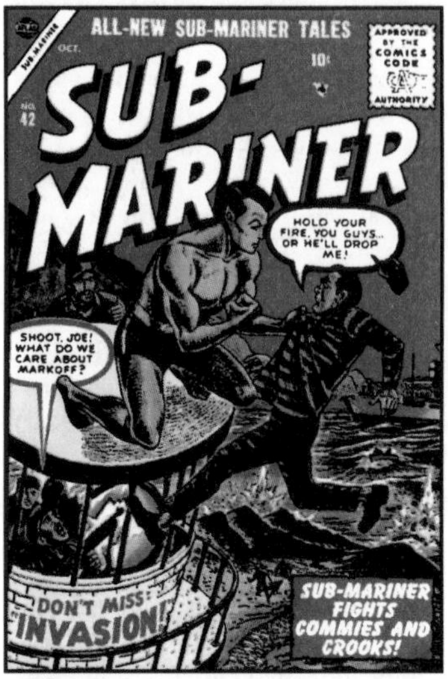
ALL-NEW SUB-MARINER TALES
OCT.
10¢
APPROVED BY THE COMICS CODE AUTHORITY
NO. 42
SUB-MARINER
HOLD YOUR FIRE, YOU GUYS... OR HE'LL DROP ME!
SHOOT, JOE! WHAT DO WE CARE ABOUT MARKOFF?
DON'T MISS: "INVASION!"
SUB-MARINER FIGHTS COMMIES AND CROOKS!

A REVIVED SUB-MARINER title lasted a full nine issues because some TV producers wanted to develop a Namor series, starring actor Richard Egan, to compete with Superman, as Everett revealed in a 1971 interview for this writer's fanzine *Alter Ego*. The TV series came to naught, and SUB-MARINER sank for a second time.

Thus, despite its promising beginning—and the fact that Everett in particular did perhaps the best work of his entire career this time around— the return of Timely's Big Three turned out to be a false spring. With the Oct. 1955 demise of SUB-MARINER, the super-hero was dead at the company which had been Timely Comics, until FANTASTIC FOUR #1 was born in 1961.

Dead? Well, perhaps not quite.

IN 1955, HAVING DISCONTINUED its "New Trend" horror comics amid a public outcry, the Entertaining Comics Group (EC) had introduced several "New Direction" titles to replace them. One of these, *Valor*, featured stories set in the 19th century and earlier, with a heavy reliance upon knights and Roman gladiators.

Timely was among several comics companies which opined that, since EC had initiated one trend, maybe it was onto another. Editor Stan Lee sat down and wrote at least the first issue of THE BLACK KNIGHT (May 1955), which combined aspects of the super hero, *Prince Valiant*, and *The Scarlet Pimpernel*. It was a laudable effort, combining exemplary writing with exciting art by Bullpen mainstay Joe Maneely. Stan must have been justly proud of the series, since he (as well as the artist) signed both stories in the first issue. Whether or not Stan wrote future issues no one remembers, least of all Stan himself.

However, EC and Timely were both wrong about young America's latent interest in things chivalric, and THE BLACK KNIGHT lasted only five issues. Still, Stan would remember the name and use it for a villain in the early days of 1960s Marvel. And the 1955 series made such a strong impression on the writer of this introduction that, soon after coming to Marvel in the mid-60s, I developed a modern-day heroic Black Knight whose origins sprang directly from Stan and Joe's Pendragonian paladin.

But the final Timely creation which would cast its long shadow into the looming Marvel Age of Comics was still to come.

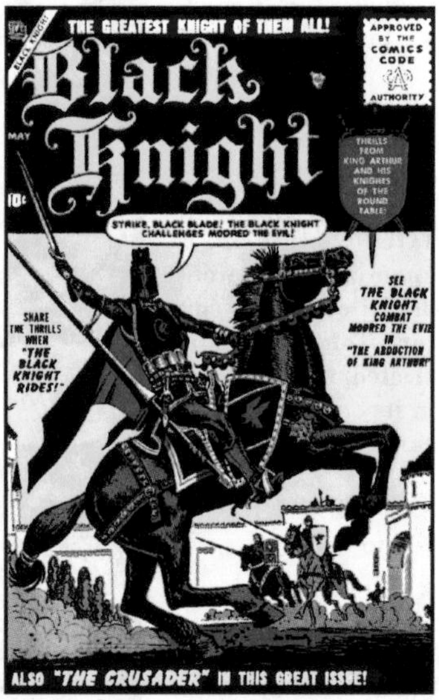
THE GREATEST KNIGHT OF THEM ALL!
APPROVED BY THE COMICS CODE AUTHORITY
MAY
Black Knight
10¢
THRILLS FROM KING ARTHUR AND HIS KNIGHTS OF THE ROUND TABLE!
STRIKE, BLACK BLADE! THE BLACK KNIGHT CHALLENGES MODRED THE EVIL!
SEE THE BLACK KNIGHT COMBAT MODRED THE EVIL IN "THE ABDUCTION OF KING ARTHUR!"
SHARE THE THRILLS WHEN "THE BLACK KNIGHT RIDES!"
ALSO "THE CRUSADER" IN THIS GREAT ISSUE!

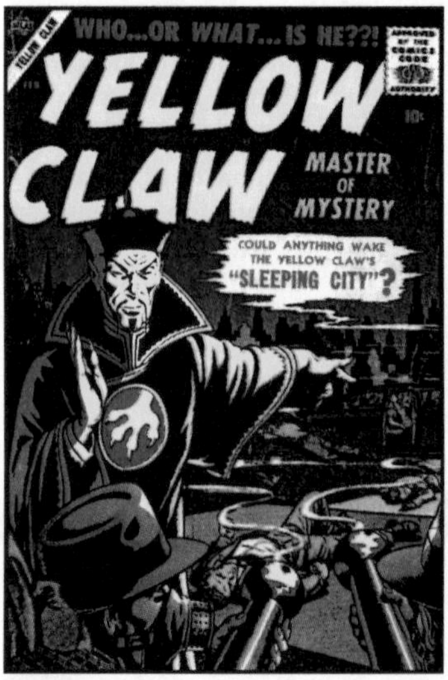
WHO...OR WHAT...IS HE??!
APPROVED BY THE COMICS CODE AUTHORITY
10¢
YELLOW CLAW
MASTER OF MYSTERY
COULD ANYTHING WAKE THE YELLOW CLAW'S "SLEEPING CITY"?

THE YELLOW CLAW, A FU Manchu-inspired creation which lasted just four issues in 1956-57, was blessed with art by Joe Maneely, John Severin, and the newly-returned Jack Kirby. But it suffered from a curse which had also crippled the 1950s incarnations of the Big Three and THE BLACK KNIGHT: the dictate that, in order to squeeze four or even five tales into each issue (and thus allegedly give the reader "his money's worth"), few stories could be longer than six or seven pages— and some were as short as four or five!

Jack Kirby breathed particular life into the comic when he drew (and is often credited with writing) three 5-page stories and one 4-pager for #3, from which this volume's "The Microscopic Army" is reprinted, but it was a doomed effort, even though the Yellow Claw would be heard from a decade later, in another comic book era.

For, only a few months after the end of YELLOW CLAW came Timely's own demise, due to a combination of market and business factors— so that Timely became a tiny stump of a company which would limp along from '57 through the early 60s, when Stan Lee, Jack Kirby, and others would follow the Golden Age of Timely/Marvel—with the unabashed Marvel Age of Comics!

ALL THINGS COME TO HIM WHO waits—including this glorious collection of Golden Age goodies!

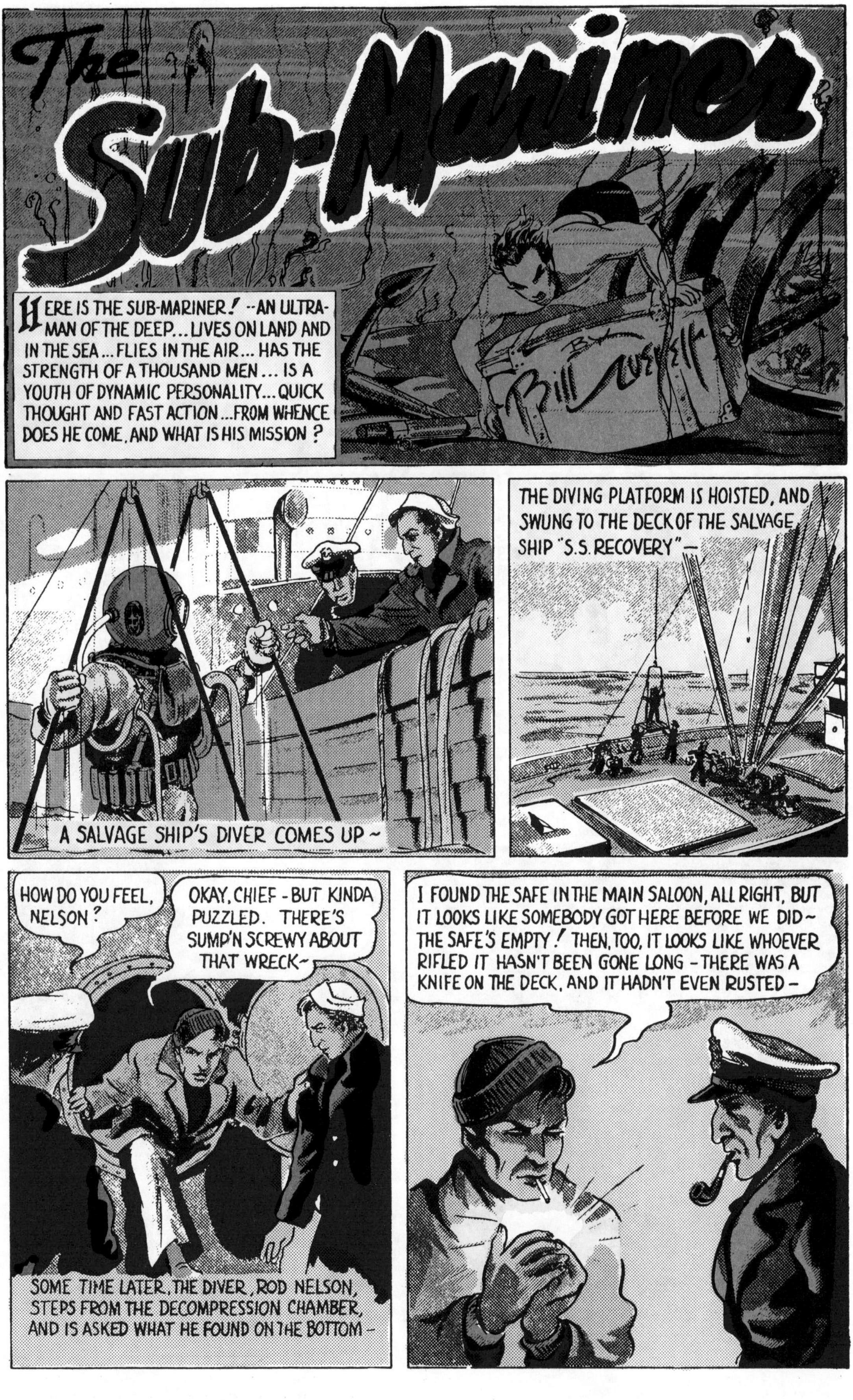
The Sub-Mariner
By Bill Everett
HERE IS THE SUB-MARINER! --AN ULTRA-MAN OF THE DEEP... LIVES ON LAND AND IN THE SEA... FLIES IN THE AIR... HAS THE STRENGTH OF A THOUSAND MEN... IS A YOUTH OF DYNAMIC PERSONALITY... QUICK THOUGHT AND FAST ACTION...FROM WHENCE DOES HE COME, AND WHAT IS HIS MISSION?
A SALVAGE SHIP'S DIVER COMES UP ~
THE DIVING PLATFORM IS HOISTED, AND SWUNG TO THE DECK OF THE SALVAGE SHIP "S.S. RECOVERY" —
HOW DO YOU FEEL, NELSON?
OKAY, CHIEF - BUT KINDA PUZZLED. THERE'S SUMP'N SCREWY ABOUT THAT WRECK~
SOME TIME LATER, THE DIVER, ROD NELSON, STEPS FROM THE DECOMPRESSION CHAMBER, AND IS ASKED WHAT HE FOUND ON THE BOTTOM -
I FOUND THE SAFE IN THE MAIN SALOON, ALL RIGHT, BUT IT LOOKS LIKE SOMEBODY GOT HERE BEFORE WE DID ~ THE SAFE'S EMPTY! THEN, TOO, IT LOOKS LIKE WHOEVER RIFLED IT HASN'T BEEN GONE LONG - THERE WAS A KNIFE ON THE DECK, AND IT HADN'T EVEN RUSTED -

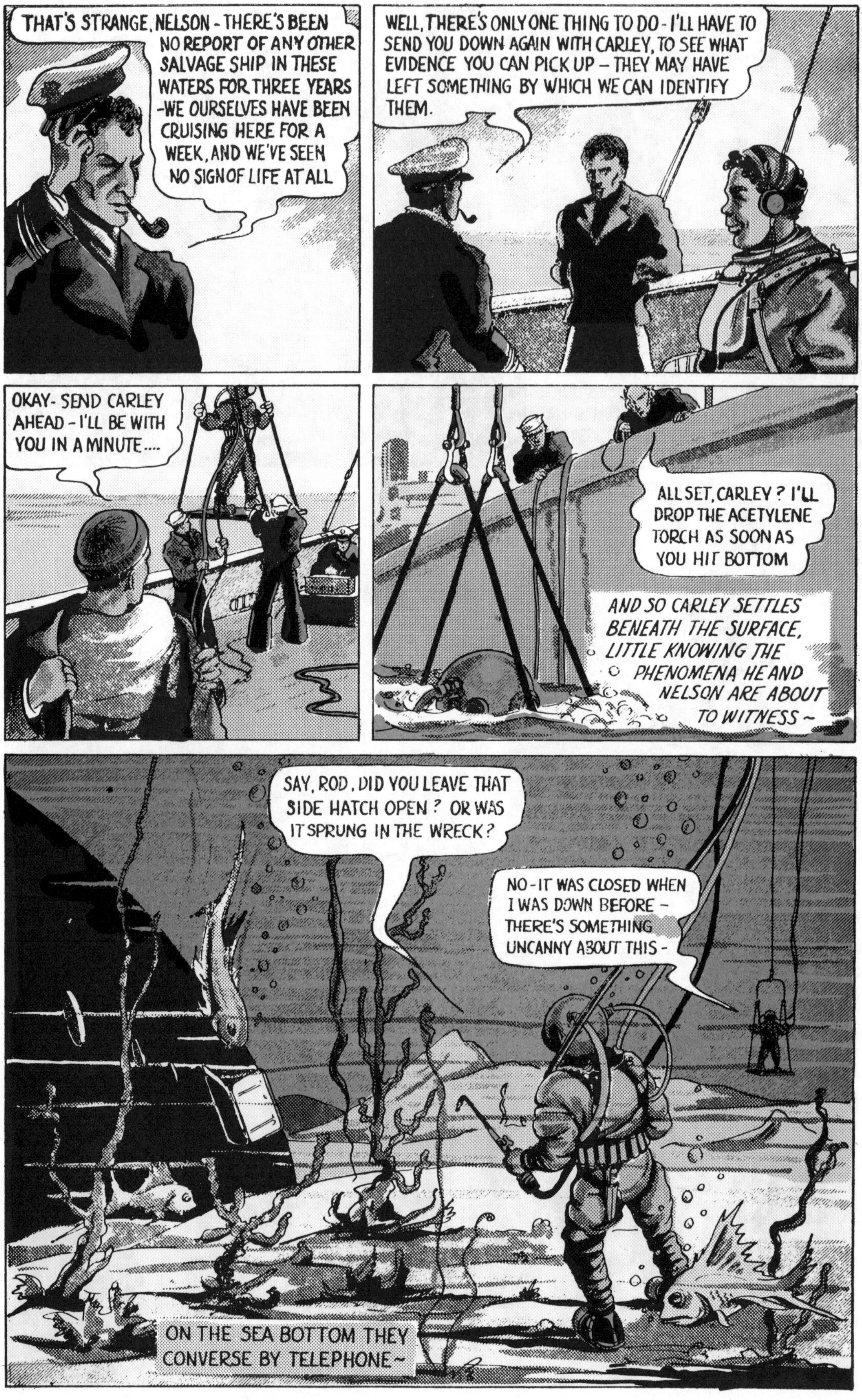
THAT'S STRANGE, NELSON - THERE'S BEEN NO REPORT OF ANY OTHER SALVAGE SHIP IN THESE WATERS FOR THREE YEARS -WE OURSELVES HAVE BEEN CRUISING HERE FOR A WEEK, AND WE'VE SEEN NO SIGN OF LIFE AT ALL
WELL, THERE'S ONLY ONE THING TO DO - I'LL HAVE TO SEND YOU DOWN AGAIN WITH CARLEY, TO SEE WHAT EVIDENCE YOU CAN PICK UP - THEY MAY HAVE LEFT SOMETHING BY WHICH WE CAN IDENTIFY THEM.
OKAY- SEND CARLEY AHEAD - I'LL BE WITH YOU IN A MINUTE....
ALL SET, CARLEY ? I'LL DROP THE ACETYLENE TORCH AS SOON AS YOU HIT BOTTOM
AND SO CARLEY SETTLES BENEATH THE SURFACE, LITTLE KNOWING THE PHENOMENA HE AND NELSON ARE ABOUT TO WITNESS ~
SAY, ROD, DID YOU LEAVE THAT SIDE HATCH OPEN ? OR WAS IT SPRUNG IN THE WRECK?
NO - IT WAS CLOSED WHEN I WAS DOWN BEFORE - THERE'S SOMETHING UNCANNY ABOUT THIS -
ON THE SEA BOTTOM THEY CONVERSE BY TELEPHONE ~

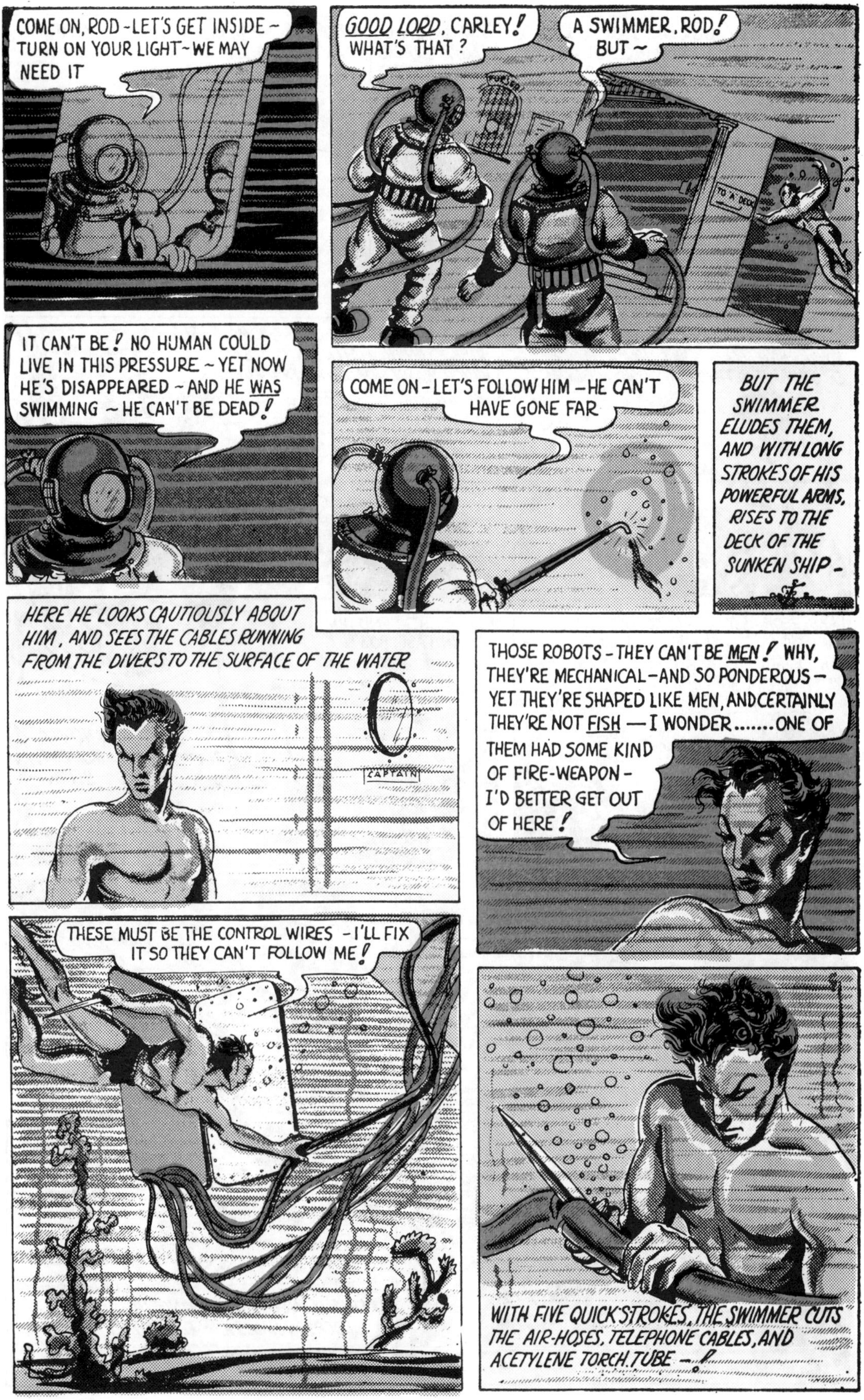
COME ON, ROD - LET'S GET INSIDE - TURN ON YOUR LIGHT - WE MAY NEED IT
GOOD LORD, CARLEY! WHAT'S THAT?
A SWIMMER, ROD! BUT ~
TO A DECK
IT CAN'T BE! NO HUMAN COULD LIVE IN THIS PRESSURE ~ YET NOW HE'S DISAPPEARED ~ AND HE WAS SWIMMING ~ HE CAN'T BE DEAD!
COME ON - LET'S FOLLOW HIM - HE CAN'T HAVE GONE FAR
BUT THE SWIMMER ELUDES THEM, AND WITH LONG STROKES OF HIS POWERFUL ARMS, RISES TO THE DECK OF THE SUNKEN SHIP -
HERE HE LOOKS CAUTIOUSLY ABOUT HIM, AND SEES THE CABLES RUNNING FROM THE DIVERS TO THE SURFACE OF THE WATER
CAPTAIN
THOSE ROBOTS - THEY CAN'T BE MEN! WHY, THEY'RE MECHANICAL - AND SO PONDEROUS - YET THEY'RE SHAPED LIKE MEN, AND CERTAINLY THEY'RE NOT FISH — I WONDER....... ONE OF THEM HAD SOME KIND OF FIRE-WEAPON - I'D BETTER GET OUT OF HERE!
THESE MUST BE THE CONTROL WIRES - I'LL FIX IT SO THEY CAN'T FOLLOW ME!
WITH FIVE QUICK STROKES, THE SWIMMER CUTS THE AIR-HOSES, TELEPHONE CABLES, AND ACETYLENE TORCH TUBE —!

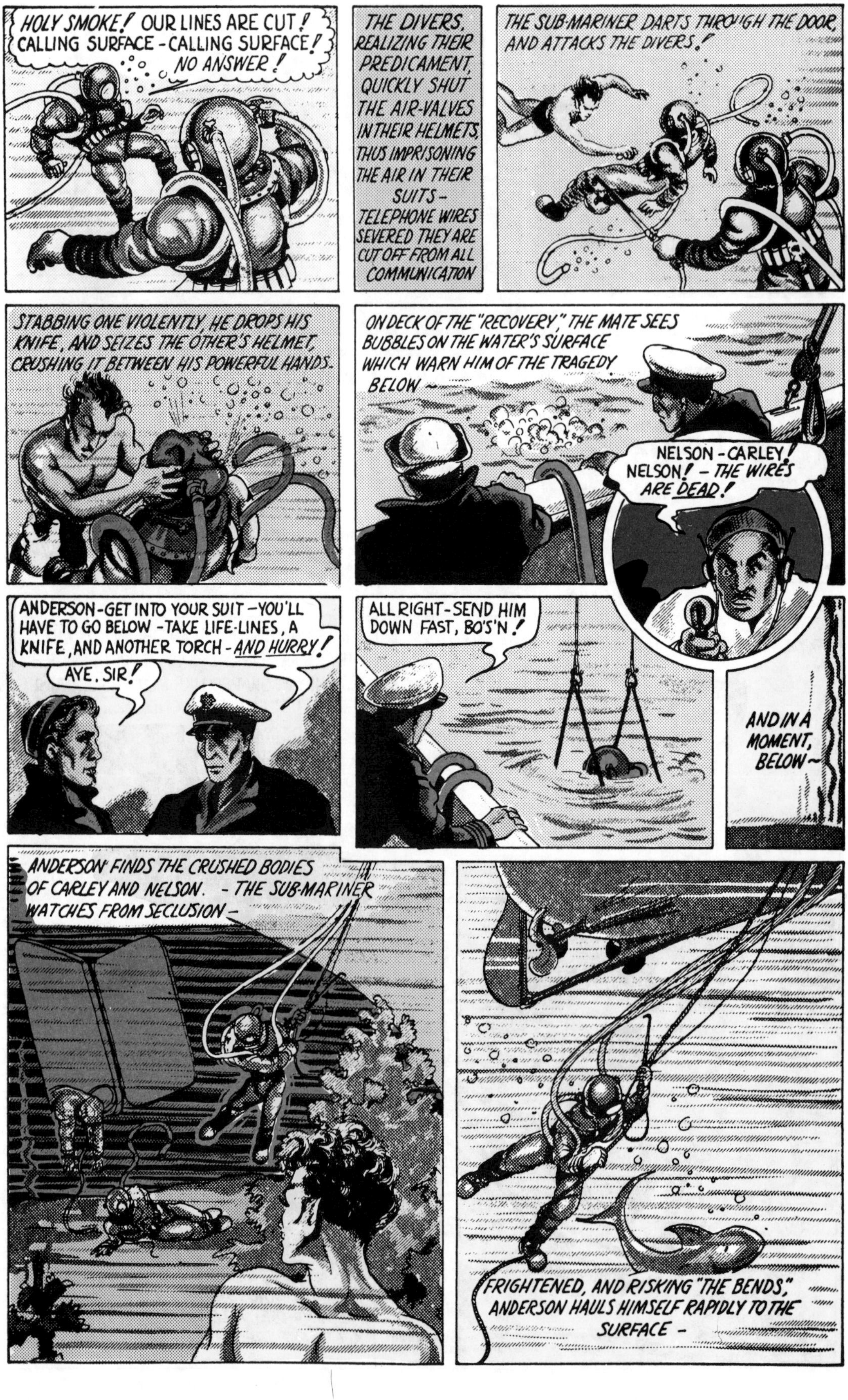
HOLY SMOKE! OUR LINES ARE CUT! CALLING SURFACE - CALLING SURFACE! NO ANSWER!
THE DIVERS, REALIZING THEIR PREDICAMENT, QUICKLY SHUT THE AIR-VALVES IN THEIR HELMETS, THUS IMPRISONING THE AIR IN THEIR SUITS - TELEPHONE WIRES SEVERED THEY ARE CUT OFF FROM ALL COMMUNICATION
THE SUB-MARINER DARTS THROUGH THE DOOR, AND ATTACKS THE DIVERS!
STABBING ONE VIOLENTLY, HE DROPS HIS KNIFE, AND SEIZES THE OTHER'S HELMET, CRUSHING IT BETWEEN HIS POWERFUL HANDS-
ON DECK OF THE "RECOVERY," THE MATE SEES BUBBLES ON THE WATER'S SURFACE WHICH WARN HIM OF THE TRAGEDY BELOW -
NELSON - CARLEY! NELSON! - THE WIRES ARE DEAD!
ANDERSON - GET INTO YOUR SUIT - YOU'LL HAVE TO GO BELOW - TAKE LIFE-LINES, A KNIFE, AND ANOTHER TORCH - AND HURRY!
AYE, SIR!
ALL RIGHT - SEND HIM DOWN FAST, BO'S'N!
AND IN A MOMENT, BELOW~
ANDERSON FINDS THE CRUSHED BODIES OF CARLEY AND NELSON. - THE SUB-MARINER WATCHES FROM SECLUSION -
FRIGHTENED, AND RISKING "THE BENDS," ANDERSON HAULS HIMSELF RAPIDLY TO THE SURFACE -

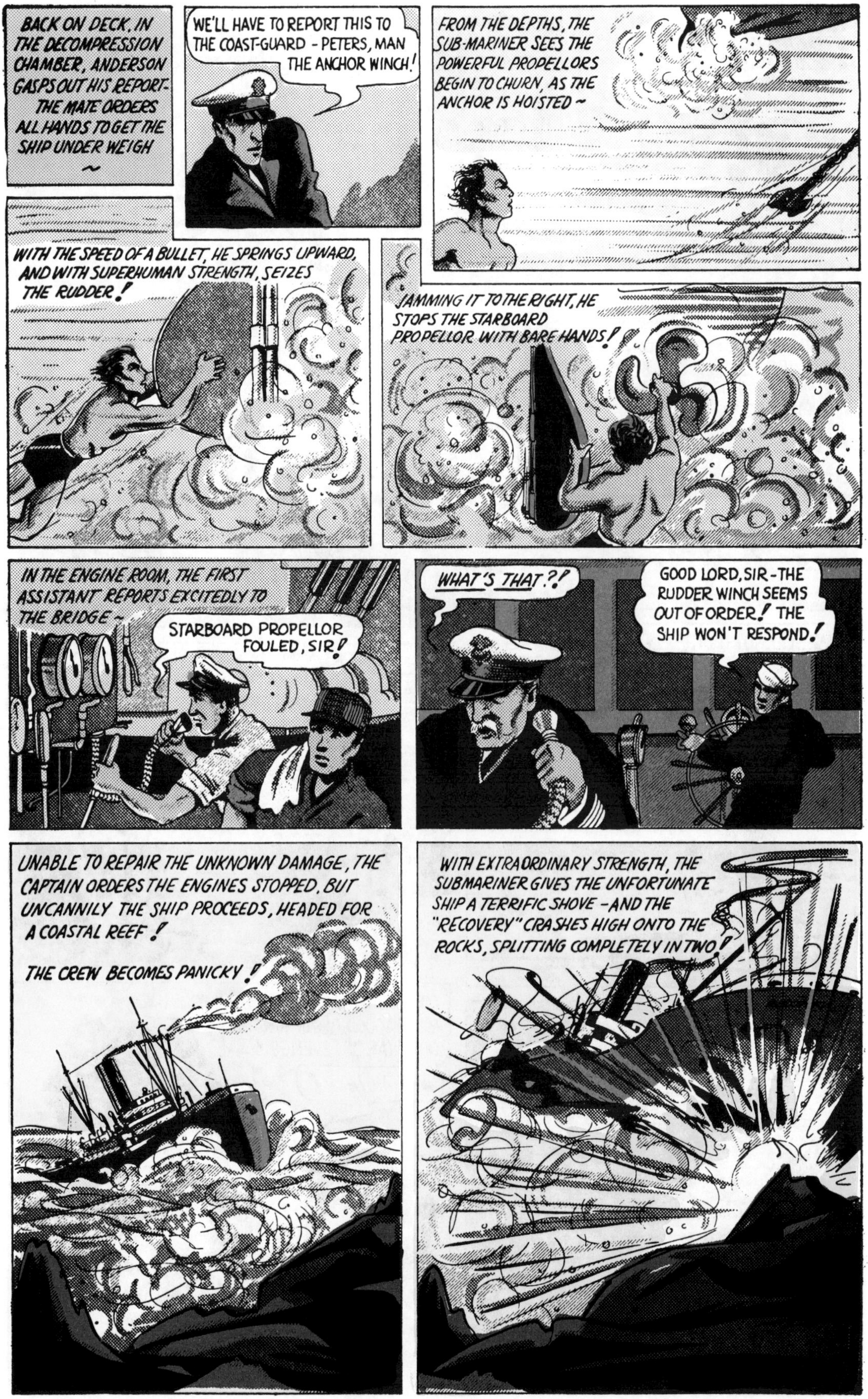
BACK ON DECK. IN THE DECOMPRESSION CHAMBER, ANDERSON GASPS OUT HIS REPORT- THE MATE ORDERS ALL HANDS TO GET THE SHIP UNDER WEIGH ~
WE'LL HAVE TO REPORT THIS TO THE COAST-GUARD - PETERS, MAN THE ANCHOR WINCH!
FROM THE DEPTHS, THE SUB-MARINER SEES THE POWERFUL PROPELLORS BEGIN TO CHURN, AS THE ANCHOR IS HOISTED ~
WITH THE SPEED OF A BULLET, HE SPRINGS UPWARD, AND WITH SUPERHUMAN STRENGTH, SEIZES THE RUDDER!
JAMMING IT TO THE RIGHT, HE STOPS THE STARBOARD PROPELLOR WITH BARE HANDS!
IN THE ENGINE ROOM, THE FIRST ASSISTANT REPORTS EXCITEDLY TO THE BRIDGE ~
STARBOARD PROPELLOR FOULED, SIR!
WHAT'S THAT?!
GOOD LORD, SIR - THE RUDDER WINCH SEEMS OUT OF ORDER! THE SHIP WON'T RESPOND!
UNABLE TO REPAIR THE UNKNOWN DAMAGE, THE CAPTAIN ORDERS THE ENGINES STOPPED. BUT UNCANNILY THE SHIP PROCEEDS, HEADED FOR A COASTAL REEF!
THE CREW BECOMES PANICKY!
WITH EXTRAORDINARY STRENGTH, THE SUBMARINER GIVES THE UNFORTUNATE SHIP A TERRIFIC SHOVE - AND THE "RECOVERY" CRASHES HIGH ONTO THE ROCKS, SPLITTING COMPLETELY IN TWO!

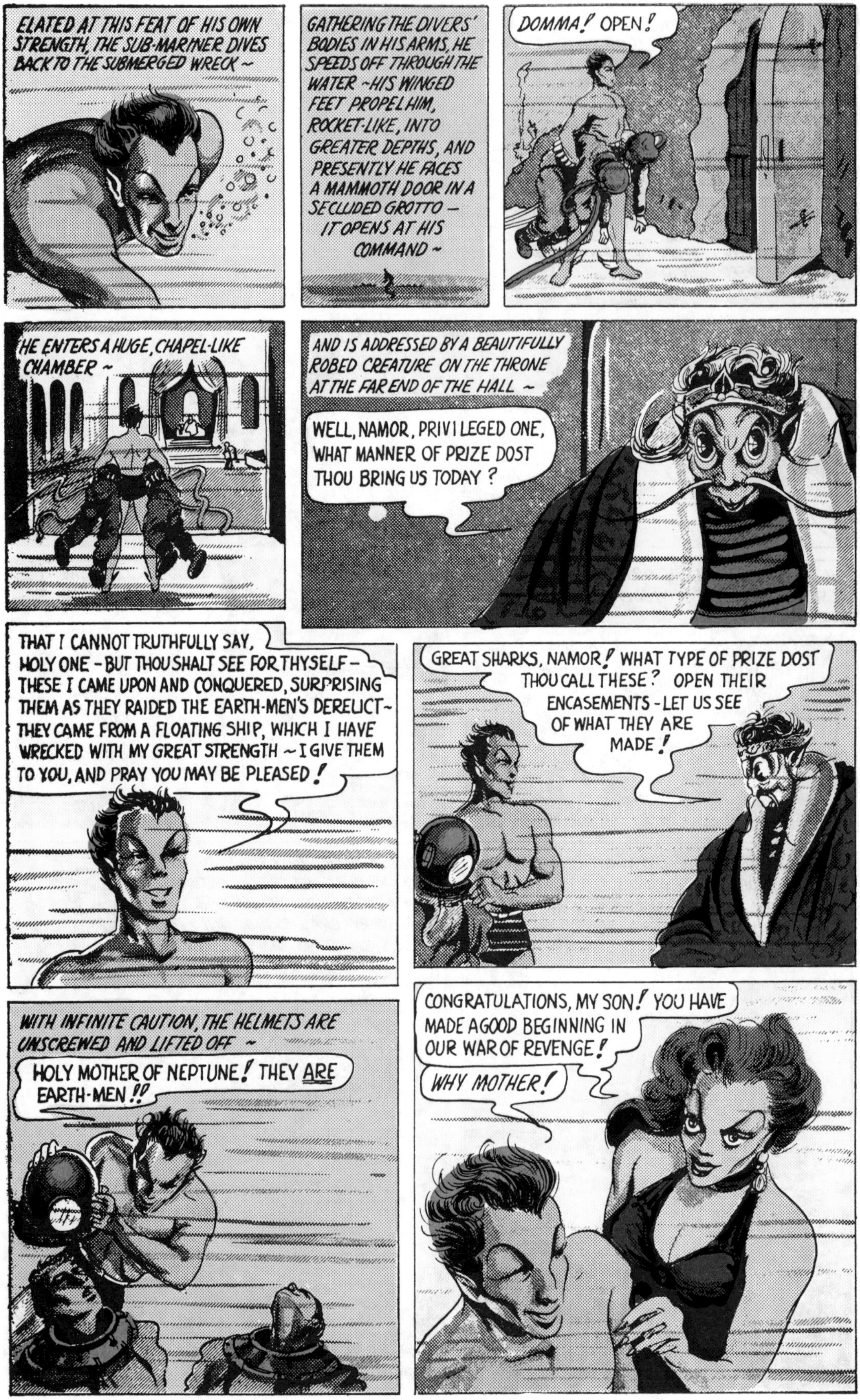
ELATED AT THIS FEAT OF HIS OWN STRENGTH, THE SUB-MARINER DIVES BACK TO THE SUBMERGED WRECK ~
GATHERING THE DIVERS' BODIES IN HIS ARMS, HE SPEEDS OFF THROUGH THE WATER ~HIS WINGED FEET PROPEL HIM, ROCKET-LIKE, INTO GREATER DEPTHS, AND PRESENTLY HE FACES A MAMMOTH DOOR IN A SECLUDED GROTTO — IT OPENS AT HIS COMMAND ~
DOMMA! OPEN!
HE ENTERS A HUGE, CHAPEL-LIKE CHAMBER ~
AND IS ADDRESSED BY A BEAUTIFULLY ROBED CREATURE ON THE THRONE AT THE FAR END OF THE HALL ~
WELL, NAMOR, PRIVILEGED ONE, WHAT MANNER OF PRIZE DOST THOU BRING US TODAY?
THAT I CANNOT TRUTHFULLY SAY, HOLY ONE - BUT THOU SHALT SEE FOR THYSELF - THESE I CAME UPON AND CONQUERED, SURPRISING THEM AS THEY RAIDED THE EARTH-MEN'S DERELICT - THEY CAME FROM A FLOATING SHIP, WHICH I HAVE WRECKED WITH MY GREAT STRENGTH ~ I GIVE THEM TO YOU, AND PRAY YOU MAY BE PLEASED!
GREAT SHARKS, NAMOR! WHAT TYPE OF PRIZE DOST THOU CALL THESE? OPEN THEIR ENCASEMENTS - LET US SEE OF WHAT THEY ARE MADE!
WITH INFINITE CAUTION, THE HELMETS ARE UNSCREWED AND LIFTED OFF ~
HOLY MOTHER OF NEPTUNE! THEY ARE EARTH-MEN!?
CONGRATULATIONS, MY SON! YOU HAVE MADE A GOOD BEGINNING IN OUR WAR OF REVENGE!
WHY MOTHER!

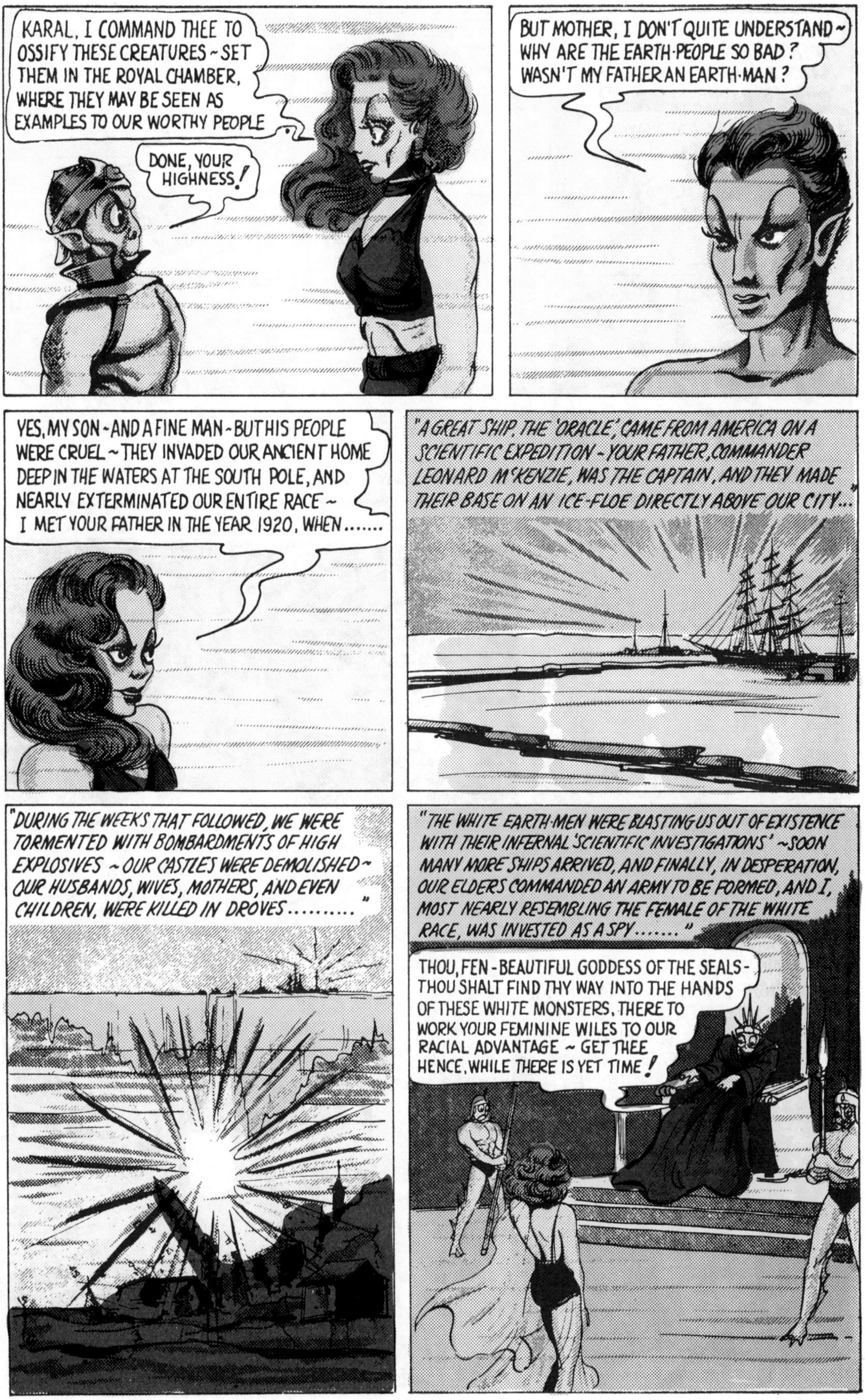
KARAL, I COMMAND THEE TO OSSIFY THESE CREATURES ~ SET THEM IN THE ROYAL CHAMBER, WHERE THEY MAY BE SEEN AS EXAMPLES TO OUR WORTHY PEOPLE
DONE, YOUR HIGHNESS!
BUT MOTHER, I DON'T QUITE UNDERSTAND ~ WHY ARE THE EARTH-PEOPLE SO BAD? WASN'T MY FATHER AN EARTH-MAN?
YES, MY SON ~ AND A FINE MAN ~ BUT HIS PEOPLE WERE CRUEL ~ THEY INVADED OUR ANCIENT HOME DEEP IN THE WATERS AT THE SOUTH POLE, AND NEARLY EXTERMINATED OUR ENTIRE RACE ~ I MET YOUR FATHER IN THE YEAR 1920, WHEN.......
"A GREAT SHIP, THE 'ORACLE', CAME FROM AMERICA ON A SCIENTIFIC EXPEDITION ~ YOUR FATHER, COMMANDER LEONARD McKENZIE, WAS THE CAPTAIN, AND THEY MADE THEIR BASE ON AN ICE-FLOE DIRECTLY ABOVE OUR CITY..."
"DURING THE WEEKS THAT FOLLOWED, WE WERE TORMENTED WITH BOMBARDMENTS OF HIGH EXPLOSIVES ~ OUR CASTLES WERE DEMOLISHED ~ OUR HUSBANDS, WIVES, MOTHERS, AND EVEN CHILDREN, WERE KILLED IN DROVES.........."
"THE WHITE EARTH-MEN WERE BLASTING US OUT OF EXISTENCE WITH THEIR INFERNAL 'SCIENTIFIC INVESTIGATIONS' ~ SOON MANY MORE SHIPS ARRIVED, AND FINALLY, IN DESPERATION, OUR ELDERS COMMANDED AN ARMY TO BE FORMED, AND I, MOST NEARLY RESEMBLING THE FEMALE OF THE WHITE RACE, WAS INVESTED AS A SPY......."
THOU, FEN ~ BEAUTIFUL GODDESS OF THE SEALS ~ THOU SHALT FIND THY WAY INTO THE HANDS OF THESE WHITE MONSTERS, THERE TO WORK YOUR FEMININE WILES TO OUR RACIAL ADVANTAGE ~ GET THEE HENCE, WHILE THERE IS YET TIME!

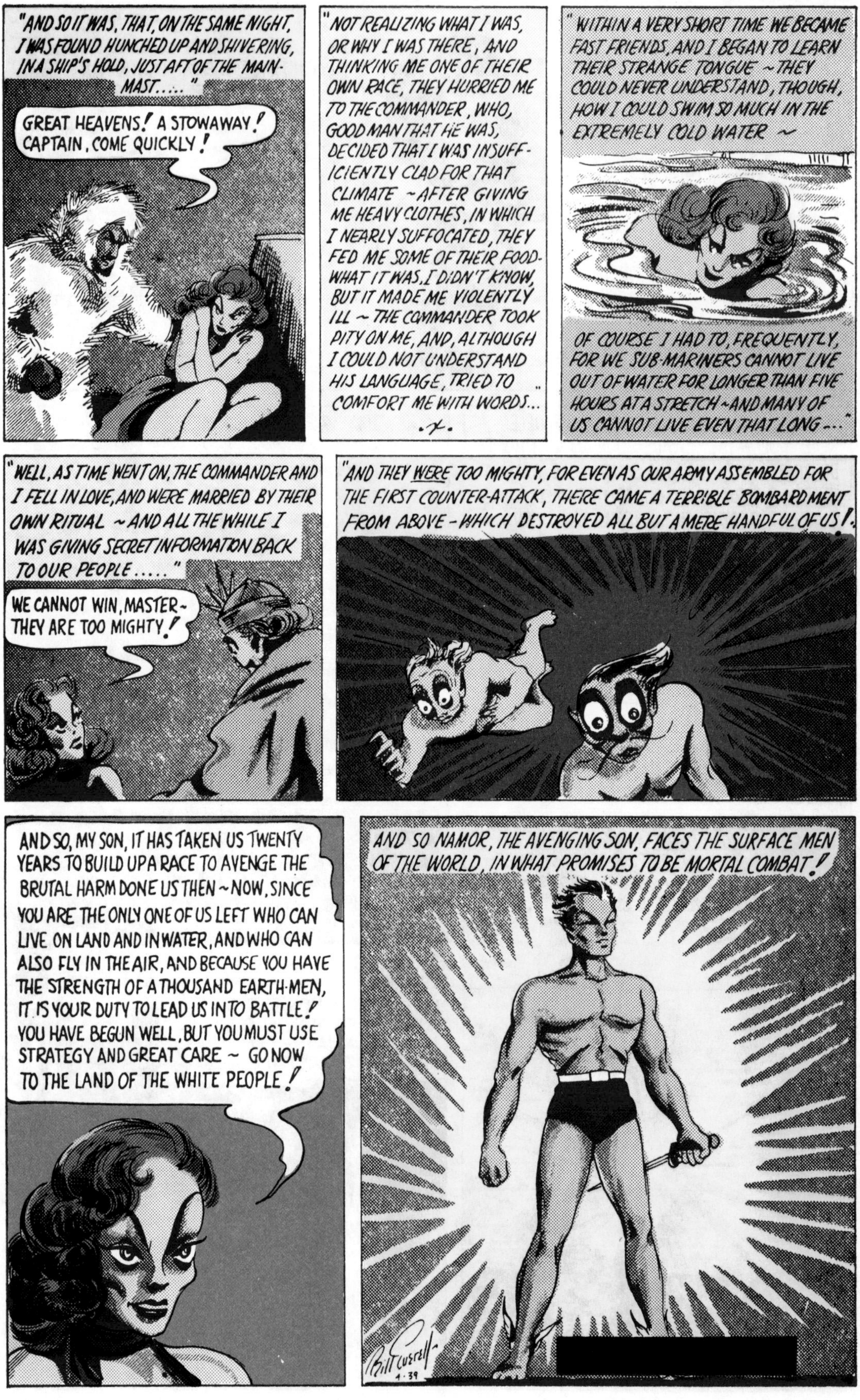
"AND SO IT WAS, THAT, ON THE SAME NIGHT, I WAS FOUND HUNCHED UP AND SHIVERING, IN A SHIP'S HOLD, JUST AFT OF THE MAIN-MAST....."
GREAT HEAVENS! A STOWAWAY! CAPTAIN, COME QUICKLY!
"NOT REALIZING WHAT I WAS, OR WHY I WAS THERE, AND THINKING ME ONE OF THEIR OWN RACE, THEY HURRIED ME TO THE COMMANDER, WHO, GOOD MAN THAT HE WAS, DECIDED THAT I WAS INSUFFICIENTLY CLAD FOR THAT CLIMATE ~ AFTER GIVING ME HEAVY CLOTHES, IN WHICH I NEARLY SUFFOCATED, THEY FED ME SOME OF THEIR FOOD- WHAT IT WAS, I DIDN'T KNOW, BUT IT MADE ME VIOLENTLY ILL ~ THE COMMANDER TOOK PITY ON ME, AND, ALTHOUGH I COULD NOT UNDERSTAND HIS LANGUAGE, TRIED TO COMFORT ME WITH WORDS..."
"WITHIN A VERY SHORT TIME WE BECAME FAST FRIENDS, AND I BEGAN TO LEARN THEIR STRANGE TONGUE ~ THEY COULD NEVER UNDERSTAND, THOUGH, HOW I COULD SWIM SO MUCH IN THE EXTREMELY COLD WATER ~
OF COURSE I HAD TO, FREQUENTLY, FOR WE SUB-MARINERS CANNOT LIVE OUT OF WATER FOR LONGER THAN FIVE HOURS AT A STRETCH ~ AND MANY OF US CANNOT LIVE EVEN THAT LONG..."
"WELL, AS TIME WENT ON, THE COMMANDER AND I FELL IN LOVE, AND WERE MARRIED BY THEIR OWN RITUAL ~ AND ALL THE WHILE I WAS GIVING SECRET INFORMATION BACK TO OUR PEOPLE....."
WE CANNOT WIN, MASTER- THEY ARE TOO MIGHTY!
"AND THEY WERE TOO MIGHTY, FOR EVEN AS OUR ARMY ASSEMBLED FOR THE FIRST COUNTER-ATTACK, THERE CAME A TERRIBLE BOMBARDMENT FROM ABOVE - WHICH DESTROYED ALL BUT A MERE HANDFUL OF US!.
AND SO, MY SON, IT HAS TAKEN US TWENTY YEARS TO BUILD UP A RACE TO AVENGE THE BRUTAL HARM DONE US THEN ~ NOW, SINCE YOU ARE THE ONLY ONE OF US LEFT WHO CAN LIVE ON LAND AND IN WATER, AND WHO CAN ALSO FLY IN THE AIR, AND BECAUSE YOU HAVE THE STRENGTH OF A THOUSAND EARTH-MEN, IT IS YOUR DUTY TO LEAD US INTO BATTLE! YOU HAVE BEGUN WELL, BUT YOU MUST USE STRATEGY AND GREAT CARE ~ GO NOW TO THE LAND OF THE WHITE PEOPLE!
AND SO NAMOR, THE AVENGING SON, FACES THE SURFACE MEN OF THE WORLD, IN WHAT PROMISES TO BE MORTAL COMBAT!
Bill Everett 4-39
[redacted]

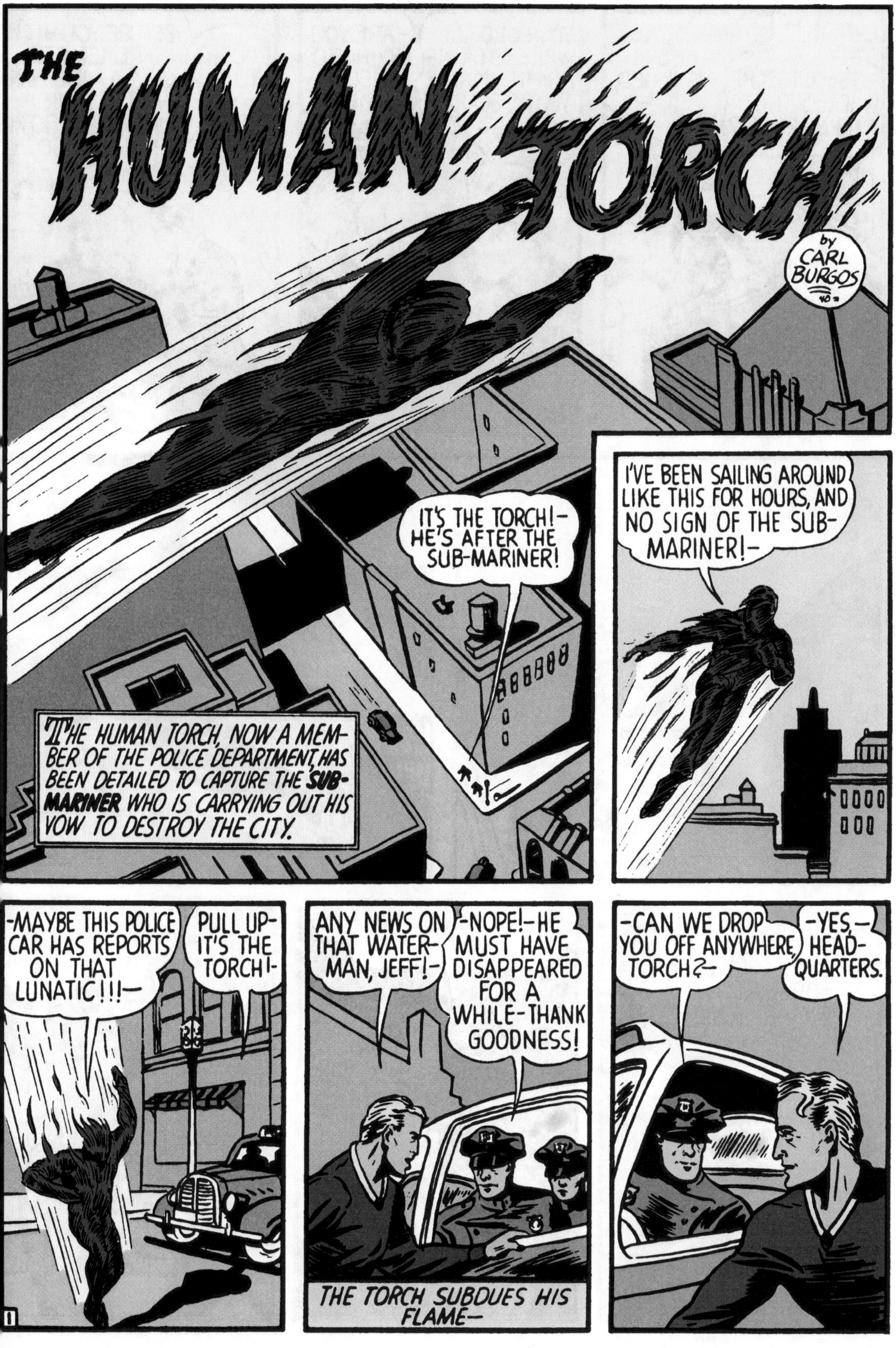
THE HUMAN TORCH
by CARL BURGOS '40
IT'S THE TORCH!- HE'S AFTER THE SUB-MARINER!
THE HUMAN TORCH, NOW A MEMBER OF THE POLICE DEPARTMENT, HAS BEEN DETAILED TO CAPTURE THE SUB-MARINER WHO IS CARRYING OUT HIS VOW TO DESTROY THE CITY.
I'VE BEEN SAILING AROUND LIKE THIS FOR HOURS, AND NO SIGN OF THE SUB-MARINER!-
-MAYBE THIS POLICE CAR HAS REPORTS ON THAT LUNATIC!!!-
PULL UP- IT'S THE TORCH!-
1
ANY NEWS ON THAT WATER-MAN, JEFF!-
-NOPE!-HE MUST HAVE DISAPPEARED FOR A WHILE-THANK GOODNESS!
THE TORCH SUBDUES HIS FLAME-
-CAN WE DROP YOU OFF ANYWHERE, TORCH?-
-YES,- HEAD-QUARTERS.

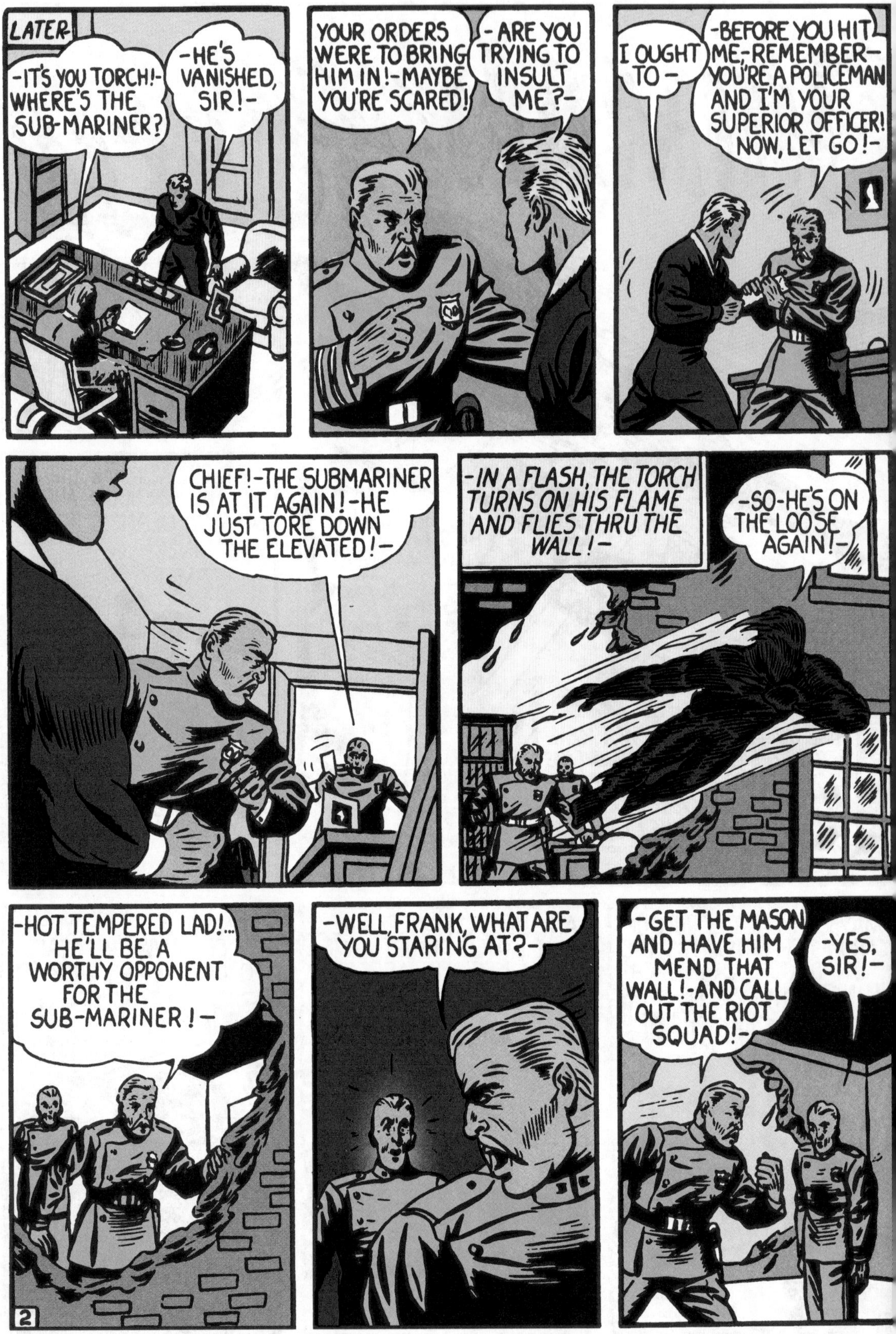
LATER-
-IT'S YOU TORCH!-WHERE'S THE SUB-MARINER?
-HE'S VANISHED, SIR!-
YOUR ORDERS WERE TO BRING HIM IN!-MAYBE YOU'RE SCARED!
-ARE YOU TRYING TO INSULT ME?-
I OUGHT TO-
-BEFORE YOU HIT ME,-REMEMBER-YOU'RE A POLICEMAN AND I'M YOUR SUPERIOR OFFICER! NOW, LET GO!-
CHIEF!-THE SUBMARINER IS AT IT AGAIN!-HE JUST TORE DOWN THE ELEVATED!-
-IN A FLASH, THE TORCH TURNS ON HIS FLAME AND FLIES THRU THE WALL!-
-SO-HE'S ON THE LOOSE AGAIN!-
-HOT TEMPERED LAD!... HE'LL BE A WORTHY OPPONENT FOR THE SUB-MARINER!-
-WELL, FRANK, WHAT ARE YOU STARING AT?-
-GET THE MASON AND HAVE HIM MEND THAT WALL!-AND CALL OUT THE RIOT SQUAD!-
-YES, SIR!-
2

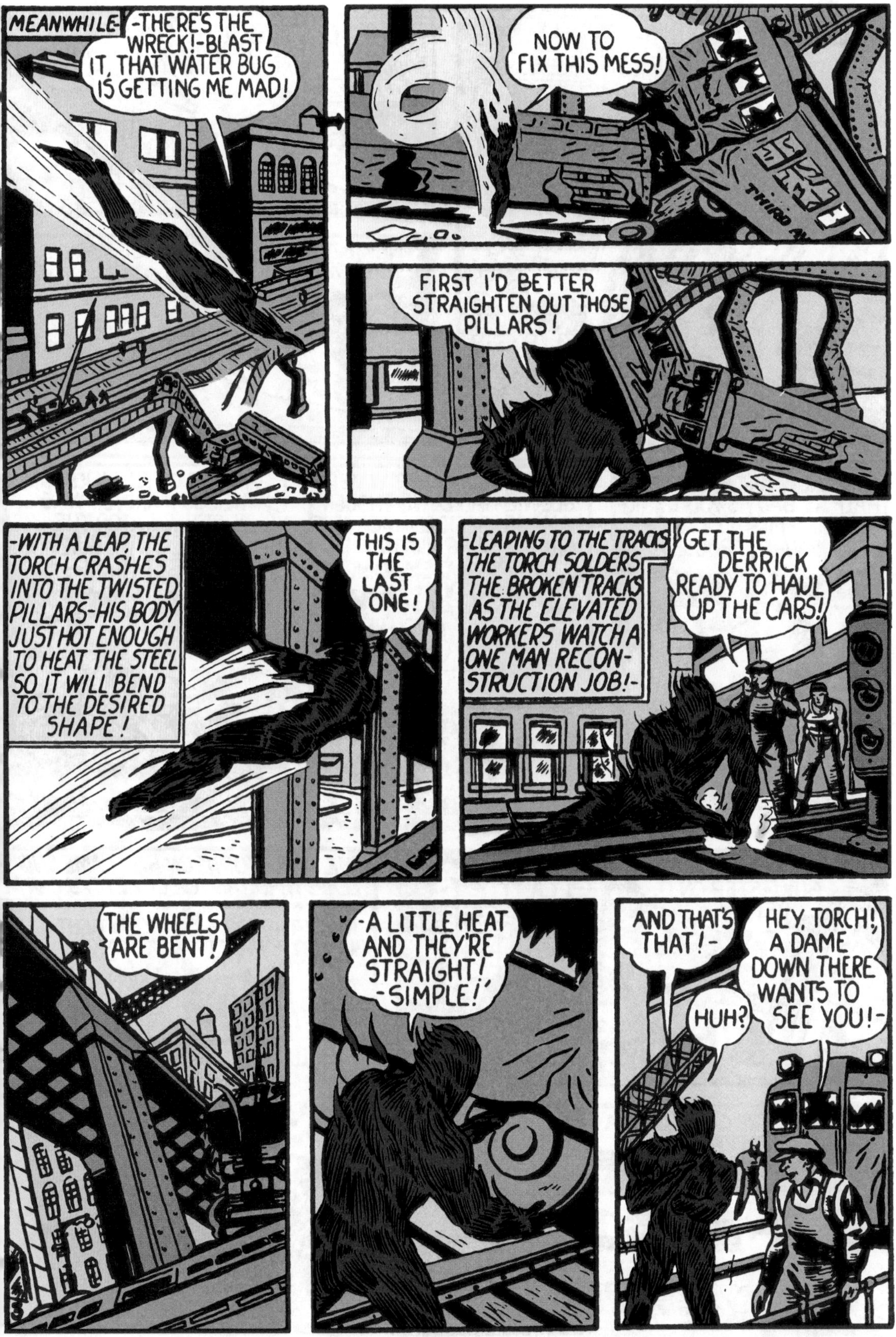
MEANWHILE-
-THERE'S THE WRECK!-BLAST IT, THAT WATER BUG IS GETTING ME MAD!
NOW TO FIX THIS MESS!
FIRST I'D BETTER STRAIGHTEN OUT THOSE PILLARS!
-WITH A LEAP, THE TORCH CRASHES INTO THE TWISTED PILLARS-HIS BODY JUST HOT ENOUGH TO HEAT THE STEEL SO IT WILL BEND TO THE DESIRED SHAPE!
THIS IS THE LAST ONE!
-LEAPING TO THE TRACKS THE TORCH SOLDERS THE BROKEN TRACKS AS THE ELEVATED WORKERS WATCH A ONE MAN RECON-STRUCTION JOB!-
GET THE DERRICK READY TO HAUL UP THE CARS!
THE WHEELS ARE BENT!
-A LITTLE HEAT AND THEY'RE STRAIGHT! -SIMPLE!
AND THAT'S THAT!-
HEY, TORCH!, A DAME DOWN THERE WANTS TO SEE YOU!-
HUH?

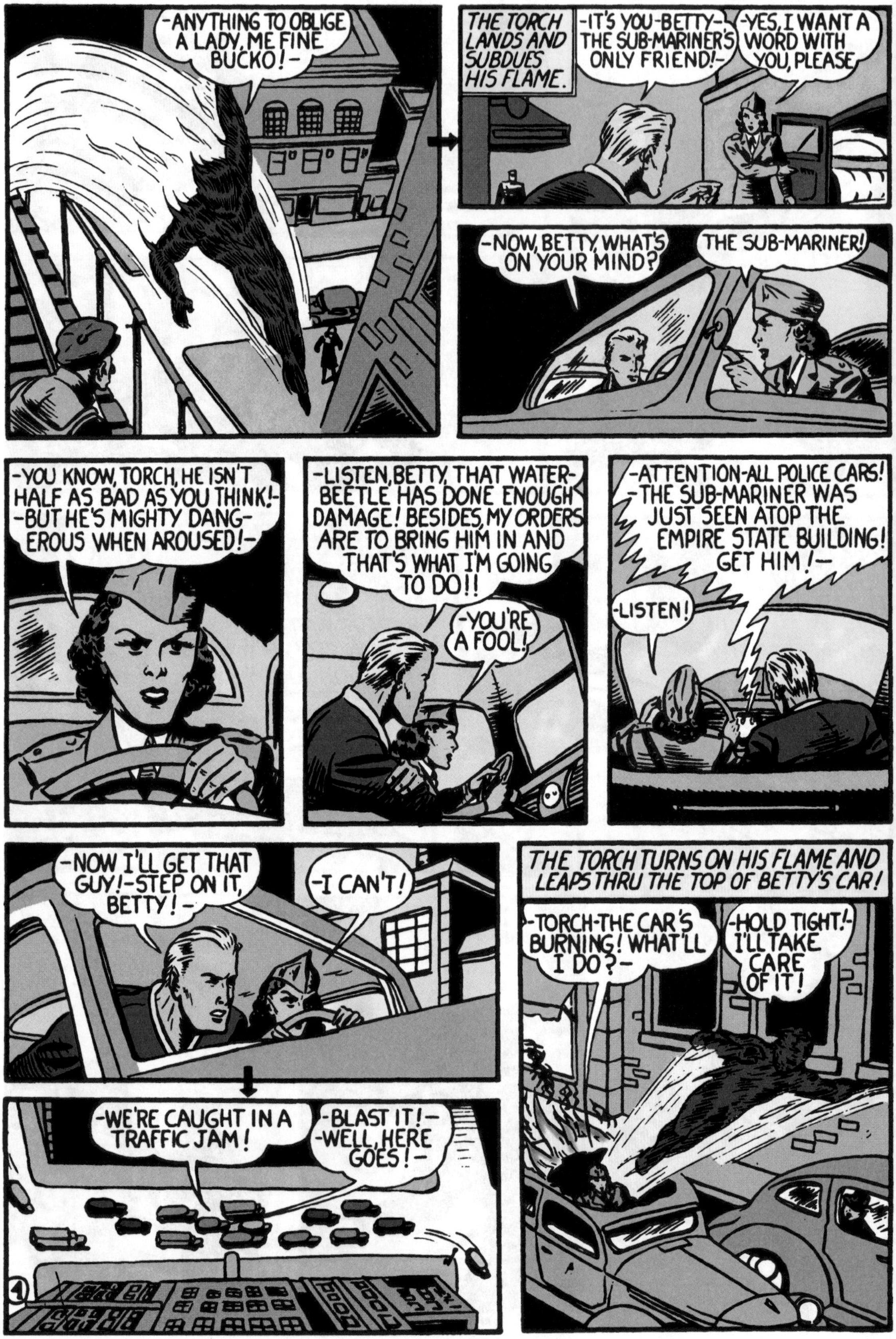
-ANYTHING TO OBLIGE A LADY, ME FINE BUCKO!-
THE TORCH LANDS AND SUBDUES HIS FLAME.
-IT'S YOU-BETTY- THE SUB-MARINER'S ONLY FRIEND!-
-YES, I WANT A WORD WITH YOU, PLEASE
-NOW, BETTY, WHAT'S ON YOUR MIND?
THE SUB-MARINER!
-YOU KNOW, TORCH, HE ISN'T HALF AS BAD AS YOU THINK!- -BUT HE'S MIGHTY DANG-EROUS WHEN AROUSED!-
-LISTEN, BETTY, THAT WATER-BEETLE HAS DONE ENOUGH DAMAGE! BESIDES, MY ORDERS ARE TO BRING HIM IN AND THAT'S WHAT I'M GOING TO DO!!
-YOU'RE A FOOL!
-ATTENTION-ALL POLICE CARS! -THE SUB-MARINER WAS JUST SEEN ATOP THE EMPIRE STATE BUILDING! GET HIM!-
-LISTEN!
-NOW I'LL GET THAT GUY!-STEP ON IT, BETTY!-
-I CAN'T!
-WE'RE CAUGHT IN A TRAFFIC JAM!
-BLAST IT!- -WELL, HERE GOES!-
THE TORCH TURNS ON HIS FLAME AND LEAPS THRU THE TOP OF BETTY'S CAR!
-TORCH-THE CAR'S BURNING! WHAT'LL I DO?-
-HOLD TIGHT!- I'LL TAKE CARE OF IT!

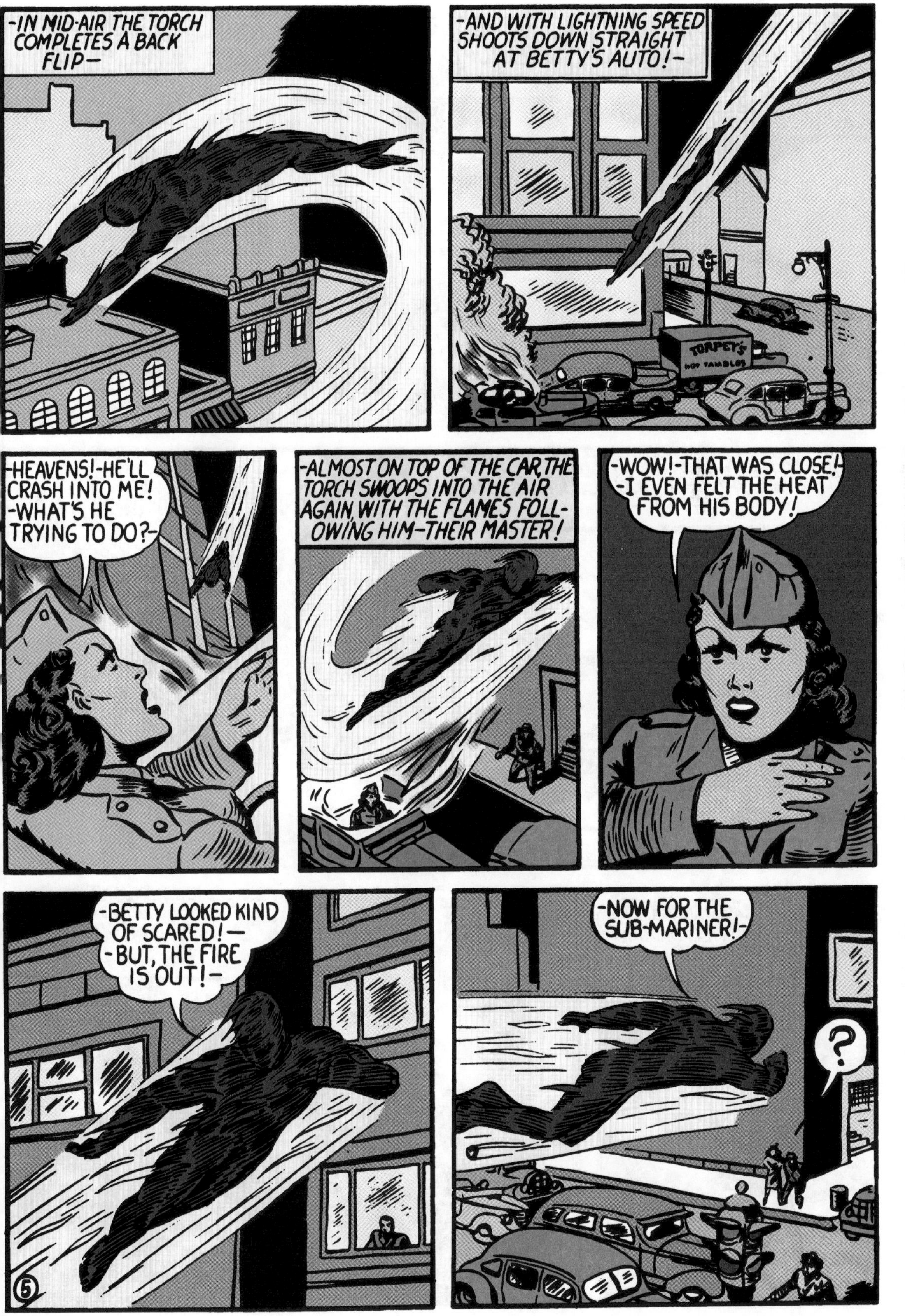
-IN MID-AIR THE TORCH COMPLETES A BACK FLIP-
-AND WITH LIGHTNING SPEED SHOOTS DOWN STRAIGHT AT BETTY'S AUTO!-
TORPEY'S
-HEAVENS!-HE'LL CRASH INTO ME! -WHAT'S HE TRYING TO DO?-
-ALMOST ON TOP OF THE CAR, THE TORCH SWOOPS INTO THE AIR AGAIN, WITH THE FLAMES FOLL-OWING HIM-THEIR MASTER!
-WOW!-THAT WAS CLOSE!- -I EVEN FELT THE HEAT FROM HIS BODY!
-BETTY LOOKED KIND OF SCARED!- -BUT, THE FIRE IS OUT!-
-NOW FOR THE SUB-MARINER!-
?

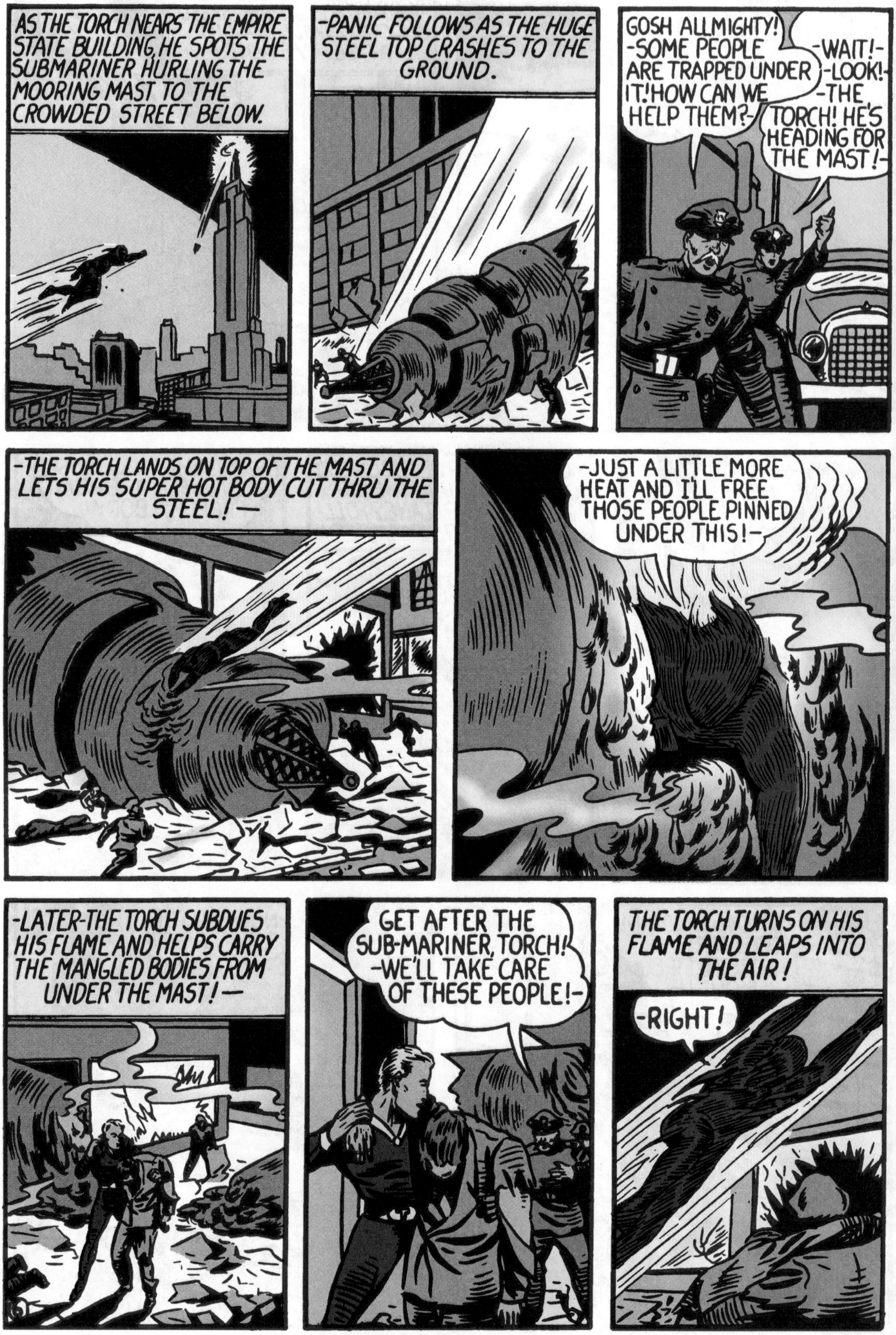
AS THE TORCH NEARS THE EMPIRE STATE BUILDING, HE SPOTS THE SUBMARINER HURLING THE MOORING MAST TO THE CROWDED STREET BELOW.
-PANIC FOLLOWS AS THE HUGE STEEL TOP CRASHES TO THE GROUND.
GOSH ALLMIGHTY! -SOME PEOPLE ARE TRAPPED UNDER IT! HOW CAN WE HELP THEM?-
-WAIT!- -LOOK!- -THE TORCH! HE'S HEADING FOR THE MAST!-
-THE TORCH LANDS ON TOP OF THE MAST AND LETS HIS SUPER HOT BODY CUT THRU THE STEEL! —
-JUST A LITTLE MORE HEAT AND I'LL FREE THOSE PEOPLE PINNED UNDER THIS!-
-LATER-THE TORCH SUBDUES HIS FLAME AND HELPS CARRY THE MANGLED BODIES FROM UNDER THE MAST! —
GET AFTER THE SUB-MARINER, TORCH! -WE'LL TAKE CARE OF THESE PEOPLE!-
THE TORCH TURNS ON HIS FLAME AND LEAPS INTO THE AIR!
-RIGHT!

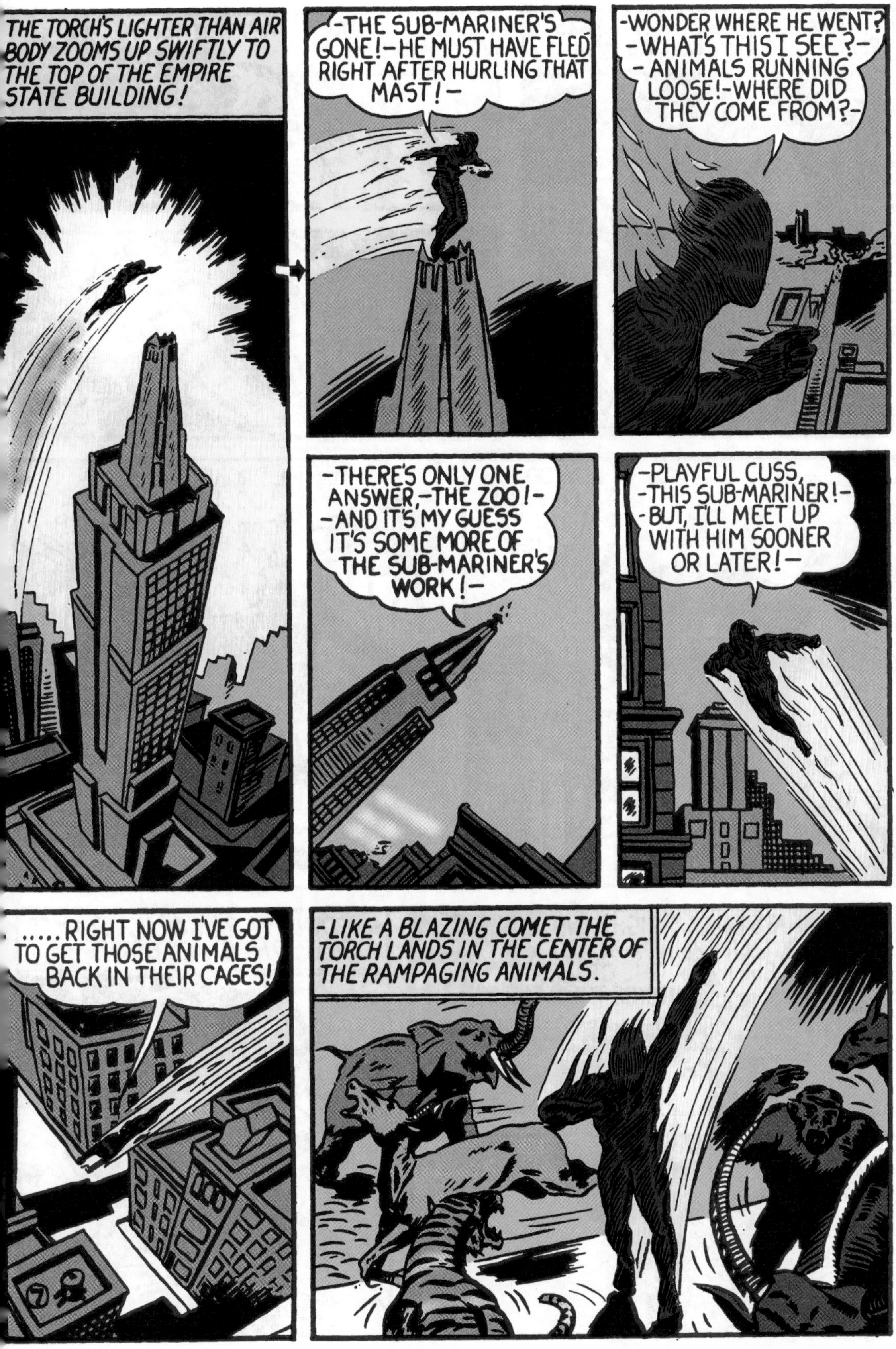

THE TORCH'S LIGHTER THAN AIR BODY ZOOMS UP SWIFTLY TO THE TOP OF THE EMPIRE STATE BUILDING!
-THE SUB-MARINER'S GONE!-HE MUST HAVE FLED RIGHT AFTER HURLING THAT MAST!-
-WONDER WHERE HE WENT? -WHAT'S THIS I SEE?- -ANIMALS RUNNING LOOSE!-WHERE DID THEY COME FROM?-
-THERE'S ONLY ONE ANSWER,-THE ZOO!- -AND IT'S MY GUESS IT'S SOME MORE OF THE SUB-MARINER'S WORK!-
-PLAYFUL CUSS, -THIS SUB-MARINER!- -BUT, I'LL MEET UP WITH HIM SOONER OR LATER!-
.....RIGHT NOW I'VE GOT TO GET THOSE ANIMALS BACK IN THEIR CAGES!
-LIKE A BLAZING COMET THE TORCH LANDS IN THE CENTER OF THE RAMPAGING ANIMALS.

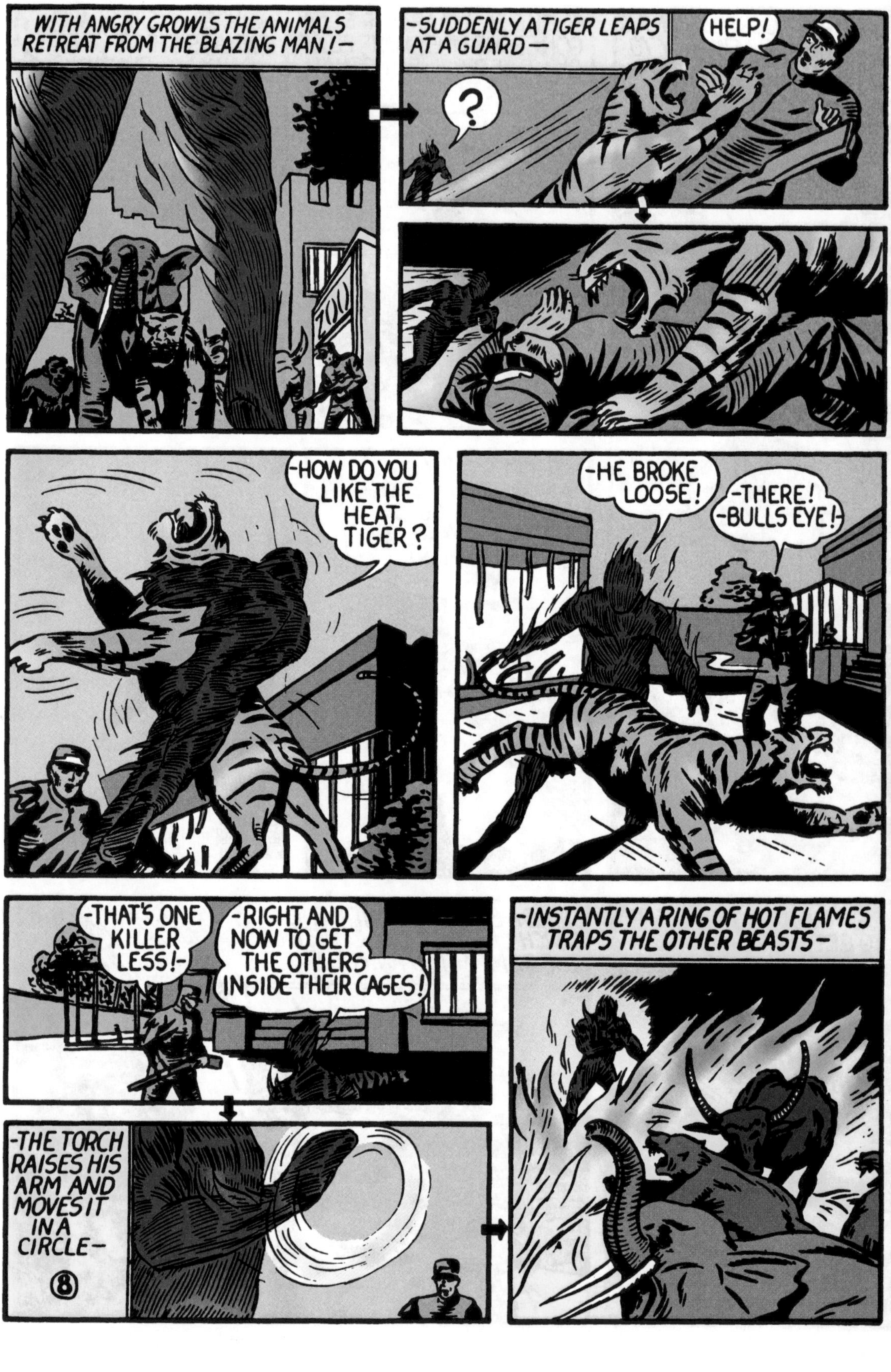
WITH ANGRY GROWLS THE ANIMALS RETREAT FROM THE BLAZING MAN!-
ZOO
-SUDDENLY A TIGER LEAPS AT A GUARD-
HELP!
?
-HOW DO YOU LIKE THE HEAT, TIGER?
-HE BROKE LOOSE!
-THERE! -BULLS EYE!-
-THAT'S ONE KILLER LESS!-
-RIGHT, AND NOW TO GET THE OTHERS INSIDE THEIR CAGES!
-THE TORCH RAISES HIS ARM AND MOVES IT IN A CIRCLE-
8
-INSTANTLY A RING OF HOT FLAMES TRAPS THE OTHER BEASTS-

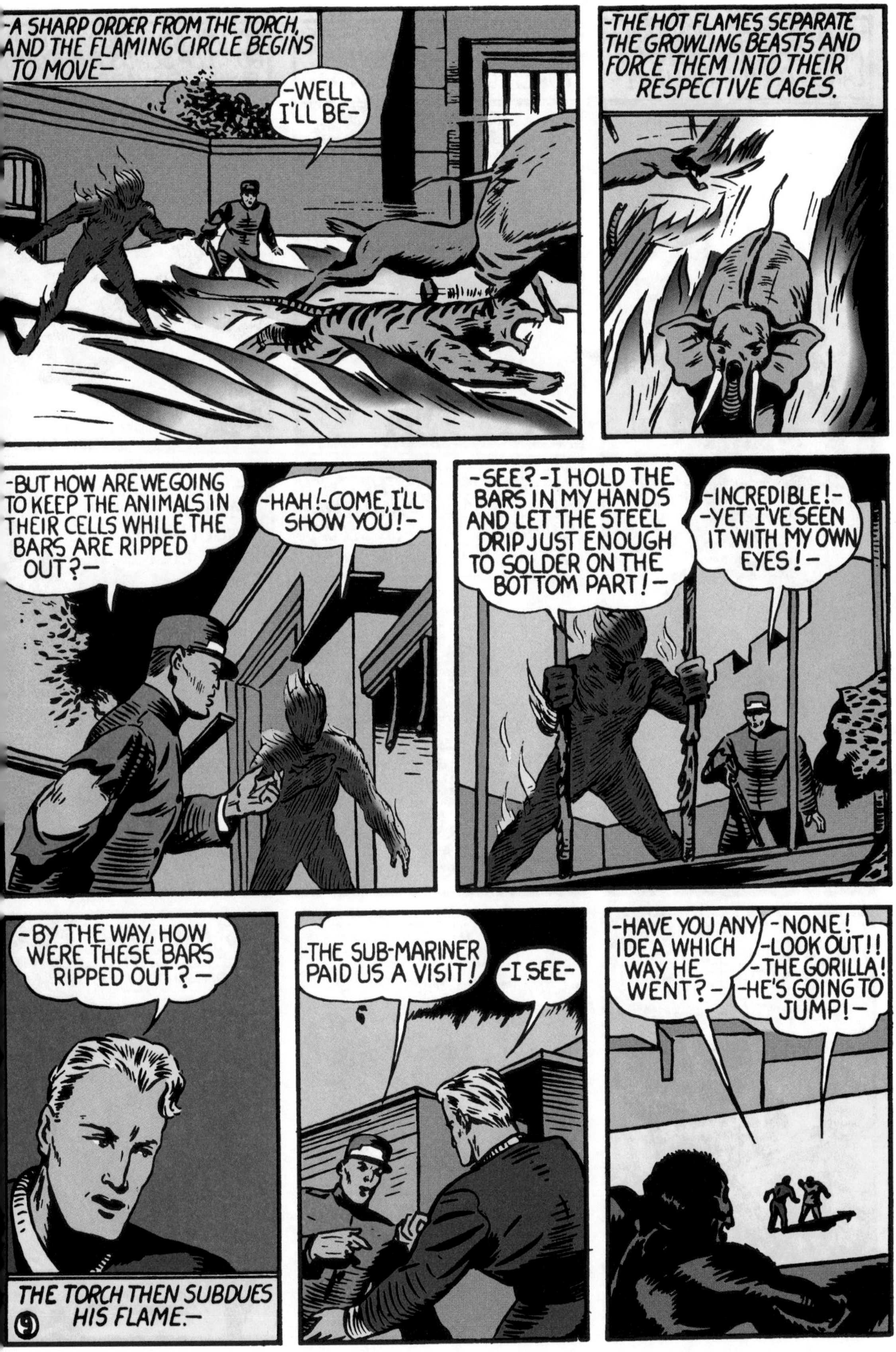
-A SHARP ORDER FROM THE TORCH, AND THE FLAMING CIRCLE BEGINS TO MOVE-
-WELL I'LL BE-
-THE HOT FLAMES SEPARATE THE GROWLING BEASTS AND FORCE THEM INTO THEIR RESPECTIVE CAGES.
-BUT HOW ARE WE GOING TO KEEP THE ANIMALS IN THEIR CELLS WHILE THE BARS ARE RIPPED OUT?-
-HAH!-COME, I'LL SHOW YOU!-
-SEE? -I HOLD THE BARS IN MY HANDS AND LET THE STEEL DRIP JUST ENOUGH TO SOLDER ON THE BOTTOM PART!-
-INCREDIBLE!- -YET I'VE SEEN IT WITH MY OWN EYES!-
-BY THE WAY, HOW WERE THESE BARS RIPPED OUT?-
THE TORCH THEN SUBDUES HIS FLAME.-
9
-THE SUB-MARINER PAID US A VISIT!
-I SEE-
-HAVE YOU ANY IDEA WHICH WAY HE WENT?-
-NONE! -LOOK OUT!! -THE GORILLA! -HE'S GOING TO JUMP!-

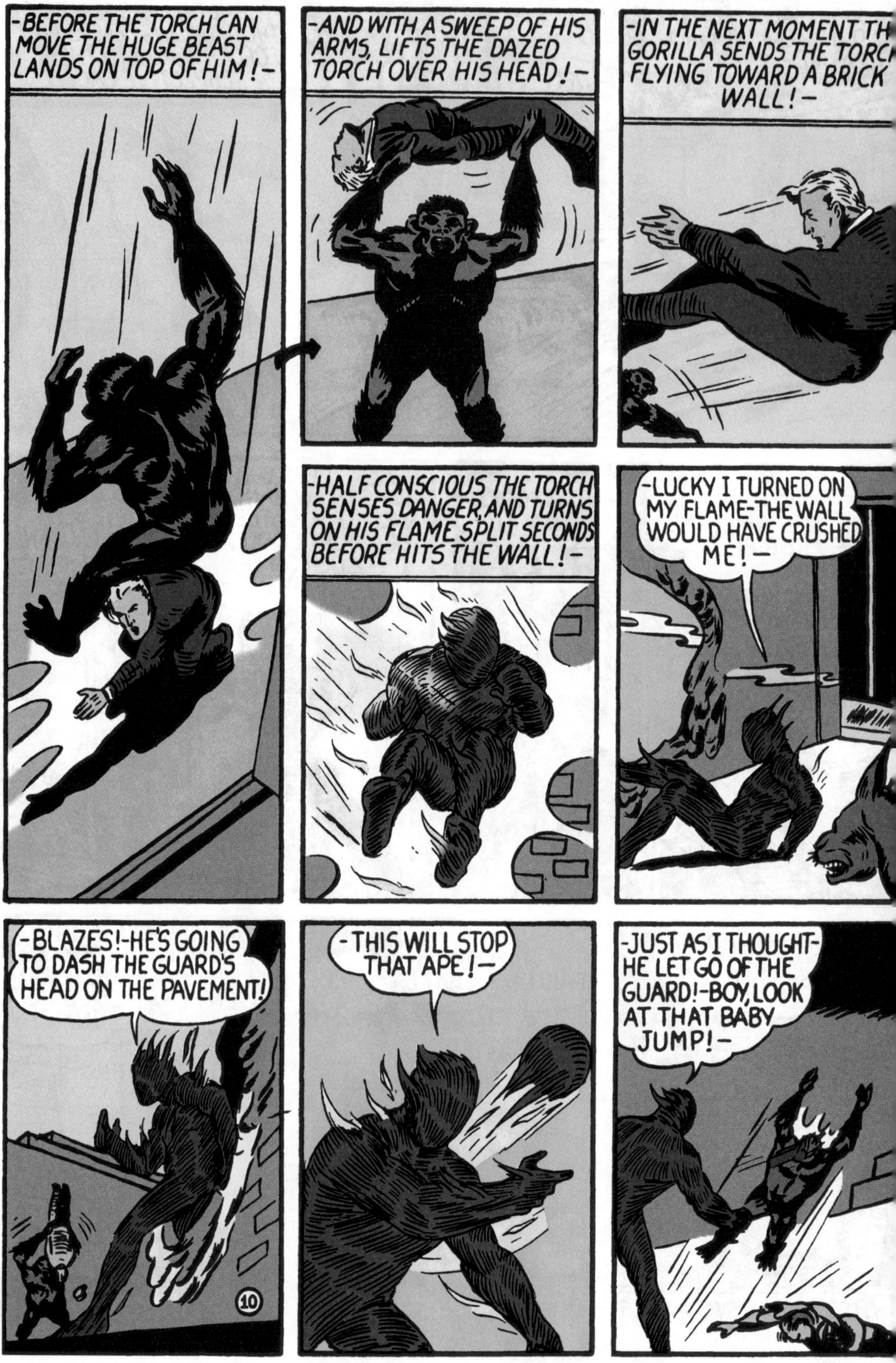

-BEFORE THE TORCH CAN MOVE THE HUGE BEAST LANDS ON TOP OF HIM!-
-AND WITH A SWEEP OF HIS ARMS, LIFTS THE DAZED TORCH OVER HIS HEAD!-
-IN THE NEXT MOMENT TH GORILLA SENDS THE TORC FLYING TOWARD A BRICK WALL!-
-HALF CONSCIOUS THE TORCH SENSES DANGER, AND TURNS ON HIS FLAME SPLIT SECONDS BEFORE HITS THE WALL!-
-LUCKY I TURNED ON MY FLAME-THE WALL WOULD HAVE CRUSHED ME!-
-BLAZES!-HE'S GOING TO DASH THE GUARD'S HEAD ON THE PAVEMENT!
10
-THIS WILL STOP THAT APE!-
-JUST AS I THOUGHT-HE LET GO OF THE GUARD!-BOY, LOOK AT THAT BABY JUMP!-

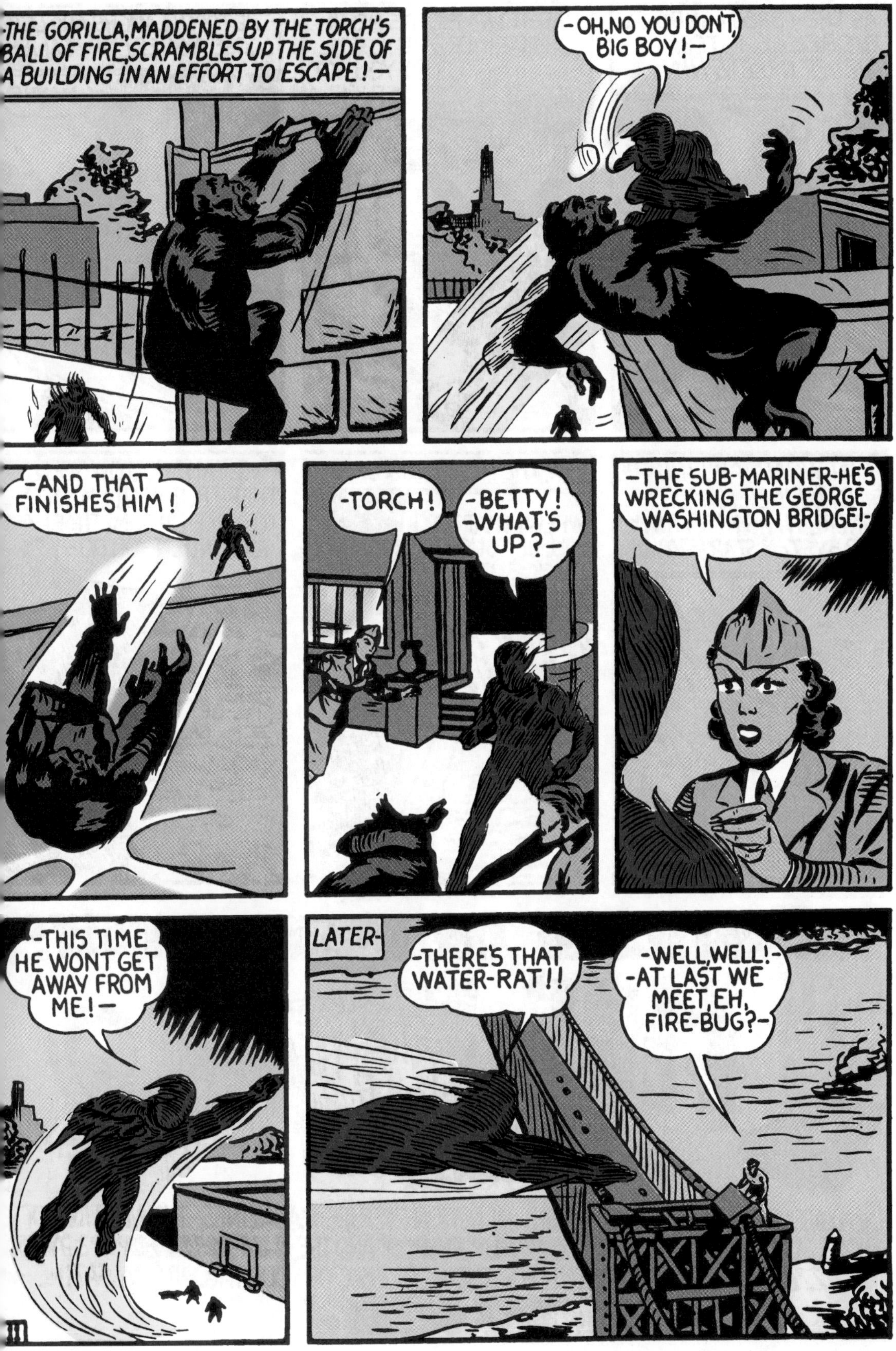
-THE GORILLA, MADDENED BY THE TORCH'S BALL OF FIRE, SCRAMBLES UP THE SIDE OF A BUILDING IN AN EFFORT TO ESCAPE! -
-OH, NO YOU DON'T, BIG BOY! -
-AND THAT FINISHES HIM!
-TORCH!
-BETTY! -WHAT'S UP? -
-THE SUB-MARINER-HE'S WRECKING THE GEORGE WASHINGTON BRIDGE! -
-THIS TIME HE WONT GET AWAY FROM ME! -
LATER-
-THERE'S THAT WATER-RAT!!
-WELL, WELL! -AT LAST WE MEET, EH, FIRE-BUG? -

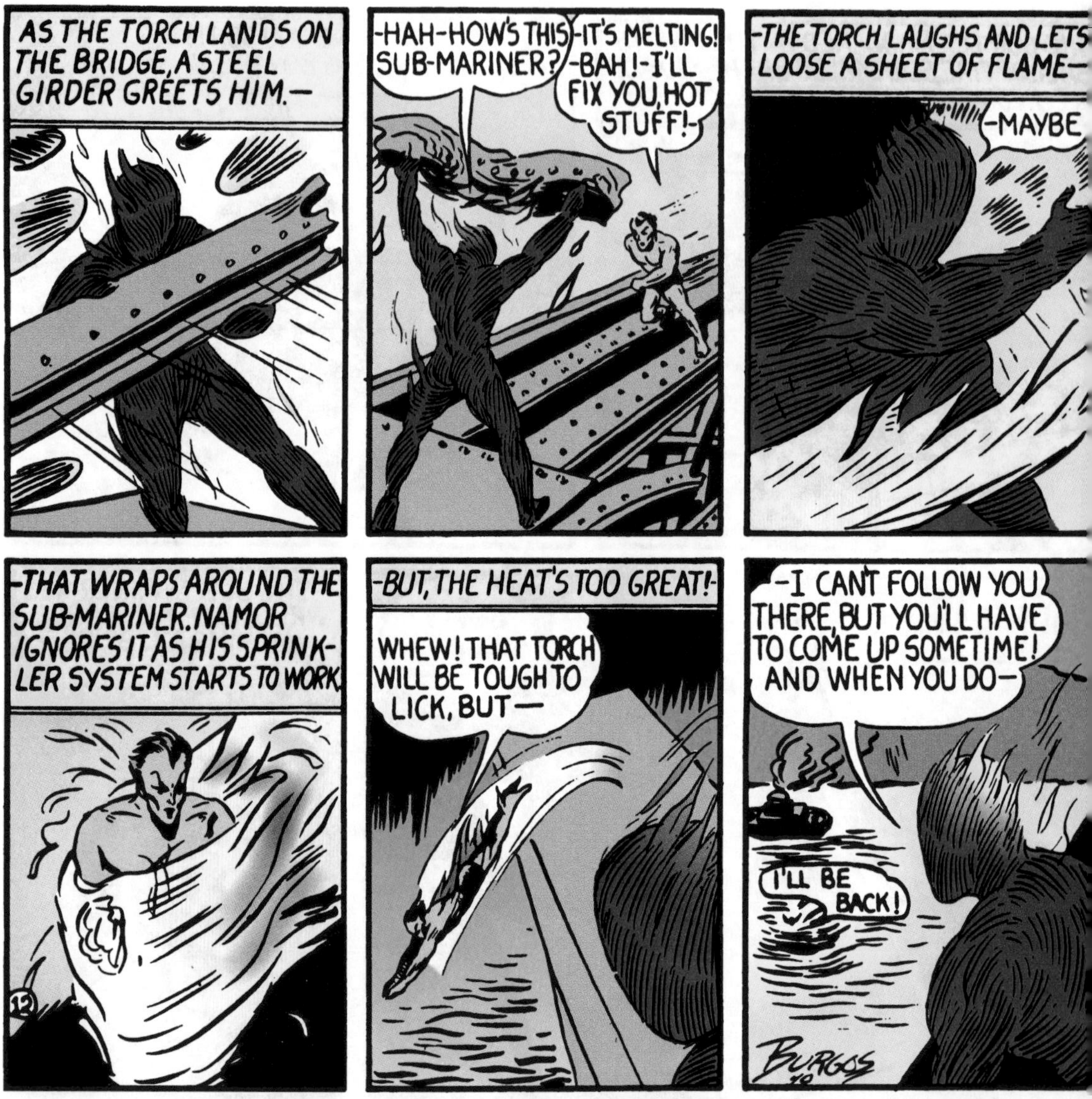
AS THE TORCH LANDS ON THE BRIDGE, A STEEL GIRDER GREETS HIM.—
-HAH-HOW'S THIS SUB-MARINER?
-IT'S MELTING! -BAH! -I'LL FIX YOU, HOT STUFF!-
-THE TORCH LAUGHS AND LETS LOOSE A SHEET OF FLAME-
-MAYBE
-THAT WRAPS AROUND THE SUB-MARINER. NAMOR IGNORES IT AS HIS SPRINK-LER SYSTEM STARTS TO WORK
-BUT, THE HEAT'S TOO GREAT!-
WHEW! THAT TORCH WILL BE TOUGH TO LICK, BUT—
-I CAN'T FOLLOW YOU THERE, BUT YOU'LL HAVE TO COME UP SOMETIME! AND WHEN YOU DO—
I'LL BE BACK!
BURGOS

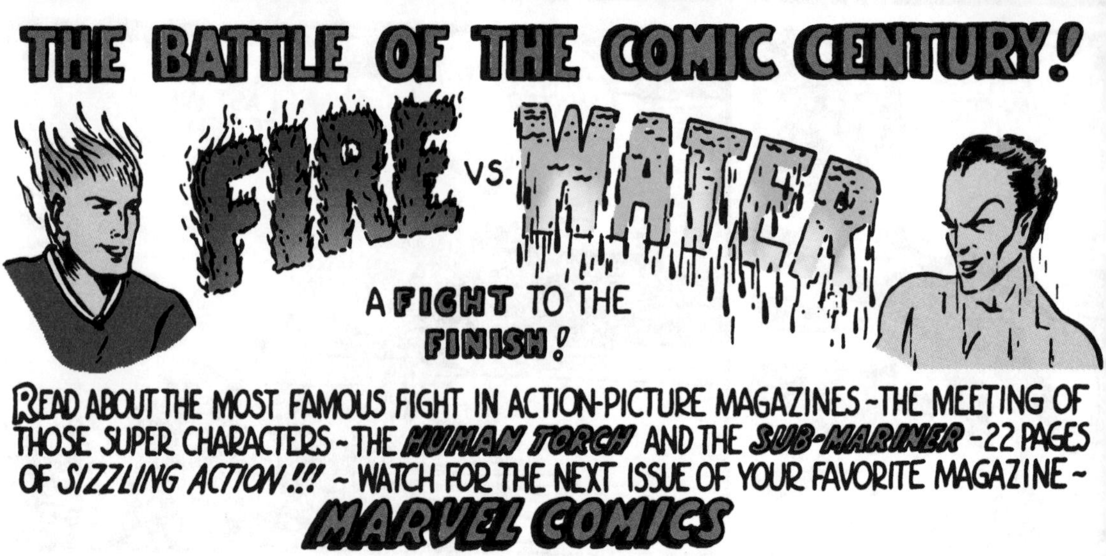
THE BATTLE OF THE COMIC CENTURY!
FIRE VS. WATER
A FIGHT TO THE FINISH!
READ ABOUT THE MOST FAMOUS FIGHT IN ACTION-PICTURE MAGAZINES - THE MEETING OF THOSE SUPER CHARACTERS - THE HUMAN TORCH AND THE SUB-MARINER - 22 PAGES OF SIZZLING ACTION!!! - WATCH FOR THE NEXT ISSUE OF YOUR FAVORITE MAGAZINE -
MARVEL COMICS

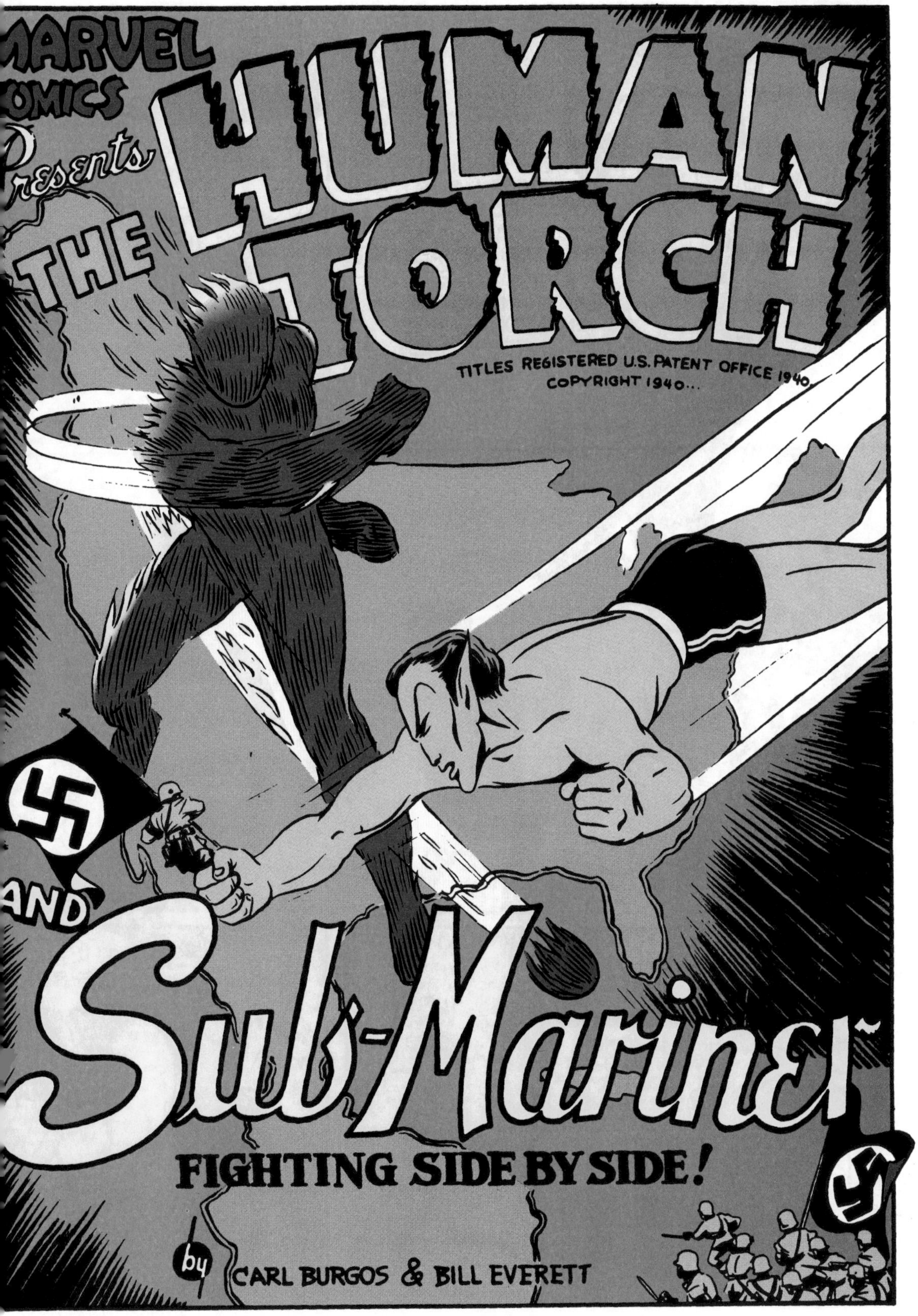
ARVEL
OMICS
Presents
THE
HUMAN
TORCH
TITLES REGISTERED U.S. PATENT OFFICE 1940.
COPYRIGHT 1940...
AND
Sub-Mariner
FIGHTING SIDE BY SIDE!
by CARL BURGOS & BILL EVERETT

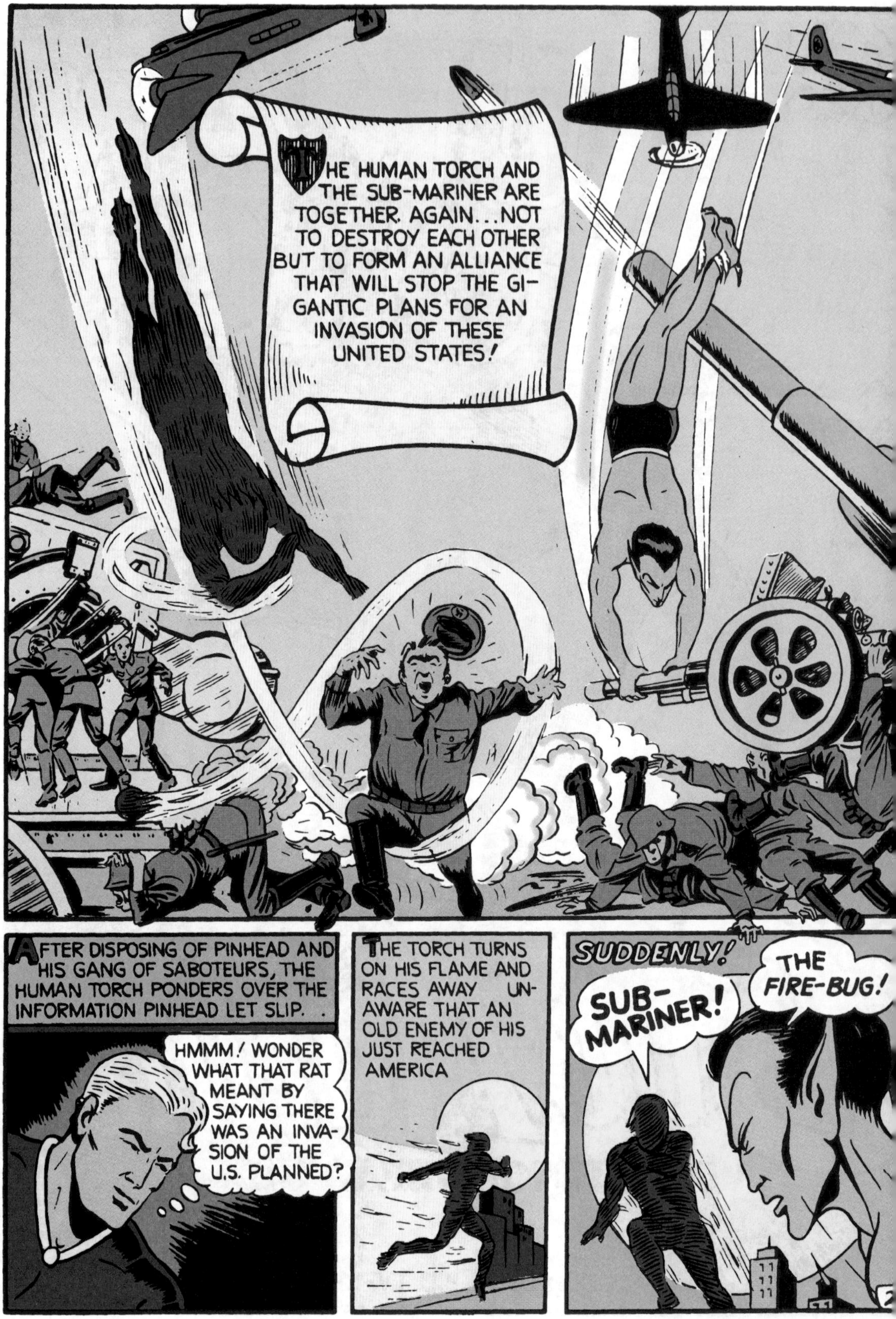
THE HUMAN TORCH AND THE SUB-MARINER ARE TOGETHER AGAIN...NOT TO DESTROY EACH OTHER BUT TO FORM AN ALLIANCE THAT WILL STOP THE GIGANTIC PLANS FOR AN INVASION OF THESE UNITED STATES!
AFTER DISPOSING OF PINHEAD AND HIS GANG OF SABOTEURS, THE HUMAN TORCH PONDERS OVER THE INFORMATION PINHEAD LET SLIP.
HMMM! WONDER WHAT THAT RAT MEANT BY SAYING THERE WAS AN INVASION OF THE U.S. PLANNED?
THE TORCH TURNS ON HIS FLAME AND RACES AWAY UNAWARE THAT AN OLD ENEMY OF HIS JUST REACHED AMERICA
SUDDENLY!
SUB-MARINER!
THE FIRE-BUG!

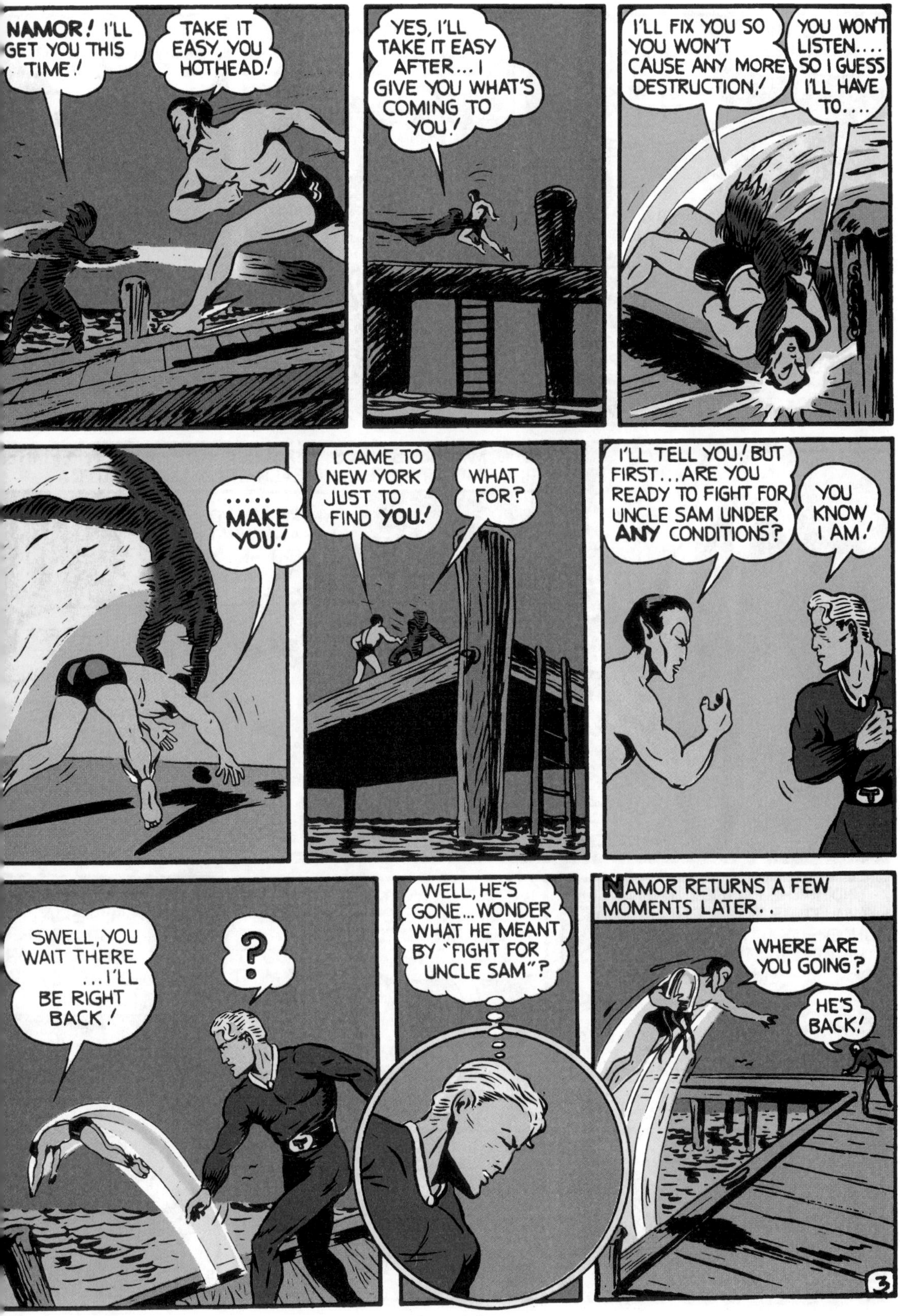
NAMOR! I'LL GET YOU THIS TIME!
TAKE IT EASY, YOU HOTHEAD!
YES, I'LL TAKE IT EASY AFTER... I GIVE YOU WHAT'S COMING TO YOU!
I'LL FIX YOU SO YOU WON'T CAUSE ANY MORE DESTRUCTION!
YOU WON'T LISTEN.... SO I GUESS I'LL HAVE TO....
..... MAKE YOU!
I CAME TO NEW YORK JUST TO FIND YOU!
WHAT FOR?
I'LL TELL YOU! BUT FIRST... ARE YOU READY TO FIGHT FOR UNCLE SAM UNDER ANY CONDITIONS?
YOU KNOW I AM!
SWELL, YOU WAIT THERE ...I'LL BE RIGHT BACK!
?
WELL, HE'S GONE... WONDER WHAT HE MEANT BY "FIGHT FOR UNCLE SAM"?
NAMOR RETURNS A FEW MOMENTS LATER..
WHERE ARE YOU GOING?
HE'S BACK!
3

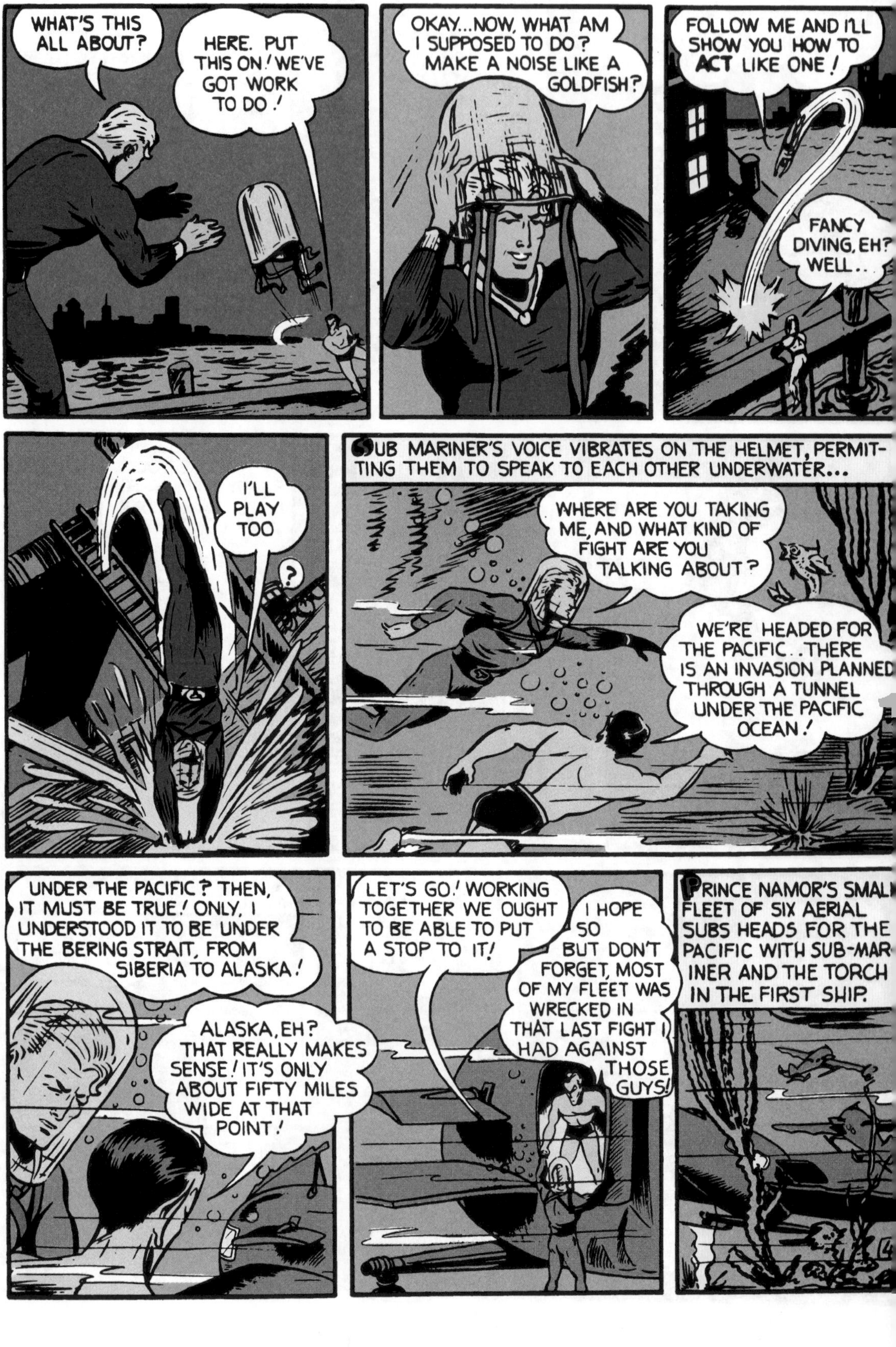
WHAT'S THIS ALL ABOUT?
HERE. PUT THIS ON! WE'VE GOT WORK TO DO!
OKAY...NOW, WHAT AM I SUPPOSED TO DO? MAKE A NOISE LIKE A GOLDFISH?
FOLLOW ME AND I'LL SHOW YOU HOW TO ACT LIKE ONE!
FANCY DIVING, EH? WELL..
I'LL PLAY TOO
?
SUB MARINER'S VOICE VIBRATES ON THE HELMET, PERMITTING THEM TO SPEAK TO EACH OTHER UNDERWATER...
WHERE ARE YOU TAKING ME, AND WHAT KIND OF FIGHT ARE YOU TALKING ABOUT?
WE'RE HEADED FOR THE PACIFIC..THERE IS AN INVASION PLANNED THROUGH A TUNNEL UNDER THE PACIFIC OCEAN!
UNDER THE PACIFIC? THEN, IT MUST BE TRUE! ONLY, I UNDERSTOOD IT TO BE UNDER THE BERING STRAIT, FROM SIBERIA TO ALASKA!
ALASKA, EH? THAT REALLY MAKES SENSE! IT'S ONLY ABOUT FIFTY MILES WIDE AT THAT POINT!
LET'S GO! WORKING TOGETHER WE OUGHT TO BE ABLE TO PUT A STOP TO IT!
I HOPE SO BUT DON'T FORGET, MOST OF MY FLEET WAS WRECKED IN THAT LAST FIGHT I HAD AGAINST THOSE GUYS!
PRINCE NAMOR'S SMAL FLEET OF SIX AERIAL SUBS HEADS FOR THE PACIFIC WITH SUB-MARINER AND THE TORCH IN THE FIRST SHIP.

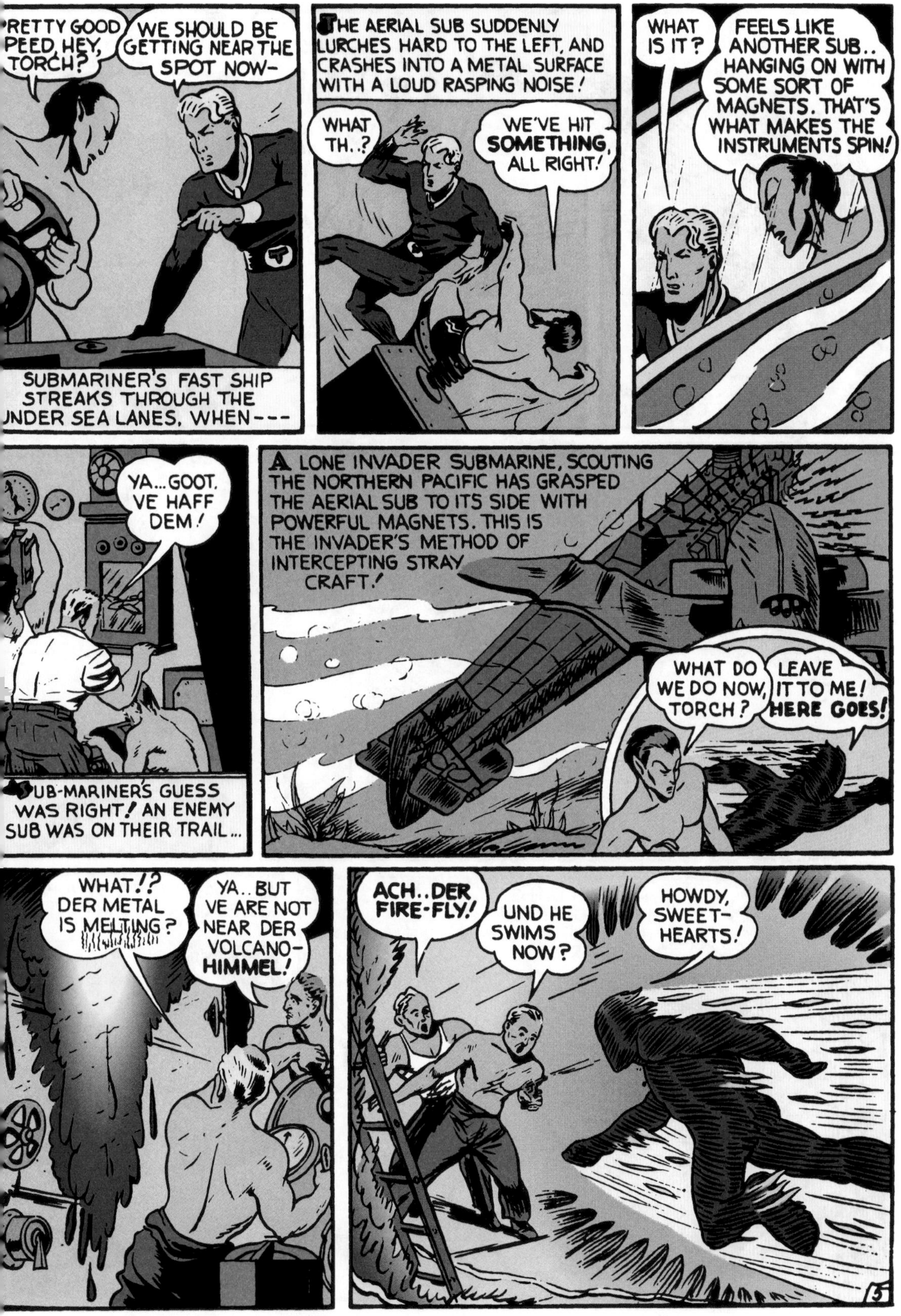

'RETTY GOOD 'PEED, HEY, TORCH?
WE SHOULD BE GETTING NEAR THE SPOT NOW-
SUBMARINER'S FAST SHIP STREAKS THROUGH THE UNDER SEA LANES, WHEN---
THE AERIAL SUB SUDDENLY LURCHES HARD TO THE LEFT, AND CRASHES INTO A METAL SURFACE WITH A LOUD RASPING NOISE!
WHAT TH..?
WE'VE HIT SOMETHING, ALL RIGHT!
WHAT IS IT?
FEELS LIKE ANOTHER SUB.. HANGING ON WITH SOME SORT OF MAGNETS. THAT'S WHAT MAKES THE INSTRUMENTS SPIN!
YA... GOOT. VE HAFF DEM!
SUB-MARINER'S GUESS WAS RIGHT! AN ENEMY SUB WAS ON THEIR TRAIL...
A LONE INVADER SUBMARINE, SCOUTING THE NORTHERN PACIFIC HAS GRASPED THE AERIAL SUB TO ITS SIDE WITH POWERFUL MAGNETS. THIS IS THE INVADER'S METHOD OF INTERCEPTING STRAY CRAFT!
WHAT DO WE DO NOW, TORCH?
LEAVE IT TO ME! HERE GOES!
WHAT!? DER METAL IS MELTING?
YA.. BUT VE ARE NOT NEAR DER VOLCANO- HIMMEL!
ACH.. DER FIRE-FLY!
UND HE SWIMS NOW?
HOWDY, SWEET- HEARTS!
5

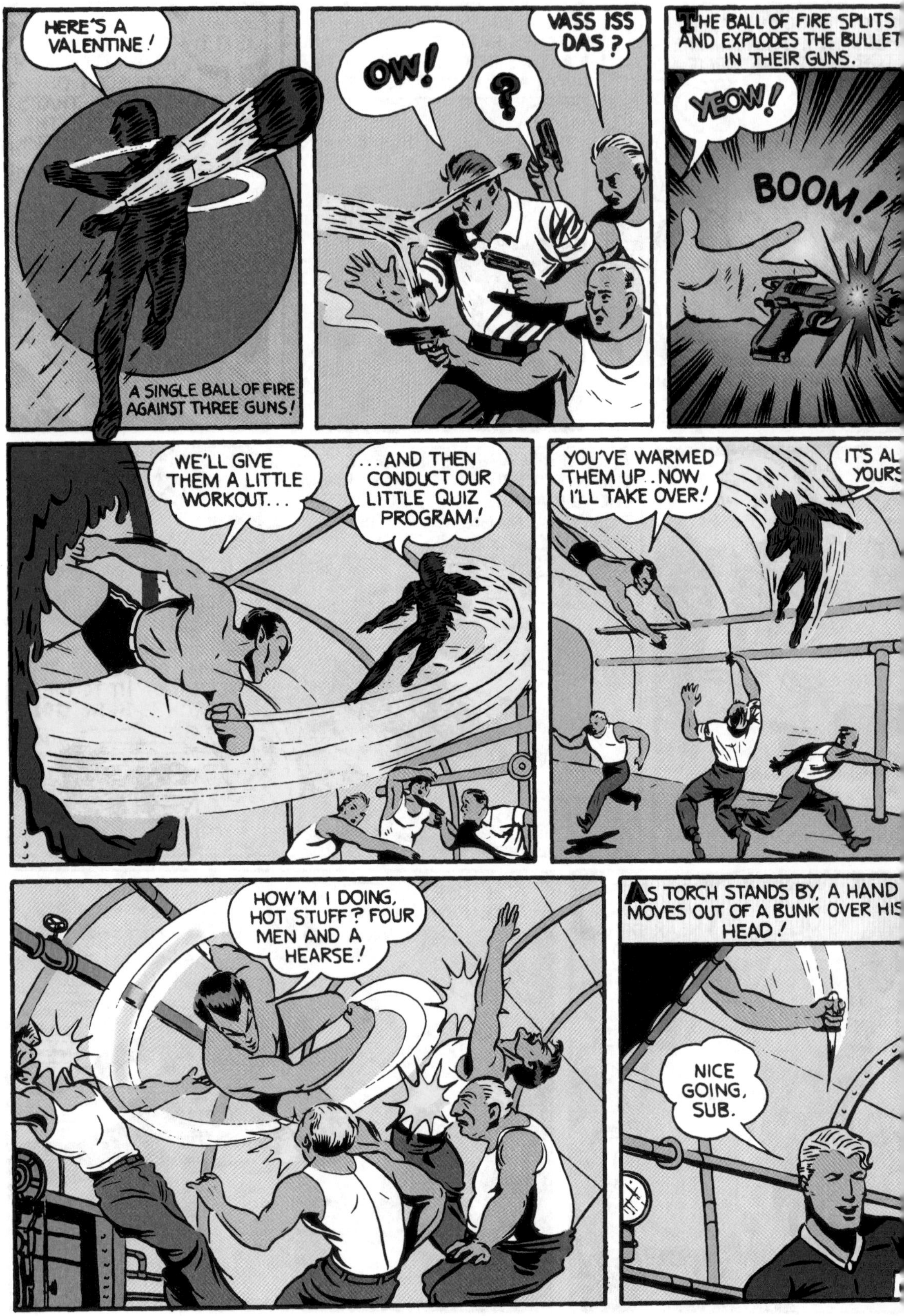
HERE'S A VALENTINE!
A SINGLE BALL OF FIRE AGAINST THREE GUNS!
OW!
?
VASS ISS DAS?
THE BALL OF FIRE SPLITS AND EXPLODES THE BULLET IN THEIR GUNS.
YEOW!
BOOM!
WE'LL GIVE THEM A LITTLE WORKOUT...
...AND THEN CONDUCT OUR LITTLE QUIZ PROGRAM!
YOU'VE WARMED THEM UP..NOW I'LL TAKE OVER!
IT'S AL YOURS
HOW'M I DOING, HOT STUFF? FOUR MEN AND A HEARSE!
AS TORCH STANDS BY, A HAND MOVES OUT OF A BUNK OVER HIS HEAD!
NICE GOING, SUB.

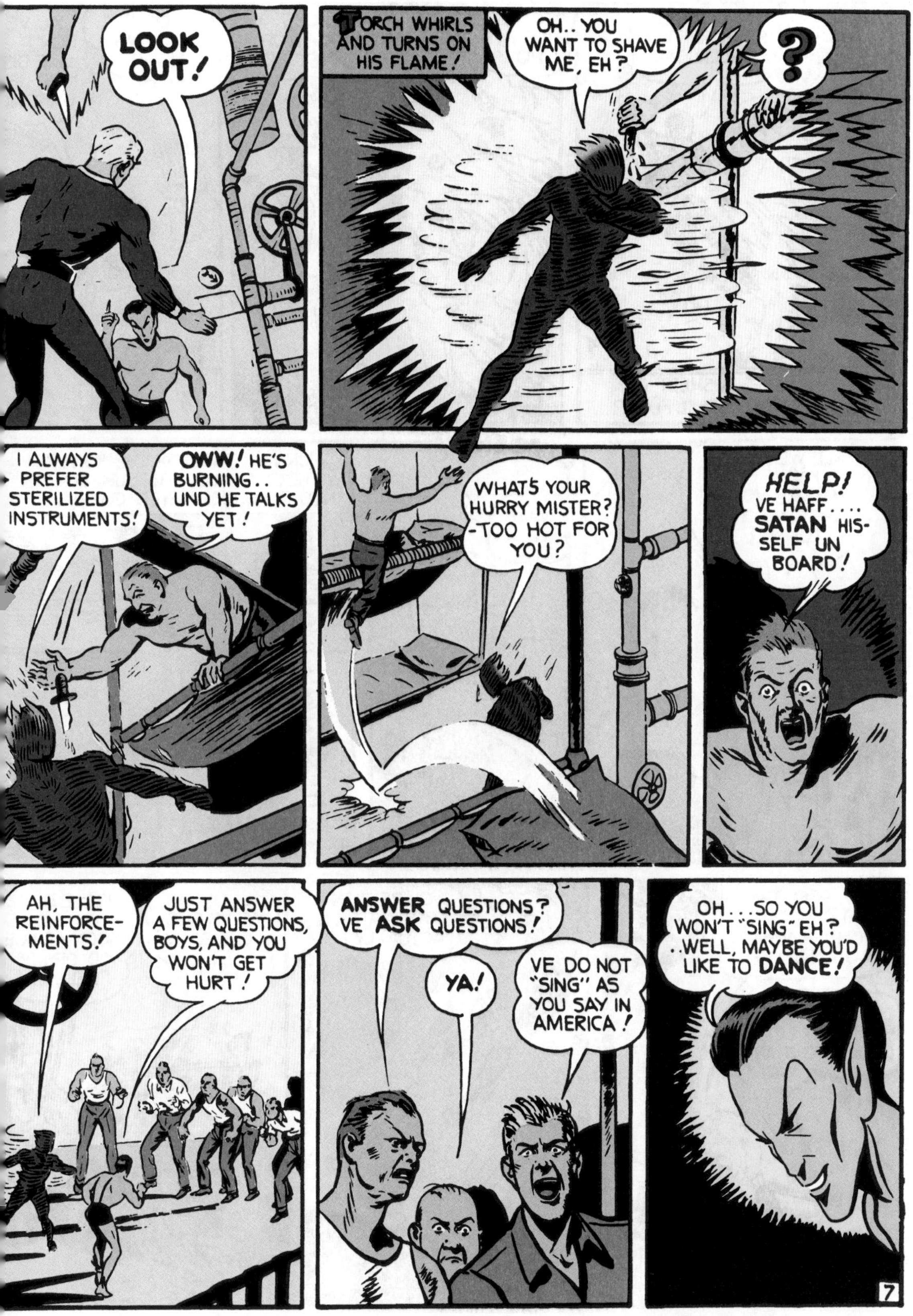
LOOK OUT!
TORCH WHIRLS AND TURNS ON HIS FLAME!
OH.. YOU WANT TO SHAVE ME, EH?
?
I ALWAYS PREFER STERILIZED INSTRUMENTS!
OWW! HE'S BURNING.. UND HE TALKS YET!
WHAT'S YOUR HURRY MISTER? -TOO HOT FOR YOU?
HELP! VE HAFF.... SATAN HIS-SELF UN BOARD!
AH, THE REINFORCE-MENTS!
JUST ANSWER A FEW QUESTIONS, BOYS, AND YOU WON'T GET HURT!
ANSWER QUESTIONS? VE ASK QUESTIONS!
YA!
VE DO NOT "SING" AS YOU SAY IN AMERICA!
OH...SO YOU WON'T "SING" EH? ..WELL, MAYBE YOU'D LIKE TO DANCE!
7

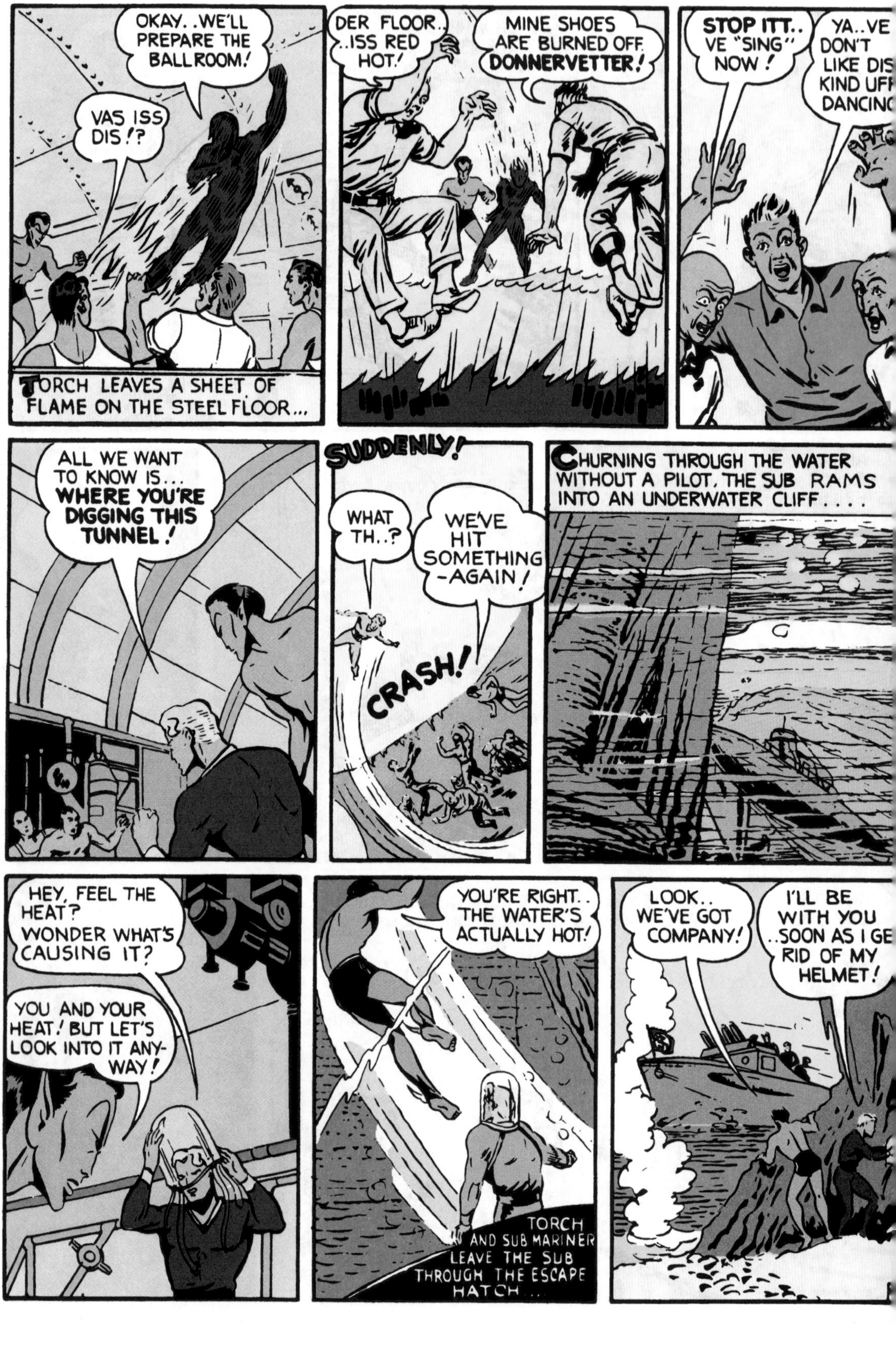
OKAY..WE'LL PREPARE THE BALLROOM!
VAS ISS DIS!?
TORCH LEAVES A SHEET OF FLAME ON THE STEEL FLOOR...
DER FLOOR.. ..ISS RED HOT!
MINE SHOES ARE BURNED OFF. DONNERVETTER!
STOP ITT.. VE "SING" NOW!
YA..VE DON'T LIKE DIS KIND UFF DANCING
ALL WE WANT TO KNOW IS... WHERE YOU'RE DIGGING THIS TUNNEL!
SUDDENLY!
WHAT TH..?
WE'VE HIT SOMETHING -AGAIN!
CRASH!
CHURNING THROUGH THE WATER WITHOUT A PILOT, THE SUB RAMS INTO AN UNDERWATER CLIFF....
HEY, FEEL THE HEAT? WONDER WHAT'S CAUSING IT?
YOU AND YOUR HEAT! BUT LET'S LOOK INTO IT ANY-WAY!
YOU'RE RIGHT.. THE WATER'S ACTUALLY HOT!
TORCH AND SUB MARINER LEAVE THE SUB THROUGH THE ESCAPE HATCH...
LOOK.. WE'VE GOT COMPANY!
I'LL BE WITH YOU ..SOON AS I GE RID OF MY HELMET!

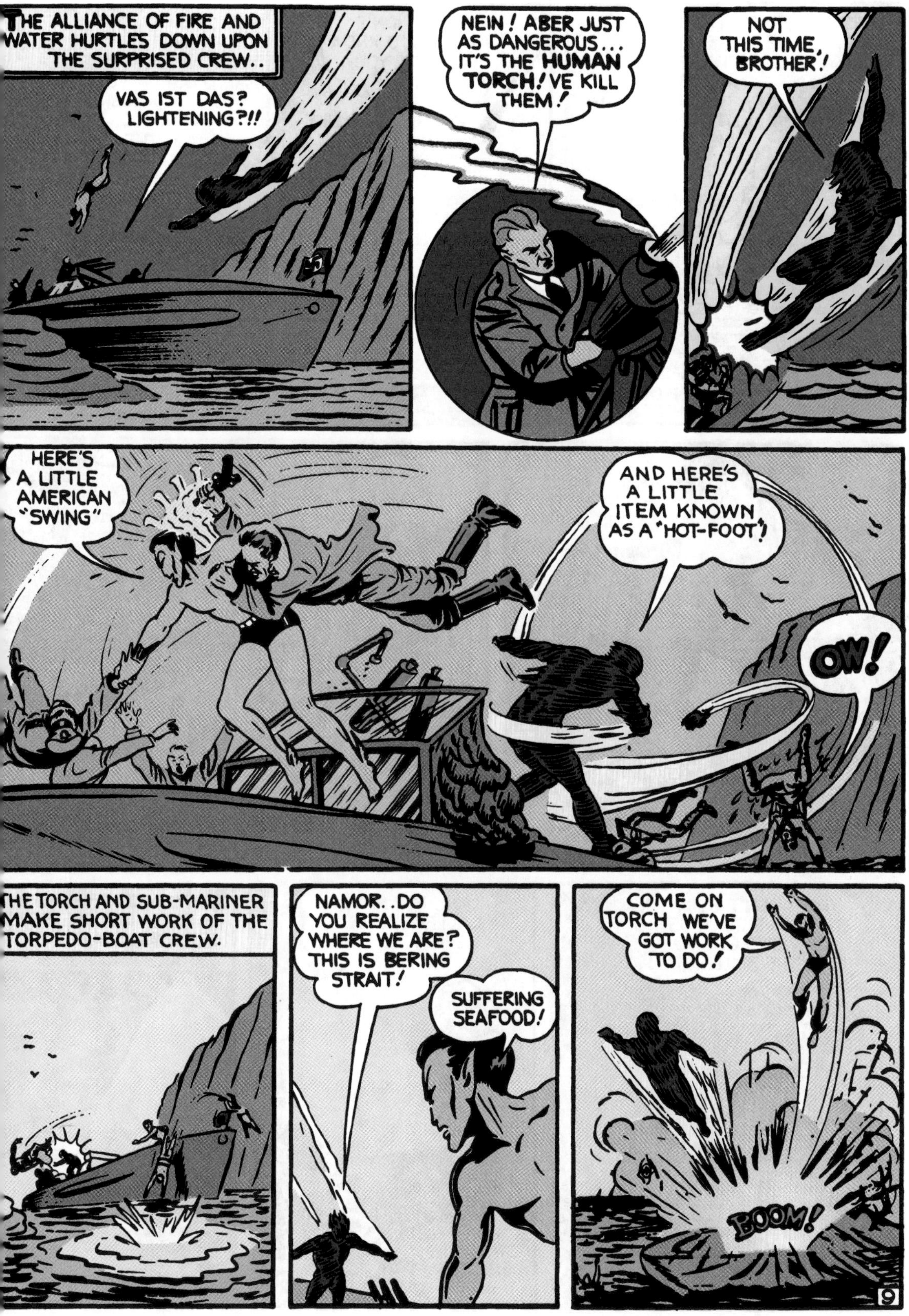
THE ALLIANCE OF FIRE AND WATER HURTLES DOWN UPON THE SURPRISED CREW..
VAS IST DAS? LIGHTENING?!!
NEIN! ABER JUST AS DANGEROUS... IT'S THE HUMAN TORCH! VE KILL THEM!
NOT THIS TIME, BROTHER!
HERE'S A LITTLE AMERICAN "SWING"
AND HERE'S A LITTLE ITEM KNOWN AS A "HOT-FOOT"!
OW!
THE TORCH AND SUB-MARINER MAKE SHORT WORK OF THE TORPEDO-BOAT CREW.
NAMOR..DO YOU REALIZE WHERE WE ARE? THIS IS BERING STRAIT!
SUFFERING SEAFOOD!
COME ON TORCH WE'VE GOT WORK TO DO!
BOOM!
9

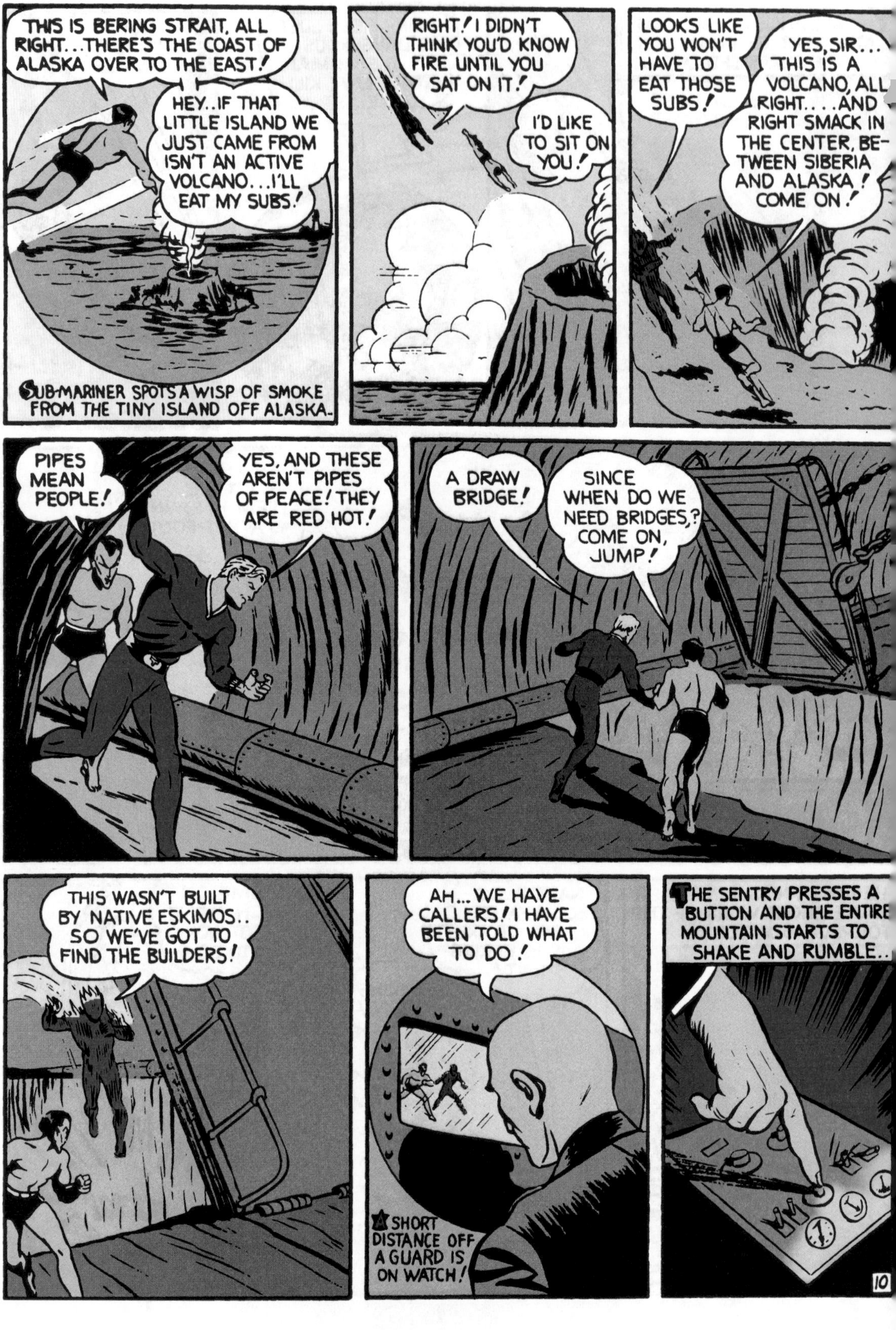
THIS IS BERING STRAIT, ALL RIGHT...THERE'S THE COAST OF ALASKA OVER TO THE EAST!
HEY..IF THAT LITTLE ISLAND WE JUST CAME FROM ISN'T AN ACTIVE VOLCANO...I'LL EAT MY SUBS!
SUB-MARINER SPOTS A WISP OF SMOKE FROM THE TINY ISLAND OFF ALASKA.
RIGHT! I DIDN'T THINK YOU'D KNOW FIRE UNTIL YOU SAT ON IT!
I'D LIKE TO SIT ON YOU!
LOOKS LIKE YOU WON'T HAVE TO EAT THOSE SUBS!
YES, SIR... THIS IS A VOLCANO, ALL RIGHT....AND RIGHT SMACK IN THE CENTER, BE-TWEEN SIBERIA AND ALASKA! COME ON!
PIPES MEAN PEOPLE!
YES, AND THESE AREN'T PIPES OF PEACE! THEY ARE RED HOT!
A DRAW BRIDGE!
SINCE WHEN DO WE NEED BRIDGES,? COME ON, JUMP!
THIS WASN'T BUILT BY NATIVE ESKIMOS.. SO WE'VE GOT TO FIND THE BUILDERS!
AH... WE HAVE CALLERS! I HAVE BEEN TOLD WHAT TO DO!
A SHORT DISTANCE OFF A GUARD IS ON WATCH!
THE SENTRY PRESSES A BUTTON AND THE ENTIRE MOUNTAIN STARTS TO SHAKE AND RUMBLE..
10

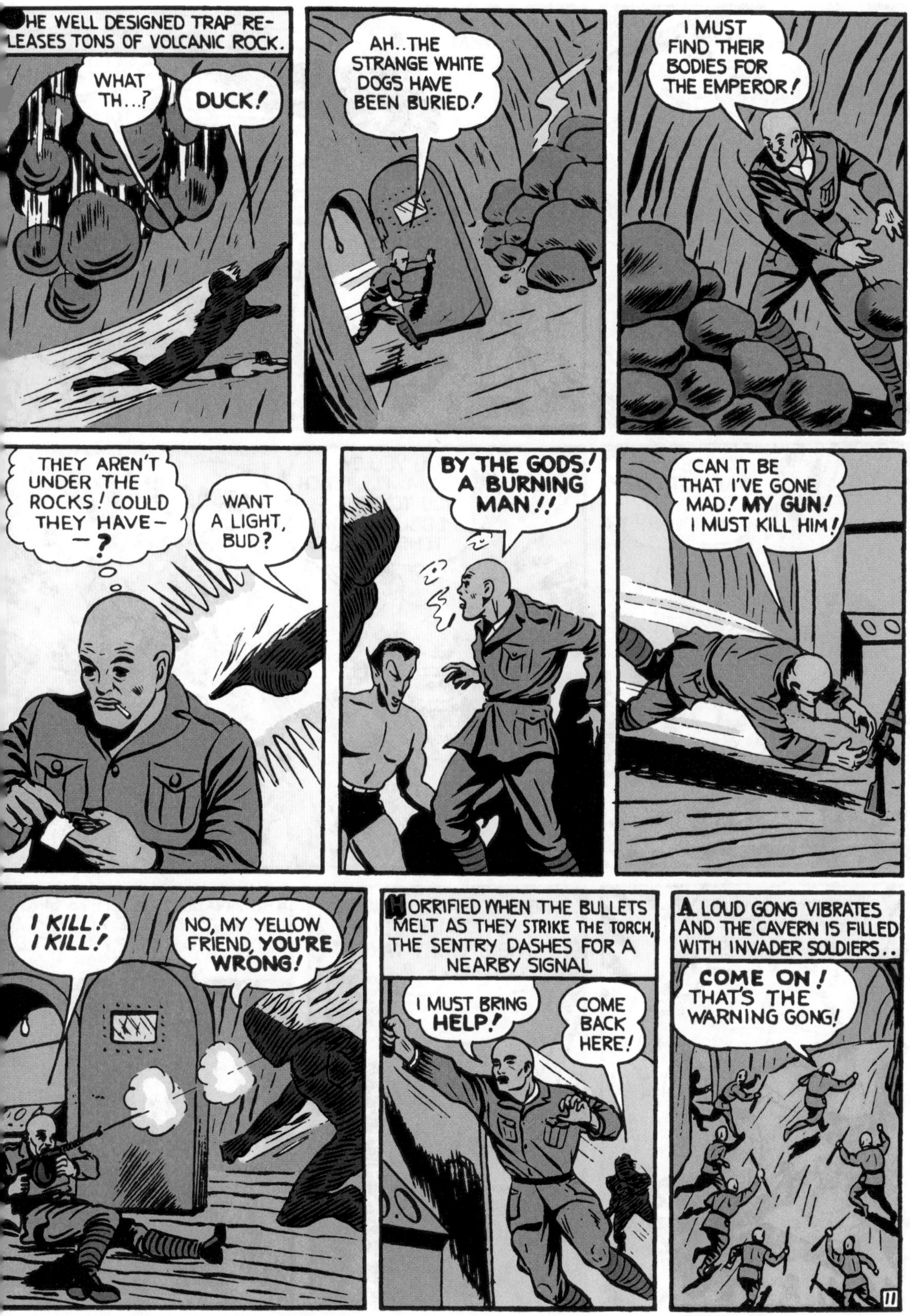
THE WELL DESIGNED TRAP RE-LEASES TONS OF VOLCANIC ROCK.
WHAT TH...?
DUCK!
AH..THE STRANGE WHITE DOGS HAVE BEEN BURIED!
I MUST FIND THEIR BODIES FOR THE EMPEROR!
THEY AREN'T UNDER THE ROCKS! COULD THEY HAVE— —?
WANT A LIGHT, BUD?
BY THE GODS! A BURNING MAN!!
CAN IT BE THAT I'VE GONE MAD! MY GUN! I MUST KILL HIM!
I KILL! I KILL!
NO, MY YELLOW FRIEND, YOU'RE WRONG!
HORRIFIED WHEN THE BULLETS MELT AS THEY STRIKE THE TORCH, THE SENTRY DASHES FOR A NEARBY SIGNAL
I MUST BRING HELP!
COME BACK HERE!
A LOUD GONG VIBRATES AND THE CAVERN IS FILLED WITH INVADER SOLDIERS..
COME ON! THAT'S THE WARNING GONG!
11

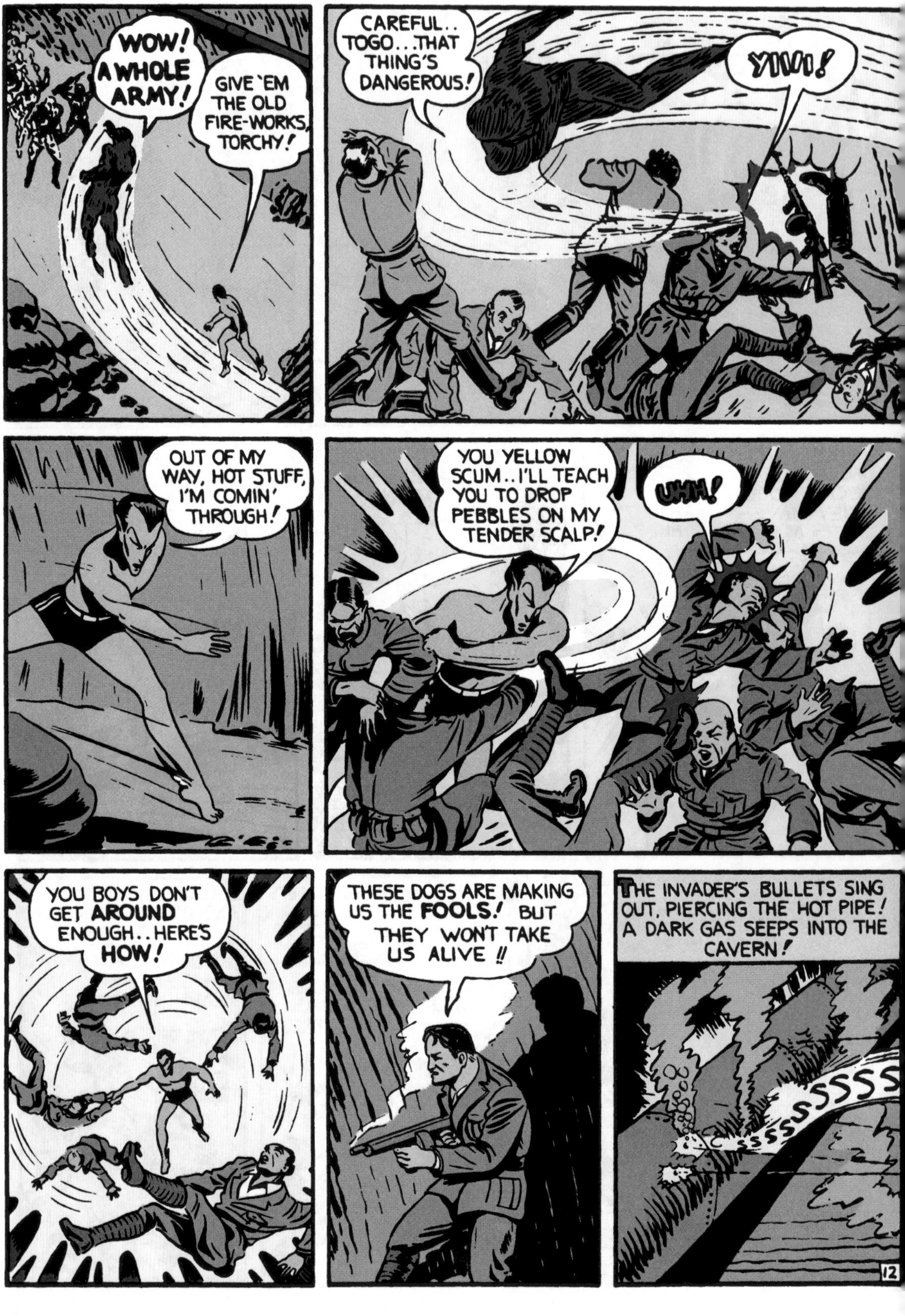
WOW! A WHOLE ARMY!
GIVE 'EM THE OLD FIRE-WORKS, TORCHY!
CAREFUL.. TOGO...THAT THING'S DANGEROUS!
YIIII!
OUT OF MY WAY, HOT STUFF, I'M COMIN' THROUGH!
YOU YELLOW SCUM..I'LL TEACH YOU TO DROP PEBBLES ON MY TENDER SCALP!
UHH!
YOU BOYS DON'T GET AROUND ENOUGH..HERE'S HOW!
THESE DOGS ARE MAKING US THE FOOLS! BUT THEY WON'T TAKE US ALIVE !!
THE INVADER'S BULLETS SING OUT, PIERCING THE HOT PIPE! A DARK GAS SEEPS INTO THE CAVERN!
SSSSSSSSS
12

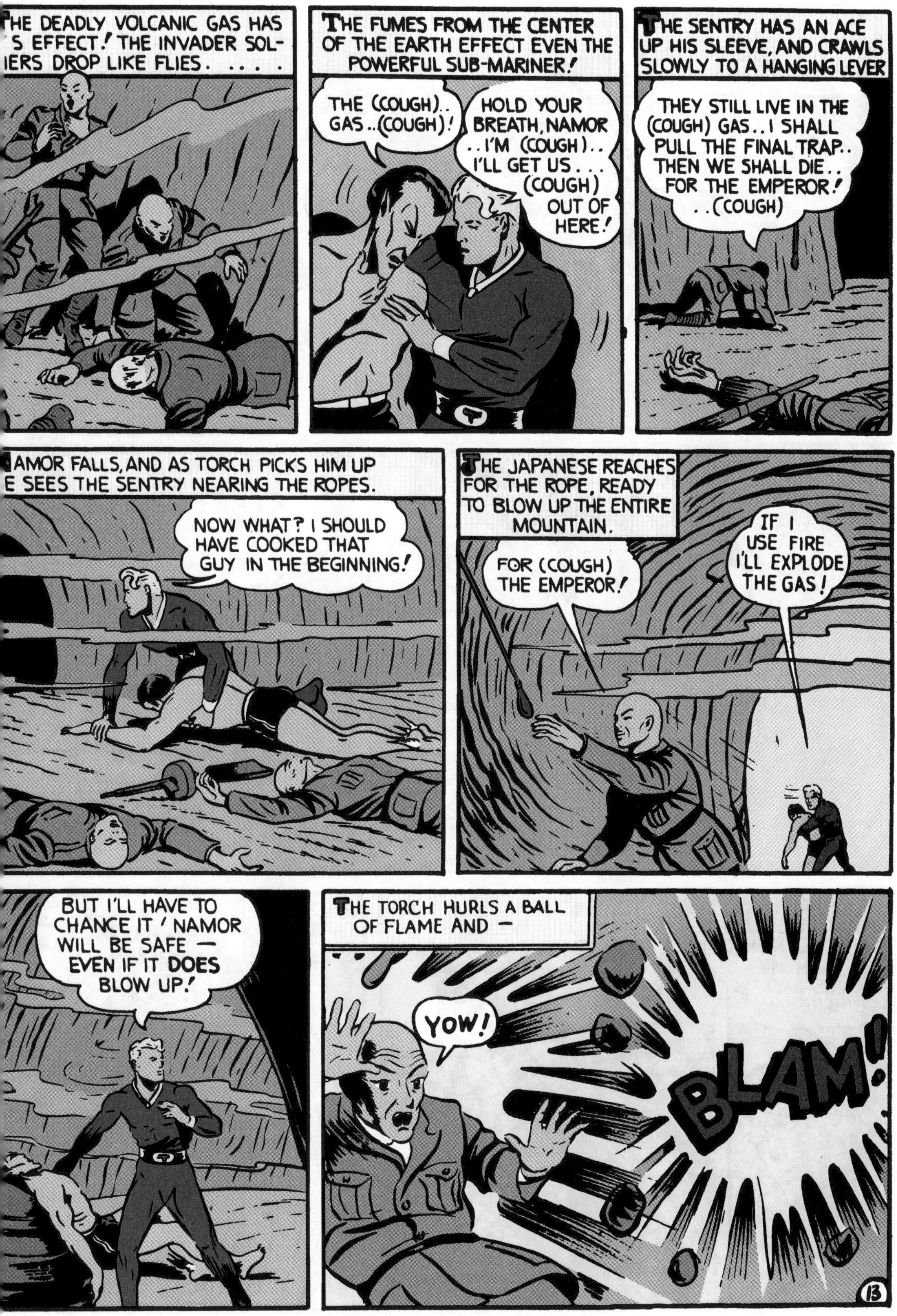
THE DEADLY VOLCANIC GAS HAS
S EFFECT! THE INVADER SOL-
IERS DROP LIKE FLIES. . . . .
THE FUMES FROM THE CENTER OF THE EARTH EFFECT EVEN THE POWERFUL SUB-MARINER!
THE (COUGH).. GAS..(COUGH)!
HOLD YOUR BREATH, NAMOR ..I'M (COUGH).. I'LL GET US... (COUGH) OUT OF HERE!
THE SENTRY HAS AN ACE UP HIS SLEEVE, AND CRAWLS SLOWLY TO A HANGING LEVER
THEY STILL LIVE IN THE (COUGH) GAS..I SHALL PULL THE FINAL TRAP.. THEN WE SHALL DIE.. FOR THE EMPEROR! ..(COUGH)
AMOR FALLS, AND AS TORCH PICKS HIM UP
E SEES THE SENTRY NEARING THE ROPES.
NOW WHAT? I SHOULD HAVE COOKED THAT GUY IN THE BEGINNING!
THE JAPANESE REACHES FOR THE ROPE, READY TO BLOW UP THE ENTIRE MOUNTAIN.
FOR (COUGH) THE EMPEROR!
IF I USE FIRE I'LL EXPLODE THE GAS!
BUT I'LL HAVE TO CHANCE IT! NAMOR WILL BE SAFE — EVEN IF IT DOES BLOW UP!
THE TORCH HURLS A BALL OF FLAME AND —
YOW!
BLAM!
13

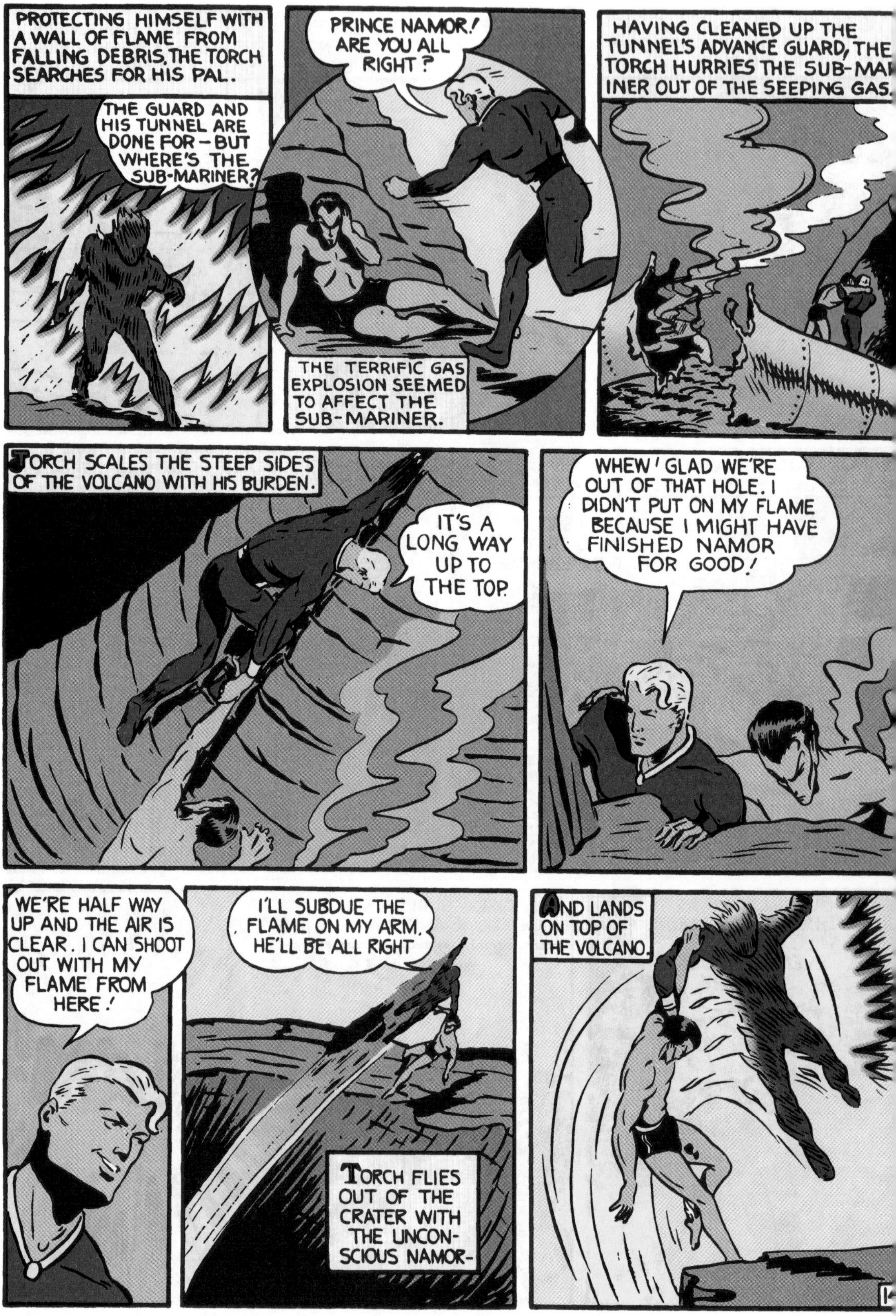
PROTECTING HIMSELF WITH A WALL OF FLAME FROM FALLING DEBRIS, THE TORCH SEARCHES FOR HIS PAL.
THE GUARD AND HIS TUNNEL ARE DONE FOR—BUT WHERE'S THE SUB-MARINER?
PRINCE NAMOR! ARE YOU ALL RIGHT?
THE TERRIFIC GAS EXPLOSION SEEMED TO AFFECT THE SUB-MARINER.
HAVING CLEANED UP THE TUNNEL'S ADVANCE GUARD, THE TORCH HURRIES THE SUB-MA INER OUT OF THE SEEPING GAS.
TORCH SCALES THE STEEP SIDES OF THE VOLCANO WITH HIS BURDEN.
IT'S A LONG WAY UP TO THE TOP.
WHEW! GLAD WE'RE OUT OF THAT HOLE. I DIDN'T PUT ON MY FLAME BECAUSE I MIGHT HAVE FINISHED NAMOR FOR GOOD!
WE'RE HALF WAY UP AND THE AIR IS CLEAR. I CAN SHOOT OUT WITH MY FLAME FROM HERE!
I'LL SUBDUE THE FLAME ON MY ARM. HE'LL BE ALL RIGHT
TORCH FLIES OUT OF THE CRATER WITH THE UNCON-SCIOUS NAMOR-
AND LANDS ON TOP OF THE VOLCANO.

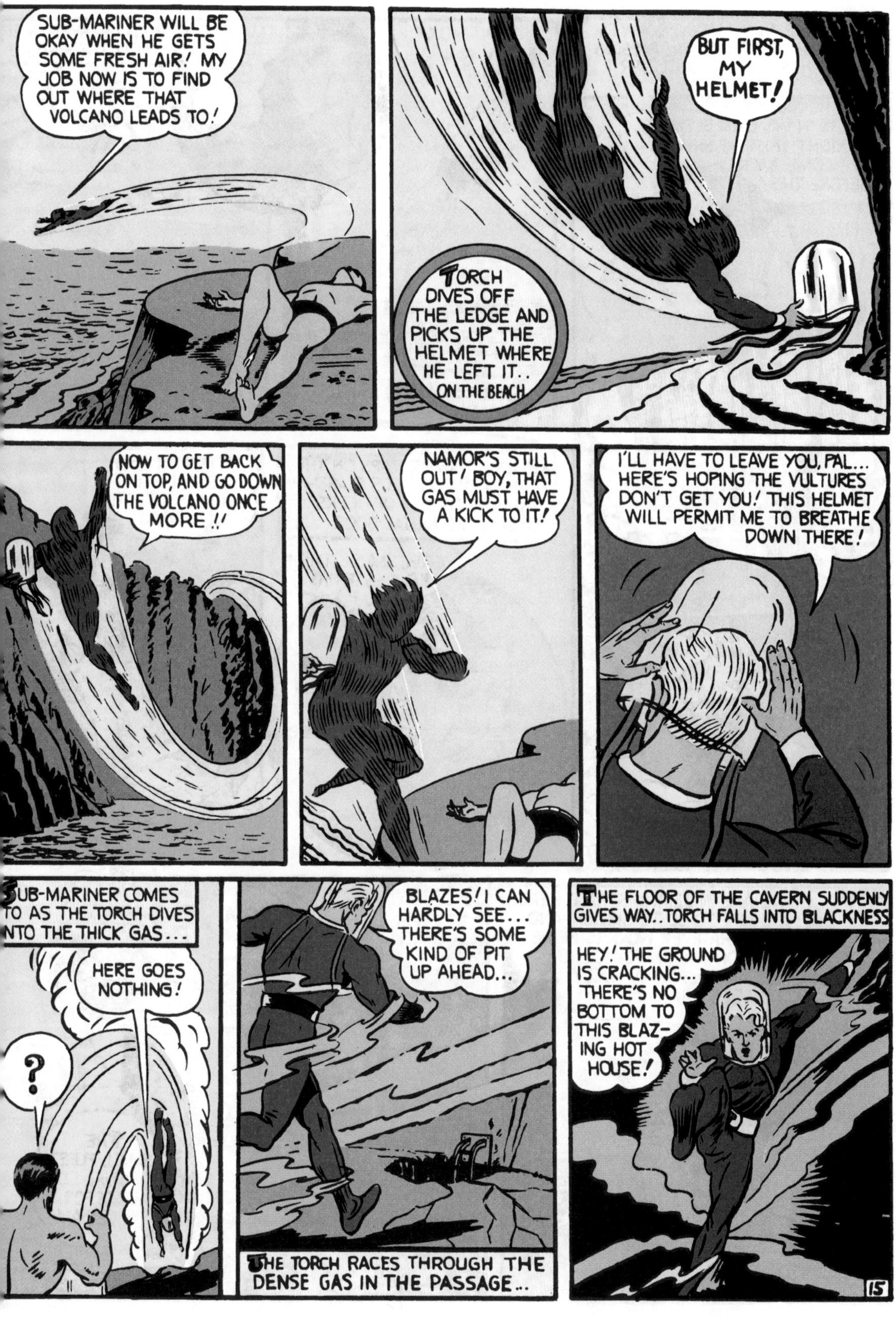
SUB-MARINER WILL BE OKAY WHEN HE GETS SOME FRESH AIR! MY JOB NOW IS TO FIND OUT WHERE THAT VOLCANO LEADS TO!
BUT FIRST, MY HELMET!
TORCH DIVES OFF THE LEDGE AND PICKS UP THE HELMET WHERE HE LEFT IT.. ON THE BEACH
NOW TO GET BACK ON TOP, AND GO DOWN THE VOLCANO ONCE MORE!!
NAMOR'S STILL OUT! BOY, THAT GAS MUST HAVE A KICK TO IT!
I'LL HAVE TO LEAVE YOU, PAL... HERE'S HOPING THE VULTURES DON'T GET YOU! THIS HELMET WILL PERMIT ME TO BREATHE DOWN THERE!
SUB-MARINER COMES TO AS THE TORCH DIVES INTO THE THICK GAS...
HERE GOES NOTHING!
?
BLAZES! I CAN HARDLY SEE... THERE'S SOME KIND OF PIT UP AHEAD...
THE TORCH RACES THROUGH THE DENSE GAS IN THE PASSAGE...
THE FLOOR OF THE CAVERN SUDDENLY GIVES WAY.. TORCH FALLS INTO BLACKNESS
HEY! THE GROUND IS CRACKING... THERE'S NO BOTTOM TO THIS BLAZ-ING HOT HOUSE!
15

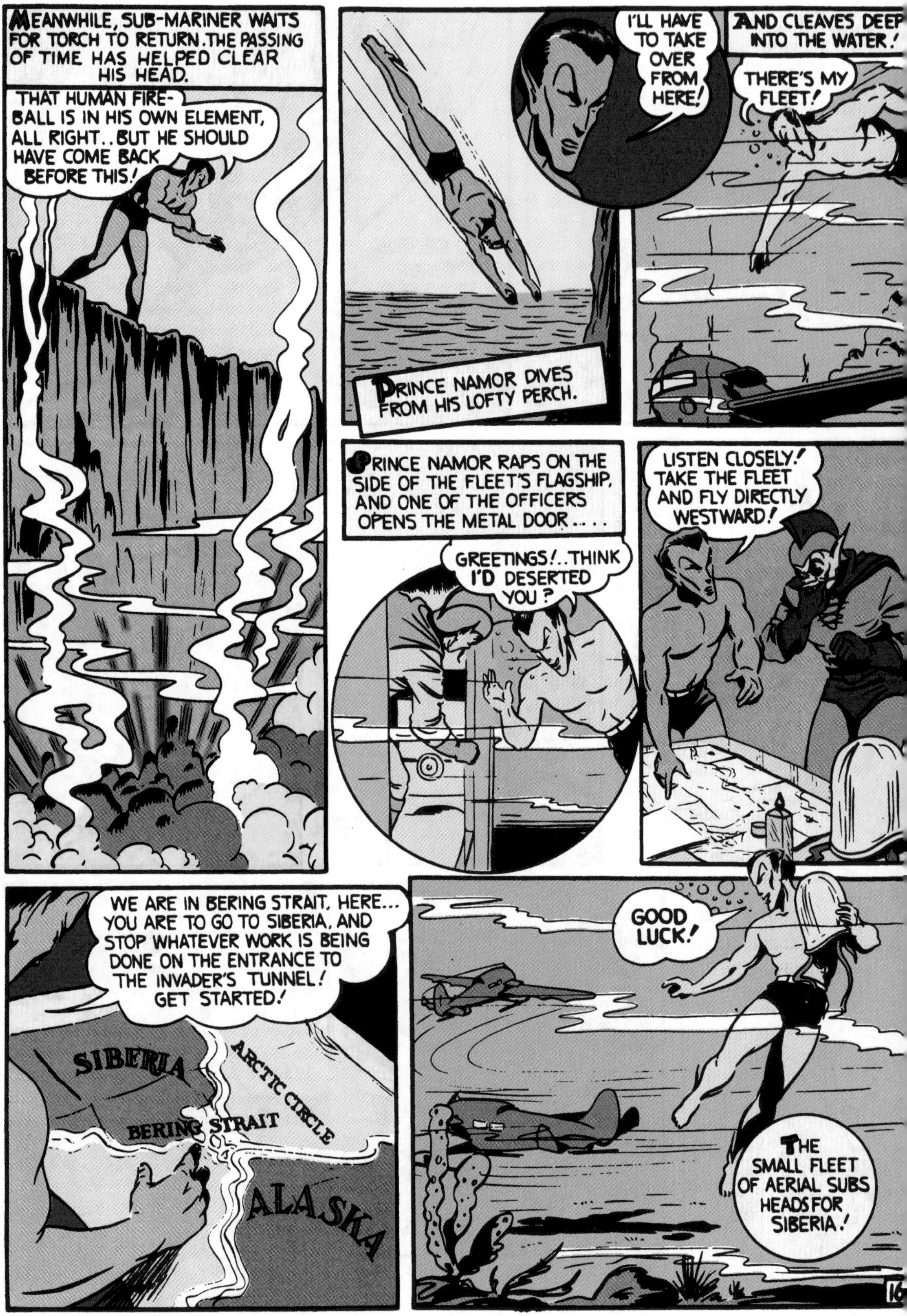

MEANWHILE, SUB-MARINER WAITS FOR TORCH TO RETURN. THE PASSING OF TIME HAS HELPED CLEAR HIS HEAD.
THAT HUMAN FIRE-BALL IS IN HIS OWN ELEMENT, ALL RIGHT.. BUT HE SHOULD HAVE COME BACK BEFORE THIS!
I'LL HAVE TO TAKE OVER FROM HERE!
PRINCE NAMOR DIVES FROM HIS LOFTY PERCH.
AND CLEAVES DEEP INTO THE WATER!
THERE'S MY FLEET!
PRINCE NAMOR RAPS ON THE SIDE OF THE FLEET'S FLAGSHIP, AND ONE OF THE OFFICERS OPENS THE METAL DOOR.....
GREETINGS!..THINK I'D DESERTED YOU?
LISTEN CLOSELY! TAKE THE FLEET AND FLY DIRECTLY WESTWARD!
WE ARE IN BERING STRAIT, HERE... YOU ARE TO GO TO SIBERIA, AND STOP WHATEVER WORK IS BEING DONE ON THE ENTRANCE TO THE INVADER'S TUNNEL! GET STARTED!
SIBERIA
ARCTIC CIRCLE
BERING STRAIT
ALASKA
GOOD LUCK!
THE SMALL FLEET OF AERIAL SUBS HEADS FOR SIBERIA!
16

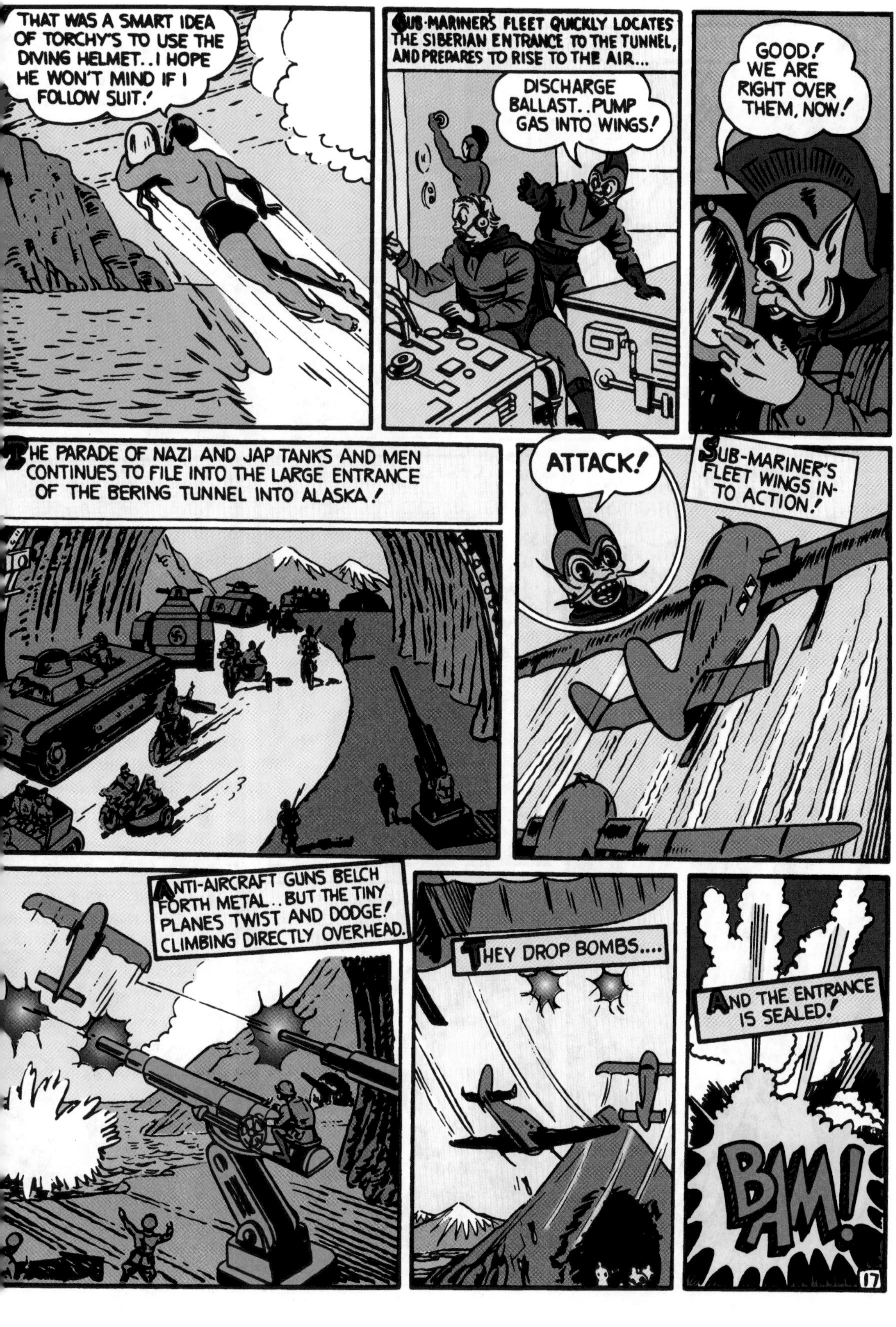
THAT WAS A SMART IDEA OF TORCHY'S TO USE THE DIVING HELMET..I HOPE HE WON'T MIND IF I FOLLOW SUIT!
SUB-MARINER'S FLEET QUICKLY LOCATES THE SIBERIAN ENTRANCE TO THE TUNNEL, AND PREPARES TO RISE TO THE AIR...
DISCHARGE BALLAST..PUMP GAS INTO WINGS!
GOOD! WE ARE RIGHT OVER THEM, NOW!
THE PARADE OF NAZI AND JAP TANKS AND MEN CONTINUES TO FILE INTO THE LARGE ENTRANCE OF THE BERING TUNNEL INTO ALASKA!
ATTACK!
SUB-MARINER'S FLEET WINGS INTO ACTION!
ANTI-AIRCRAFT GUNS BELCH FORTH METAL.. BUT THE TINY PLANES TWIST AND DODGE! CLIMBING DIRECTLY OVERHEAD.
THEY DROP BOMBS....
AND THE ENTRANCE IS SEALED!
BLAM!

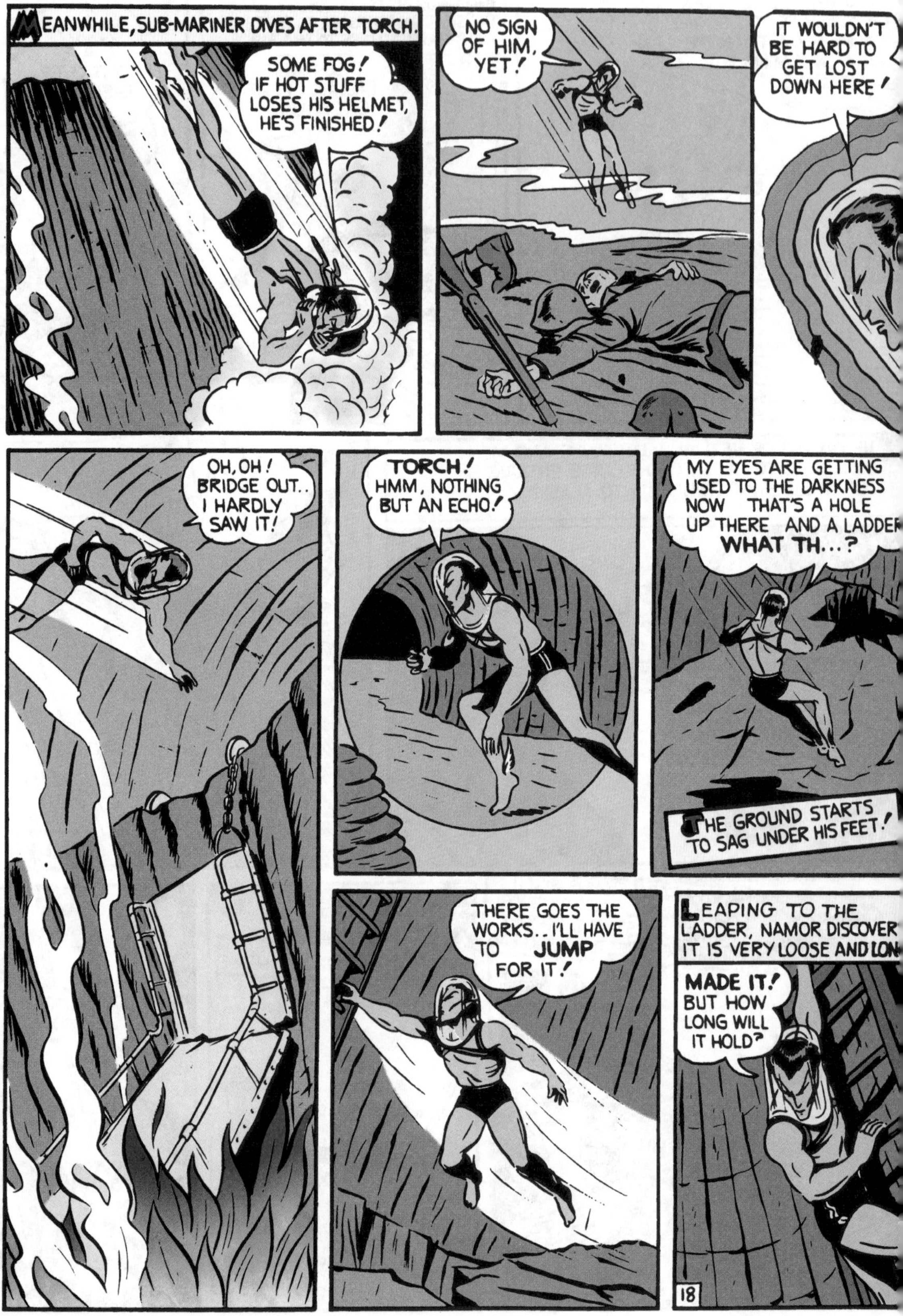
MEANWHILE, SUB-MARINER DIVES AFTER TORCH.
SOME FOG! IF HOT STUFF LOSES HIS HELMET, HE'S FINISHED!
NO SIGN OF HIM, YET!
IT WOULDN'T BE HARD TO GET LOST DOWN HERE!
OH, OH! BRIDGE OUT.. I HARDLY SAW IT!
TORCH! HMM, NOTHING BUT AN ECHO!
MY EYES ARE GETTING USED TO THE DARKNESS NOW THAT'S A HOLE UP THERE AND A LADDER
WHAT TH...?
THE GROUND STARTS TO SAG UNDER HIS FEET!
THERE GOES THE WORKS.. I'LL HAVE TO JUMP FOR IT!
LEAPING TO THE LADDER, NAMOR DISCOVER
IT IS VERY LOOSE AND LON
MADE IT! BUT HOW LONG WILL IT HOLD?

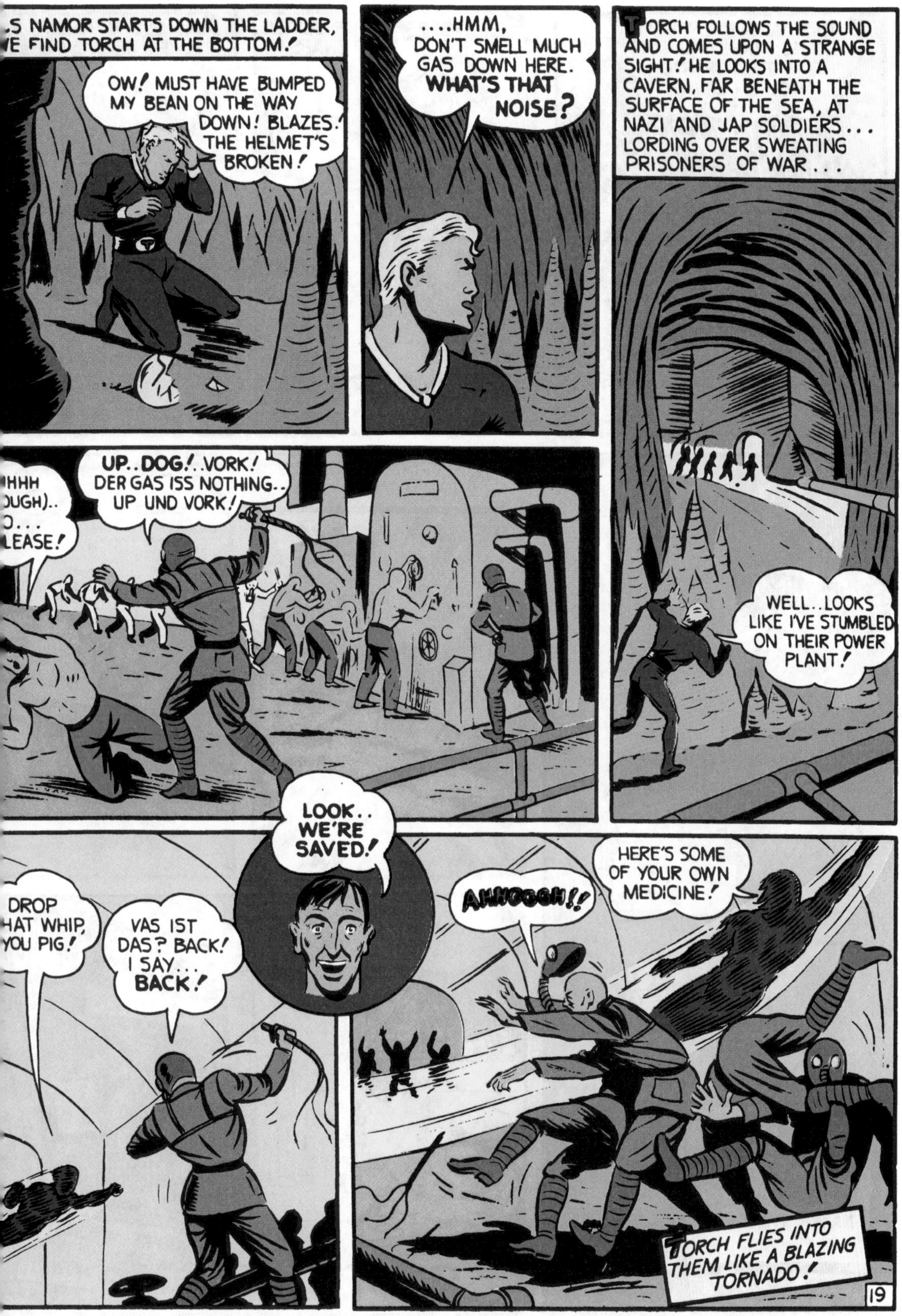

...S NAMOR STARTS DOWN THE LADDER, ...E FIND TORCH AT THE BOTTOM!
OW! MUST HAVE BUMPED MY BEAN ON THE WAY DOWN! BLAZES! THE HELMET'S BROKEN!
....HMM, DON'T SMELL MUCH GAS DOWN HERE. WHAT'S THAT NOISE?
TORCH FOLLOWS THE SOUND AND COMES UPON A STRANGE SIGHT! HE LOOKS INTO A CAVERN, FAR BENEATH THE SURFACE OF THE SEA, AT NAZI AND JAP SOLDIERS... LORDING OVER SWEATING PRISONERS OF WAR...
...HHH ...OUGH).. ...O... ...LEASE!
UP..DOG!..VORK! DER GAS ISS NOTHING.. UP UND VORK!
WELL..LOOKS LIKE I'VE STUMBLED ON THEIR POWER PLANT!
LOOK.. WE'RE SAVED!
DROP ...HAT WHIP, YOU PIG!
VAS IST DAS? BACK! I SAY... BACK!
AHHOOGGH!!
HERE'S SOME OF YOUR OWN MEDICINE!
TORCH FLIES INTO THEM LIKE A BLAZING TORNADO!

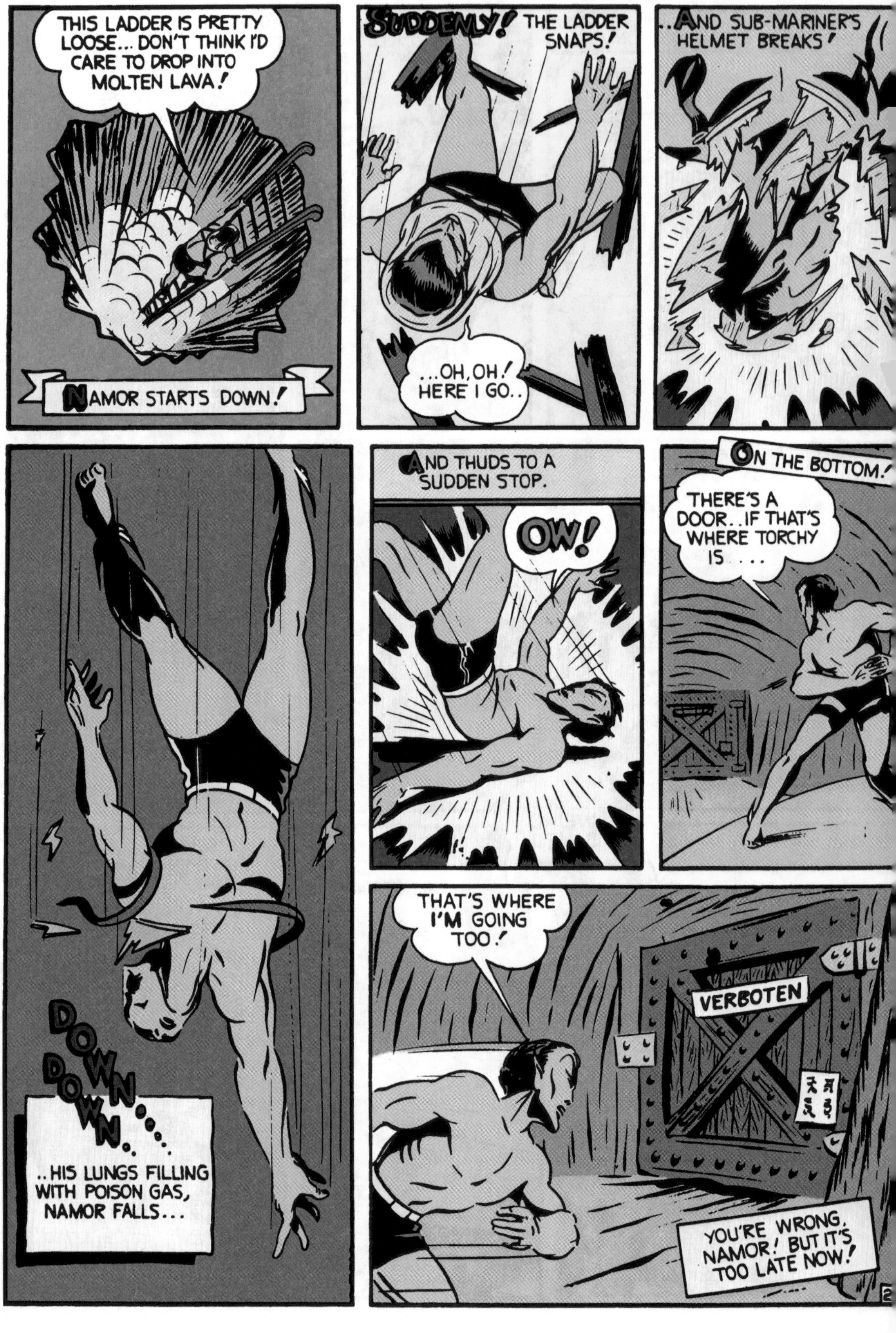
THIS LADDER IS PRETTY LOOSE... DON'T THINK I'D CARE TO DROP INTO MOLTEN LAVA!
NAMOR STARTS DOWN!
SUDDENLY! THE LADDER SNAPS!
...OH, OH! HERE I GO..
..AND SUB-MARINER'S HELMET BREAKS!
DOWN DOWN....
..HIS LUNGS FILLING WITH POISON GAS, NAMOR FALLS...
AND THUDS TO A SUDDEN STOP.
OW!
ON THE BOTTOM!
THERE'S A DOOR..IF THAT'S WHERE TORCHY IS . . .
THAT'S WHERE I'M GOING TOO!
VERBOTEN
YOU'RE WRONG, NAMOR! BUT IT'S TOO LATE NOW!

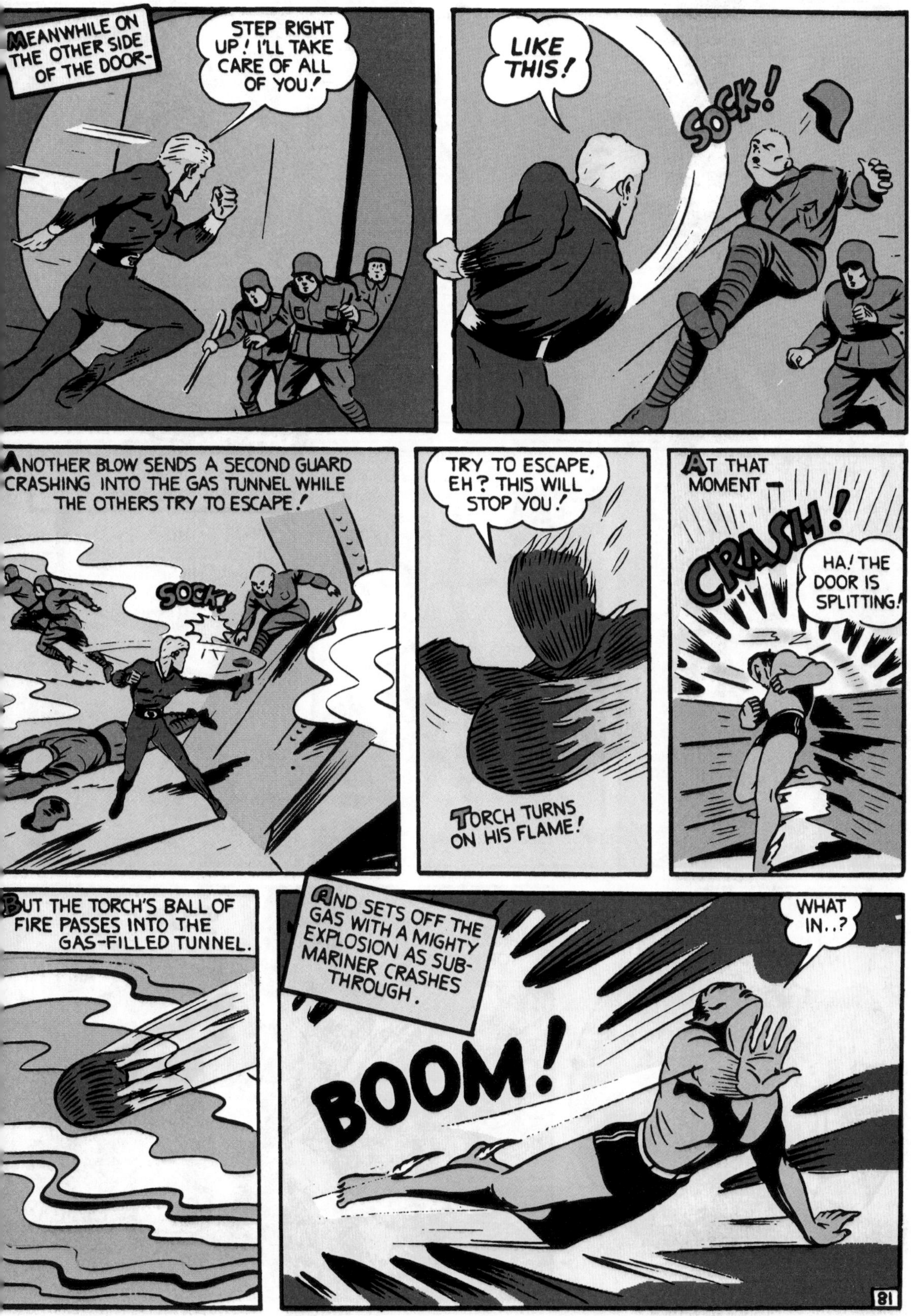
MEANWHILE ON THE OTHER SIDE OF THE DOOR-
STEP RIGHT UP! I'LL TAKE CARE OF ALL OF YOU!
LIKE THIS!
SOCK!
ANOTHER BLOW SENDS A SECOND GUARD CRASHING INTO THE GAS TUNNEL WHILE THE OTHERS TRY TO ESCAPE!
SOCK!
TRY TO ESCAPE, EH? THIS WILL STOP YOU!
TORCH TURNS ON HIS FLAME!
AT THAT MOMENT -
CRASH!
HA! THE DOOR IS SPLITTING!
BUT THE TORCH'S BALL OF FIRE PASSES INTO THE GAS-FILLED TUNNEL.
AND SETS OFF THE GAS WITH A MIGHTY EXPLOSION AS SUB-MARINER CRASHES THROUGH.
WHAT IN..?
BOOM!
81

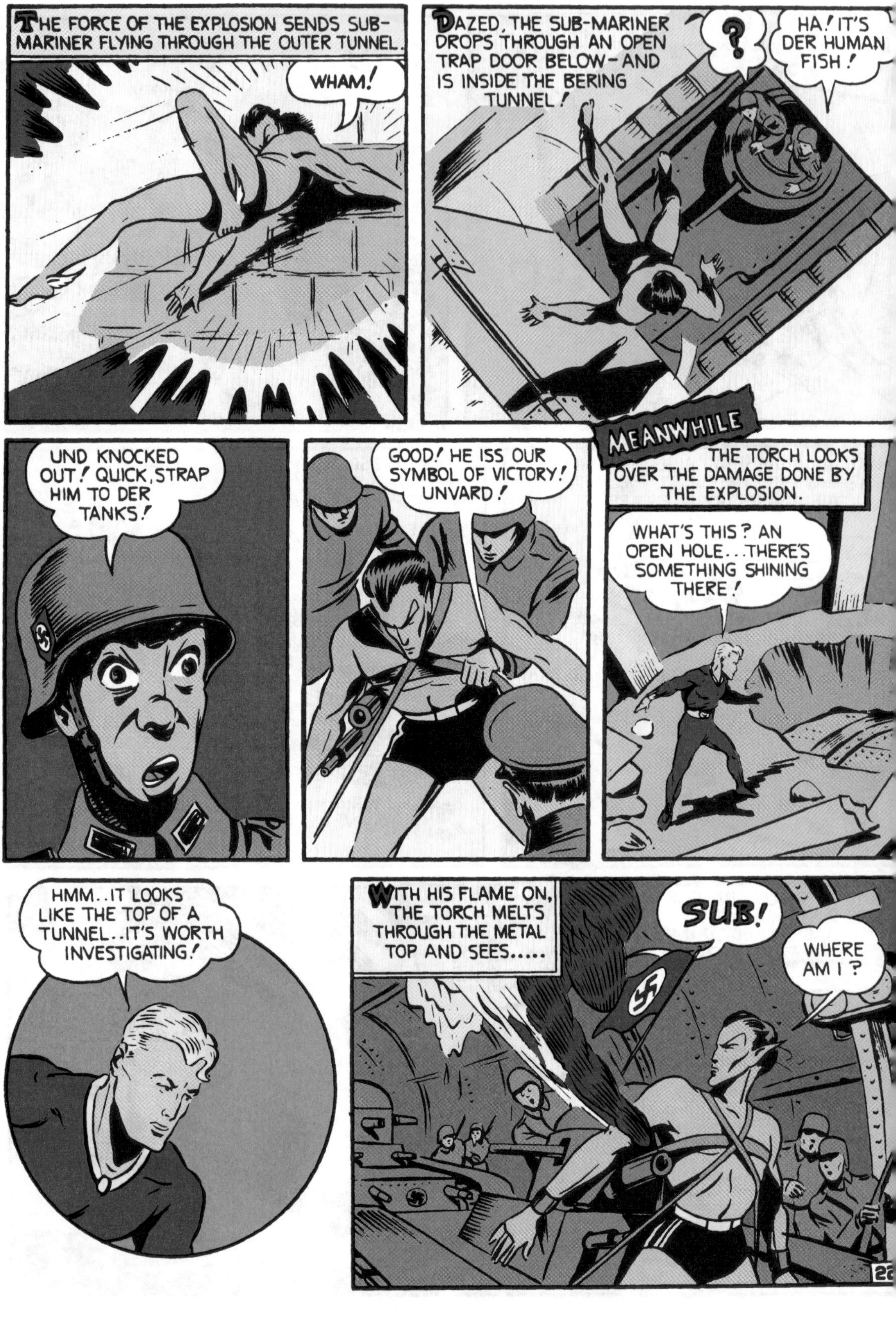
THE FORCE OF THE EXPLOSION SENDS SUB-MARINER FLYING THROUGH THE OUTER TUNNEL.
WHAM!
DAZED, THE SUB-MARINER DROPS THROUGH AN OPEN TRAP DOOR BELOW—AND IS INSIDE THE BERING TUNNEL!
?
HA! IT'S DER HUMAN FISH!
UND KNOCKED OUT! QUICK, STRAP HIM TO DER TANKS!
GOOD! HE ISS OUR SYMBOL OF VICTORY! UNVARD!
MEANWHILE
THE TORCH LOOKS OVER THE DAMAGE DONE BY THE EXPLOSION.
WHAT'S THIS? AN OPEN HOLE...THERE'S SOMETHING SHINING THERE!
HMM..IT LOOKS LIKE THE TOP OF A TUNNEL..IT'S WORTH INVESTIGATING!
WITH HIS FLAME ON, THE TORCH MELTS THROUGH THE METAL TOP AND SEES.....
SUB!
WHERE AM I?
22

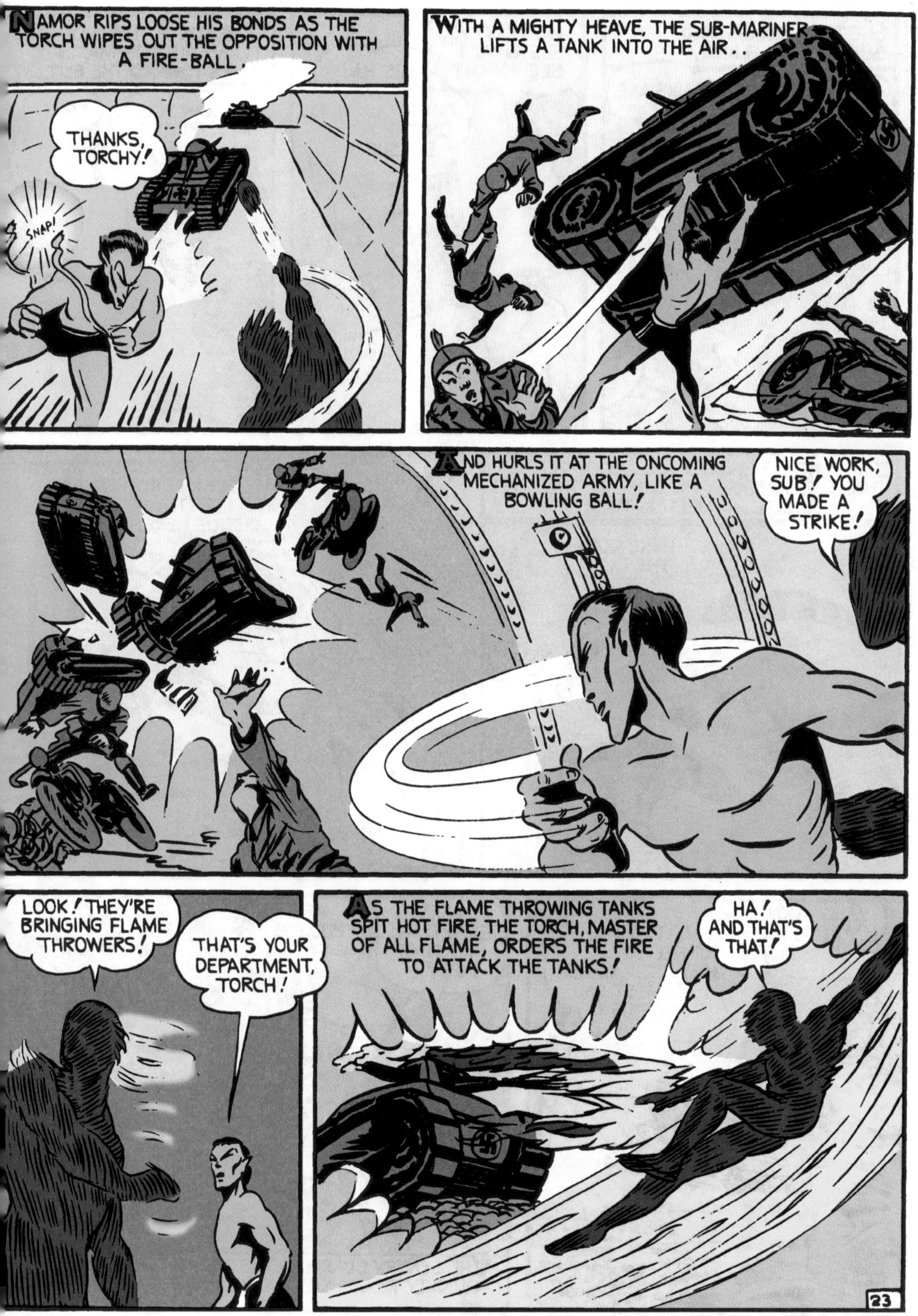
NAMOR RIPS LOOSE HIS BONDS AS THE TORCH WIPES OUT THE OPPOSITION WITH A FIRE-BALL . .
THANKS, TORCHY!
SNAP!
WITH A MIGHTY HEAVE, THE SUB-MARINER LIFTS A TANK INTO THE AIR . .
AND HURLS IT AT THE ONCOMING MECHANIZED ARMY, LIKE A BOWLING BALL!
NICE WORK, SUB! YOU MADE A STRIKE!
LOOK! THEY'RE BRINGING FLAME THROWERS!
THAT'S YOUR DEPARTMENT, TORCH!
AS THE FLAME THROWING TANKS SPIT HOT FIRE, THE TORCH, MASTER OF ALL FLAME, ORDERS THE FIRE TO ATTACK THE TANKS!
HA! AND THAT'S THAT!

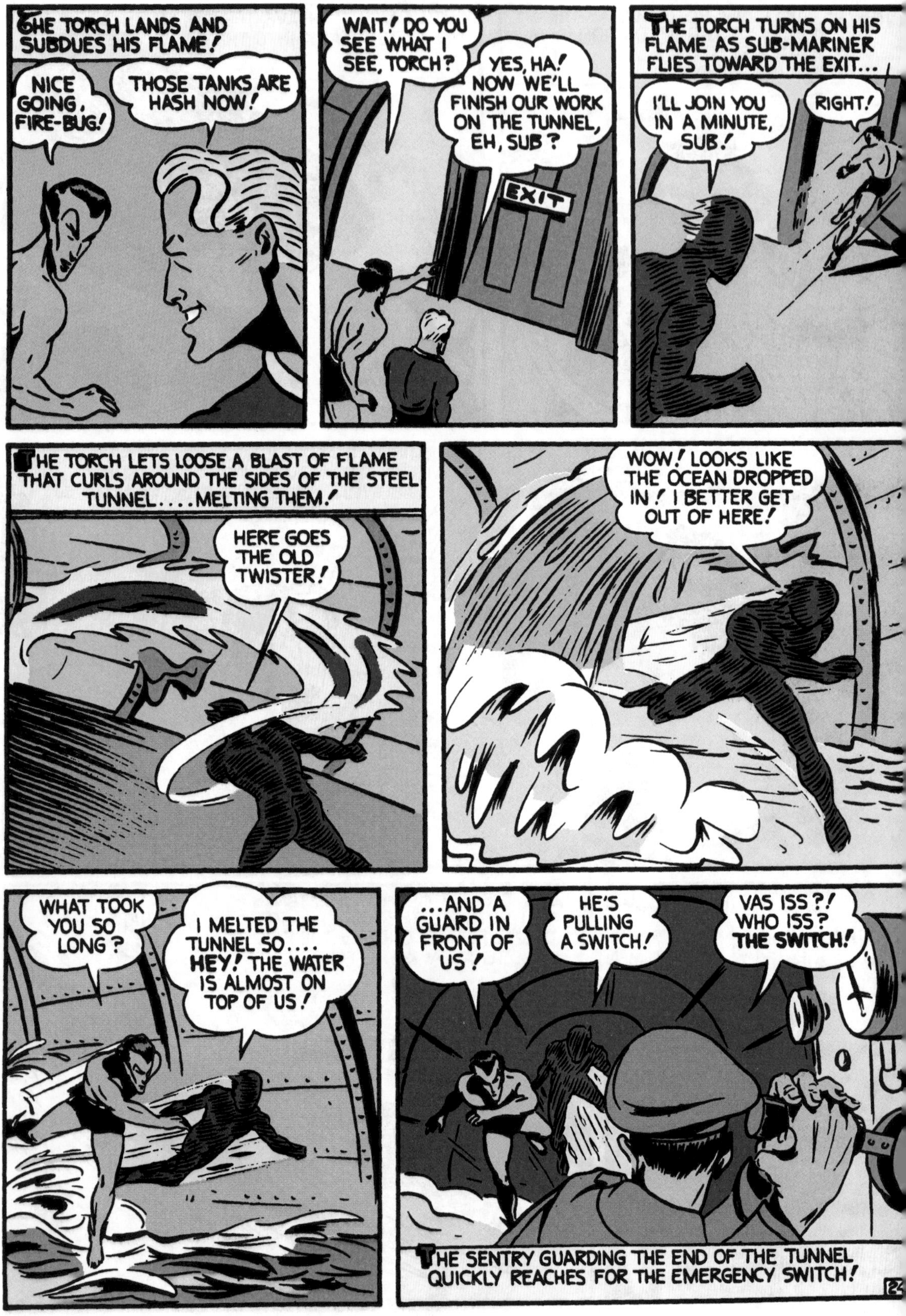
THE TORCH LANDS AND SUBDUES HIS FLAME!
NICE GOING, FIRE-BUG!
THOSE TANKS ARE HASH NOW!
WAIT! DO YOU SEE WHAT I SEE, TORCH?
YES, HA! NOW WE'LL FINISH OUR WORK ON THE TUNNEL, EH, SUB?
EXIT
THE TORCH TURNS ON HIS FLAME AS SUB-MARINER FLIES TOWARD THE EXIT...
I'LL JOIN YOU IN A MINUTE, SUB!
RIGHT!
THE TORCH LETS LOOSE A BLAST OF FLAME THAT CURLS AROUND THE SIDES OF THE STEEL TUNNEL....MELTING THEM!
HERE GOES THE OLD TWISTER!
WOW! LOOKS LIKE THE OCEAN DROPPED IN! I BETTER GET OUT OF HERE!
WHAT TOOK YOU SO LONG?
I MELTED THE TUNNEL SO.... HEY! THE WATER IS ALMOST ON TOP OF US!
...AND A GUARD IN FRONT OF US!
HE'S PULLING A SWITCH!
VAS ISS?! WHO ISS? THE SWITCH!
THE SENTRY GUARDING THE END OF THE TUNNEL QUICKLY REACHES FOR THE EMERGENCY SWITCH!

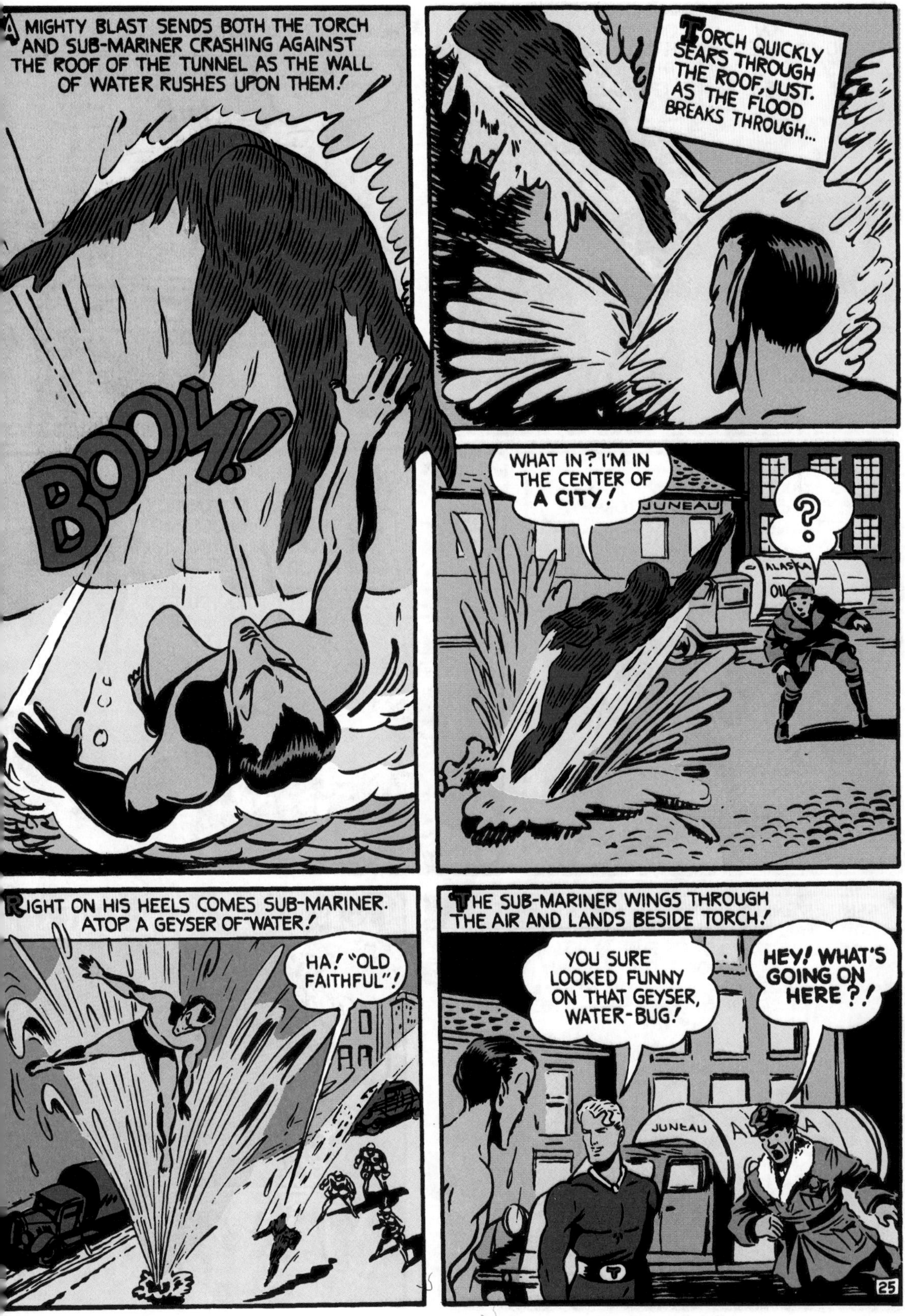
A MIGHTY BLAST SENDS BOTH THE TORCH AND SUB-MARINER CRASHING AGAINST THE ROOF OF THE TUNNEL AS THE WALL OF WATER RUSHES UPON THEM!
BOOM!!
TORCH QUICKLY SEARS THROUGH THE ROOF, JUST AS THE FLOOD BREAKS THROUGH...
WHAT IN? I'M IN THE CENTER OF A CITY!
JUNEAU
?
ALASKA
OIL
RIGHT ON HIS HEELS COMES SUB-MARINER. ATOP A GEYSER OF WATER!
HA! "OLD FAITHFUL"!
THE SUB-MARINER WINGS THROUGH THE AIR AND LANDS BESIDE TORCH!
YOU SURE LOOKED FUNNY ON THAT GEYSER, WATER-BUG!
HEY! WHAT'S GOING ON HERE?!
JUNEAU
25

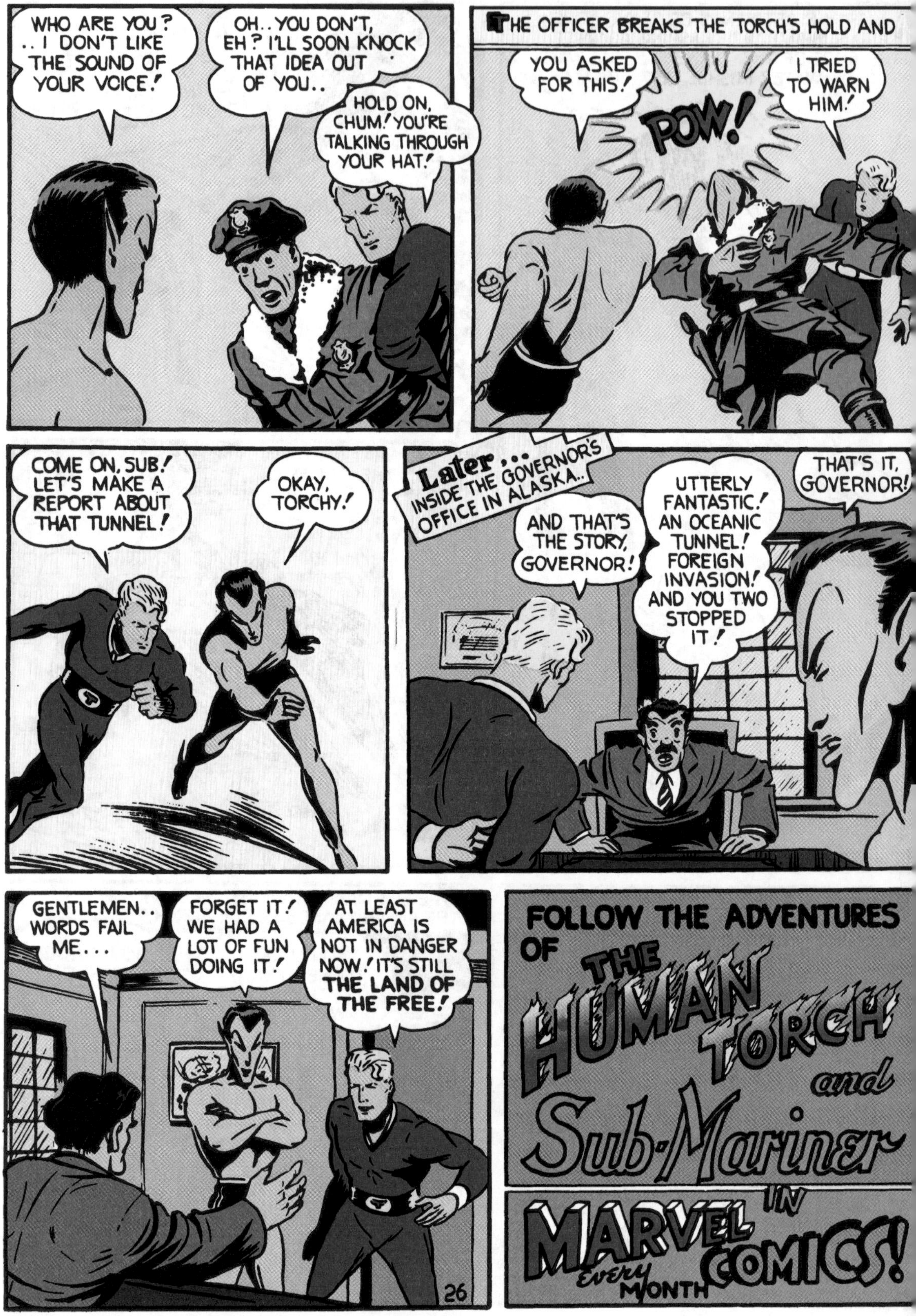
WHO ARE YOU? .. I DON'T LIKE THE SOUND OF YOUR VOICE!
OH.. YOU DON'T, EH? I'LL SOON KNOCK THAT IDEA OUT OF YOU..
HOLD ON, CHUM! YOU'RE TALKING THROUGH YOUR HAT!
THE OFFICER BREAKS THE TORCH'S HOLD AND
YOU ASKED FOR THIS!
POW!
I TRIED TO WARN HIM!
COME ON, SUB! LET'S MAKE A REPORT ABOUT THAT TUNNEL!
OKAY, TORCHY!
Later... INSIDE THE GOVERNOR'S OFFICE IN ALASKA..
AND THAT'S THE STORY, GOVERNOR!
UTTERLY FANTASTIC! AN OCEANIC TUNNEL! FOREIGN INVASION! AND YOU TWO STOPPED IT!
THAT'S IT, GOVERNOR!
GENTLEMEN.. WORDS FAIL ME...
FORGET IT! WE HAD A LOT OF FUN DOING IT!
AT LEAST AMERICA IS NOT IN DANGER NOW! IT'S STILL THE LAND OF THE FREE!
26
FOLLOW THE ADVENTURES OF THE HUMAN TORCH and Sub-Mariner
IN MARVEL COMICS! EVERY MONTH

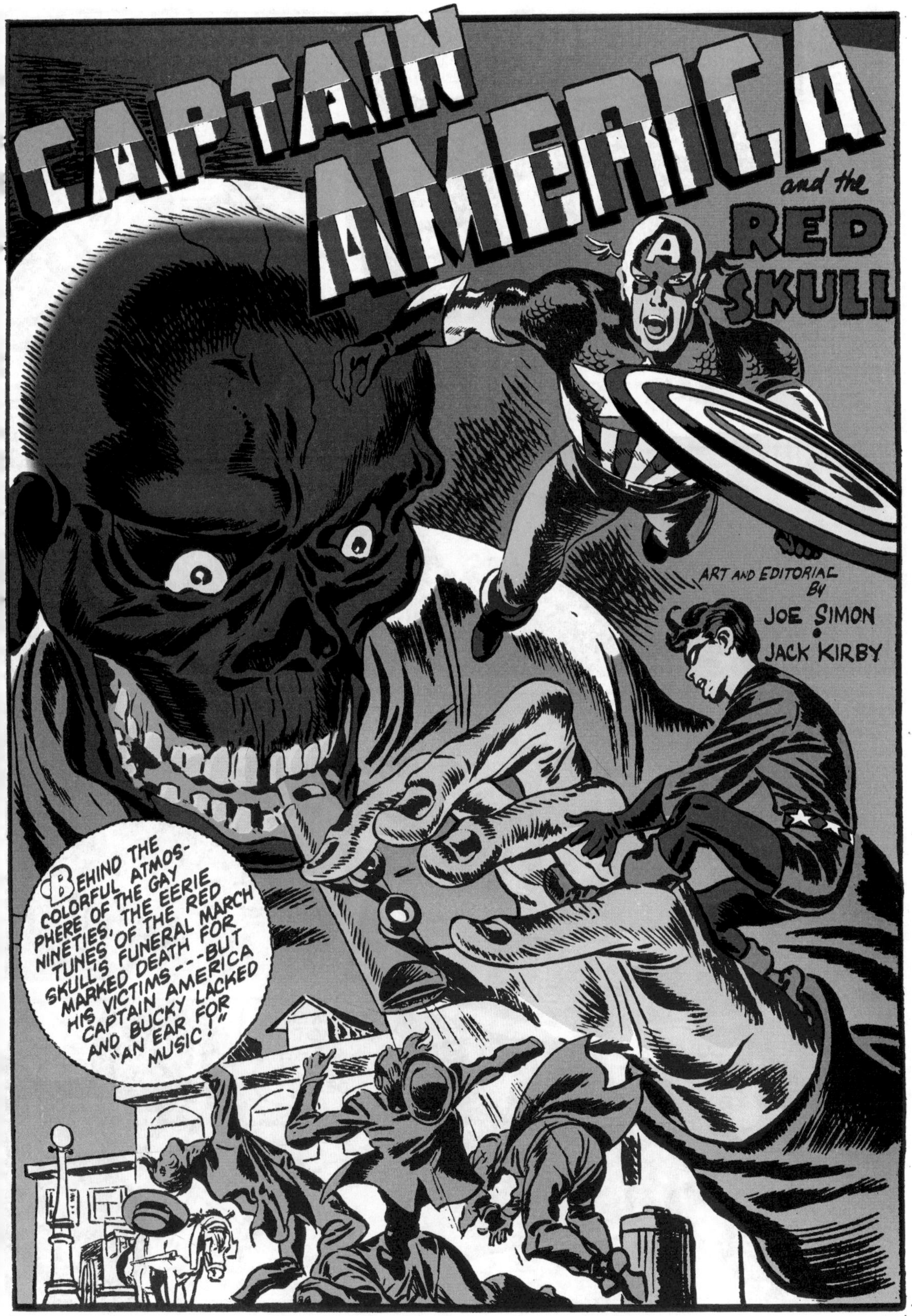
CAPTAIN AMERICA
and the
RED SKULL
ART AND EDITORIAL BY
JOE SIMON
JACK KIRBY
BEHIND THE COLORFUL ATMOSPHERE OF THE GAY NINETIES, THE EERIE TUNES OF THE RED SKULL'S FUNERAL MARCH MARKED DEATH FOR HIS VICTIMS---BUT CAPTAIN AMERICA AND BUCKY LACKED "AN EAR FOR MUSIC!"

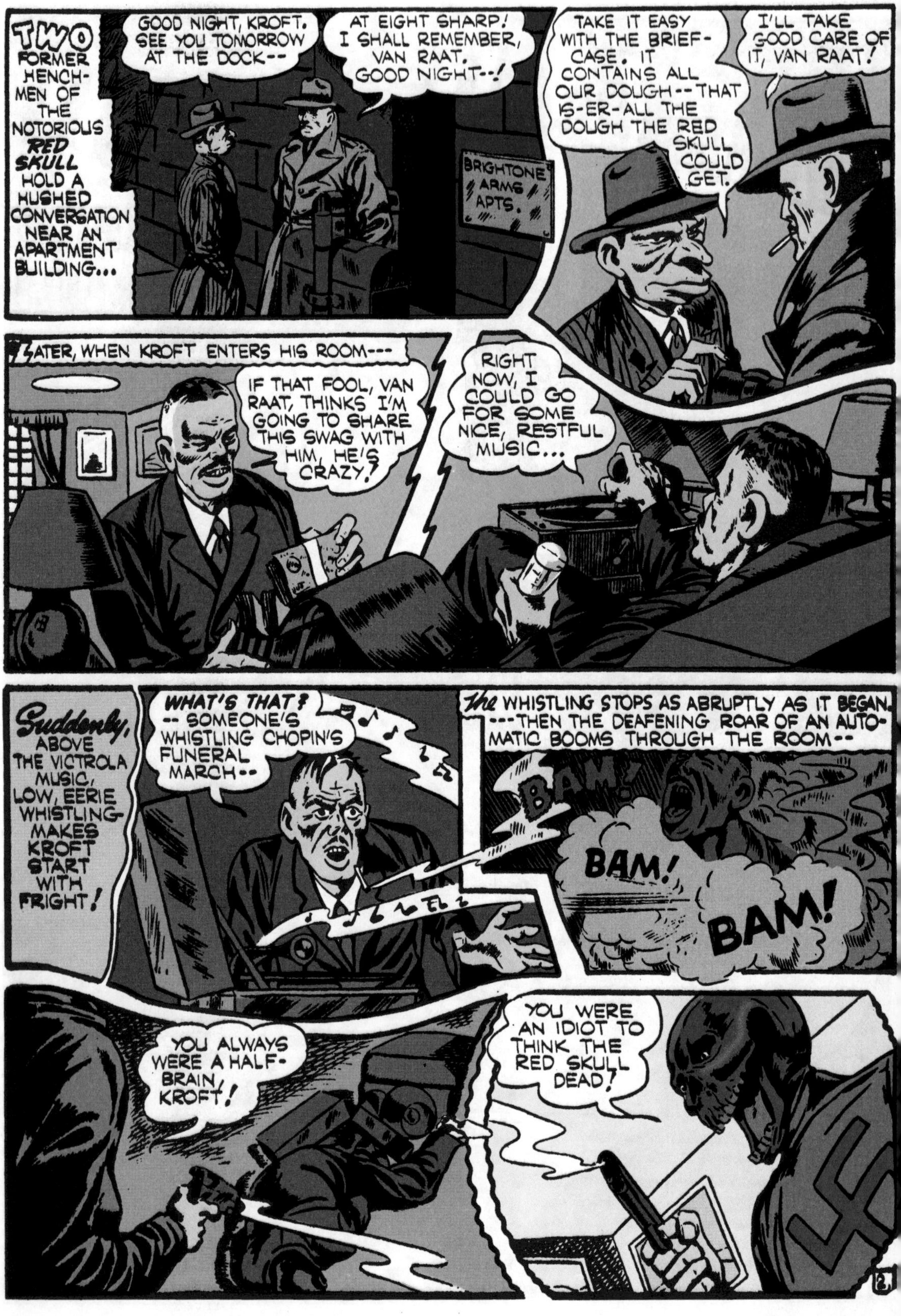
TWO FORMER HENCHMEN OF THE NOTORIOUS RED SKULL HOLD A HUSHED CONVERSATION NEAR AN APARTMENT BUILDING...
GOOD NIGHT, KROFT. SEE YOU TOMORROW AT THE DOCK--
AT EIGHT SHARP! I SHALL REMEMBER, VAN RAAT. GOOD NIGHT--!
BRIGHTONE ARMS APTS.
TAKE IT EASY WITH THE BRIEF-CASE. IT CONTAINS ALL OUR DOUGH--THAT IS-ER-ALL THE DOUGH THE RED SKULL COULD GET.
I'LL TAKE GOOD CARE OF IT, VAN RAAT!
LATER, WHEN KROFT ENTERS HIS ROOM---
IF THAT FOOL, VAN RAAT, THINKS I'M GOING TO SHARE THIS SWAG WITH HIM, HE'S CRAZY!
RIGHT NOW, I COULD GO FOR SOME NICE, RESTFUL MUSIC...
Suddenly, ABOVE THE VICTROLA MUSIC, LOW, EERIE WHISTLING MAKES KROFT START WITH FRIGHT!
WHAT'S THAT? -- SOMEONE'S WHISTLING CHOPIN'S FUNERAL MARCH--
THE WHISTLING STOPS AS ABRUPTLY AS IT BEGAN. ---THEN THE DEAFENING ROAR OF AN AUTOMATIC BOOMS THROUGH THE ROOM--
BAM!
BAM!
BAM!
YOU ALWAYS WERE A HALF-BRAIN, KROFT!
YOU WERE AN IDIOT TO THINK THE RED SKULL DEAD!
3

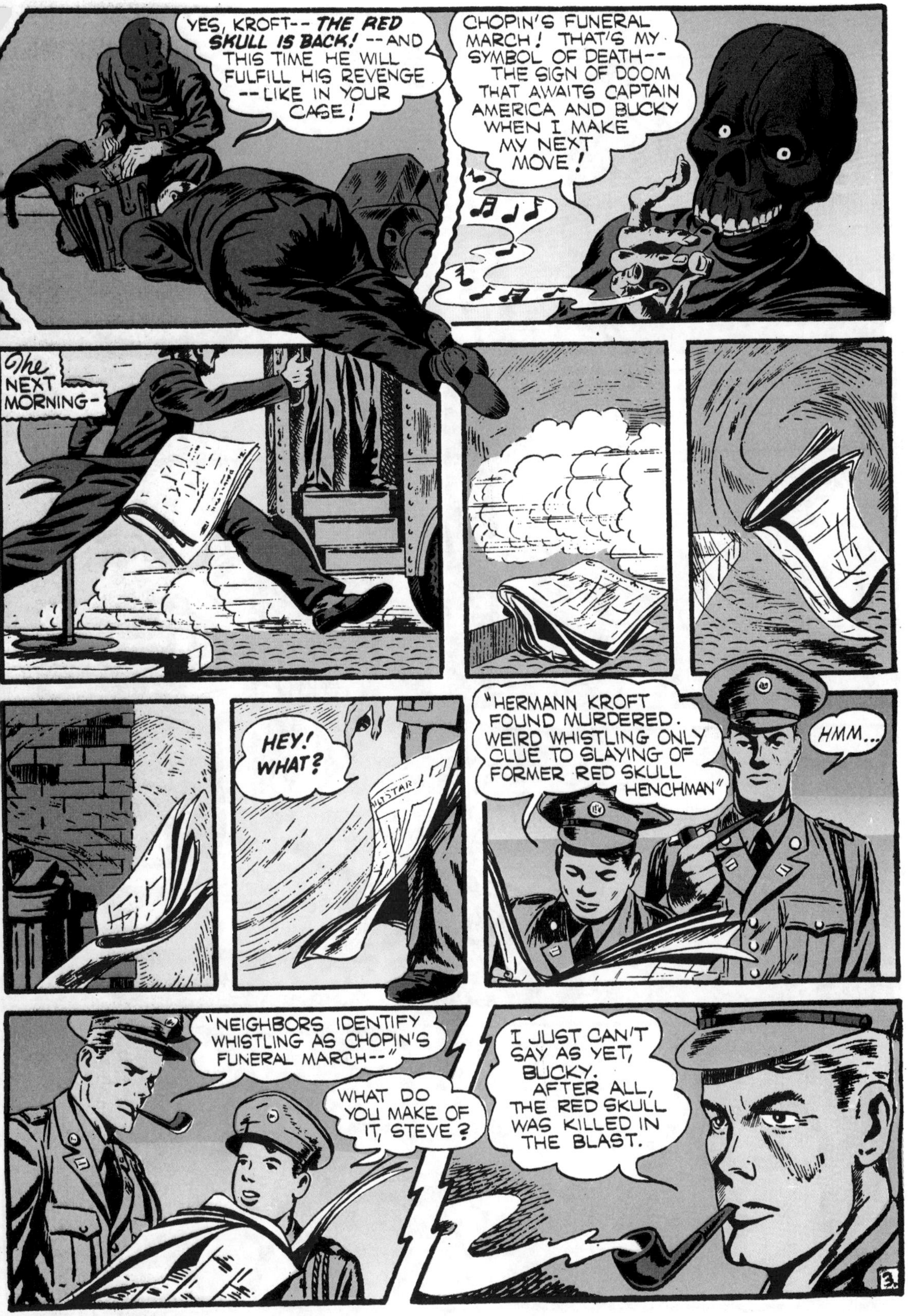
YES, KROFT-- THE RED SKULL IS BACK! --AND THIS TIME HE WILL FULFILL HIS REVENGE --LIKE IN YOUR CASE!
CHOPIN'S FUNERAL MARCH! THAT'S MY SYMBOL OF DEATH-- THE SIGN OF DOOM THAT AWAITS CAPTAIN AMERICA AND BUCKY WHEN I MAKE MY NEXT MOVE!
The NEXT MORNING-
HEY! WHAT?
"HERMANN KROFT FOUND MURDERED. WEIRD WHISTLING ONLY CLUE TO SLAYING OF FORMER RED SKULL HENCHMAN"
HMM...
"NEIGHBORS IDENTIFY WHISTLING AS CHOPIN'S FUNERAL MARCH--"
WHAT DO YOU MAKE OF IT, STEVE?
I JUST CAN'T SAY AS YET, BUCKY. AFTER ALL, THE RED SKULL WAS KILLED IN THE BLAST.
3.

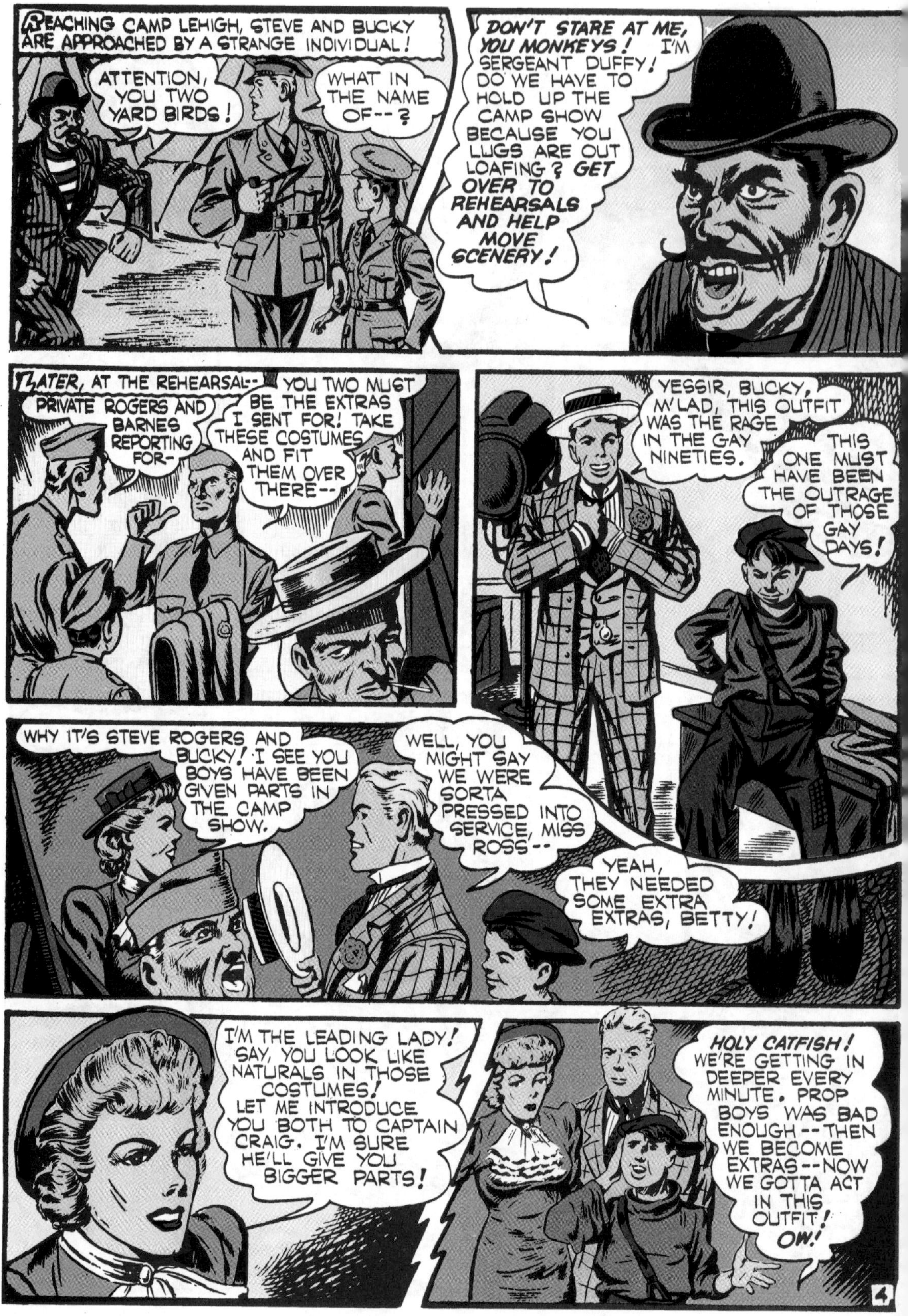
REACHING CAMP LEHIGH, STEVE AND BUCKY ARE APPROACHED BY A STRANGE INDIVIDUAL!
ATTENTION, YOU TWO YARD BIRDS!
WHAT IN THE NAME OF--?
DON'T STARE AT ME, YOU MONKEYS! I'M SERGEANT DUFFY! DO WE HAVE TO HOLD UP THE CAMP SHOW BECAUSE YOU LUGS ARE OUT LOAFING? GET OVER TO REHEARSALS AND HELP MOVE SCENERY!
LATER, AT THE REHEARSAL--
PRIVATE ROGERS AND BARNES REPORTING FOR-
YOU TWO MUST BE THE EXTRAS I SENT FOR! TAKE THESE COSTUMES AND FIT THEM OVER THERE--
YESSIR, BUCKY, M'LAD, THIS OUTFIT WAS THE RAGE IN THE GAY NINETIES.
THIS ONE MUST HAVE BEEN THE OUTRAGE OF THOSE GAY DAYS!
WHY IT'S STEVE ROGERS AND BUCKY! I SEE YOU BOYS HAVE BEEN GIVEN PARTS IN THE CAMP SHOW.
WELL, YOU MIGHT SAY WE WERE SORTA PRESSED INTO SERVICE, MISS ROSS--
YEAH, THEY NEEDED SOME EXTRA EXTRAS, BETTY!
I'M THE LEADING LADY! SAY, YOU LOOK LIKE NATURALS IN THOSE COSTUMES! LET ME INTRODUCE YOU BOTH TO CAPTAIN CRAIG. I'M SURE HE'LL GIVE YOU BIGGER PARTS!
HOLY CATFISH! WE'RE GETTING IN DEEPER EVERY MINUTE. PROP BOYS WAS BAD ENOUGH--THEN WE BECOME EXTRAS--NOW WE GOTTA ACT IN THIS OUTFIT! OW!
4

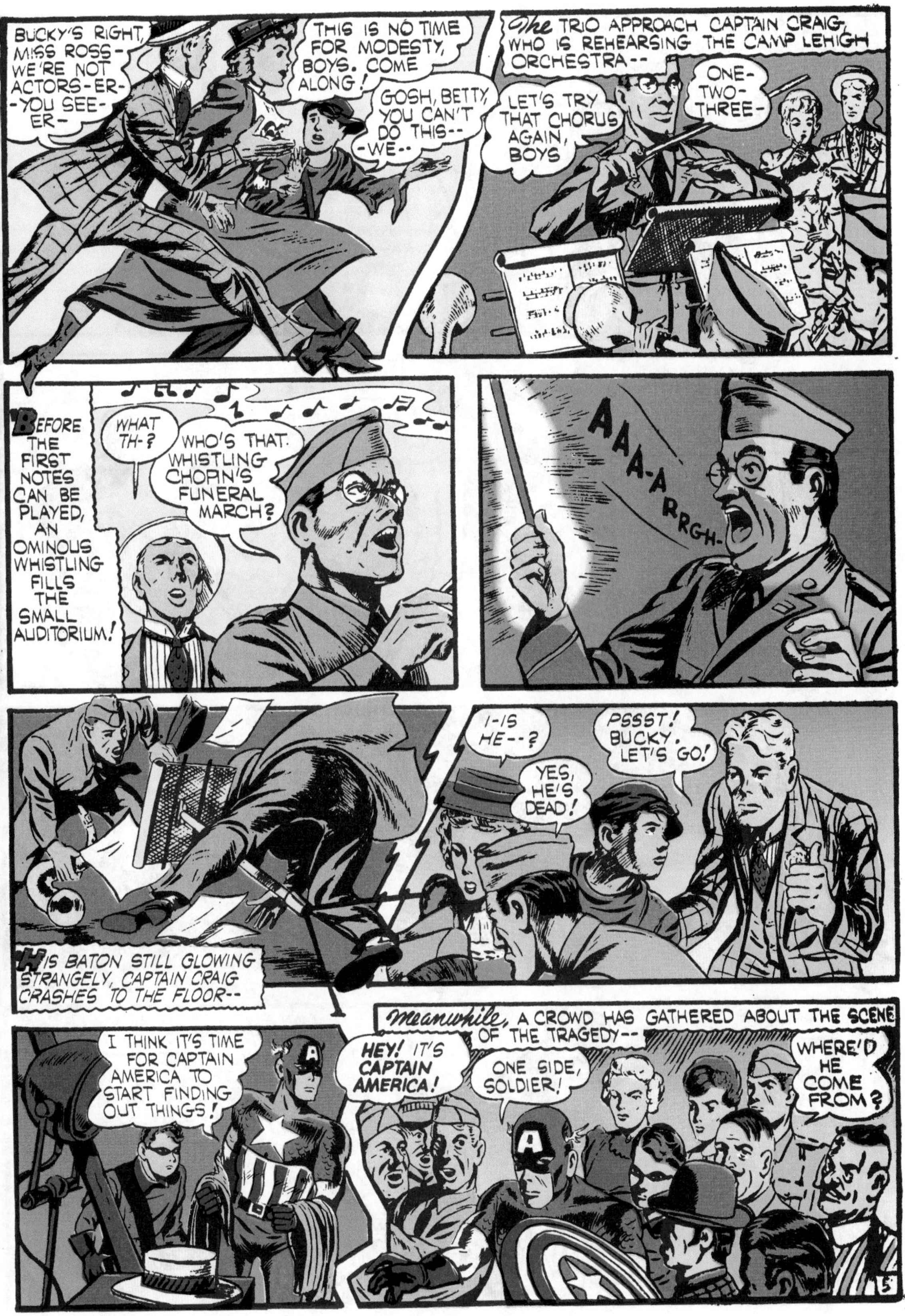
BUCKY'S RIGHT, MISS ROSS- WE'RE NOT ACTORS-ER- -YOU SEE- ER-
THIS IS NO TIME FOR MODESTY, BOYS. COME ALONG!
GOSH, BETTY, YOU CAN'T DO THIS-- -WE--
THE TRIO APPROACH CAPTAIN CRAIG, WHO IS REHEARSING THE CAMP LEHIGH ORCHESTRA--
LET'S TRY THAT CHORUS AGAIN, BOYS
ONE- TWO- THREE-
BEFORE THE FIRST NOTES CAN BE PLAYED, AN OMINOUS WHISTLING FILLS THE SMALL AUDITORIUM!
WHAT TH-?
WHO'S THAT WHISTLING CHOPIN'S FUNERAL MARCH?
AAAA-ARRGH-
HIS BATON STILL GLOWING STRANGELY, CAPTAIN CRAIG CRASHES TO THE FLOOR--
I-IS HE--?
YES, HE'S DEAD!
PSSST! BUCKY, LET'S GO!
I THINK IT'S TIME FOR CAPTAIN AMERICA TO START FINDING OUT THINGS!
MEANWHILE, A CROWD HAS GATHERED ABOUT THE SCENE OF THE TRAGEDY--
HEY! IT'S CAPTAIN AMERICA!
ONE SIDE, SOLDIER!
WHERE'D HE COME FROM?
5

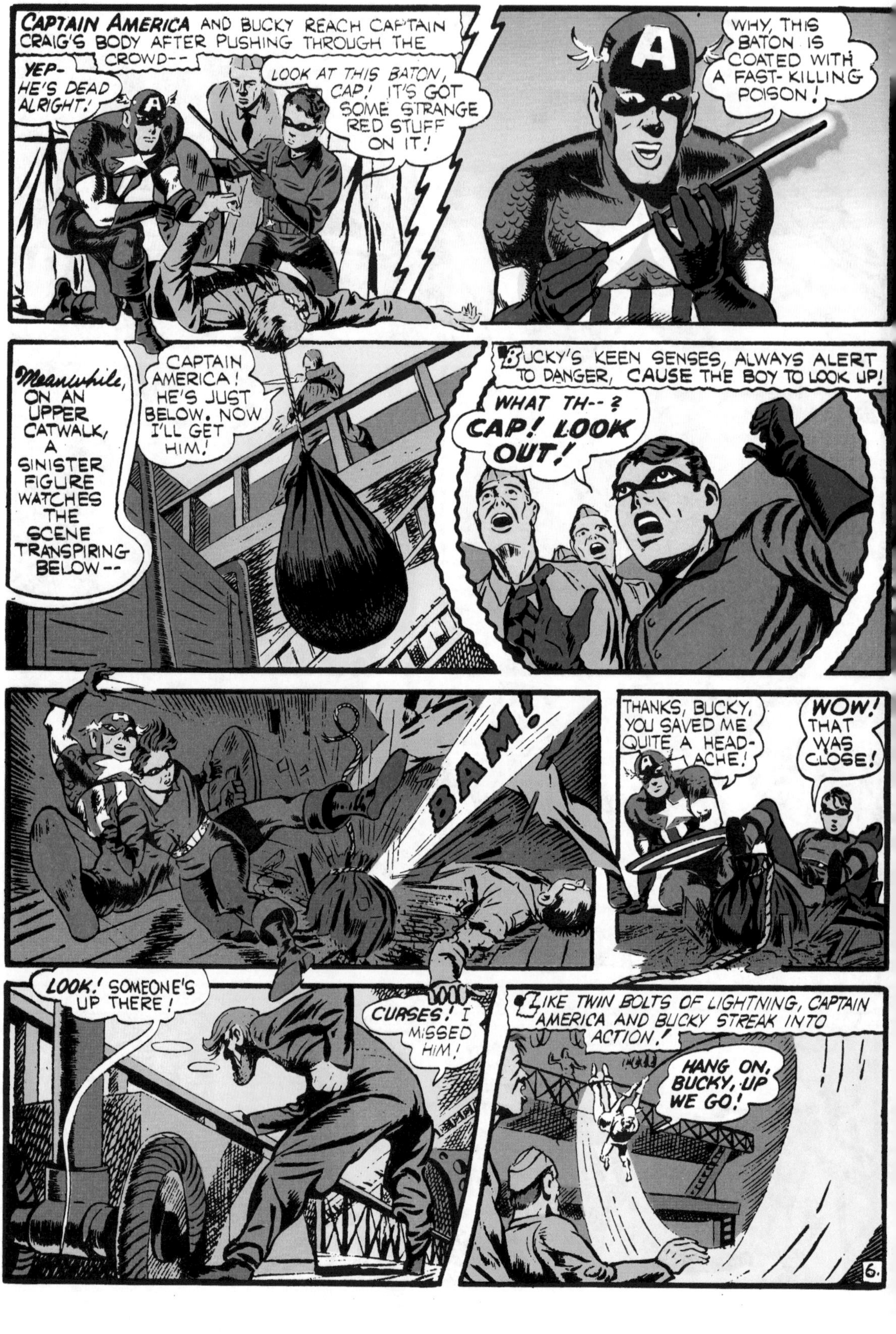

CAPTAIN AMERICA AND BUCKY REACH CAPTAIN CRAIG'S BODY AFTER PUSHING THROUGH THE CROWD--
YEP- HE'S DEAD ALRIGHT!
LOOK AT THIS BATON, CAP! IT'S GOT SOME STRANGE RED STUFF ON IT!
WHY, THIS BATON IS COATED WITH A FAST-KILLING POISON!
Meanwhile, ON AN UPPER CATWALK, A SINISTER FIGURE WATCHES THE SCENE TRANSPIRING BELOW--
CAPTAIN AMERICA! HE'S JUST BELOW. NOW I'LL GET HIM!
BUCKY'S KEEN SENSES, ALWAYS ALERT TO DANGER, CAUSE THE BOY TO LOOK UP!
WHAT TH--? CAP! LOOK OUT!
BAM!
THANKS, BUCKY, YOU SAVED ME QUITE A HEAD-ACHE!
WOW! THAT WAS CLOSE!
LOOK! SOMEONE'S UP THERE!
CURSES! I MISSED HIM!
LIKE TWIN BOLTS OF LIGHTNING, CAPTAIN AMERICA AND BUCKY STREAK INTO ACTION!
HANG ON, BUCKY, UP WE GO!
6.

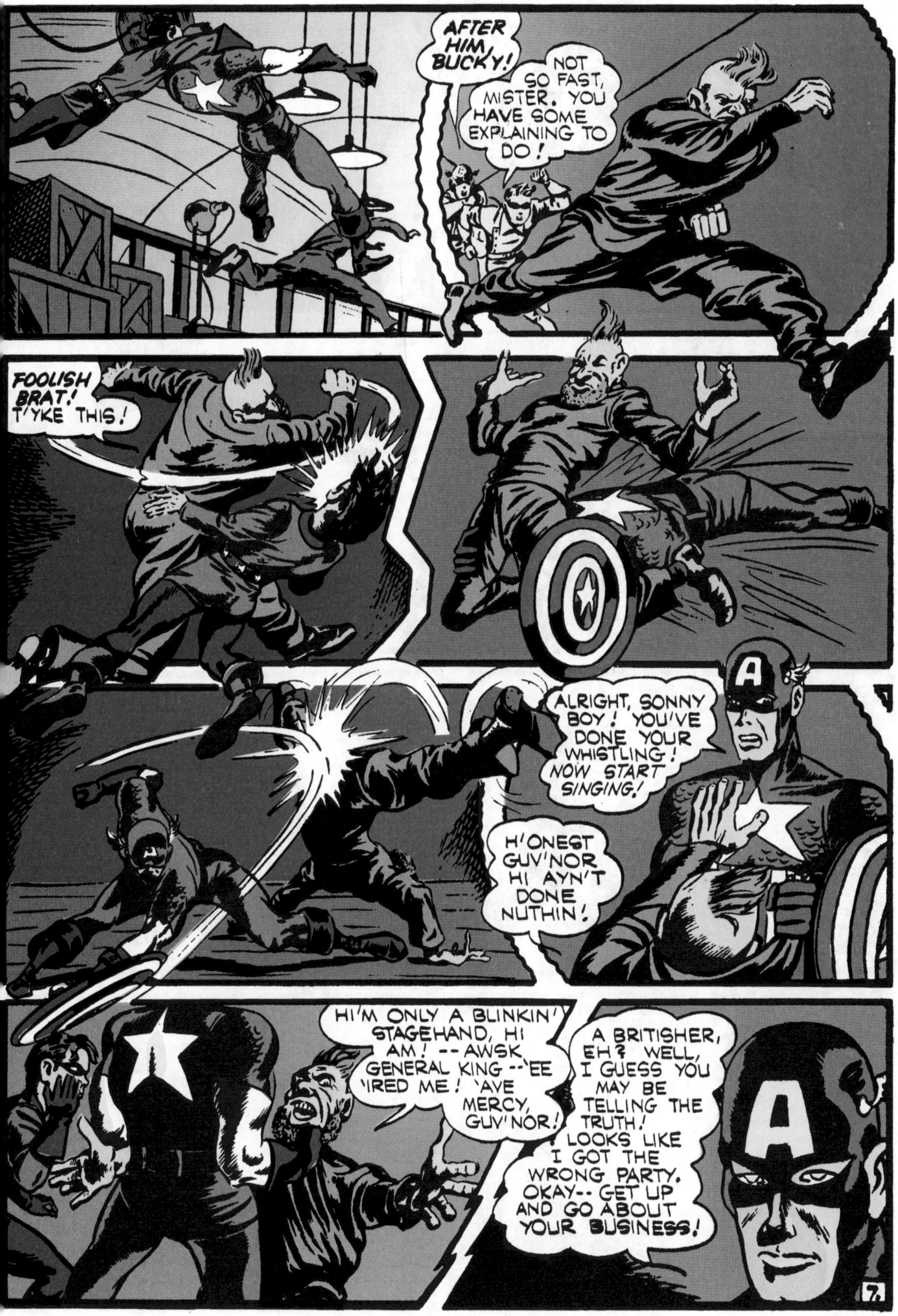
AFTER HIM, BUCKY!
NOT SO FAST, MISTER. YOU HAVE SOME EXPLAINING TO DO!
FOOLISH BRAT! T'YKE THIS!
ALRIGHT, SONNY BOY! YOU'VE DONE YOUR WHISTLING! NOW START SINGING!
H'ONEST GUV'NOR HI AYN'T DONE NUTHIN'!
HI'M ONLY A BLINKIN' STAGEHAND, HI AM! --AWSK GENERAL KING--'EE 'IRED ME! 'AVE MERCY, GUV'NOR!
A BRITISHER, EH? WELL, I GUESS YOU MAY BE TELLING THE TRUTH! LOOKS LIKE I GOT THE WRONG PARTY. OKAY-- GET UP AND GO ABOUT YOUR BUSINESS!
7

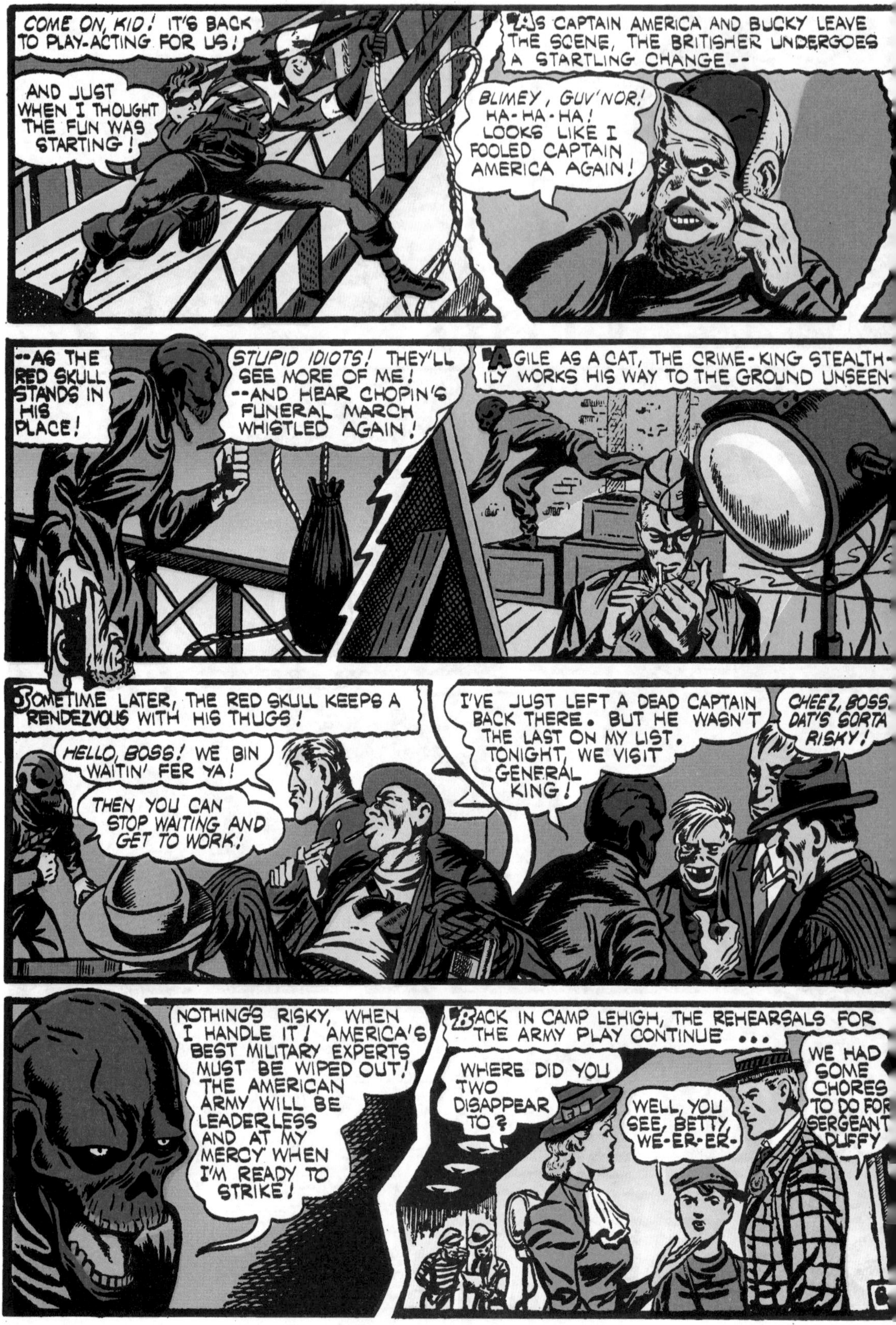
COME ON, KID! IT'S BACK TO PLAY-ACTING FOR US!
AND JUST WHEN I THOUGHT THE FUN WAS STARTING!
AS CAPTAIN AMERICA AND BUCKY LEAVE THE SCENE, THE BRITISHER UNDERGOES A STARTLING CHANGE--
BLIMEY, GUV'NOR! HA-HA-HA! LOOKS LIKE I FOOLED CAPTAIN AMERICA AGAIN!
--AS THE RED SKULL STANDS IN HIS PLACE!
STUPID IDIOTS! THEY'LL SEE MORE OF ME! --AND HEAR CHOPIN'S FUNERAL MARCH WHISTLED AGAIN!
AGILE AS A CAT, THE CRIME-KING STEALTHILY WORKS HIS WAY TO THE GROUND UNSEEN-
SOMETIME LATER, THE RED SKULL KEEPS A RENDEZVOUS WITH HIS THUGS!
HELLO, BOSS! WE BIN WAITIN' FER YA!
THEN YOU CAN STOP WAITING AND GET TO WORK!
I'VE JUST LEFT A DEAD CAPTAIN BACK THERE. BUT HE WASN'T THE LAST ON MY LIST. TONIGHT, WE VISIT GENERAL KING!
CHEEZ, BOSS, DAT'S SORTA RISKY!
NOTHING'S RISKY, WHEN I HANDLE IT! AMERICA'S BEST MILITARY EXPERTS MUST BE WIPED OUT! THE AMERICAN ARMY WILL BE LEADERLESS AND AT MY MERCY WHEN I'M READY TO STRIKE!
BACK IN CAMP LEHIGH, THE REHEARSALS FOR THE ARMY PLAY CONTINUE...
WHERE DID YOU TWO DISAPPEAR TO?
WELL, YOU SEE, BETTY, WE-ER-ER-
WE HAD SOME CHORES TO DO FOR SERGEANT DUFFY

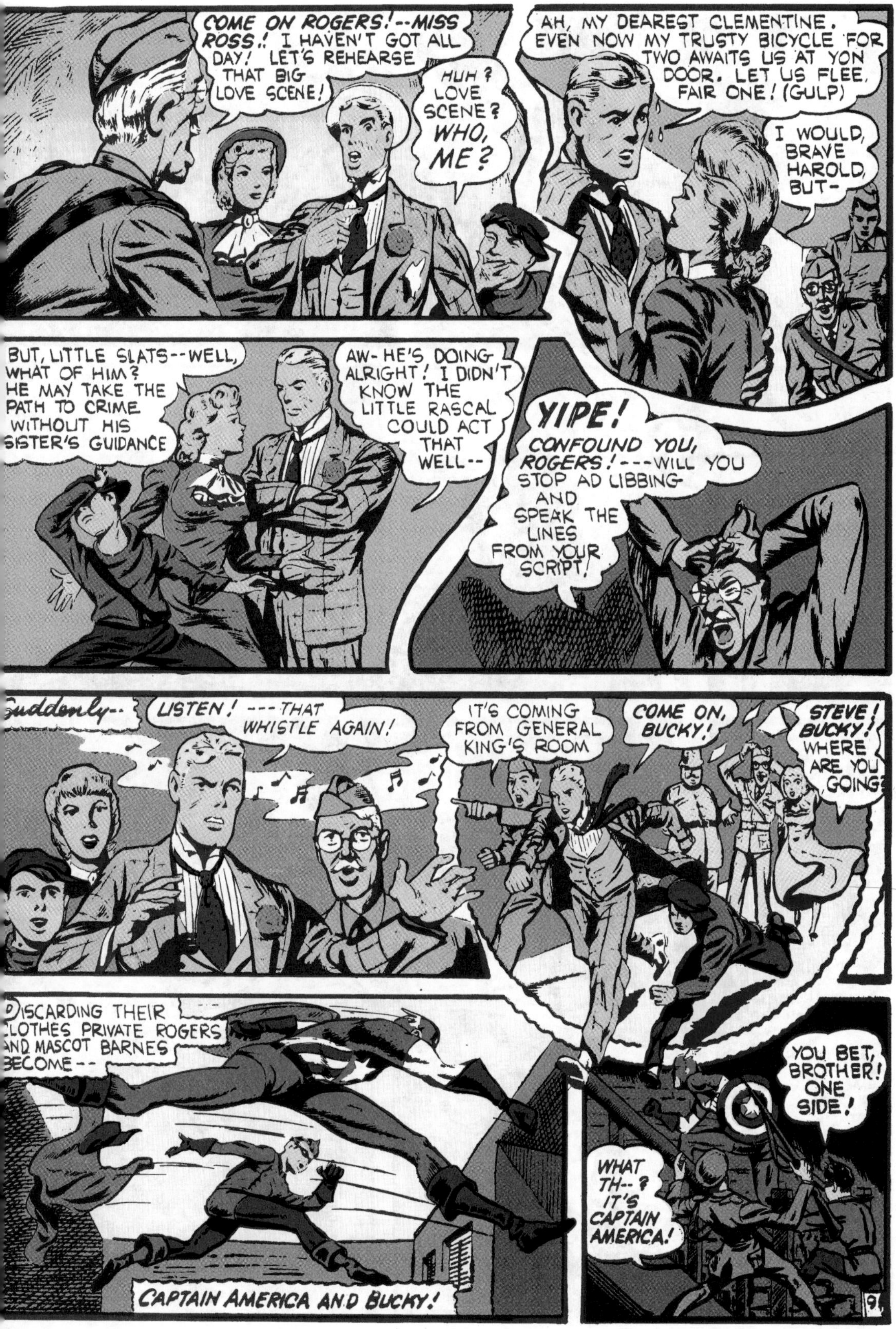
COME ON ROGERS! --MISS ROSS! I HAVEN'T GOT ALL DAY! LET'S REHEARSE THAT BIG LOVE SCENE!
HUH? LOVE SCENE? WHO, ME?
AH, MY DEAREST CLEMENTINE. EVEN NOW MY TRUSTY BICYCLE FOR TWO AWAITS US AT YON DOOR. LET US FLEE, FAIR ONE! (GULP)
I WOULD, BRAVE HAROLD, BUT-
BUT, LITTLE SLATS--WELL, WHAT OF HIM? HE MAY TAKE THE PATH TO CRIME WITHOUT HIS SISTER'S GUIDANCE
AW- HE'S DOING ALRIGHT! I DIDN'T KNOW THE LITTLE RASCAL COULD ACT THAT WELL--
YIPE!
CONFOUND YOU, ROGERS! ---WILL YOU STOP AD LIBBING AND SPEAK THE LINES FROM YOUR SCRIPT!
Suddenly--
LISTEN! ---THAT WHISTLE AGAIN!
IT'S COMING FROM GENERAL KING'S ROOM
COME ON, BUCKY!
STEVE! BUCKY! WHERE ARE YOU GOING?
DISCARDING THEIR CLOTHES PRIVATE ROGERS AND MASCOT BARNES BECOME--
CAPTAIN AMERICA AND BUCKY!
YOU BET, BROTHER! ONE SIDE!
WHAT TH--? IT'S CAPTAIN AMERICA!
9

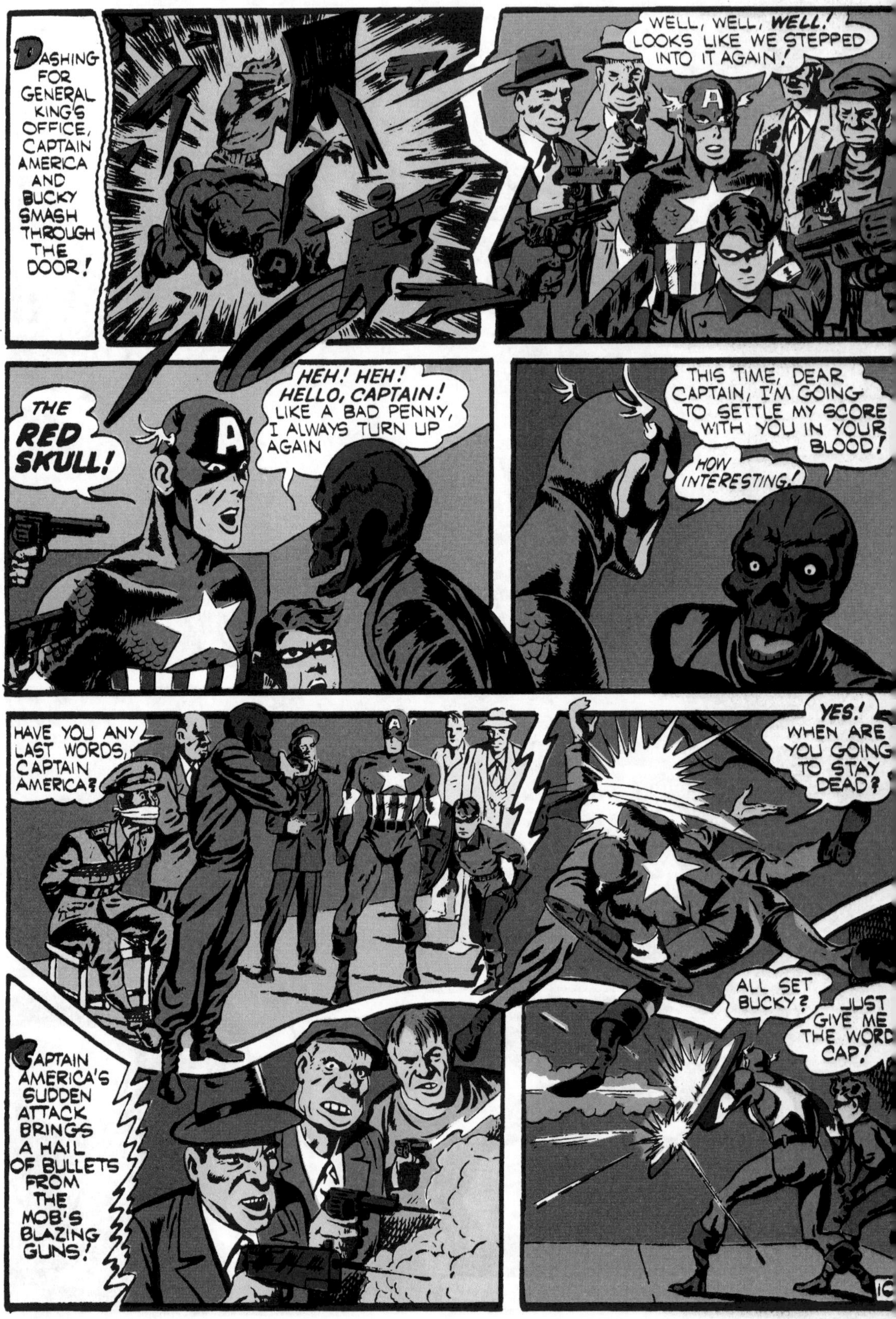
DASHING FOR GENERAL KING'S OFFICE, CAPTAIN AMERICA AND BUCKY SMASH THROUGH THE DOOR!
WELL, WELL, WELL! LOOKS LIKE WE STEPPED INTO IT AGAIN!
THE RED SKULL!
HEH! HEH! HELLO, CAPTAIN! LIKE A BAD PENNY, I ALWAYS TURN UP AGAIN
THIS TIME, DEAR CAPTAIN, I'M GOING TO SETTLE MY SCORE WITH YOU IN YOUR BLOOD!
HOW INTERESTING!
HAVE YOU ANY LAST WORDS, CAPTAIN AMERICA?
YES! WHEN ARE YOU GOING TO STAY DEAD?
CAPTAIN AMERICA'S SUDDEN ATTACK BRINGS A HAIL OF BULLETS FROM THE MOB'S BLAZING GUNS!
ALL SET BUCKY?
JUST GIVE ME THE WORD CAP!
10

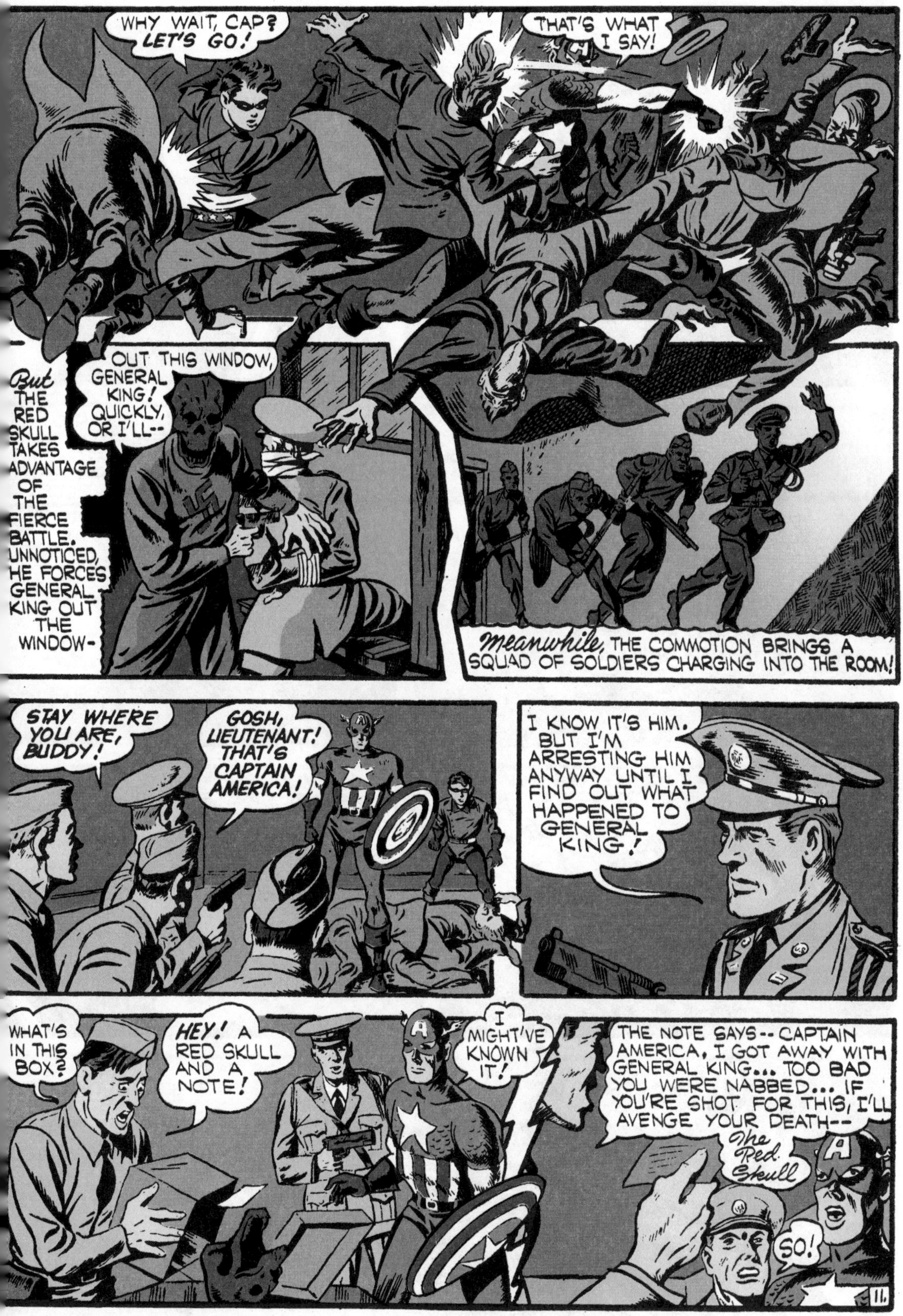
WHY WAIT, CAP? LET'S GO!
THAT'S WHAT I SAY!
But THE RED SKULL TAKES ADVANTAGE OF THE FIERCE BATTLE. UNNOTICED, HE FORCES GENERAL KING OUT THE WINDOW-
OUT THIS WINDOW, GENERAL KING! QUICKLY, OR I'LL--
Meanwhile, THE COMMOTION BRINGS A SQUAD OF SOLDIERS CHARGING INTO THE ROOM!
STAY WHERE YOU ARE, BUDDY!
GOSH, LIEUTENANT! THAT'S CAPTAIN AMERICA!
I KNOW IT'S HIM. BUT I'M ARRESTING HIM ANYWAY UNTIL I FIND OUT WHAT HAPPENED TO GENERAL KING!
WHAT'S IN THIS BOX?
HEY! A RED SKULL AND A NOTE!
I MIGHT'VE KNOWN IT!
THE NOTE SAYS-- CAPTAIN AMERICA, I GOT AWAY WITH GENERAL KING... TOO BAD YOU WERE NABBED... IF YOU'RE SHOT FOR THIS, I'LL AVENGE YOUR DEATH-- The Red Skull
SO!
11

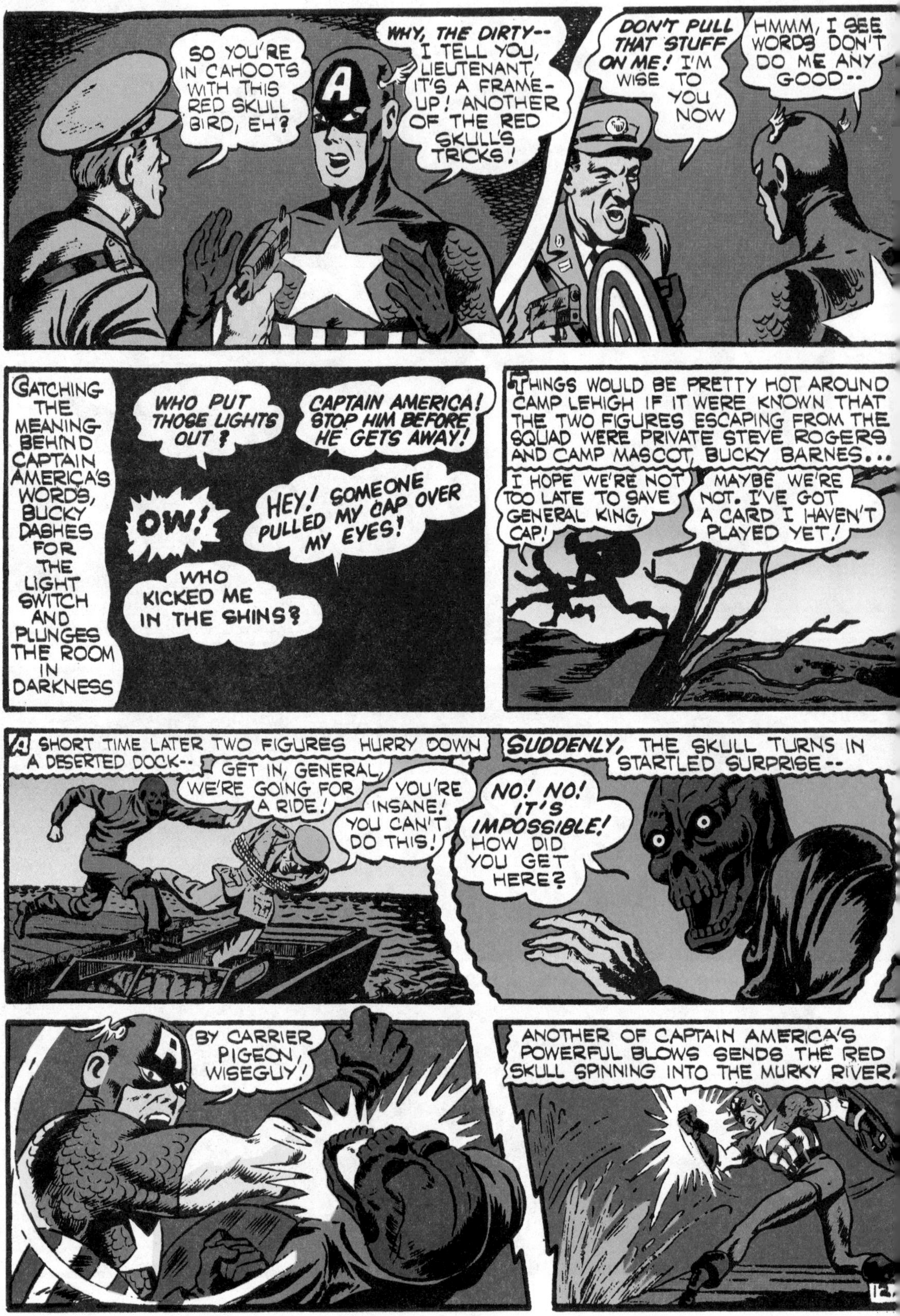
SO YOU'RE IN CAHOOTS WITH THIS RED SKULL BIRD, EH?
WHY, THE DIRTY-- I TELL YOU, LIEUTENANT, IT'S A FRAME-UP! ANOTHER OF THE RED SKULL'S TRICKS!
DON'T PULL THAT STUFF ON ME! I'M WISE TO YOU NOW
HMMM, I SEE WORDS DON'T DO ME ANY GOOD--
CATCHING THE MEANING BEHIND CAPTAIN AMERICA'S WORDS, BUCKY DASHES FOR THE LIGHT SWITCH AND PLUNGES THE ROOM IN DARKNESS
WHO PUT THOSE LIGHTS OUT?
CAPTAIN AMERICA! STOP HIM BEFORE HE GETS AWAY!
OW!
HEY! SOMEONE PULLED MY CAP OVER MY EYES!
WHO KICKED ME IN THE SHINS?
THINGS WOULD BE PRETTY HOT AROUND CAMP LEHIGH IF IT WERE KNOWN THAT THE TWO FIGURES ESCAPING FROM THE SQUAD WERE PRIVATE STEVE ROGERS AND CAMP MASCOT, BUCKY BARNES...
I HOPE WE'RE NOT TOO LATE TO SAVE GENERAL KING, CAP!
MAYBE WE'RE NOT. I'VE GOT A CARD I HAVEN'T PLAYED YET!
A SHORT TIME LATER TWO FIGURES HURRY DOWN A DESERTED DOCK--
GET IN, GENERAL, WE'RE GOING FOR A RIDE!
YOU'RE INSANE! YOU CAN'T DO THIS!
SUDDENLY, THE SKULL TURNS IN STARTLED SURPRISE--
NO! NO! IT'S IMPOSSIBLE! HOW DID YOU GET HERE?
BY CARRIER PIGEON, WISEGUY!
ANOTHER OF CAPTAIN AMERICA'S POWERFUL BLOWS SENDS THE RED SKULL SPINNING INTO THE MURKY RIVER.
12.

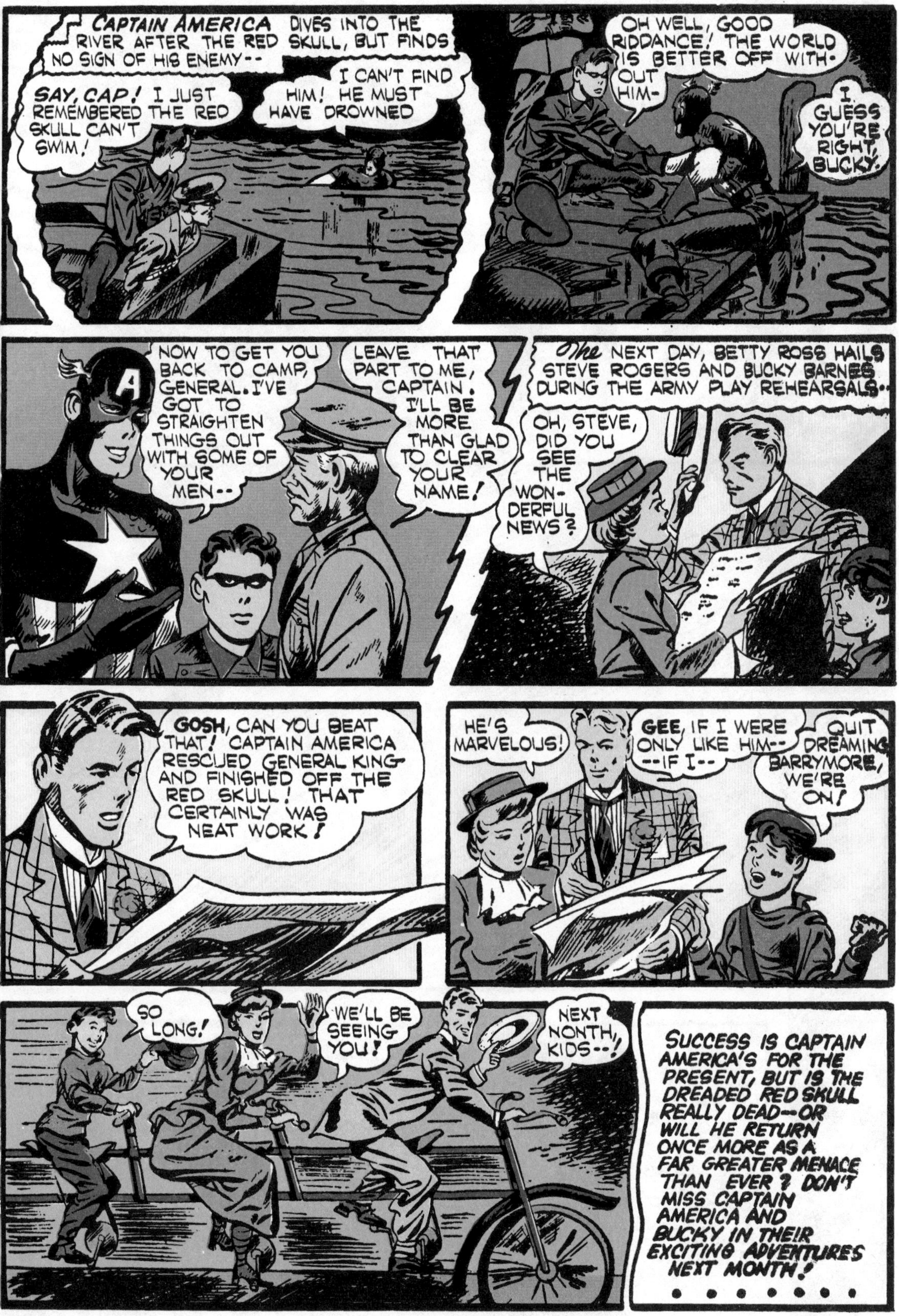
CAPTAIN AMERICA DIVES INTO THE RIVER AFTER THE RED SKULL, BUT FINDS NO SIGN OF HIS ENEMY--
SAY, CAP! I JUST REMEMBERED THE RED SKULL CAN'T SWIM!
I CAN'T FIND HIM! HE MUST HAVE DROWNED
OH WELL, GOOD RIDDANCE! THE WORLD IS BETTER OFF WITHOUT HIM-
I GUESS YOU'RE RIGHT, BUCKY.
NOW TO GET YOU BACK TO CAMP, GENERAL. I'VE GOT TO STRAIGHTEN THINGS OUT WITH SOME OF YOUR MEN--
LEAVE THAT PART TO ME, CAPTAIN. I'LL BE MORE THAN GLAD TO CLEAR YOUR NAME!
The NEXT DAY, BETTY ROSS HAILS STEVE ROGERS AND BUCKY BARNES DURING THE ARMY PLAY REHEARSALS--
OH, STEVE, DID YOU SEE THE WONDERFUL NEWS?
GOSH, CAN YOU BEAT THAT! CAPTAIN AMERICA RESCUED GENERAL KING AND FINISHED OFF THE RED SKULL! THAT CERTAINLY WAS NEAT WORK!
HE'S MARVELOUS!
GEE, IF I WERE ONLY LIKE HIM-- --IF I--
QUIT DREAMING BARRYMORE, WE'RE ON!
SO LONG!
WE'LL BE SEEING YOU!
NEXT MONTH, KIDS--!
SUCCESS IS CAPTAIN AMERICA'S FOR THE PRESENT, BUT IS THE DREADED RED SKULL REALLY DEAD--OR WILL HE RETURN ONCE MORE AS A FAR GREATER MENACE THAN EVER? DON'T MISS CAPTAIN AMERICA AND BUCKY IN THEIR EXCITING ADVENTURES NEXT MONTH!

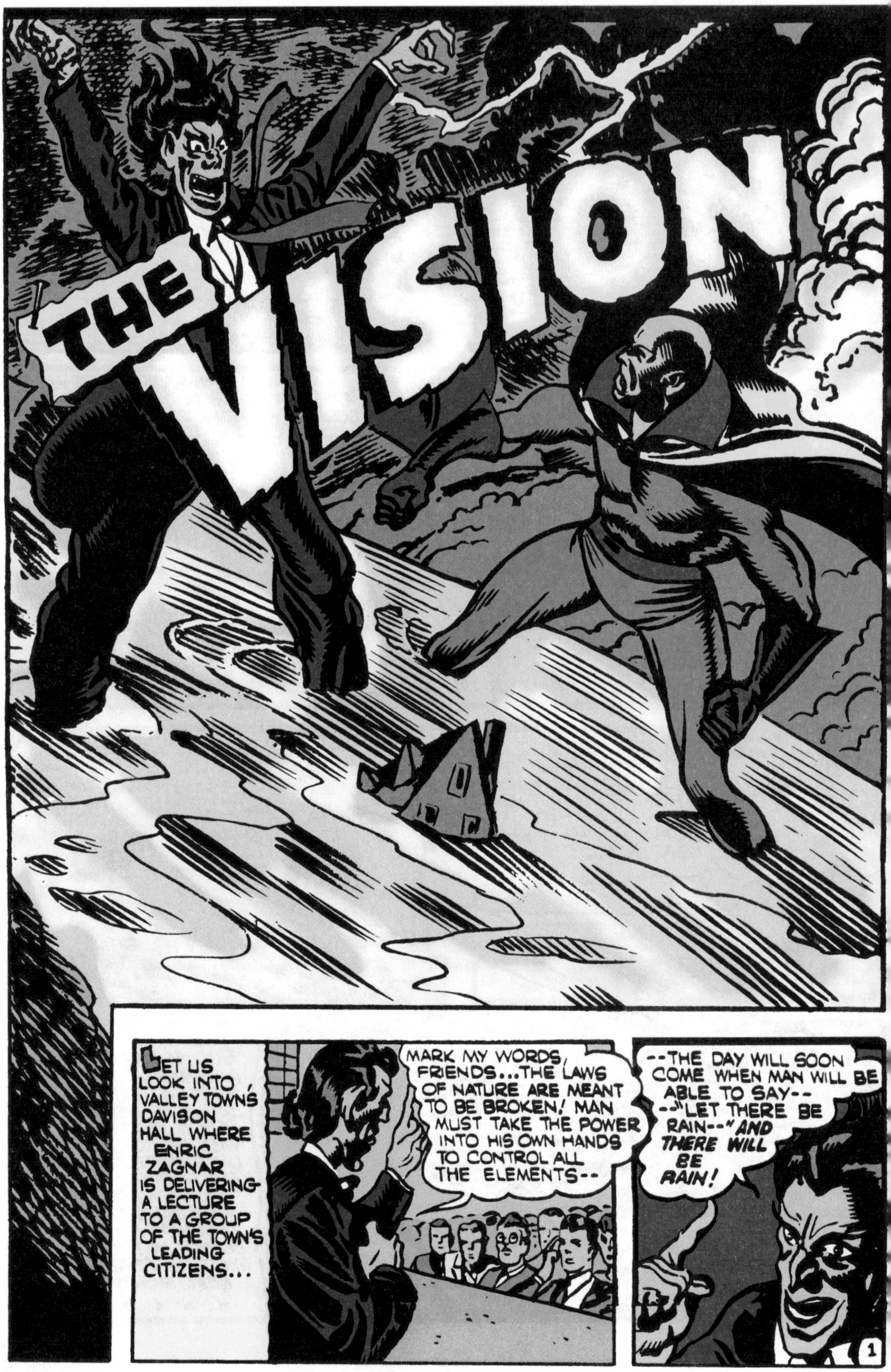
THE VISION
LET US LOOK INTO VALLEY TOWN'S DAVISON HALL WHERE ENRIC ZAGNAR IS DELIVERING A LECTURE TO A GROUP OF THE TOWN'S LEADING CITIZENS...
MARK MY WORDS, FRIENDS...THE LAWS OF NATURE ARE MEANT TO BE BROKEN! MAN MUST TAKE THE POWER INTO HIS OWN HANDS TO CONTROL ALL THE ELEMENTS--
--THE DAY WILL SOON COME WHEN MAN WILL BE ABLE TO SAY-- --"LET THERE BE RAIN--" AND THERE WILL BE RAIN!
1

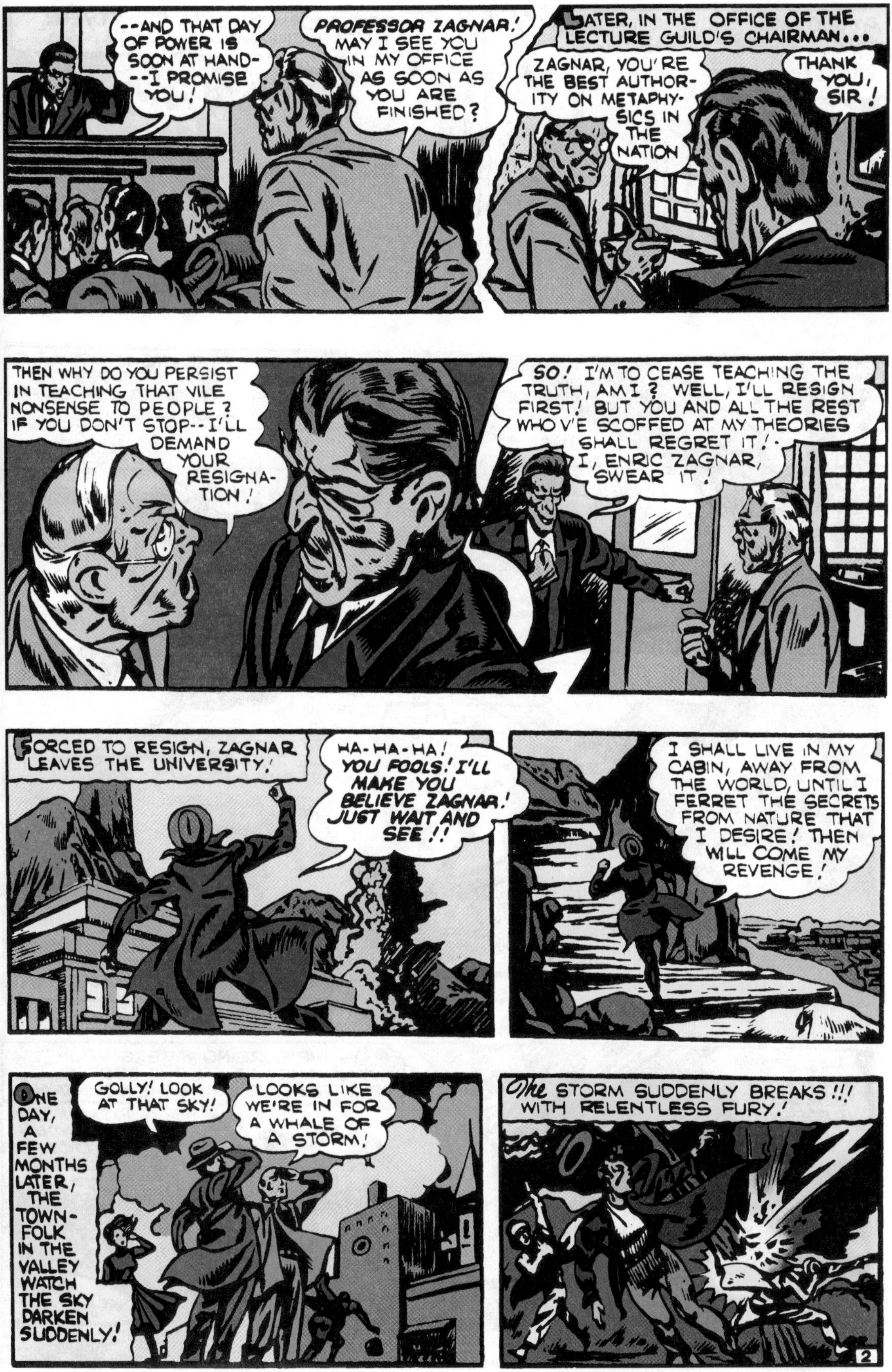
--AND THAT DAY OF POWER IS SOON AT HAND- --I PROMISE YOU!
PROFESSOR ZAGNAR! MAY I SEE YOU IN MY OFFICE AS SOON AS YOU ARE FINISHED?
LATER, IN THE OFFICE OF THE LECTURE GUILD'S CHAIRMAN...
ZAGNAR, YOU'RE THE BEST AUTHORITY ON METAPHYSICS IN THE NATION
THANK YOU, SIR!
THEN WHY DO YOU PERSIST IN TEACHING THAT VILE NONSENSE TO PEOPLE? IF YOU DON'T STOP--I'LL DEMAND YOUR RESIGNATION!
SO! I'M TO CEASE TEACHING THE TRUTH, AM I? WELL, I'LL RESIGN FIRST! BUT YOU AND ALL THE REST WHO'VE SCOFFED AT MY THEORIES SHALL REGRET IT! I, ENRIC ZAGNAR, SWEAR IT!
FORCED TO RESIGN, ZAGNAR LEAVES THE UNIVERSITY!
HA-HA-HA! YOU FOOLS! I'LL MAKE YOU BELIEVE ZAGNAR! JUST WAIT AND SEE!!
I SHALL LIVE IN MY CABIN, AWAY FROM THE WORLD, UNTIL I FERRET THE SECRETS FROM NATURE THAT I DESIRE! THEN WILL COME MY REVENGE!
ONE DAY, A FEW MONTHS LATER, THE TOWNFOLK IN THE VALLEY WATCH THE SKY DARKEN SUDDENLY!
GOLLY! LOOK AT THAT SKY!
LOOKS LIKE WE'RE IN FOR A WHALE OF A STORM!
THE STORM SUDDENLY BREAKS!!! WITH RELENTLESS FURY!
2

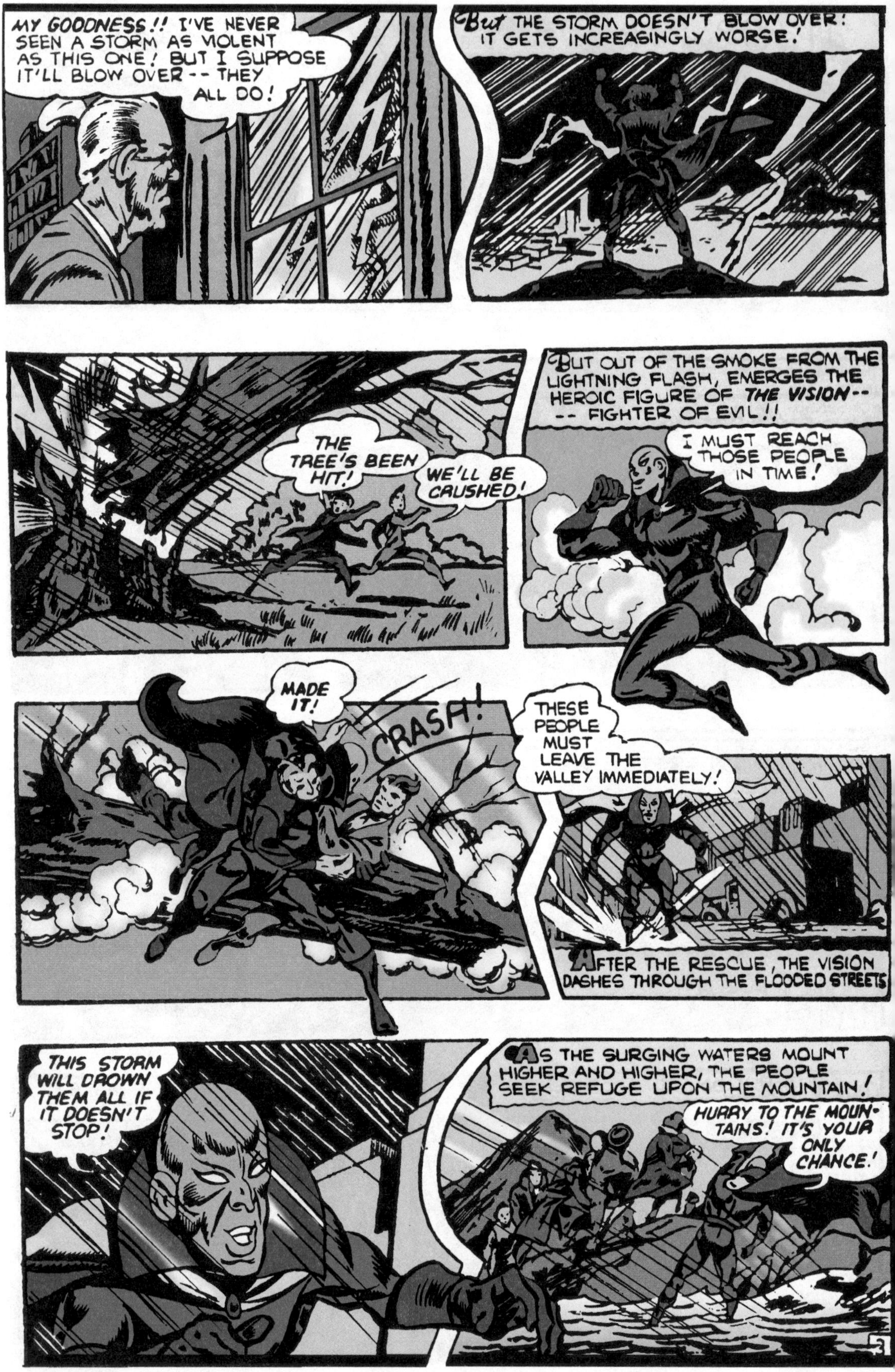
MY GOODNESS!! I'VE NEVER SEEN A STORM AS VIOLENT AS THIS ONE! BUT I SUPPOSE IT'LL BLOW OVER -- THEY ALL DO!
But THE STORM DOESN'T BLOW OVER! IT GETS INCREASINGLY WORSE!
THE TREE'S BEEN HIT!
WE'LL BE CRUSHED!
BUT OUT OF THE SMOKE FROM THE LIGHTNING FLASH, EMERGES THE HEROIC FIGURE OF THE VISION -- -- FIGHTER OF EVIL!!
I MUST REACH THOSE PEOPLE IN TIME!
MADE IT!
CRASH!
THESE PEOPLE MUST LEAVE THE VALLEY IMMEDIATELY!
AFTER THE RESCUE, THE VISION DASHES THROUGH THE FLOODED STREETS
THIS STORM WILL DROWN THEM ALL IF IT DOESN'T STOP!
AS THE SURGING WATERS MOUNT HIGHER AND HIGHER, THE PEOPLE SEEK REFUGE UPON THE MOUNTAIN!
HURRY TO THE MOUNTAINS! IT'S YOUR ONLY CHANCE!
3

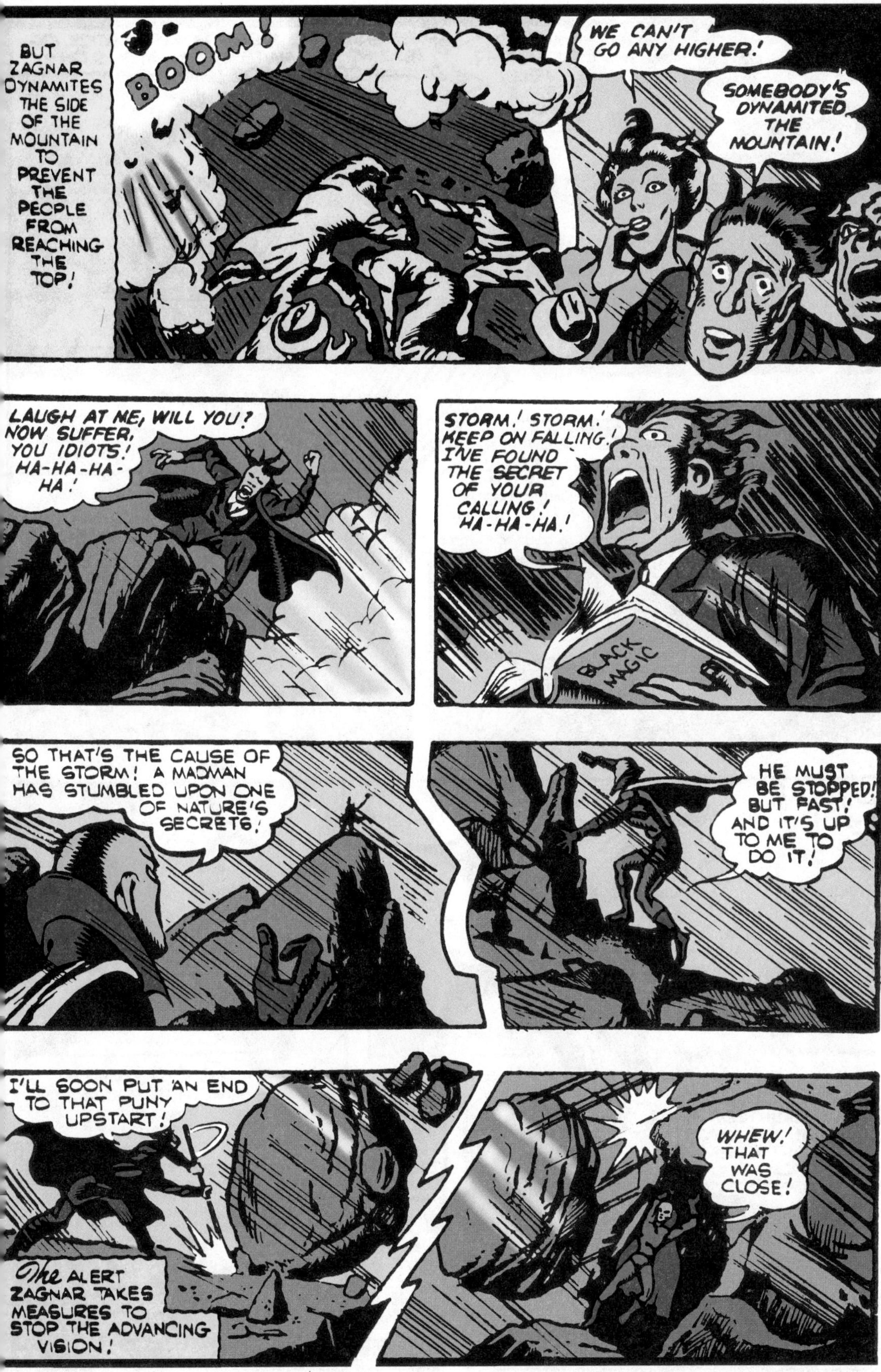
BUT ZAGNAR DYNAMITES THE SIDE OF THE MOUNTAIN TO PREVENT THE PEOPLE FROM REACHING THE TOP!
BOOM!
WE CAN'T GO ANY HIGHER!
SOMEBODY'S DYNAMITED THE MOUNTAIN!
LAUGH AT ME, WILL YOU? NOW SUFFER, YOU IDIOTS! HA-HA-HA-HA!
STORM! STORM! KEEP ON FALLING! I'VE FOUND THE SECRET OF YOUR CALLING! HA-HA-HA!
BLACK MAGIC
SO THAT'S THE CAUSE OF THE STORM! A MADMAN HAS STUMBLED UPON ONE OF NATURE'S SECRETS!
HE MUST BE STOPPED! BUT FAST! AND IT'S UP TO ME TO DO IT!
I'LL SOON PUT AN END TO THAT PUNY UPSTART!
The ALERT ZAGNAR TAKES MEASURES TO STOP THE ADVANCING VISION!
WHEW! THAT WAS CLOSE!

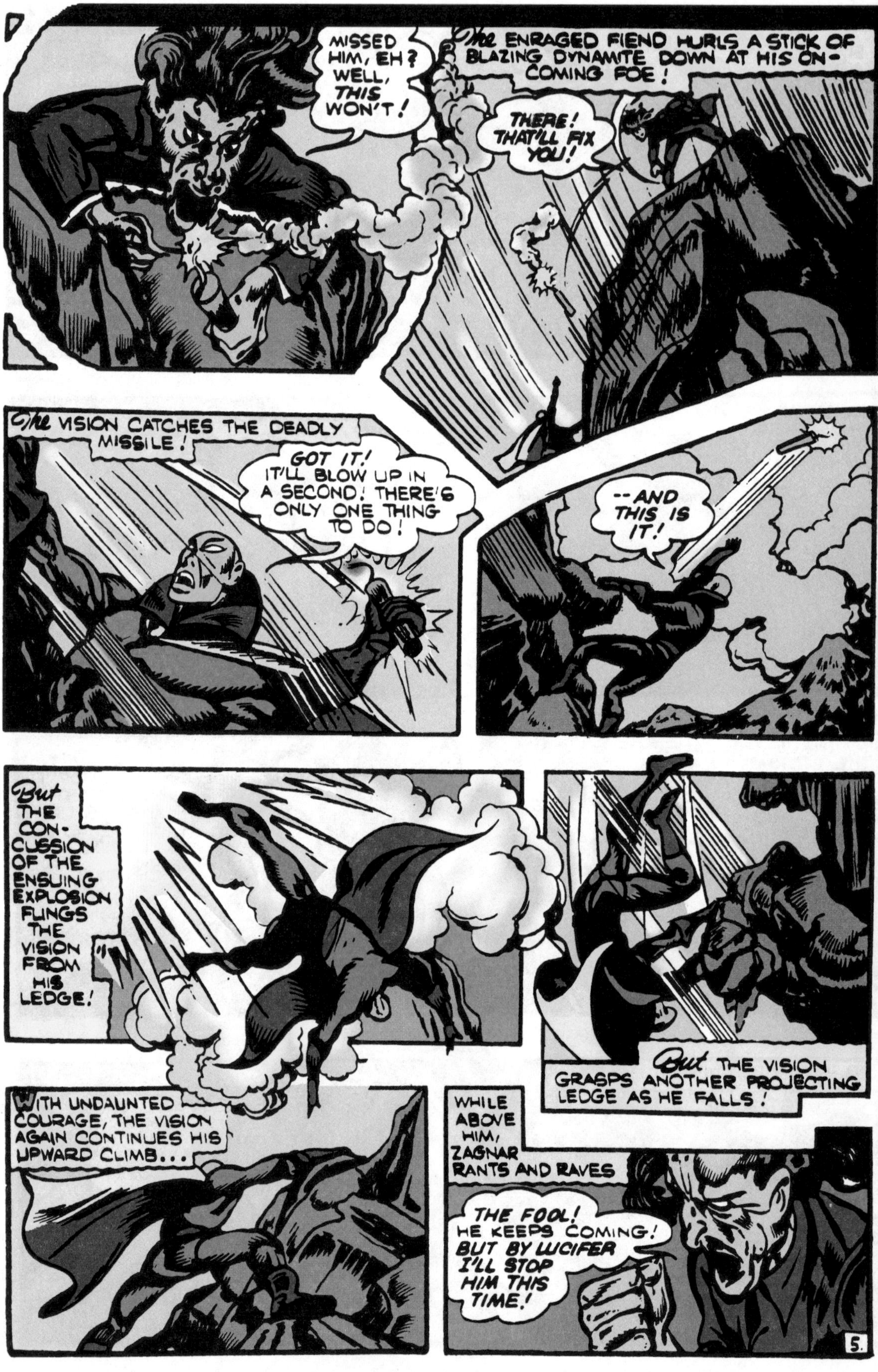

MISSED HIM, EH? WELL, THIS WON'T!
THE ENRAGED FIEND HURLS A STICK OF BLAZING DYNAMITE DOWN AT HIS ON-COMING FOE!
THERE! THAT'LL FIX YOU!
THE VISION CATCHES THE DEADLY MISSILE!
GOT IT! IT'LL BLOW UP IN A SECOND! THERE'S ONLY ONE THING TO DO!
--AND THIS IS IT!
BUT THE CONCUSSION OF THE ENSUING EXPLOSION FLINGS THE VISION FROM HIS LEDGE!
BUT THE VISION GRASPS ANOTHER PROJECTING LEDGE AS HE FALLS!
WITH UNDAUNTED COURAGE, THE VISION AGAIN CONTINUES HIS UPWARD CLIMB...
WHILE ABOVE HIM, ZAGNAR RANTS AND RAVES
THE FOOL! HE KEEPS COMING! BUT BY LUCIFER I'LL STOP HIM THIS TIME!

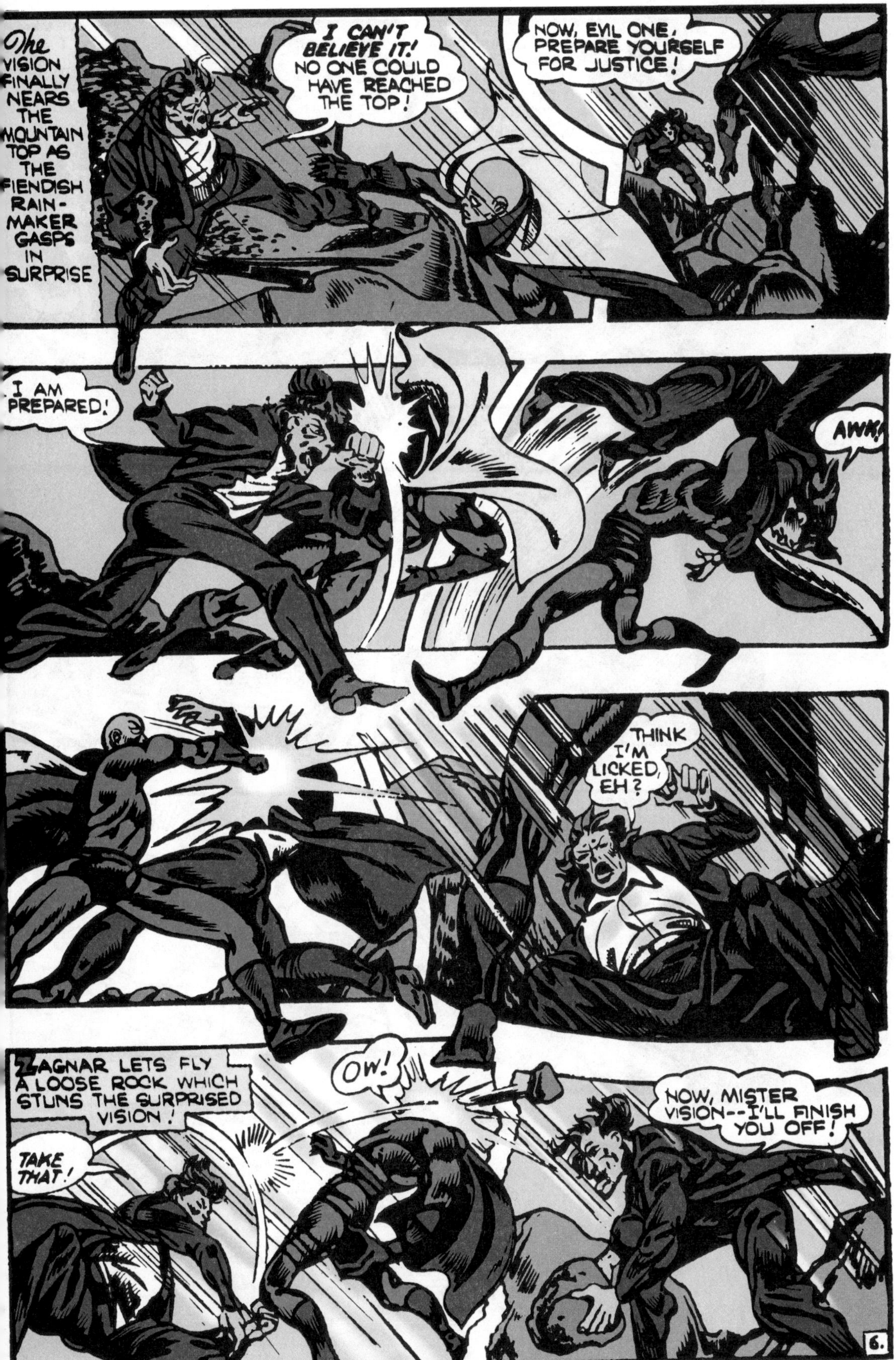
The VISION FINALLY NEARS THE MOUNTAIN TOP AS THE FIENDISH RAIN-MAKER GASPS IN SURPRISE
I CAN'T BELIEVE IT! NO ONE COULD HAVE REACHED THE TOP!
NOW, EVIL ONE, PREPARE YOURSELF FOR JUSTICE!
I AM PREPARED!
AWK!
THINK I'M LICKED, EH?
ZAGNAR LETS FLY A LOOSE ROCK WHICH STUNS THE SURPRISED VISION!
OW!
NOW, MISTER VISION--I'LL FINISH YOU OFF!
TAKE THAT!

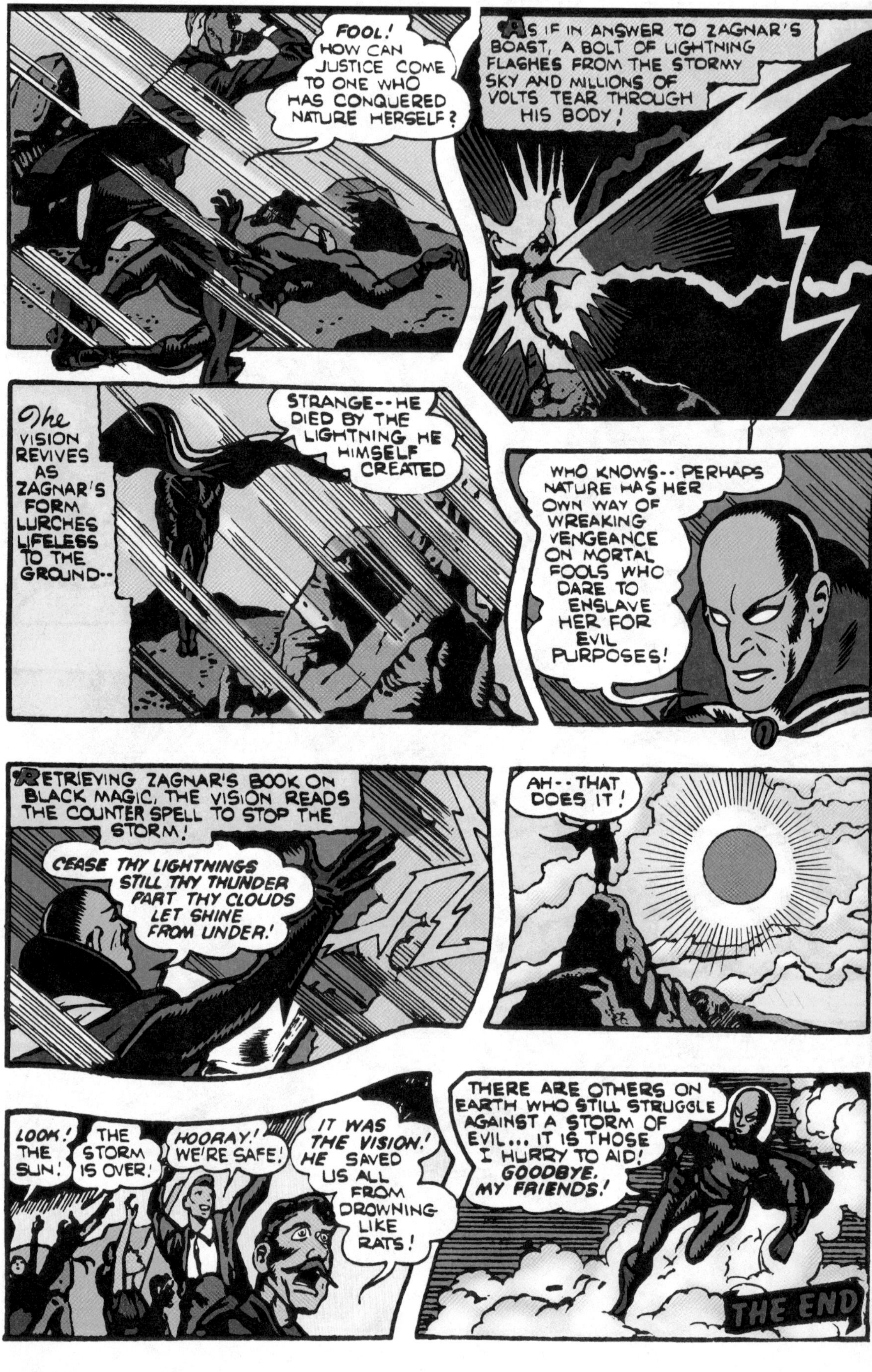
FOOL! HOW CAN JUSTICE COME TO ONE WHO HAS CONQUERED NATURE HERSELF?
AS IF IN ANSWER TO ZAGNAR'S BOAST, A BOLT OF LIGHTNING FLASHES FROM THE STORMY SKY AND MILLIONS OF VOLTS TEAR THROUGH HIS BODY!
THE VISION REVIVES AS ZAGNAR'S FORM LURCHES LIFELESS TO THE GROUND--
STRANGE--HE DIED BY THE LIGHTNING HE HIMSELF CREATED
WHO KNOWS--PERHAPS NATURE HAS HER OWN WAY OF WREAKING VENGEANCE ON MORTAL FOOLS WHO DARE TO ENSLAVE HER FOR EVIL PURPOSES!
RETRIEVING ZAGNAR'S BOOK ON BLACK MAGIC, THE VISION READS THE COUNTER SPELL TO STOP THE STORM!
CEASE THY LIGHTNINGS STILL THY THUNDER PART THY CLOUDS LET SHINE FROM UNDER!
AH--THAT DOES IT!
LOOK! THE SUN!
THE STORM IS OVER!
HOORAY! WE'RE SAFE!
IT WAS THE VISION! HE SAVED US ALL FROM DROWNING LIKE RATS!
THERE ARE OTHERS ON EARTH WHO STILL STRUGGLE AGAINST A STORM OF EVIL... IT IS THOSE I HURRY TO AID! GOODBYE, MY FRIENDS!
THE END

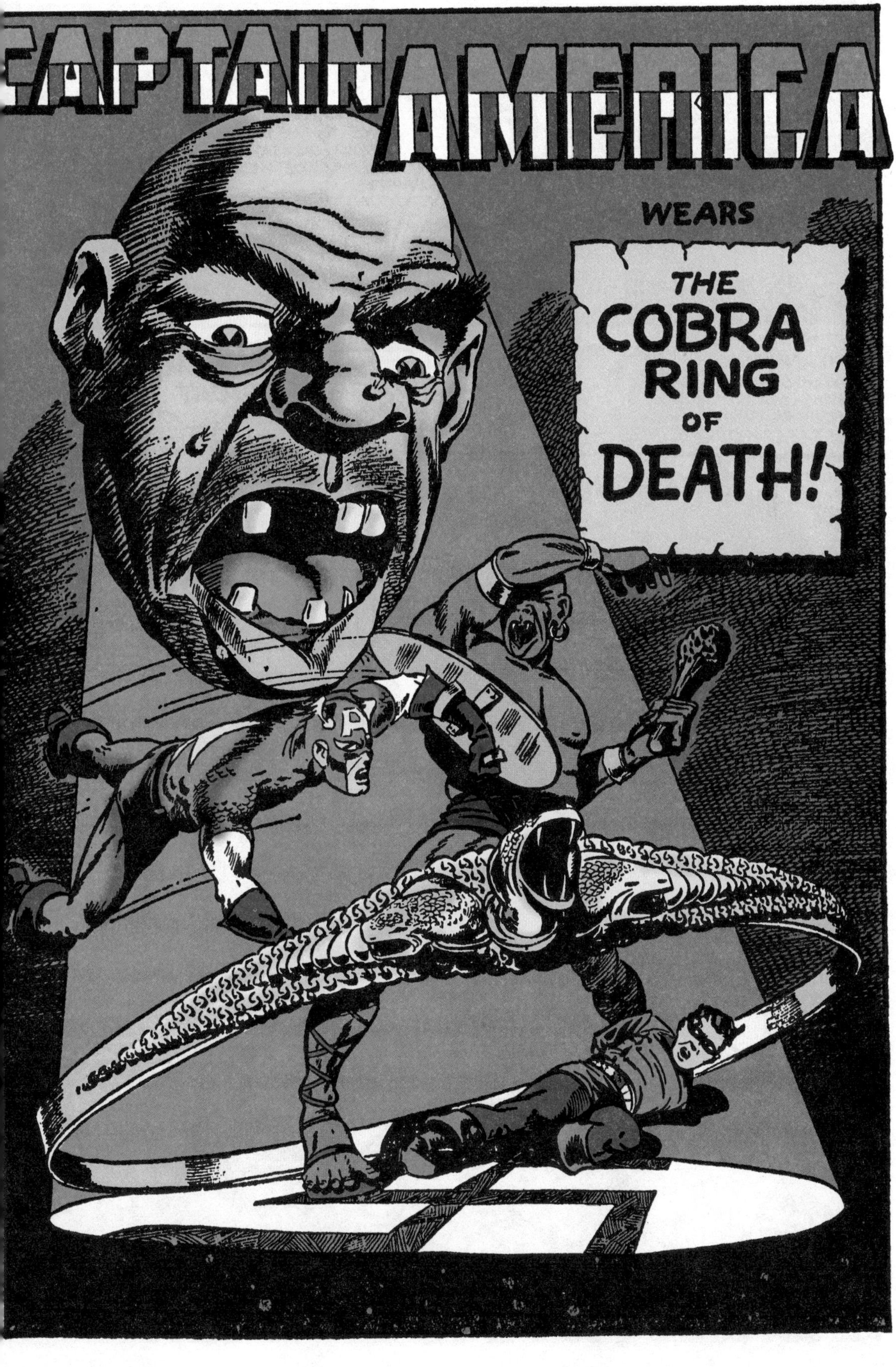
CAPTAIN AMERICA
WEARS
THE COBRA RING OF DEATH!

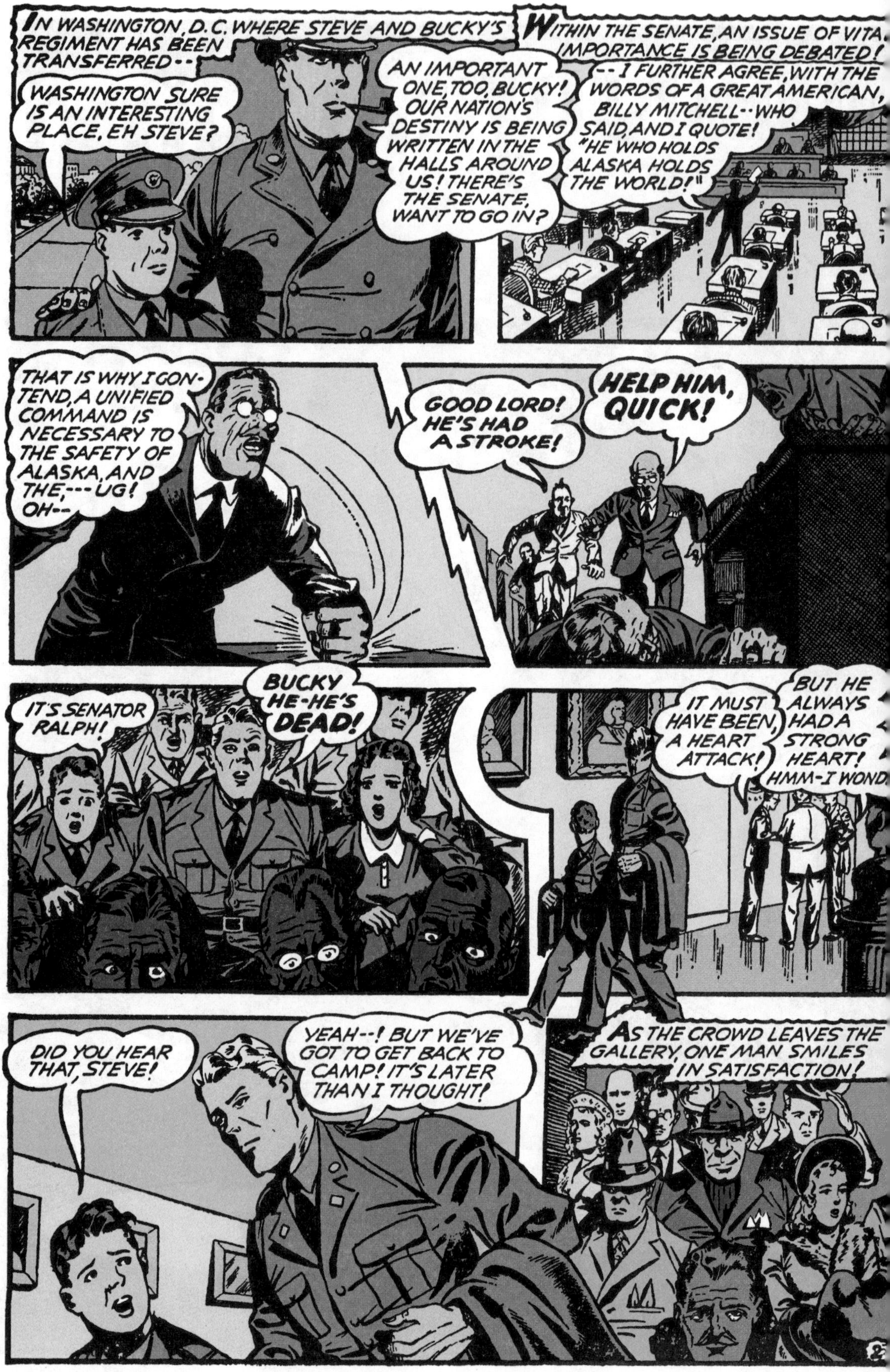
IN WASHINGTON, D.C. WHERE STEVE AND BUCKY'S REGIMENT HAS BEEN TRANSFERRED--
WASHINGTON SURE IS AN INTERESTING PLACE, EH STEVE?
AN IMPORTANT ONE, TOO, BUCKY! OUR NATION'S DESTINY IS BEING WRITTEN IN THE HALLS AROUND US! THERE'S THE SENATE, WANT TO GO IN?
WITHIN THE SENATE, AN ISSUE OF VITA IMPORTANCE IS BEING DEBATED!
-- I FURTHER AGREE, WITH THE WORDS OF A GREAT AMERICAN, BILLY MITCHELL--WHO SAID, AND I QUOTE! "HE WHO HOLDS ALASKA HOLDS THE WORLD!"
THAT IS WHY I CONTEND, A UNIFIED COMMAND IS NECESSARY TO THE SAFETY OF ALASKA, AND THE,---UG! OH--
GOOD LORD! HE'S HAD A STROKE!
HELP HIM, QUICK!
IT'S SENATOR RALPH!
BUCKY HE-HE'S DEAD!
IT MUST HAVE BEEN, A HEART ATTACK!
BUT HE ALWAYS HAD A STRONG HEART! HMM-I WOND
DID YOU HEAR THAT, STEVE!
YEAH--! BUT WE'VE GOT TO GET BACK TO CAMP! IT'S LATER THAN I THOUGHT!
AS THE CROWD LEAVES THE GALLERY, ONE MAN SMILES IN SATISFACTION!

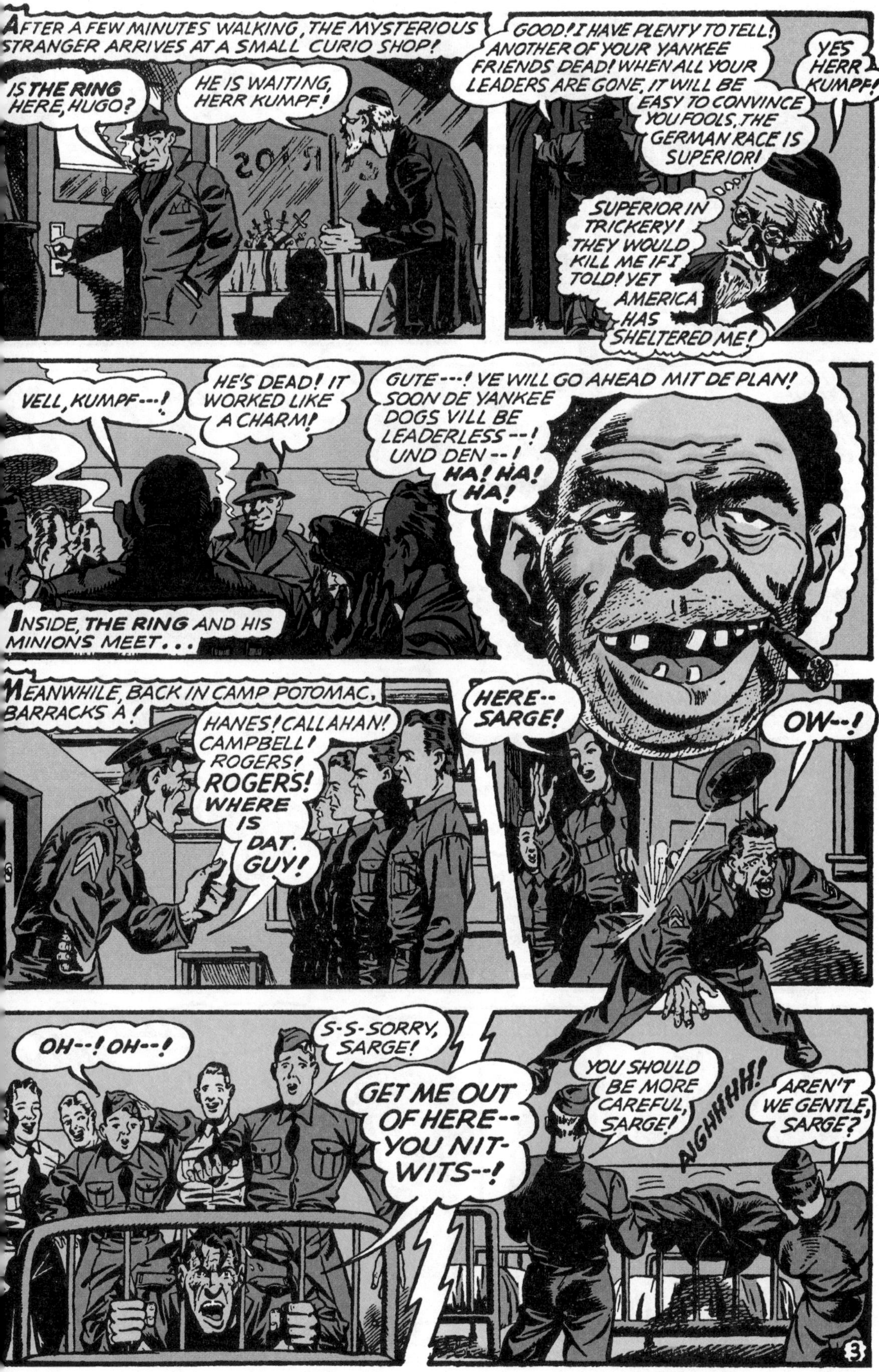
AFTER A FEW MINUTES WALKING, THE MYSTERIOUS STRANGER ARRIVES AT A SMALL CURIO SHOP!
IS THE RING HERE, HUGO?
HE IS WAITING, HERR KUMPF!
GOOD! I HAVE PLENTY TO TELL! ANOTHER OF YOUR YANKEE FRIENDS DEAD! WHEN ALL YOUR LEADERS ARE GONE, IT WILL BE EASY TO CONVINCE YOU FOOLS, THE GERMAN RACE IS SUPERIOR!
YES HERR KUMPF!
SUPERIOR IN TRICKERY! THEY WOULD KILL ME IF I TOLD! YET AMERICA HAS SHELTERED ME!
VELL, KUMPF---!
HE'S DEAD! IT WORKED LIKE A CHARM!
GUTE---! VE WILL GO AHEAD MIT DE PLAN! SOON DE YANKEE DOGS VILL BE LEADERLESS--! UND DEN--! HA! HA! HA!
INSIDE, THE RING AND HIS MINIONS MEET...
MEANWHILE, BACK IN CAMP POTOMAC, BARRACKS A!
HANES! CALLAHAN! CAMPBELL! ROGERS! ROGERS! WHERE IS DAT GUY!
HERE-- SARGE!
OW--!
OH--! OH--!
S-S-SORRY, SARGE!
GET ME OUT OF HERE-- YOU NIT-WITS--!
YOU SHOULD BE MORE CAREFUL, SARGE!
AIGHHHH!
AREN'T WE GENTLE, SARGE?

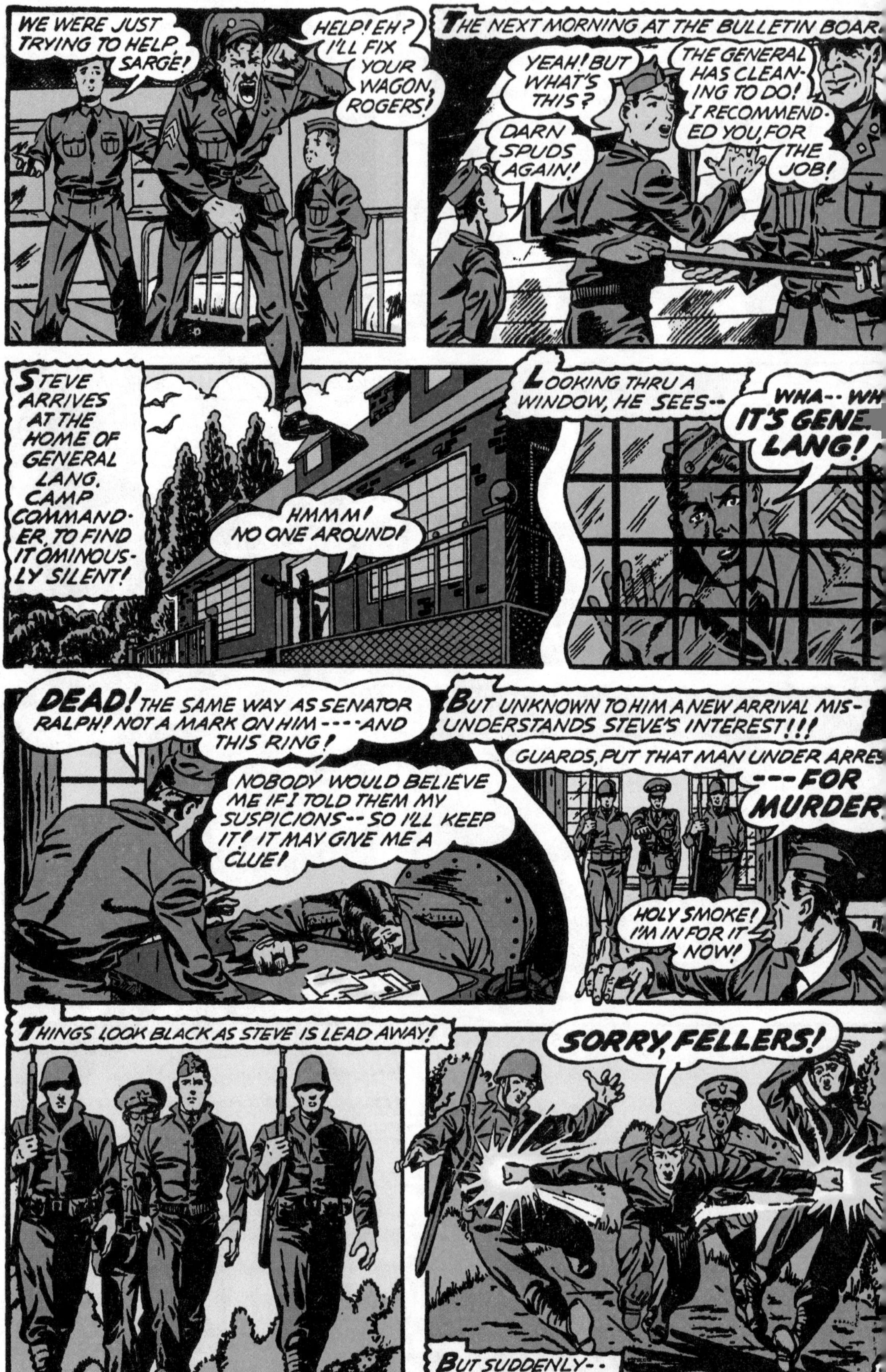
WE WERE JUST TRYING TO HELP, SARGE!
HELP! EH? I'LL FIX YOUR WAGON, ROGERS!
THE NEXT MORNING AT THE BULLETIN BOAR
YEAH! BUT WHAT'S THIS?
THE GENERAL HAS CLEANING TO DO! I RECOMMENDED YOU, FOR THE JOB!
DARN SPUDS AGAIN!
STEVE ARRIVES AT THE HOME OF GENERAL LANG, CAMP COMMANDER, TO FIND IT OMINOUSLY SILENT!
HMMM! NO ONE AROUND!
LOOKING THRU A WINDOW, HE SEES--
WHA-- WH IT'S GENE LANG!
DEAD! THE SAME WAY AS SENATOR RALPH! NOT A MARK ON HIM ----AND THIS RING!
NOBODY WOULD BELIEVE ME IF I TOLD THEM MY SUSPICIONS-- SO I'LL KEEP IT! IT MAY GIVE ME A CLUE!
BUT UNKNOWN TO HIM A NEW ARRIVAL MISUNDERSTANDS STEVE'S INTEREST!!!
GUARDS, PUT THAT MAN UNDER ARRES ---FOR MURDER
HOLY SMOKE! I'M IN FOR IT NOW!
THINGS LOOK BLACK AS STEVE IS LEAD AWAY!
SORRY, FELLERS!
BUT SUDDENLY--

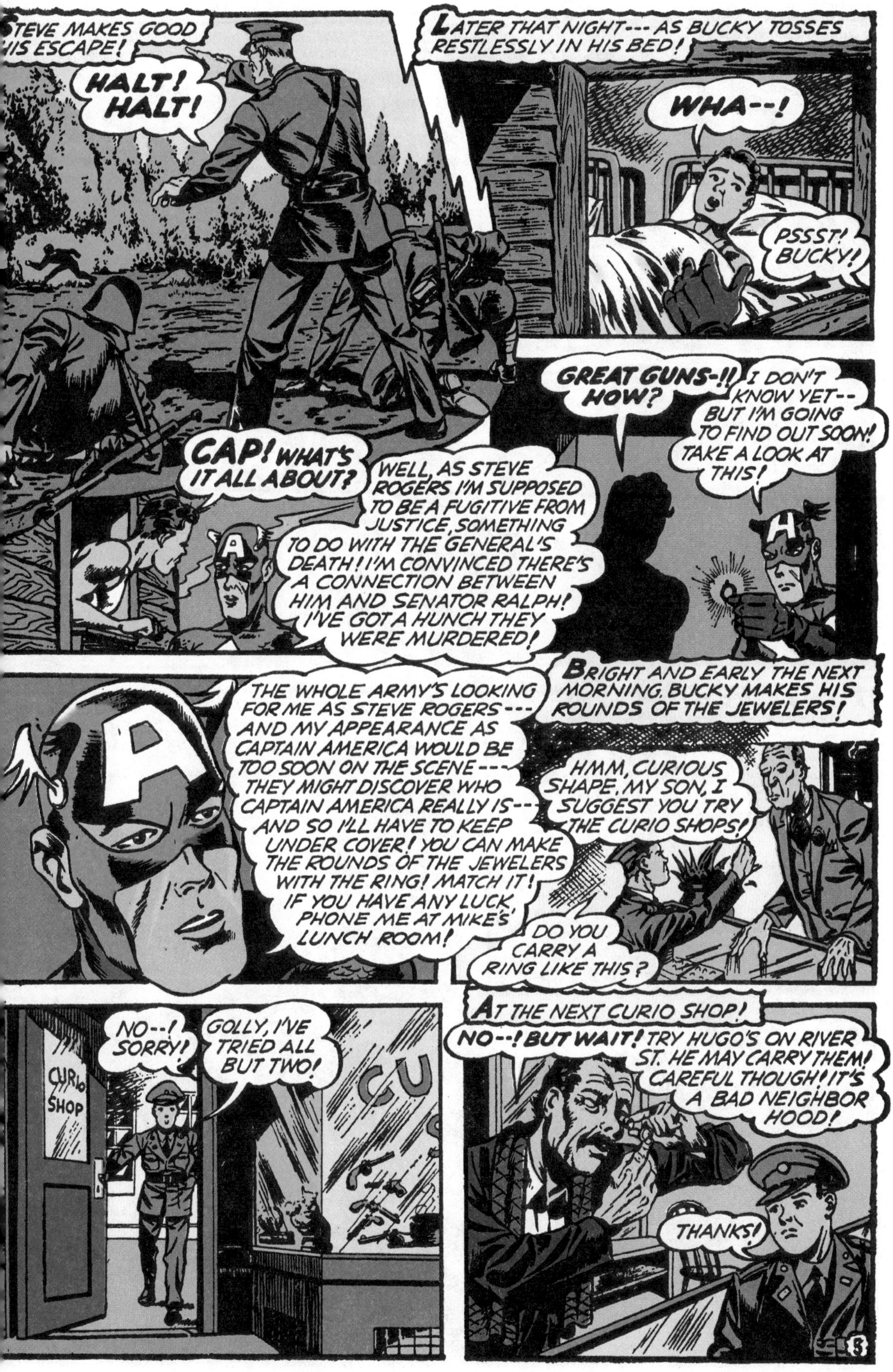
STEVE MAKES GOOD HIS ESCAPE!
HALT! HALT!
LATER THAT NIGHT--- AS BUCKY TOSSES RESTLESSLY IN HIS BED!
WHA--!
PSSST! BUCKY!
CAP! WHAT'S IT ALL ABOUT?
WELL, AS STEVE ROGERS I'M SUPPOSED TO BE A FUGITIVE FROM JUSTICE, SOMETHING TO DO WITH THE GENERAL'S DEATH! I'M CONVINCED THERE'S A CONNECTION BETWEEN HIM AND SENATOR RALPH! I'VE GOT A HUNCH THEY WERE MURDERED!
GREAT GUNS-!! HOW?
I DON'T KNOW YET-- BUT I'M GOING TO FIND OUT SOON! TAKE A LOOK AT THIS!
THE WHOLE ARMY'S LOOKING FOR ME AS STEVE ROGERS--- AND MY APPEARANCE AS CAPTAIN AMERICA WOULD BE TOO SOON ON THE SCENE--- THEY MIGHT DISCOVER WHO CAPTAIN AMERICA REALLY IS--- AND SO I'LL HAVE TO KEEP UNDER COVER! YOU CAN MAKE THE ROUNDS OF THE JEWELERS WITH THE RING! MATCH IT! IF YOU HAVE ANY LUCK, PHONE ME AT MIKE'S LUNCH ROOM!
BRIGHT AND EARLY THE NEXT MORNING, BUCKY MAKES HIS ROUNDS OF THE JEWELERS!
DO YOU CARRY A RING LIKE THIS?
HMM, CURIOUS SHAPE, MY SON, I SUGGEST YOU TRY THE CURIO SHOPS!
CURIO SHOP
NO--! SORRY!
GOLLY, I'VE TRIED ALL BUT TWO!
CU
AT THE NEXT CURIO SHOP!
NO--! BUT WAIT! TRY HUGO'S ON RIVER ST. HE MAY CARRY THEM! CAREFUL THOUGH! IT'S A BAD NEIGHBOR HOOD!
THANKS!
5

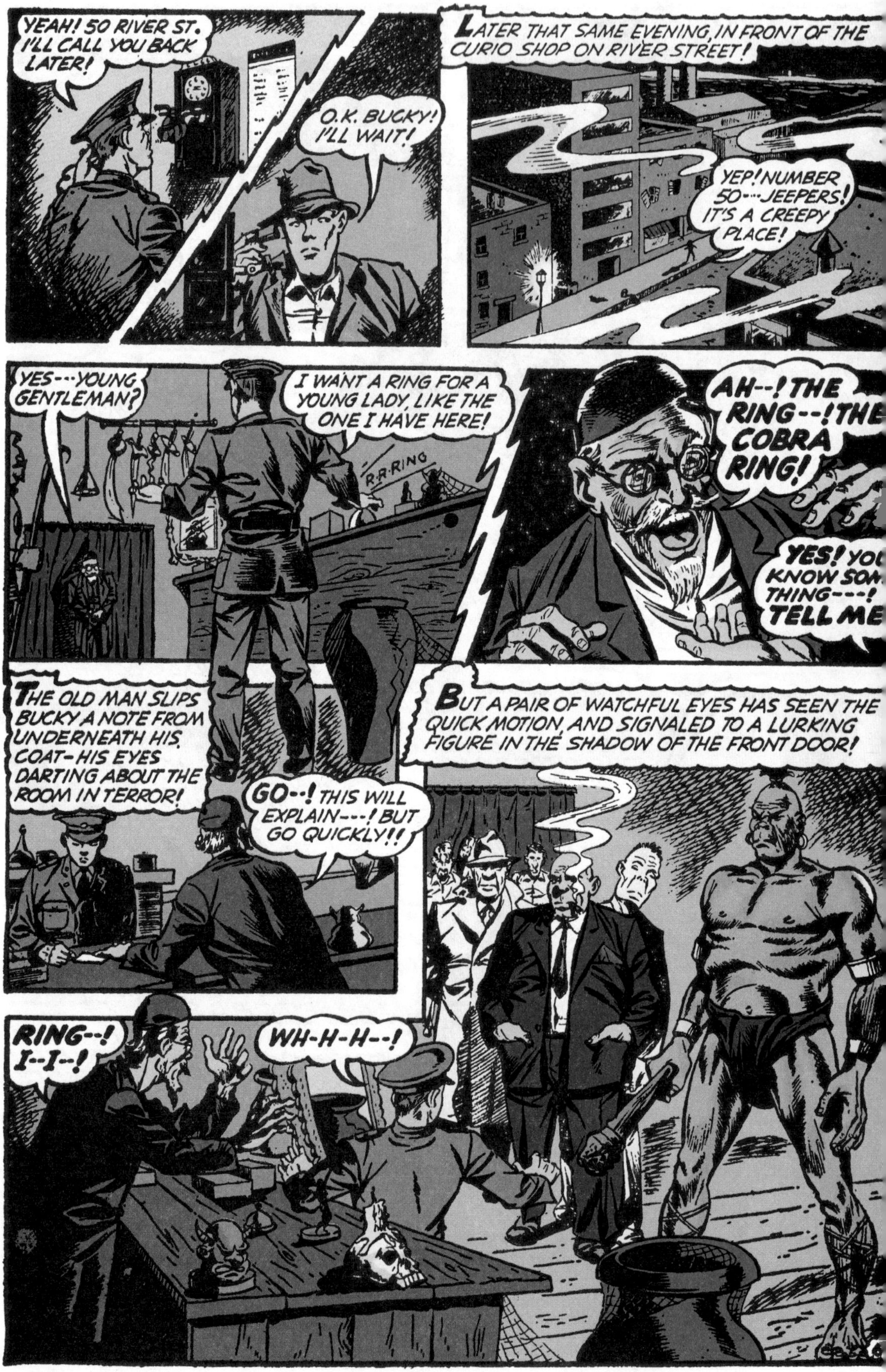
YEAH! 50 RIVER ST. I'LL CALL YOU BACK LATER!
O.K. BUCKY! I'LL WAIT!
LATER THAT SAME EVENING, IN FRONT OF THE CURIO SHOP ON RIVER STREET!
YEP! NUMBER 50--- JEEPERS! IT'S A CREEPY PLACE!
YES---YOUNG GENTLEMAN?
I WANT A RING FOR A YOUNG LADY, LIKE THE ONE I HAVE HERE!
R-R-RING
AH--! THE RING--! THE COBRA RING!
YES! YO KNOW SOM THING---! TELL ME
THE OLD MAN SLIPS BUCKY A NOTE FROM UNDERNEATH HIS COAT- HIS EYES DARTING ABOUT THE ROOM IN TERROR!
GO--! THIS WILL EXPLAIN---! BUT GO QUICKLY!!
BUT A PAIR OF WATCHFUL EYES HAS SEEN THE QUICK MOTION, AND SIGNALED TO A LURKING FIGURE IN THE SHADOW OF THE FRONT DOOR!
RING--! I--I--!
WH-H-H--!

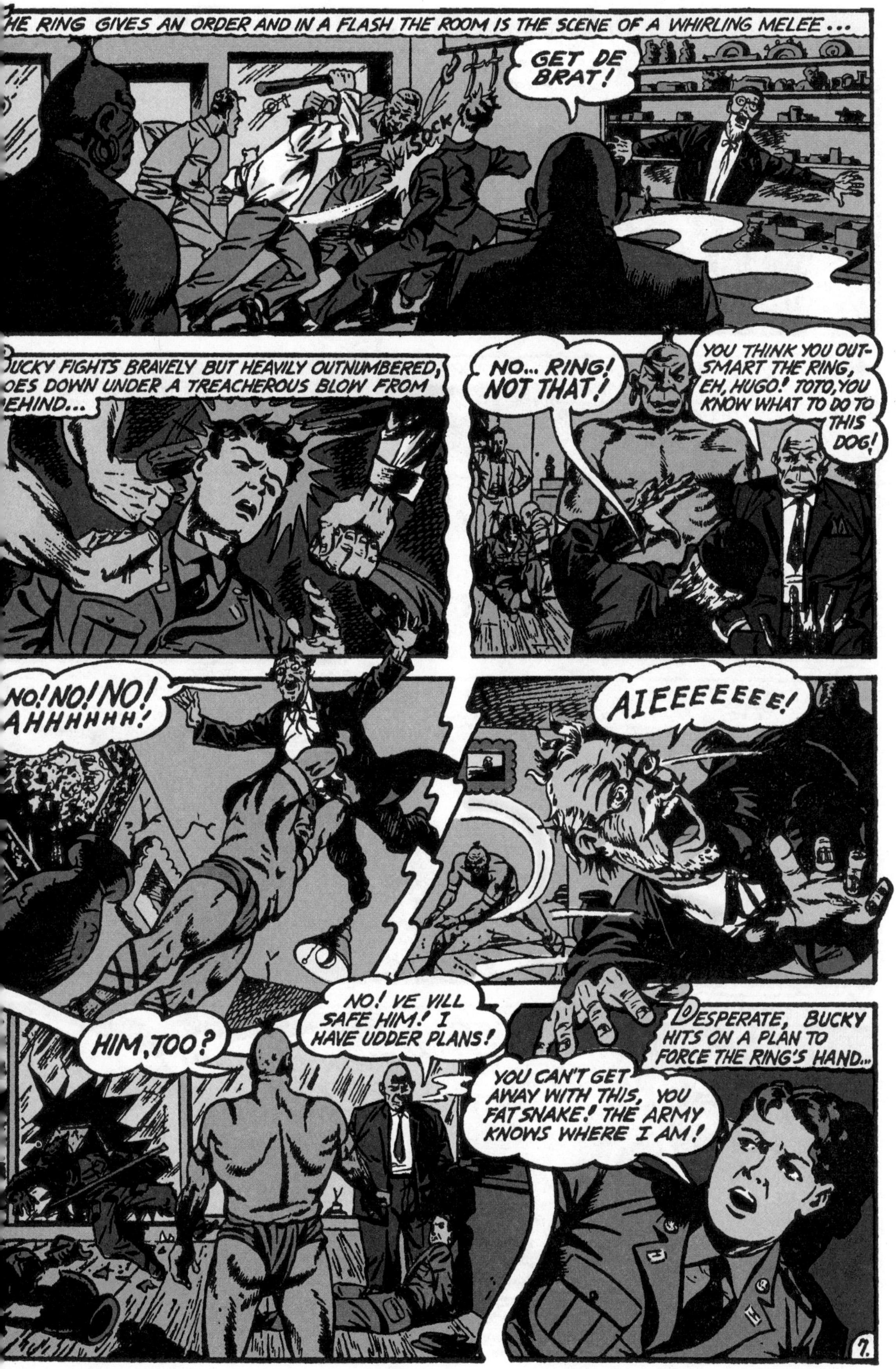
THE RING GIVES AN ORDER AND IN A FLASH THE ROOM IS THE SCENE OF A WHIRLING MELEE...
GET DE BRAT!
SOCK
BUCKY FIGHTS BRAVELY BUT HEAVILY OUTNUMBERED, GOES DOWN UNDER A TREACHEROUS BLOW FROM BEHIND...
NO... RING! NOT THAT!
YOU THINK YOU OUT-SMART THE RING, EH, HUGO! TOTO, YOU KNOW WHAT TO DO TO THIS DOG!
NO! NO! NO! AHHHHHH!
AIEEEEEEE!
HIM, TOO?
NO! VE VILL SAFE HIM! I HAVE UDDER PLANS!
DESPERATE, BUCKY HITS ON A PLAN TO FORCE THE RING'S HAND...
YOU CAN'T GET AWAY WITH THIS, YOU FAT SNAKE! THE ARMY KNOWS WHERE I AM!

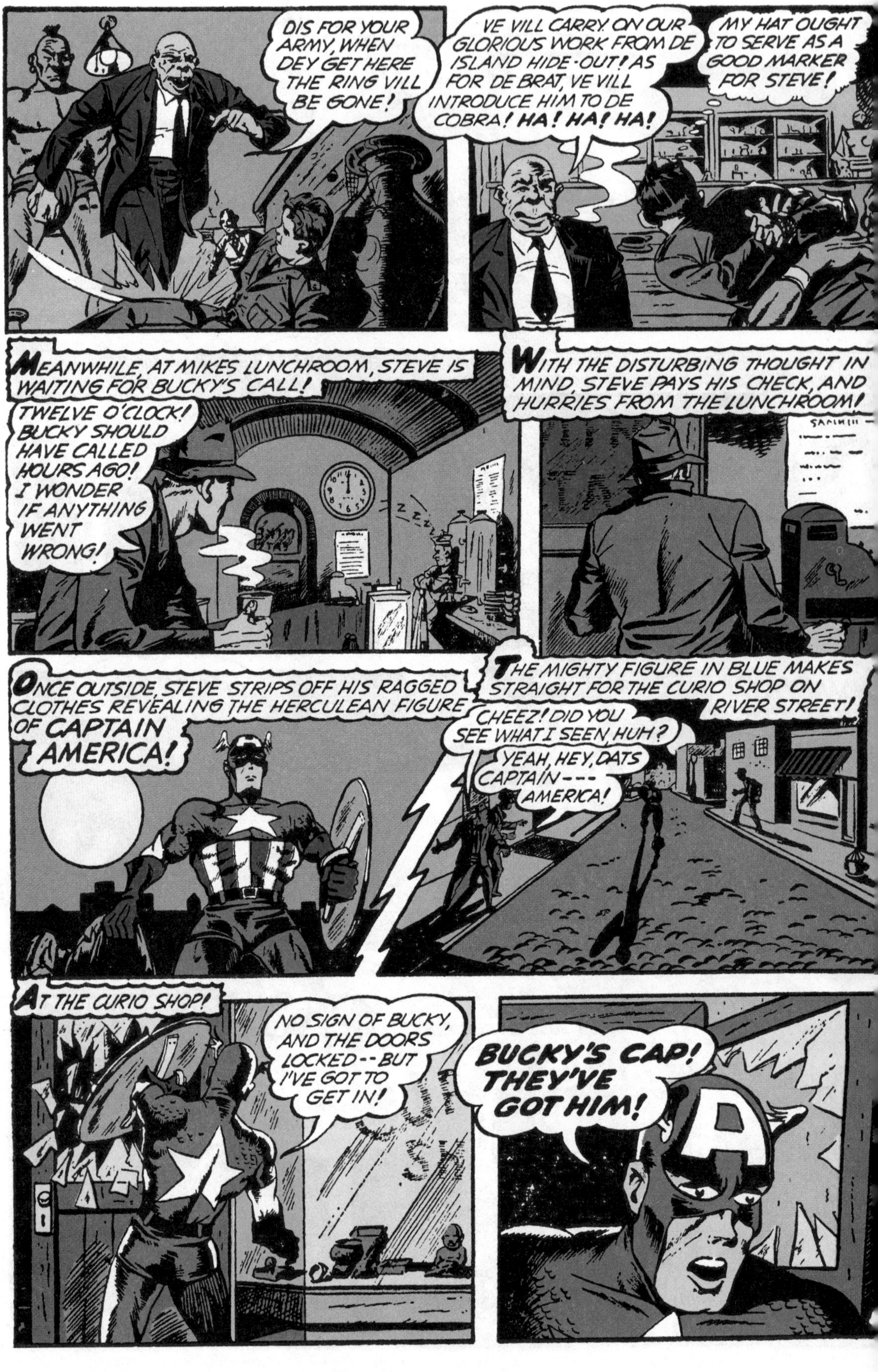
DIS FOR YOUR ARMY, WHEN DEY GET HERE THE RING VILL BE GONE!
VE VILL CARRY ON OUR GLORIOUS WORK FROM DE ISLAND HIDE-OUT! AS FOR DE BRAT, VE VILL INTRODUCE HIM TO DE COBRA! HA! HA! HA!
MY HAT OUGHT TO SERVE AS A GOOD MARKER FOR STEVE!
MEANWHILE, AT MIKES LUNCHROOM, STEVE IS WAITING FOR BUCKY'S CALL!
TWELVE O'CLOCK! BUCKY SHOULD HAVE CALLED HOURS AGO! I WONDER IF ANYTHING WENT WRONG!
WITH THE DISTURBING THOUGHT IN MIND, STEVE PAYS HIS CHECK, AND HURRIES FROM THE LUNCHROOM!
ONCE OUTSIDE, STEVE STRIPS OFF HIS RAGGED CLOTHES REVEALING THE HERCULEAN FIGURE OF CAPTAIN AMERICA!
THE MIGHTY FIGURE IN BLUE MAKES STRAIGHT FOR THE CURIO SHOP ON RIVER STREET!
CHEEZ! DID YOU SEE WHAT I SEEN, HUH?
YEAH, HEY, DATS CAPTAIN--- AMERICA!
AT THE CURIO SHOP!
NO SIGN OF BUCKY, AND THE DOORS LOCKED--BUT I'VE GOT TO GET IN!
BUCKY'S CAP! THEY'VE GOT HIM!

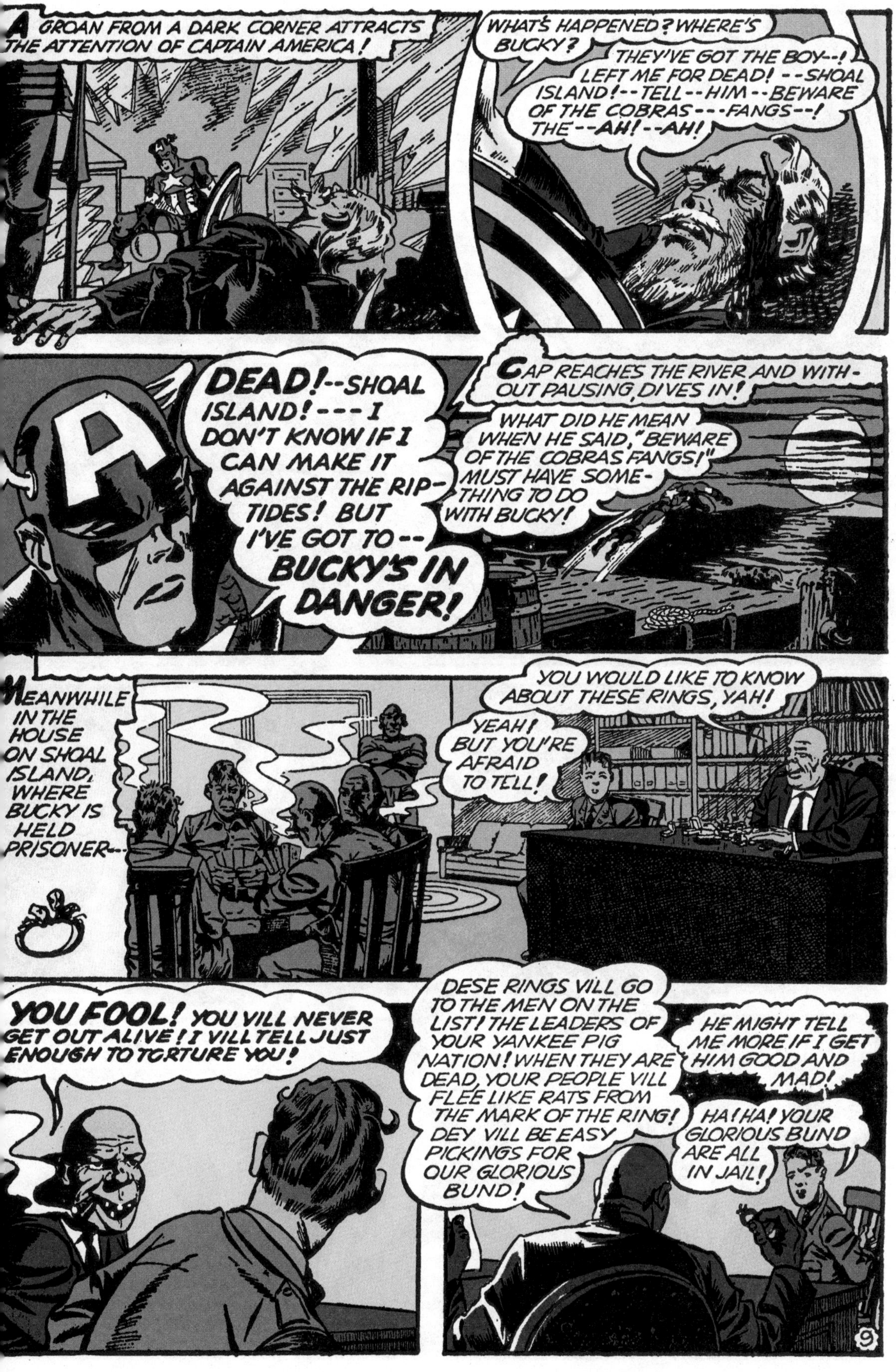
A GROAN FROM A DARK CORNER ATTRACTS THE ATTENTION OF CAPTAIN AMERICA!
WHAT'S HAPPENED? WHERE'S BUCKY?
THEY'VE GOT THE BOY--! LEFT ME FOR DEAD! --SHOAL ISLAND!--TELL--HIM--BEWARE OF THE COBRAS---FANGS--! THE--AH!--AH!
DEAD!--SHOAL ISLAND!---I DON'T KNOW IF I CAN MAKE IT AGAINST THE RIP-TIDES! BUT I'VE GOT TO--BUCKY'S IN DANGER!
CAP REACHES THE RIVER AND WITH-OUT PAUSING, DIVES IN!
WHAT DID HE MEAN WHEN HE SAID, "BEWARE OF THE COBRAS FANGS!" MUST HAVE SOME-THING TO DO WITH BUCKY!
MEANWHILE IN THE HOUSE ON SHOAL ISLAND, WHERE BUCKY IS HELD PRISONER---
YOU WOULD LIKE TO KNOW ABOUT THESE RINGS, YAH!
YEAH! BUT YOU'RE AFRAID TO TELL!
YOU FOOL! YOU VILL NEVER GET OUT ALIVE! I VILL TELL JUST ENOUGH TO TORTURE YOU!
DESE RINGS VILL GO TO THE MEN ON THE LIST! THE LEADERS OF YOUR YANKEE PIG NATION! WHEN THEY ARE DEAD, YOUR PEOPLE VILL FLEE LIKE RATS FROM THE MARK OF THE RING! DEY VILL BE EASY PICKINGS FOR OUR GLORIOUS BUND!
HE MIGHT TELL ME MORE IF I GET HIM GOOD AND MAD!
HA! HA! YOUR GLORIOUS BUND ARE ALL IN JAIL!
9

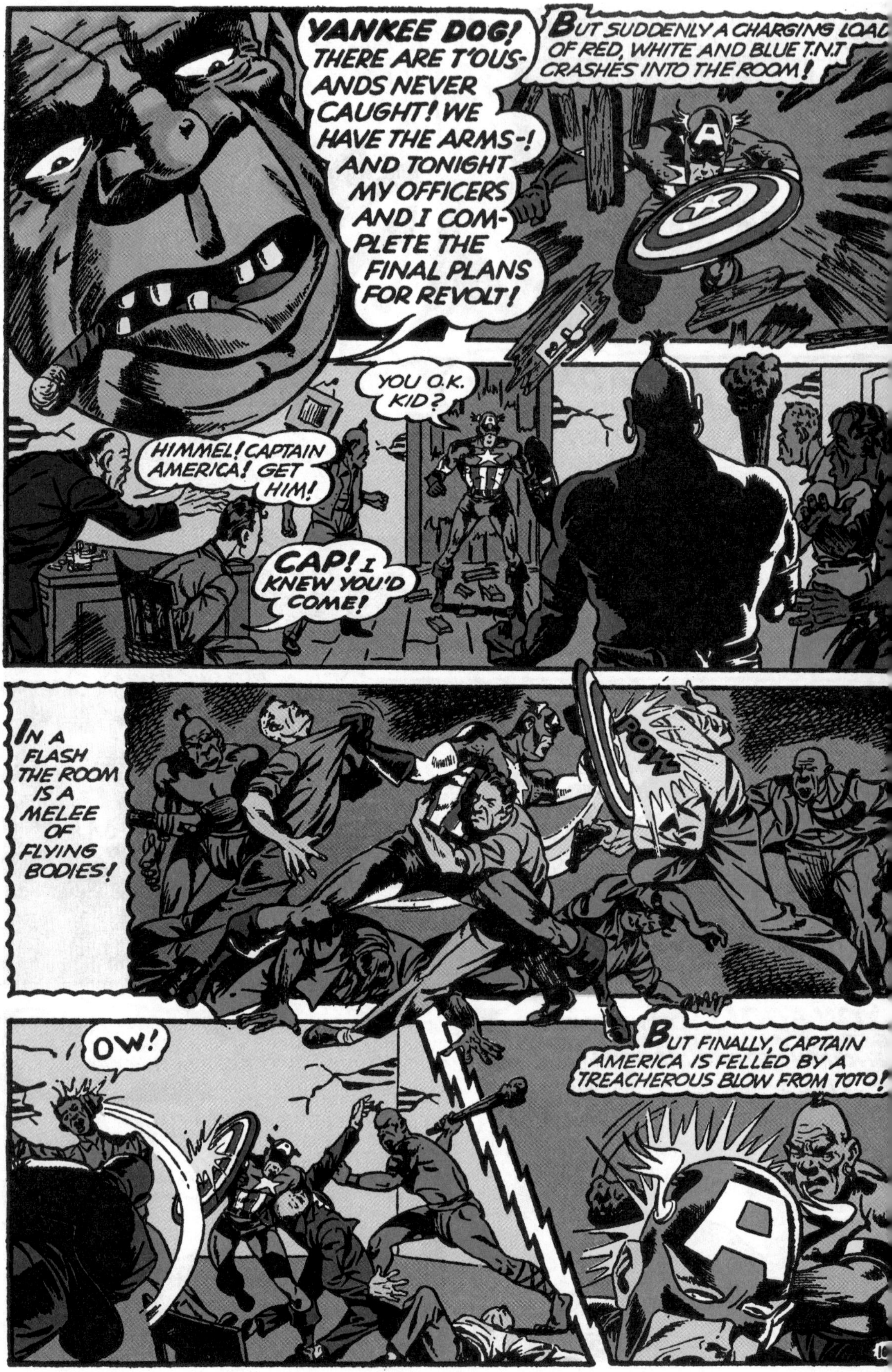
YANKEE DOG! THERE ARE T'OUS-ANDS NEVER CAUGHT! WE HAVE THE ARMS-! AND TONIGHT MY OFFICERS AND I COM-PLETE THE FINAL PLANS FOR REVOLT!
BUT SUDDENLY A CHARGING LOAD OF RED, WHITE AND BLUE T.N.T CRASHES INTO THE ROOM!
YOU O.K. KID?
HIMMEL! CAPTAIN AMERICA! GET HIM!
CAP! I KNEW YOU'D COME!
IN A FLASH THE ROOM IS A MELEE OF FLYING BODIES!
POW
OW!
BUT FINALLY, CAPTAIN AMERICA IS FELLED BY A TREACHEROUS BLOW FROM TOTO!
16

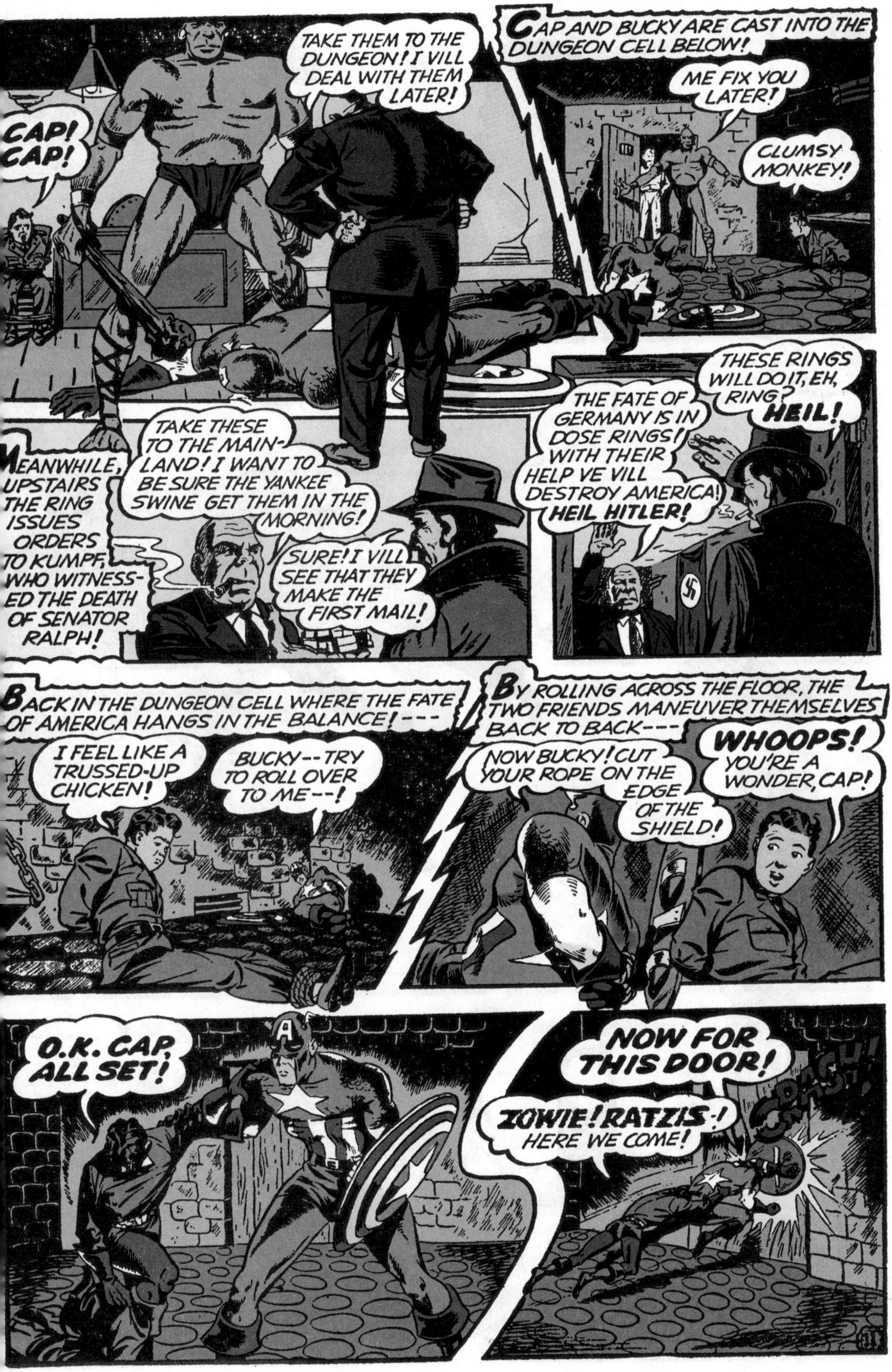

TAKE THEM TO THE DUNGEON! I VILL DEAL WITH THEM LATER!
CAP! CAP!
CAP AND BUCKY ARE CAST INTO THE DUNGEON CELL BELOW!
ME FIX YOU LATER!
CLUMSY MONKEY!
MEANWHILE, UPSTAIRS THE RING ISSUES ORDERS TO KUMPF, WHO WITNESSED THE DEATH OF SENATOR RALPH!
TAKE THESE TO THE MAINLAND! I WANT TO BE SURE THE YANKEE SWINE GET THEM IN THE MORNING!
SURE! I VILL SEE THAT THEY MAKE THE FIRST MAIL!
THESE RINGS WILL DO IT, EH, RING? HEIL!
THE FATE OF GERMANY IS IN DOSE RINGS! WITH THEIR HELP VE VILL DESTROY AMERICA! HEIL HITLER!
BACK IN THE DUNGEON CELL WHERE THE FATE OF AMERICA HANGS IN THE BALANCE! ---
I FEEL LIKE A TRUSSED-UP CHICKEN!
BUCKY -- TRY TO ROLL OVER TO ME --!
BY ROLLING ACROSS THE FLOOR, THE TWO FRIENDS MANEUVER THEMSELVES BACK TO BACK ---
NOW BUCKY! CUT YOUR ROPE ON THE EDGE OF THE SHIELD!
WHOOPS! YOU'RE A WONDER, CAP!
O.K. CAP, ALL SET!
NOW FOR THIS DOOR!
ZOWIE! RATZIS -! HERE WE COME!
CRASH!!
11

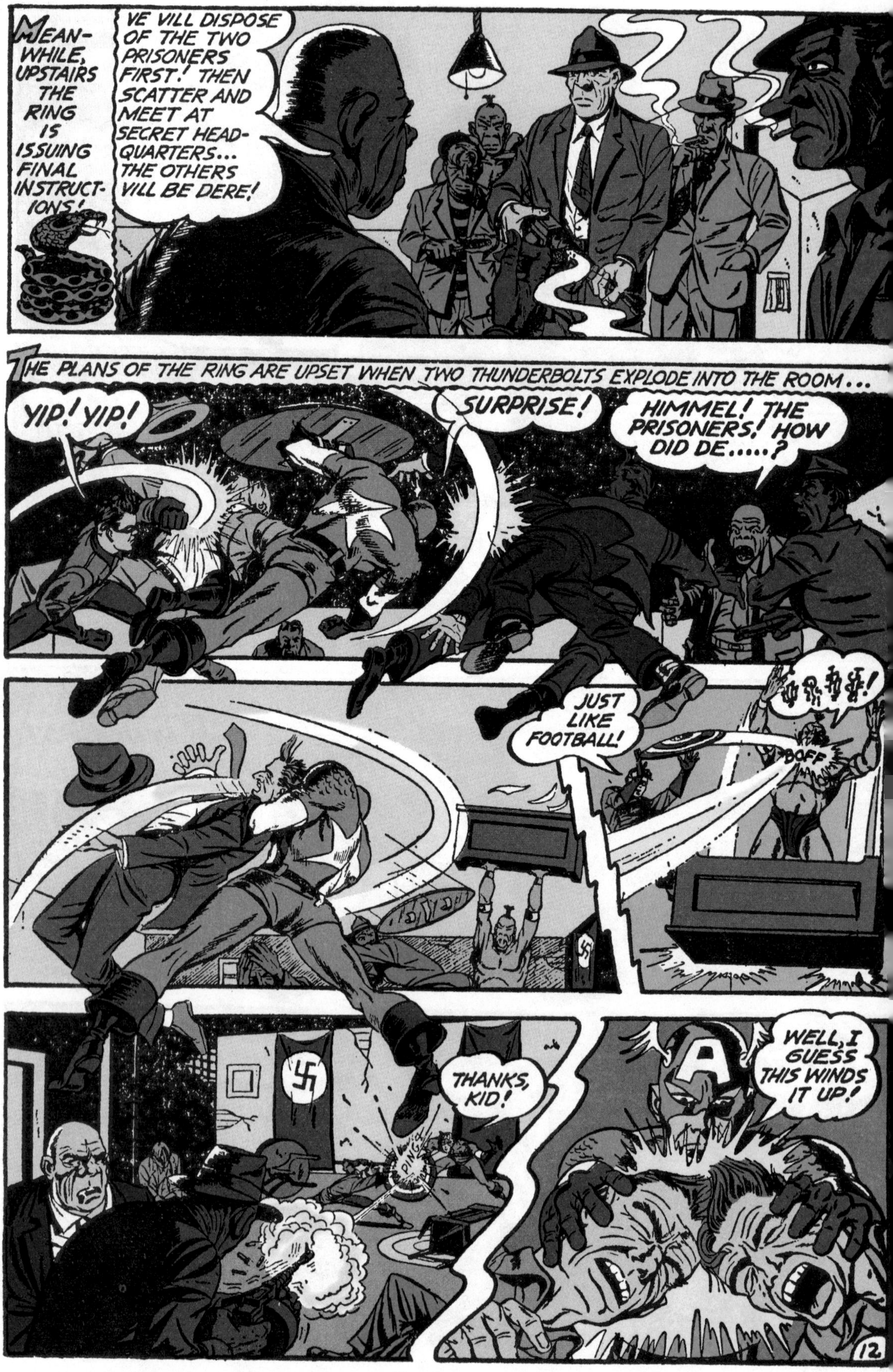
MEANWHILE, UPSTAIRS THE RING IS ISSUING FINAL INSTRUCTIONS!
VE VILL DISPOSE OF THE TWO PRISONERS FIRST! THEN SCATTER AND MEET AT SECRET HEADQUARTERS... THE OTHERS VILL BE DERE!
THE PLANS OF THE RING ARE UPSET WHEN TWO THUNDERBOLTS EXPLODE INTO THE ROOM...
YIP! YIP!
SURPRISE!
HIMMEL! THE PRISONERS! HOW DID DE.....?
JUST LIKE FOOTBALL!
BOFF
THANKS, KID!
PING
WELL, I GUESS THIS WINDS IT UP!

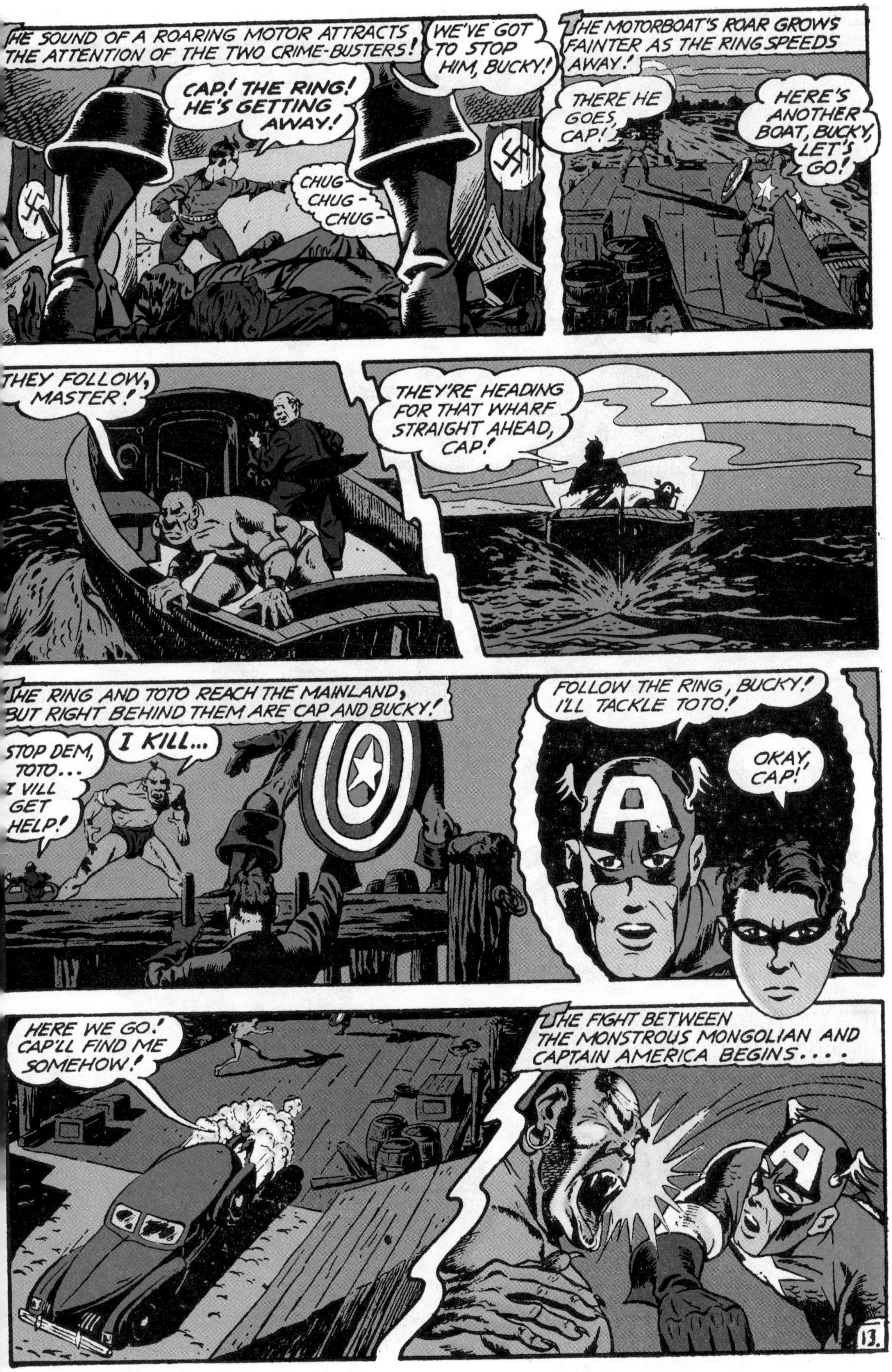
THE SOUND OF A ROARING MOTOR ATTRACTS THE ATTENTION OF THE TWO CRIME-BUSTERS!
CAP! THE RING! HE'S GETTING AWAY!
CHUG CHUG-CHUG-
WE'VE GOT TO STOP HIM, BUCKY!
THE MOTORBOAT'S ROAR GROWS FAINTER AS THE RING SPEEDS AWAY!
THERE HE GOES, CAP!
HERE'S ANOTHER BOAT, BUCKY, LET'S GO!
THEY FOLLOW, MASTER!
THEY'RE HEADING FOR THAT WHARF STRAIGHT AHEAD, CAP!
THE RING AND TOTO REACH THE MAINLAND, BUT RIGHT BEHIND THEM ARE CAP AND BUCKY!
STOP DEM, TOTO... I VILL GET HELP!
I KILL...
FOLLOW THE RING, BUCKY! I'LL TACKLE TOTO!
OKAY, CAP!
HERE WE GO! CAP'LL FIND ME SOMEHOW!
THE FIGHT BETWEEN THE MONSTROUS MONGOLIAN AND CAPTAIN AMERICA BEGINS....

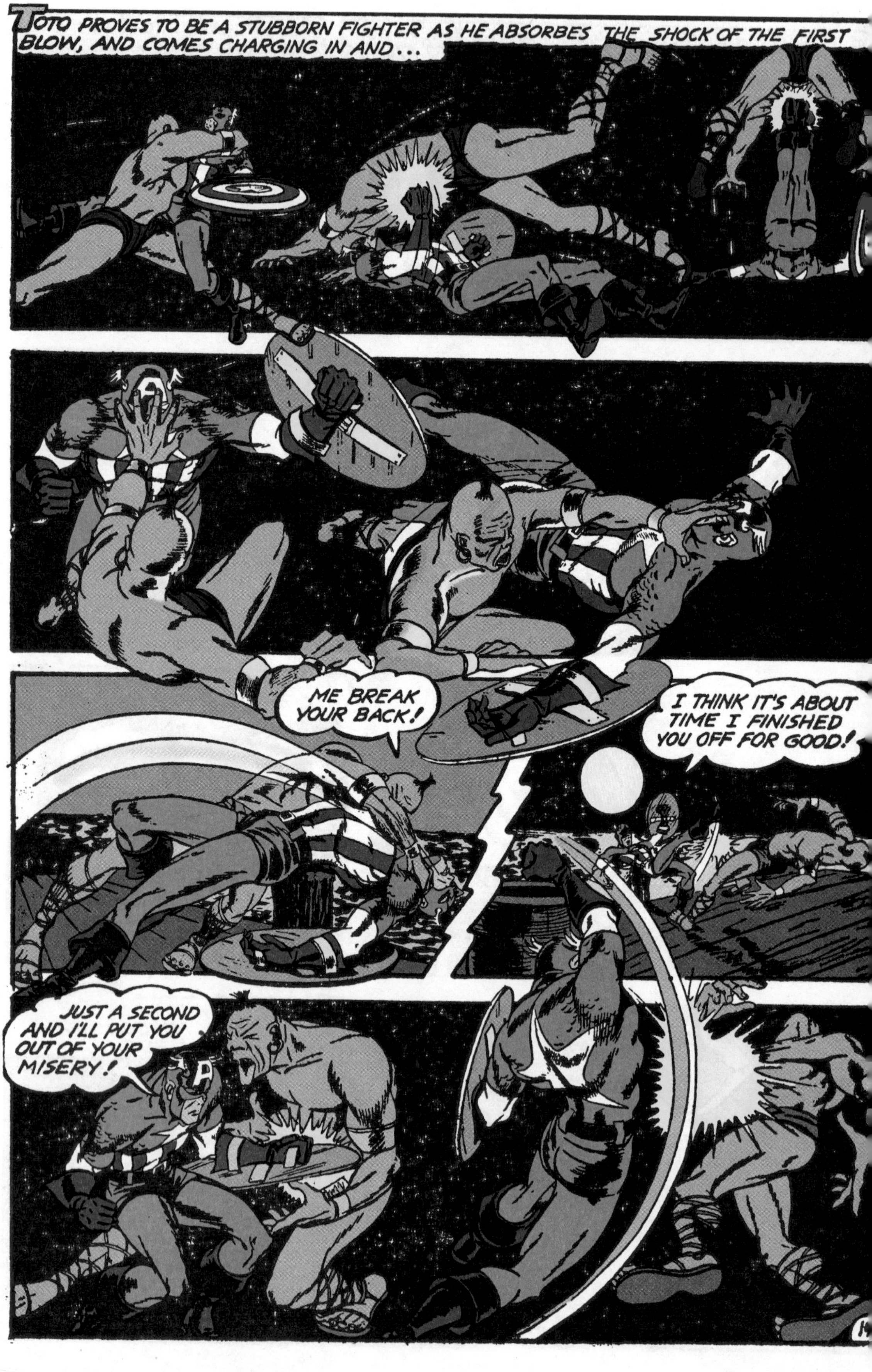
TOTO PROVES TO BE A STUBBORN FIGHTER AS HE ABSORBES THE SHOCK OF THE FIRST BLOW, AND COMES CHARGING IN AND...
ME BREAK YOUR BACK!
I THINK IT'S ABOUT TIME I FINISHED YOU OFF FOR GOOD!
JUST A SECOND AND I'LL PUT YOU OUT OF YOUR MISERY!

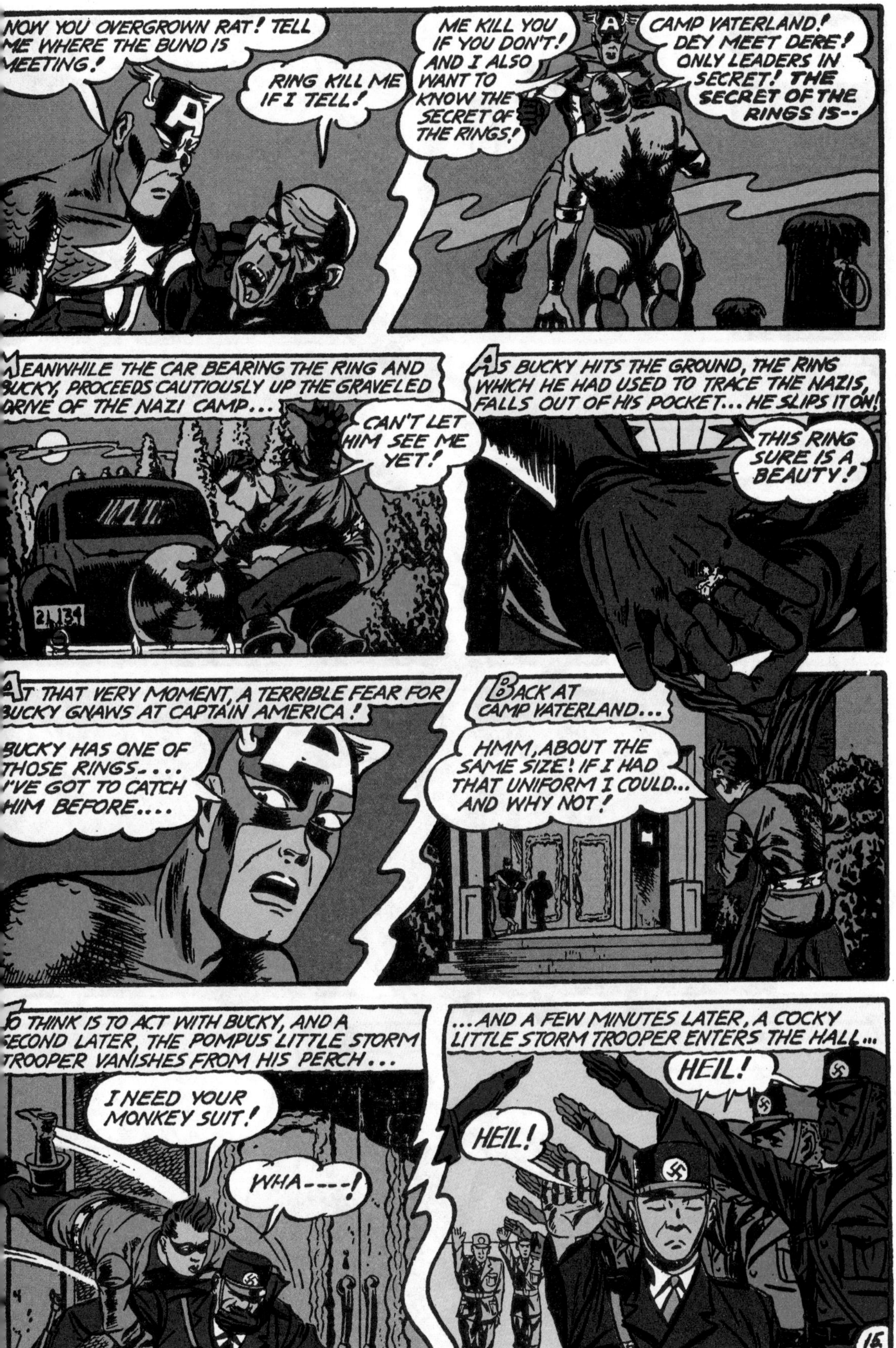

NOW YOU OVERGROWN RAT! TELL ME WHERE THE BUND IS MEETING!
RING KILL ME IF I TELL!
ME KILL YOU IF YOU DON'T! AND I ALSO WANT TO KNOW THE SECRET OF THE RINGS!
CAMP VATERLAND! DEY MEET DERE! ONLY LEADERS IN SECRET! THE SECRET OF THE RINGS IS--
MEANWHILE THE CAR BEARING THE RING AND BUCKY, PROCEEDS CAUTIOUSLY UP THE GRAVELED DRIVE OF THE NAZI CAMP...
CAN'T LET HIM SEE ME YET!
AS BUCKY HITS THE GROUND, THE RING WHICH HE HAD USED TO TRACE THE NAZIS, FALLS OUT OF HIS POCKET... HE SLIPS IT ON!
THIS RING SURE IS A BEAUTY!
AT THAT VERY MOMENT, A TERRIBLE FEAR FOR BUCKY GNAWS AT CAPTAIN AMERICA!
BUCKY HAS ONE OF THOSE RINGS.... I'VE GOT TO CATCH HIM BEFORE....
BACK AT CAMP VATERLAND...
HMM, ABOUT THE SAME SIZE! IF I HAD THAT UNIFORM I COULD... AND WHY NOT!
TO THINK IS TO ACT WITH BUCKY, AND A SECOND LATER, THE POMPUS LITTLE STORM TROOPER VANISHES FROM HIS PERCH...
I NEED YOUR MONKEY SUIT!
WHA----!
...AND A FEW MINUTES LATER, A COCKY LITTLE STORM TROOPER ENTERS THE HALL...
HEIL!
HEIL!
16

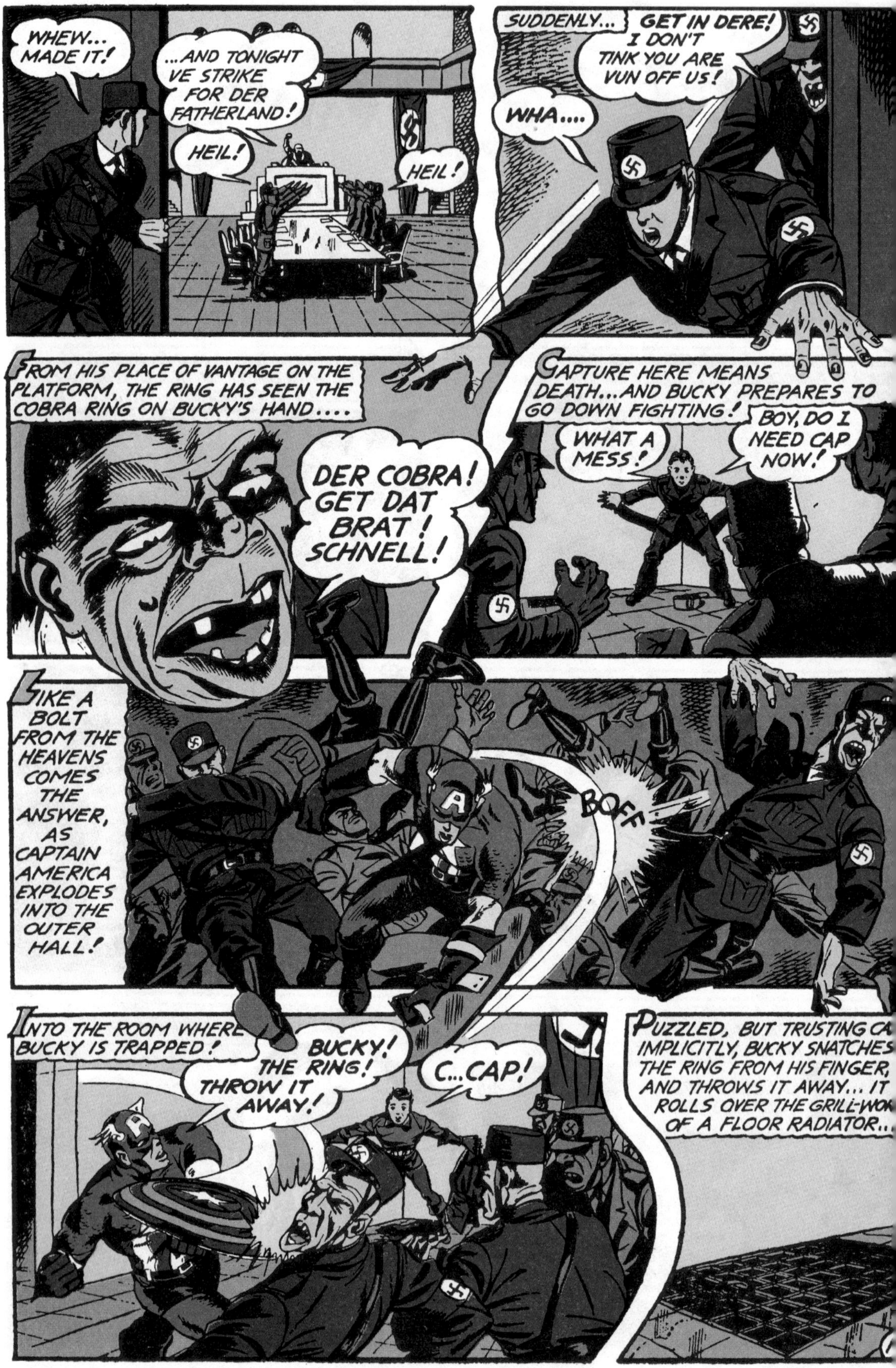
WHEW... MADE IT!
...AND TONIGHT VE STRIKE FOR DER FATHERLAND!
HEIL!
HEIL!
SUDDENLY...
GET IN DERE! I DON'T TINK YOU ARE VUN OFF US!
WHA....
FROM HIS PLACE OF VANTAGE ON THE PLATFORM, THE RING HAS SEEN THE COBRA RING ON BUCKY'S HAND....
DER COBRA! GET DAT BRAT! SCHNELL!
CAPTURE HERE MEANS DEATH...AND BUCKY PREPARES TO GO DOWN FIGHTING!
WHAT A MESS!
BOY, DO I NEED CAP NOW!
LIKE A BOLT FROM THE HEAVENS COMES THE ANSWER, AS CAPTAIN AMERICA EXPLODES INTO THE OUTER HALL!
BOFF
INTO THE ROOM WHERE BUCKY IS TRAPPED!
BUCKY! THE RING! THROW IT AWAY!
C...CAP!
PUZZLED, BUT TRUSTING CA IMPLICITLY, BUCKY SNATCHES THE RING FROM HIS FINGER, AND THROWS IT AWAY... IT ROLLS OVER THE GRILL-WOR OF A FLOOR RADIATOR...

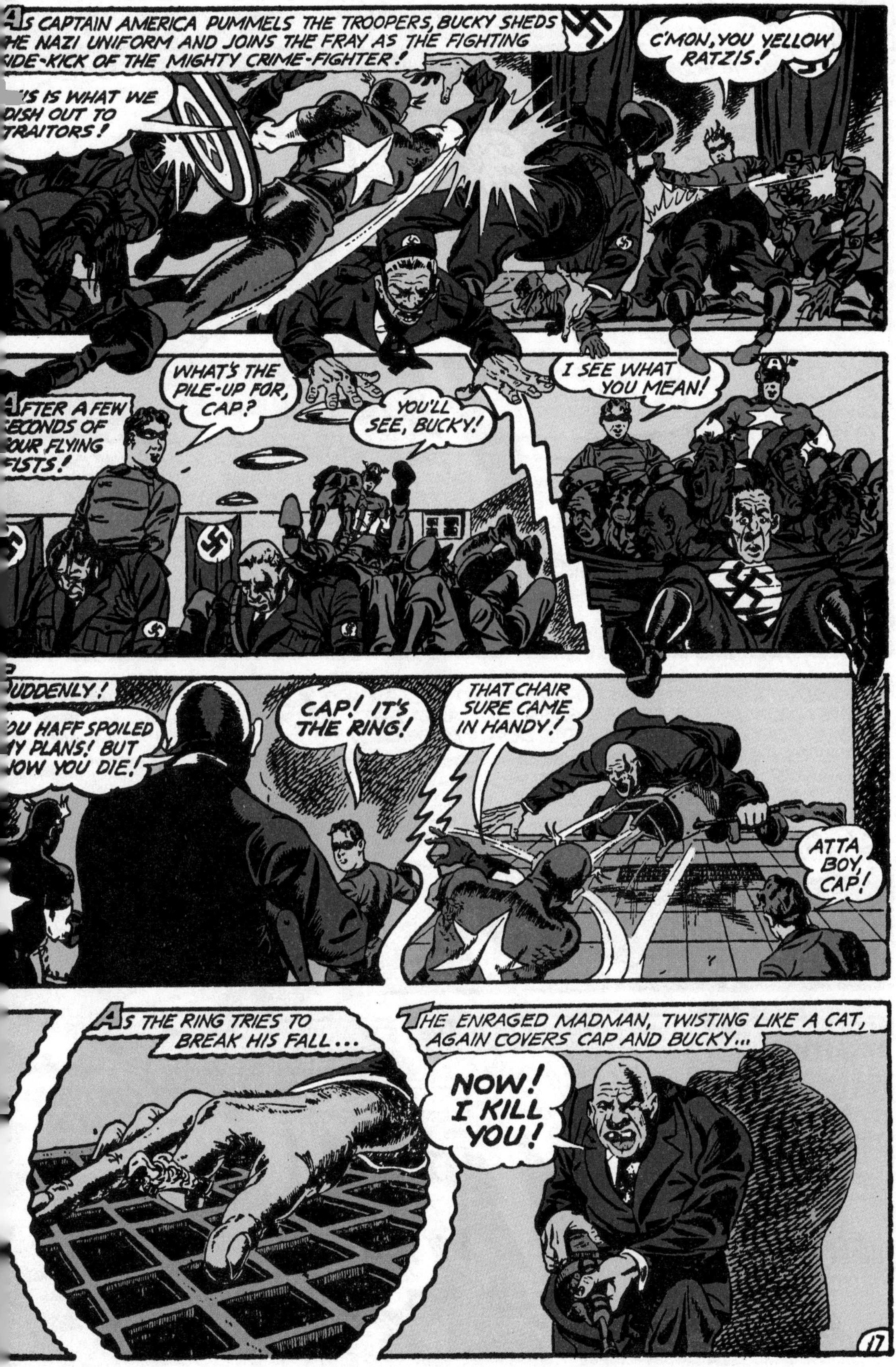

AS CAPTAIN AMERICA PUMMELS THE TROOPERS, BUCKY SHEDS HE NAZI UNIFORM AND JOINS THE FRAY AS THE FIGHTING IDE-KICK OF THE MIGHTY CRIME-FIGHTER!
C'MON, YOU YELLOW RATZIS!
IS IS WHAT WE DISH OUT TO TRAITORS!
AFTER A FEW ECONDS OF OUR FLYING FISTS!
WHAT'S THE PILE-UP FOR, CAP?
YOU'LL SEE, BUCKY!
I SEE WHAT YOU MEAN!
UDDENLY!
OU HAFF SPOILED MY PLANS! BUT NOW YOU DIE!
CAP! IT'S THE RING!
THAT CHAIR SURE CAME IN HANDY!
ATTA BOY, CAP!
AS THE RING TRIES TO BREAK HIS FALL...
THE ENRAGED MADMAN, TWISTING LIKE A CAT, AGAIN COVERS CAP AND BUCKY...
NOW! I KILL YOU!

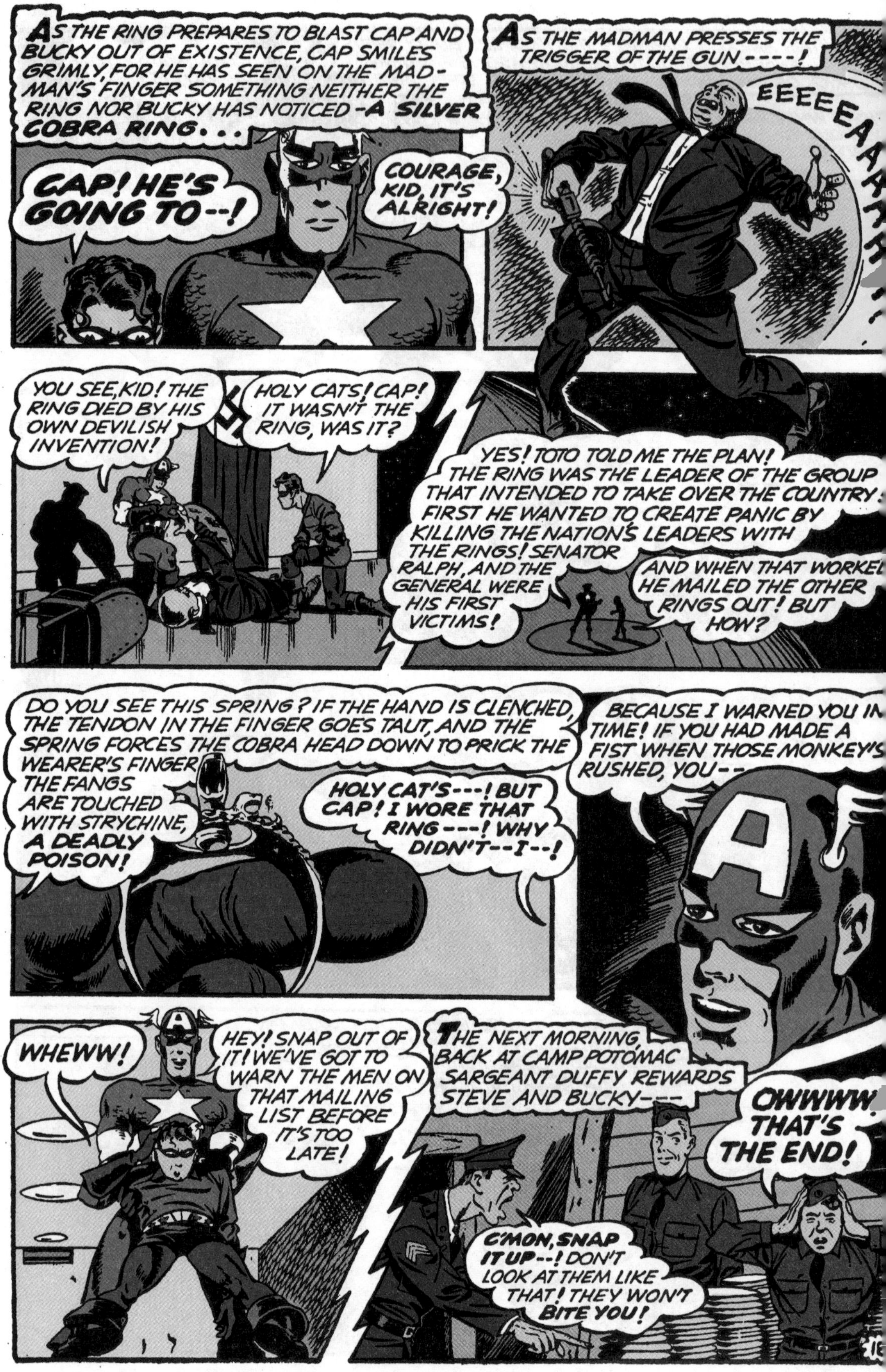

AS THE RING PREPARES TO BLAST CAP AND BUCKY OUT OF EXISTENCE, CAP SMILES GRIMLY, FOR HE HAS SEEN ON THE MAD-MAN'S FINGER SOMETHING NEITHER THE RING NOR BUCKY HAS NOTICED -A SILVER COBRA RING...
CAP! HE'S GOING TO--!
COURAGE, KID, IT'S ALRIGHT!
AS THE MADMAN PRESSES THE TRIGGER OF THE GUN----!
EEEEEAAARR!!
YOU SEE, KID! THE RING DIED BY HIS OWN DEVILISH INVENTION!
HOLY CATS! CAP! IT WASN'T THE RING, WAS IT?
YES! TOTO TOLD ME THE PLAN! THE RING WAS THE LEADER OF THE GROUP THAT INTENDED TO TAKE OVER THE COUNTRY! FIRST HE WANTED TO CREATE PANIC BY KILLING THE NATION'S LEADERS WITH THE RINGS! SENATOR RALPH, AND THE GENERAL WERE HIS FIRST VICTIMS!
AND WHEN THAT WORKED HE MAILED THE OTHER RINGS OUT! BUT HOW?
DO YOU SEE THIS SPRING? IF THE HAND IS CLENCHED, THE TENDON IN THE FINGER GOES TAUT, AND THE SPRING FORCES THE COBRA HEAD DOWN TO PRICK THE WEARER'S FINGER. THE FANGS ARE TOUCHED WITH STRYCHINE, A DEADLY POISON!
HOLY CAT'S---! BUT CAP! I WORE THAT RING---! WHY DIDN'T--I--!
BECAUSE I WARNED YOU IN TIME! IF YOU HAD MADE A FIST WHEN THOSE MONKEY'S RUSHED, YOU--
WHEWW!
HEY! SNAP OUT OF IT! WE'VE GOT TO WARN THE MEN ON THAT MAILING LIST BEFORE IT'S TOO LATE!
THE NEXT MORNING, BACK AT CAMP POTOMAC SARGEANT DUFFY REWARDS STEVE AND BUCKY---
OWWWW. THAT'S THE END!
C'MON, SNAP IT UP--! DON'T LOOK AT THEM LIKE THAT! THEY WON'T BITE YOU!

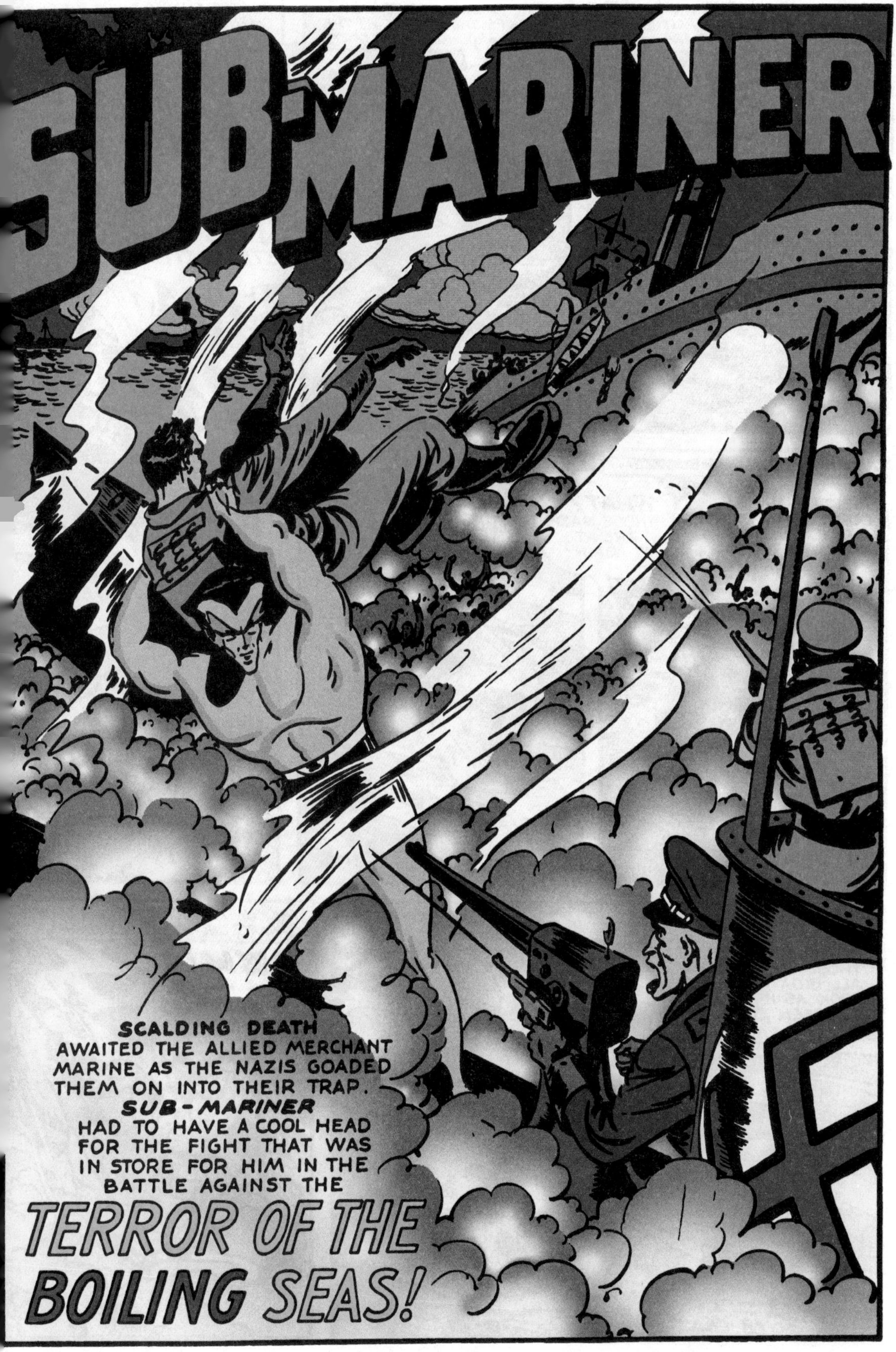
SUB-MARINER
SCALDING DEATH AWAITED THE ALLIED MERCHANT MARINE AS THE NAZIS GOADED THEM ON INTO THEIR TRAP. SUB-MARINER HAD TO HAVE A COOL HEAD FOR THE FIGHT THAT WAS IN STORE FOR HIM IN THE BATTLE AGAINST THE
TERROR OF THE BOILING SEAS!

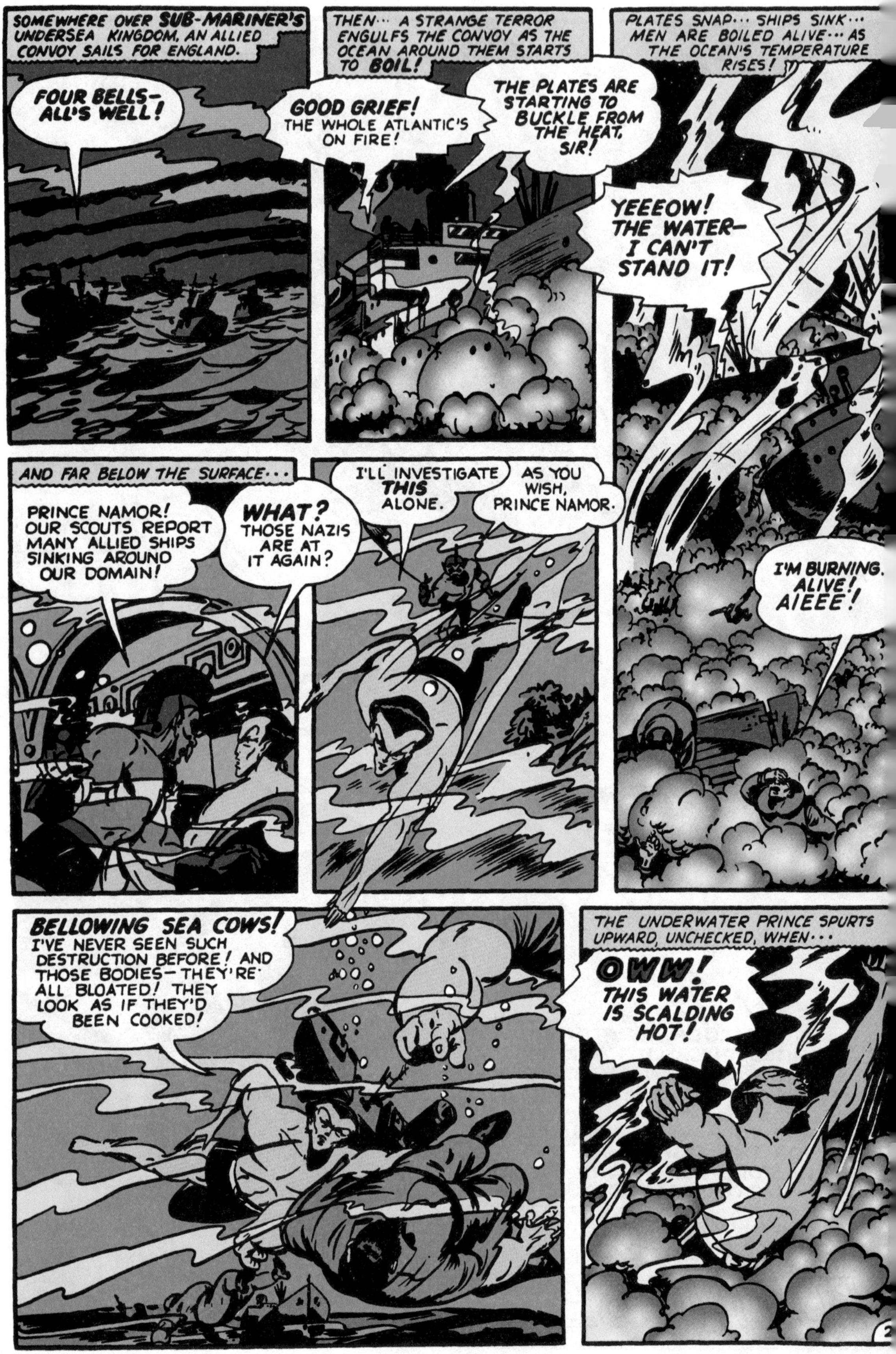
SOMEWHERE OVER SUB-MARINER'S UNDERSEA KINGDOM, AN ALLIED CONVOY SAILS FOR ENGLAND.
FOUR BELLS— ALL'S WELL!
THEN··· A STRANGE TERROR ENGULFS THE CONVOY AS THE OCEAN AROUND THEM STARTS TO BOIL!
GOOD GRIEF! THE WHOLE ATLANTIC'S ON FIRE!
THE PLATES ARE STARTING TO BUCKLE FROM THE HEAT, SIR!
PLATES SNAP··· SHIPS SINK··· MEN ARE BOILED ALIVE··· AS THE OCEAN'S TEMPERATURE RISES!
YEEEOW! THE WATER— I CAN'T STAND IT!
I'M BURNING. ALIVE! AIEEE!
AND FAR BELOW THE SURFACE···
PRINCE NAMOR! OUR SCOUTS REPORT MANY ALLIED SHIPS SINKING AROUND OUR DOMAIN!
WHAT? THOSE NAZIS ARE AT IT AGAIN?
I'LL INVESTIGATE THIS ALONE.
AS YOU WISH, PRINCE NAMOR.
BELLOWING SEA COWS! I'VE NEVER SEEN SUCH DESTRUCTION BEFORE! AND THOSE BODIES—THEY'RE ALL BLOATED! THEY LOOK AS IF THEY'D BEEN COOKED!
THE UNDERWATER PRINCE SPURTS UPWARD, UNCHECKED, WHEN···
OWW! THIS WATER IS SCALDING HOT!

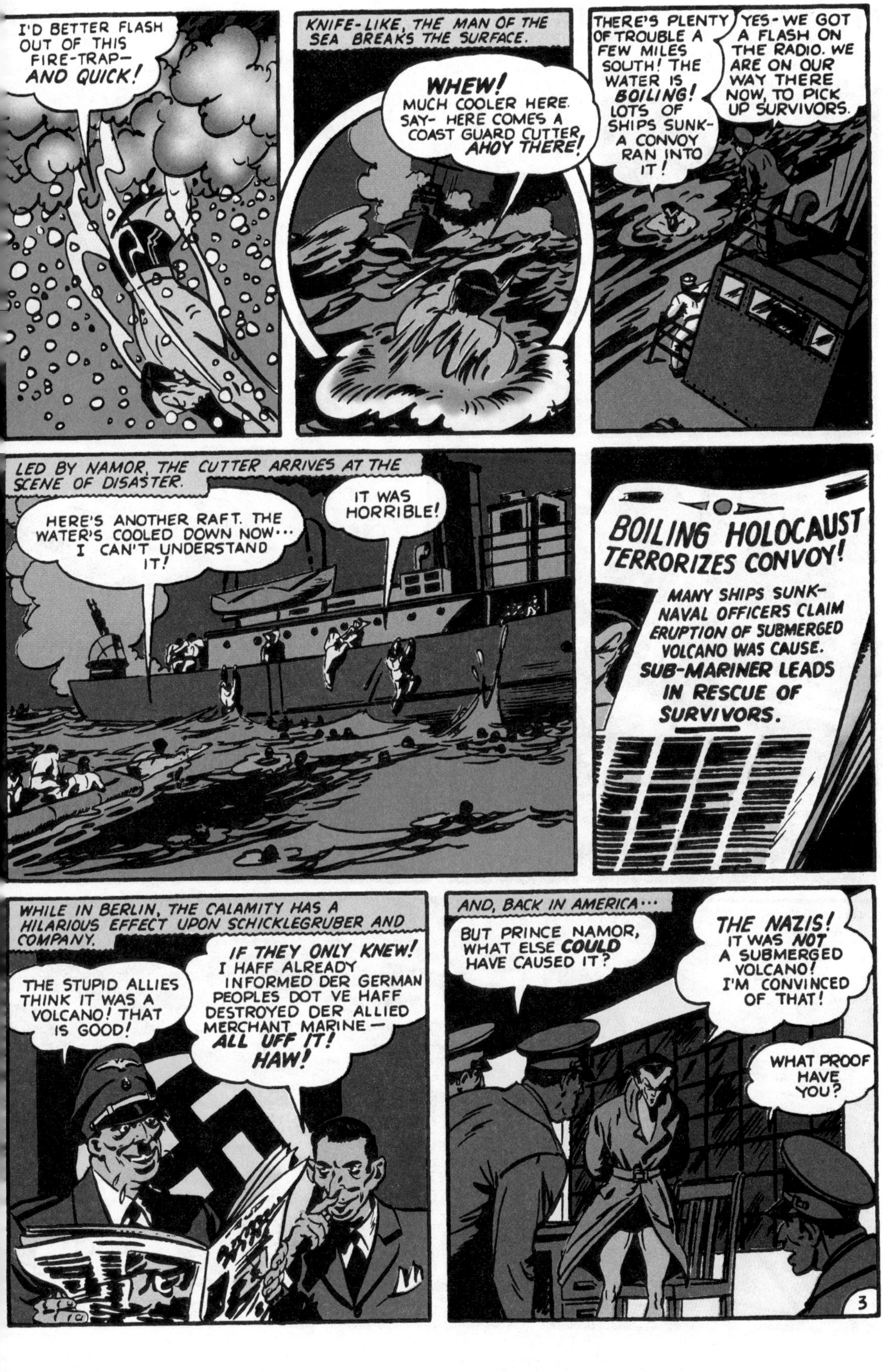
I'D BETTER FLASH OUT OF THIS FIRE-TRAP— AND QUICK!
KNIFE-LIKE, THE MAN OF THE SEA BREAKS THE SURFACE.
WHEW! MUCH COOLER HERE. SAY- HERE COMES A COAST GUARD CUTTER. AHOY THERE!
THERE'S PLENTY OF TROUBLE A FEW MILES SOUTH! THE WATER IS BOILING! LOTS OF SHIPS SUNK- A CONVOY RAN INTO IT!
YES- WE GOT A FLASH ON THE RADIO. WE ARE ON OUR WAY THERE NOW, TO PICK UP SURVIVORS.
LED BY NAMOR, THE CUTTER ARRIVES AT THE SCENE OF DISASTER.
HERE'S ANOTHER RAFT. THE WATER'S COOLED DOWN NOW... I CAN'T UNDERSTAND IT!
IT WAS HORRIBLE!
BOILING HOLOCAUST TERRORIZES CONVOY!
MANY SHIPS SUNK- NAVAL OFFICERS CLAIM ERUPTION OF SUBMERGED VOLCANO WAS CAUSE. SUB-MARINER LEADS IN RESCUE OF SURVIVORS.
WHILE IN BERLIN, THE CALAMITY HAS A HILARIOUS EFFECT UPON SCHICKLEGRUBER AND COMPANY.
THE STUPID ALLIES THINK IT WAS A VOLCANO! THAT IS GOOD!
IF THEY ONLY KNEW! I HAFF ALREADY INFORMED DER GERMAN PEOPLES DOT VE HAFF DESTROYED DER ALLIED MERCHANT MARINE— ALL UFF IT! HAW!
AND, BACK IN AMERICA...
BUT PRINCE NAMOR, WHAT ELSE COULD HAVE CAUSED IT?
THE NAZIS! IT WAS NOT A SUBMERGED VOLCANO! I'M CONVINCED OF THAT!
WHAT PROOF HAVE YOU?
3

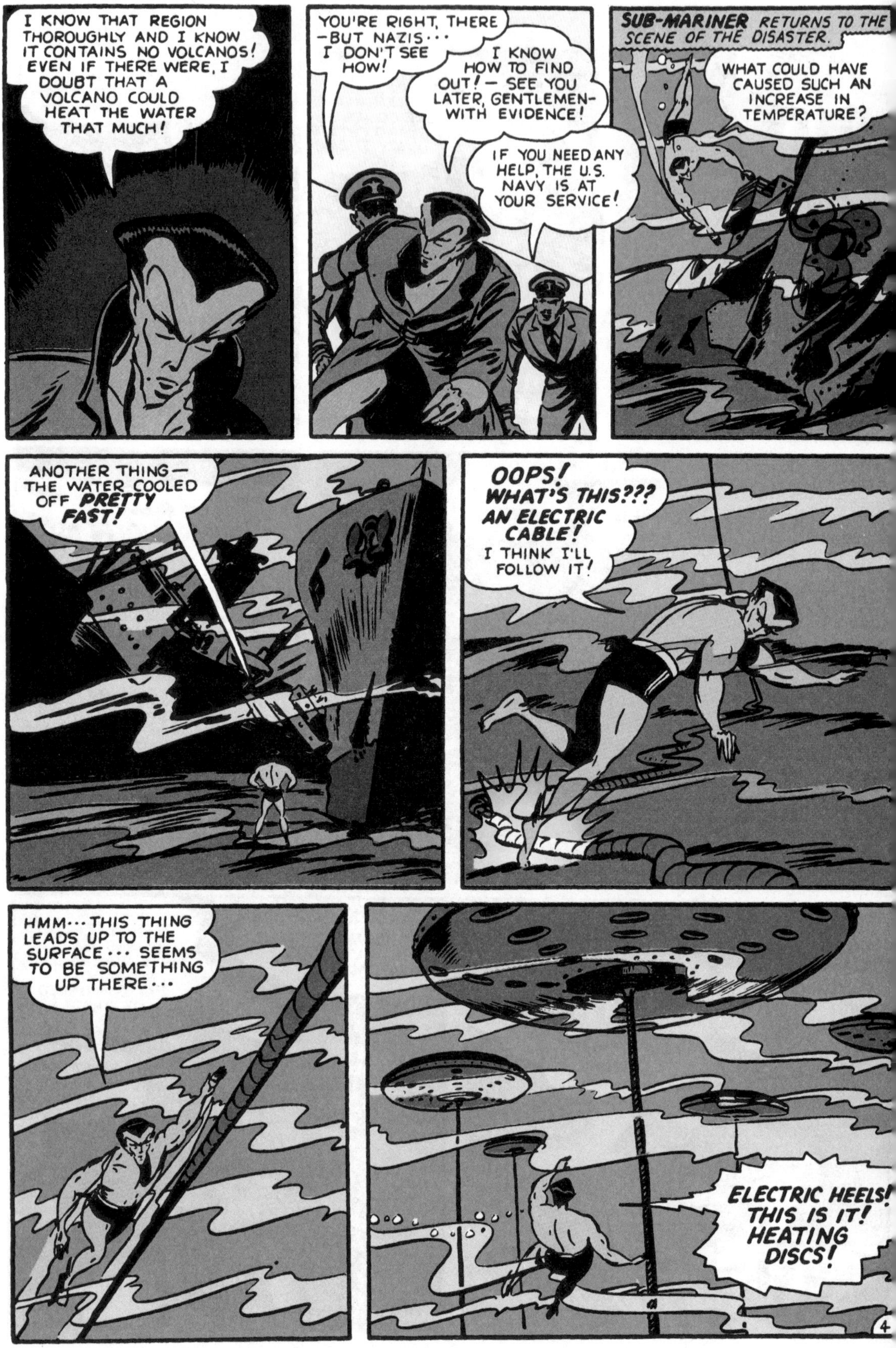
I KNOW THAT REGION THOROUGHLY AND I KNOW IT CONTAINS NO VOLCANOS! EVEN IF THERE WERE, I DOUBT THAT A VOLCANO COULD HEAT THE WATER THAT MUCH!
YOU'RE RIGHT, THERE —BUT NAZIS··· I DON'T SEE HOW!
I KNOW HOW TO FIND OUT! — SEE YOU LATER, GENTLEMEN- WITH EVIDENCE!
IF YOU NEED ANY HELP, THE U.S. NAVY IS AT YOUR SERVICE!
SUB-MARINER RETURNS TO THE SCENE OF THE DISASTER.
WHAT COULD HAVE CAUSED SUCH AN INCREASE IN TEMPERATURE?
ANOTHER THING— THE WATER COOLED OFF PRETTY FAST!
OOPS! WHAT'S THIS??? AN ELECTRIC CABLE! I THINK I'LL FOLLOW IT!
HMM··· THIS THING LEADS UP TO THE SURFACE··· SEEMS TO BE SOMETHING UP THERE···
ELECTRIC HEELS! THIS IS IT! HEATING DISCS!
4

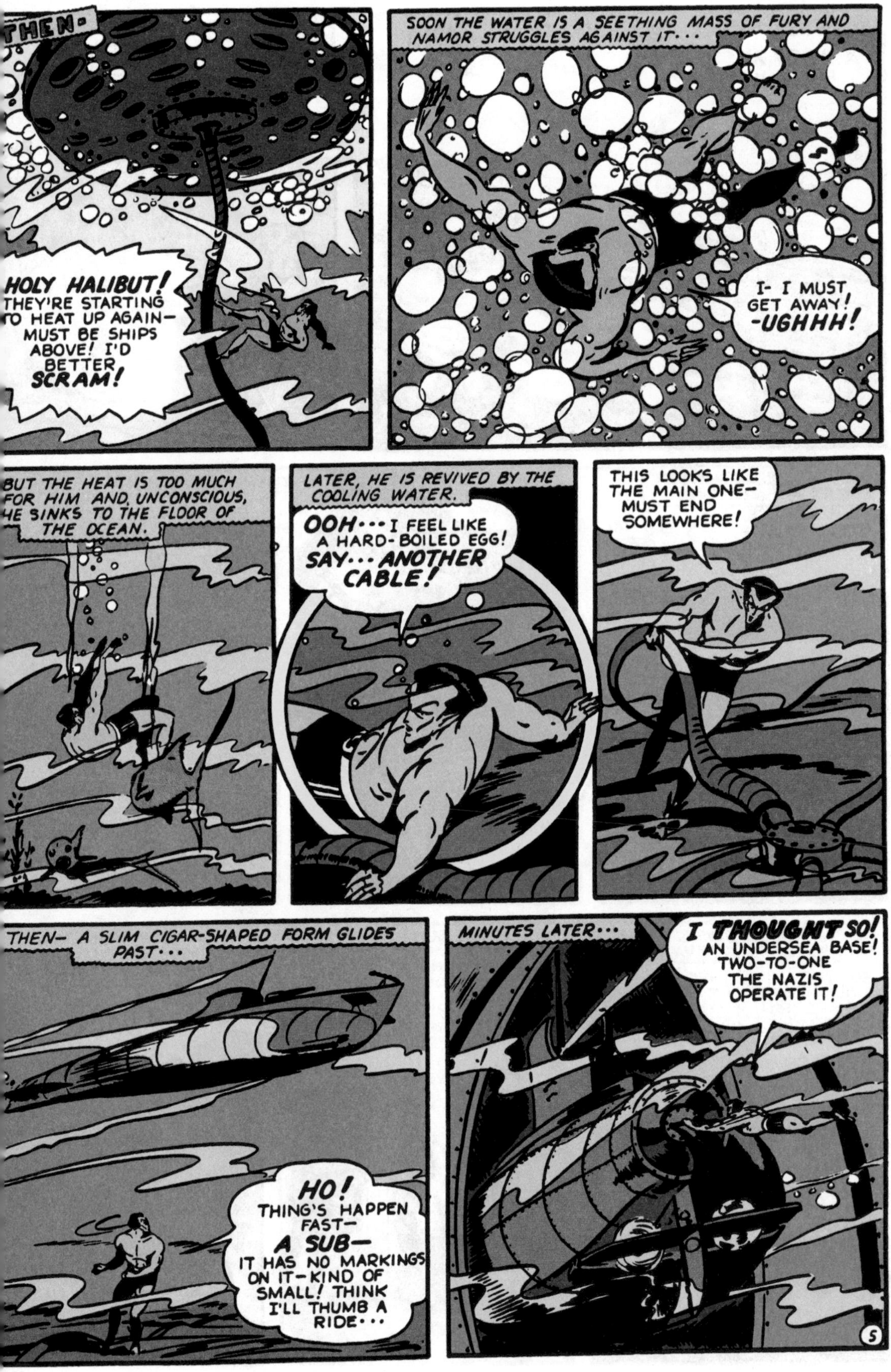
THEN-
HOLY HALIBUT! THEY'RE STARTING TO HEAT UP AGAIN— MUST BE SHIPS ABOVE! I'D BETTER SCRAM!
SOON THE WATER IS A SEETHING MASS OF FURY AND NAMOR STRUGGLES AGAINST IT...
I- I MUST GET AWAY! -UGHHH!
BUT THE HEAT IS TOO MUCH FOR HIM AND, UNCONSCIOUS, HE SINKS TO THE FLOOR OF THE OCEAN.
LATER, HE IS REVIVED BY THE COOLING WATER.
OOH... I FEEL LIKE A HARD-BOILED EGG! SAY... ANOTHER CABLE!
THIS LOOKS LIKE THE MAIN ONE— MUST END SOMEWHERE!
THEN— A SLIM CIGAR-SHAPED FORM GLIDES PAST...
HO! THING'S HAPPEN FAST— A SUB— IT HAS NO MARKINGS ON IT—KIND OF SMALL! THINK I'LL THUMB A RIDE...
MINUTES LATER...
I THOUGHT SO! AN UNDERSEA BASE! TWO-TO-ONE THE NAZIS OPERATE IT!
5

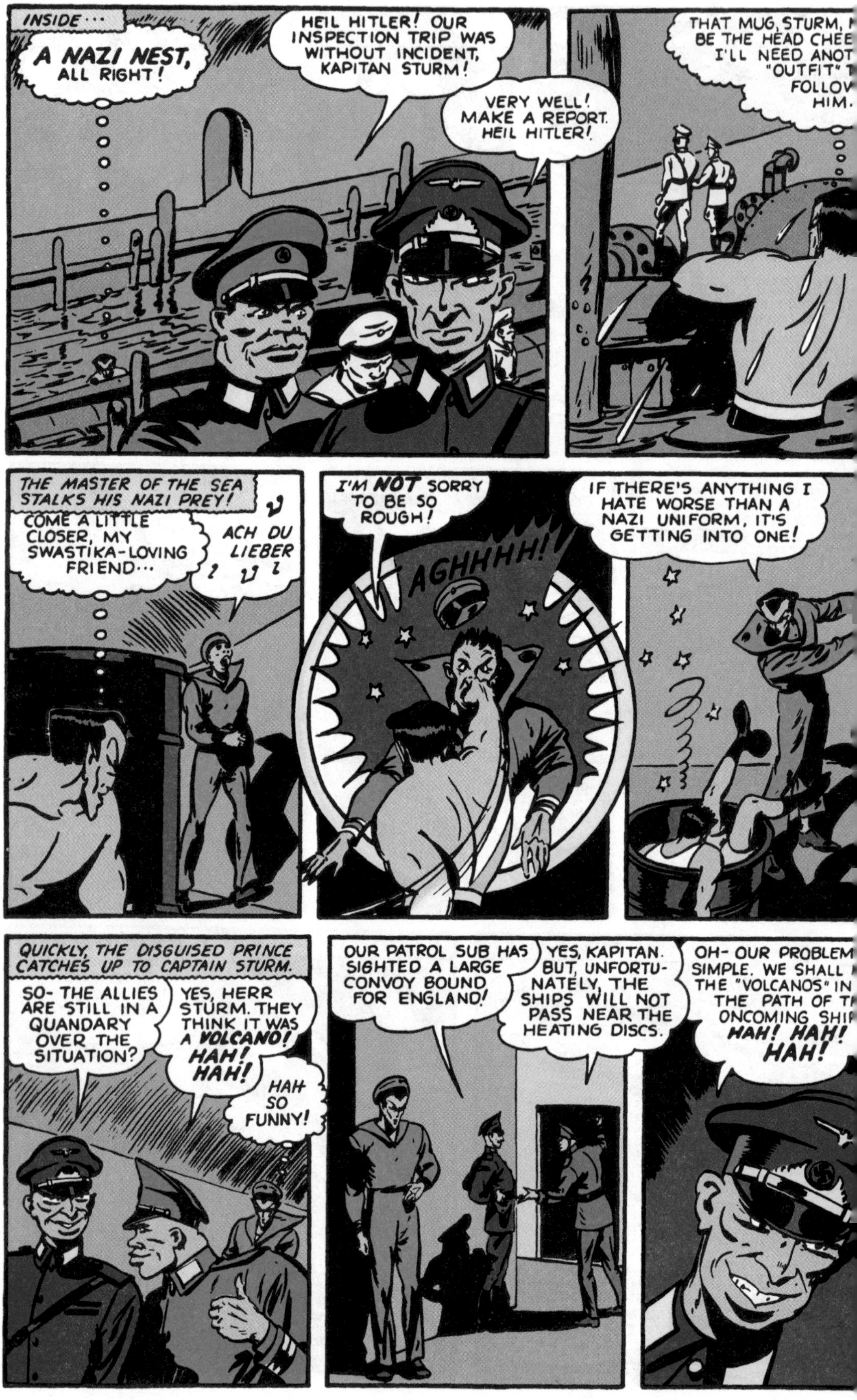

INSIDE...
A NAZI NEST, ALL RIGHT!
HEIL HITLER! OUR INSPECTION TRIP WAS WITHOUT INCIDENT, KAPITAN STURM!
VERY WELL! MAKE A REPORT. HEIL HITLER!
THE MASTER OF THE SEA STALKS HIS NAZI PREY!
COME A LITTLE CLOSER, MY SWASTIKA-LOVING FRIEND...
ACH DU LIEBER
I'M NOT SORRY TO BE SO ROUGH!
AGHHHH!
IF THERE'S ANYTHING I HATE WORSE THAN A NAZI UNIFORM, IT'S GETTING INTO ONE!
QUICKLY, THE DISGUISED PRINCE CATCHES UP TO CAPTAIN STURM.
SO- THE ALLIES ARE STILL IN A QUANDARY OVER THE SITUATION?
YES, HERR STURM. THEY THINK IT WAS A VOLCANO! HAH! HAH!
HAH SO FUNNY!
OUR PATROL SUB HAS SIGHTED A LARGE CONVOY BOUND FOR ENGLAND!
YES, KAPITAN. BUT, UNFORTUNATELY, THE SHIPS WILL NOT PASS NEAR THE HEATING DISCS.

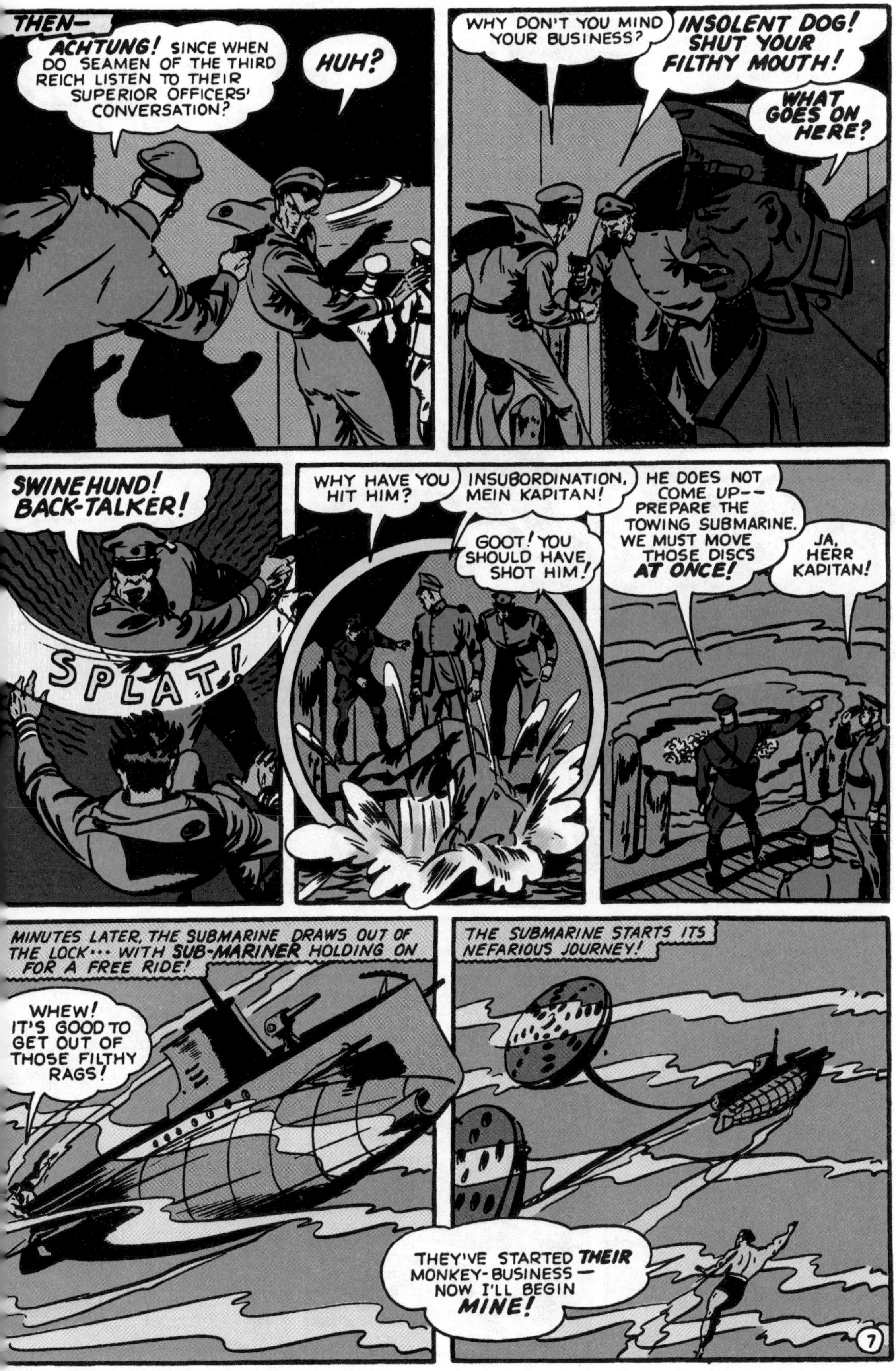
THEN—
ACHTUNG! SINCE WHEN DO SEAMEN OF THE THIRD REICH LISTEN TO THEIR SUPERIOR OFFICERS' CONVERSATION?
HUH?
WHY DON'T YOU MIND YOUR BUSINESS?
INSOLENT DOG! SHUT YOUR FILTHY MOUTH!
WHAT GOES ON HERE?
SWINEHUND! BACK-TALKER!
SPLAT!
WHY HAVE YOU HIT HIM?
INSUBORDINATION, MEIN KAPITAN!
GOOT! YOU SHOULD HAVE SHOT HIM!
HE DOES NOT COME UP-- PREPARE THE TOWING SUBMARINE. WE MUST MOVE THOSE DISCS AT ONCE!
JA, HERR KAPITAN!
MINUTES LATER, THE SUBMARINE DRAWS OUT OF THE LOCK··· WITH SUB-MARINER HOLDING ON FOR A FREE RIDE!
WHEW! IT'S GOOD TO GET OUT OF THOSE FILTHY RAGS!
THE SUBMARINE STARTS ITS NEFARIOUS JOURNEY!
THEY'VE STARTED THEIR MONKEY-BUSINESS— NOW I'LL BEGIN MINE!
7

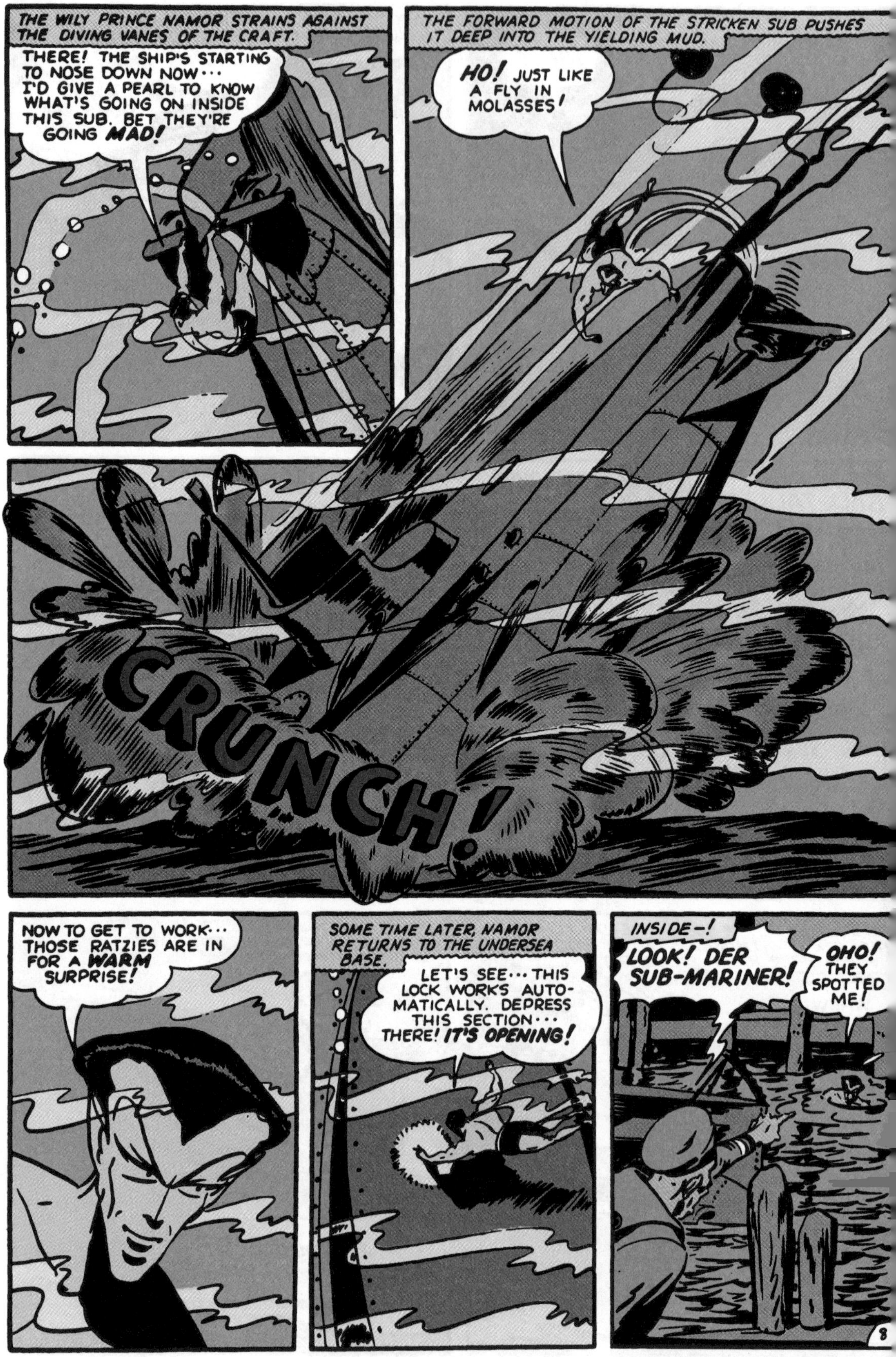

THE WILY PRINCE NAMOR STRAINS AGAINST THE DIVING VANES OF THE CRAFT.
THERE! THE SHIP'S STARTING TO NOSE DOWN NOW··· I'D GIVE A PEARL TO KNOW WHAT'S GOING ON INSIDE THIS SUB. BET THEY'RE GOING MAD!
THE FORWARD MOTION OF THE STRICKEN SUB PUSHES IT DEEP INTO THE YIELDING MUD.
HO! JUST LIKE A FLY IN MOLASSES!
CRUNCH!
NOW TO GET TO WORK··· THOSE RATZIES ARE IN FOR A WARM SURPRISE!
SOME TIME LATER, NAMOR RETURNS TO THE UNDERSEA BASE.
LET'S SEE··· THIS LOCK WORKS AUTOMATICALLY. DEPRESS THIS SECTION··· THERE! IT'S OPENING!
INSIDE—!
LOOK! DER SUB-MARINER!
OHO! THEY SPOTTED ME!

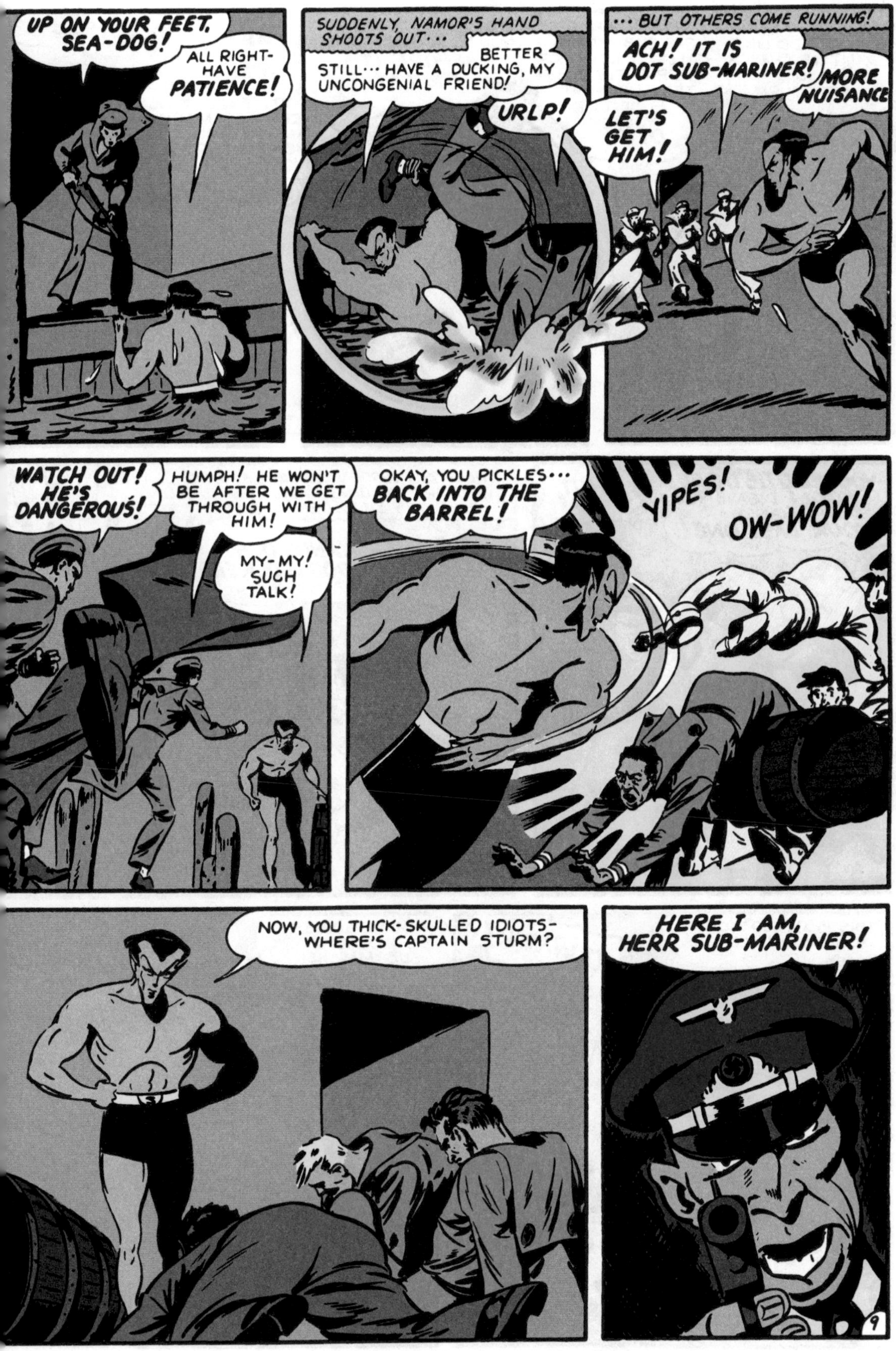

UP ON YOUR FEET, SEA-DOG!
ALL RIGHT- HAVE PATIENCE!
SUDDENLY, NAMOR'S HAND SHOOTS OUT...
BETTER STILL... HAVE A DUCKING, MY UNCONGENIAL FRIEND!
URLP!
...BUT OTHERS COME RUNNING!
ACH! IT IS DOT SUB-MARINER!
MORE NUISANCE
LET'S GET HIM!
WATCH OUT! HE'S DANGEROUS!
HUMPH! HE WON'T BE AFTER WE GET THROUGH WITH HIM!
MY-MY! SUCH TALK!
OKAY, YOU PICKLES... BACK INTO THE BARREL!
YIPES!
OW-WOW!
NOW, YOU THICK-SKULLED IDIOTS- WHERE'S CAPTAIN STURM?
HERE I AM, HERR SUB-MARINER!
9

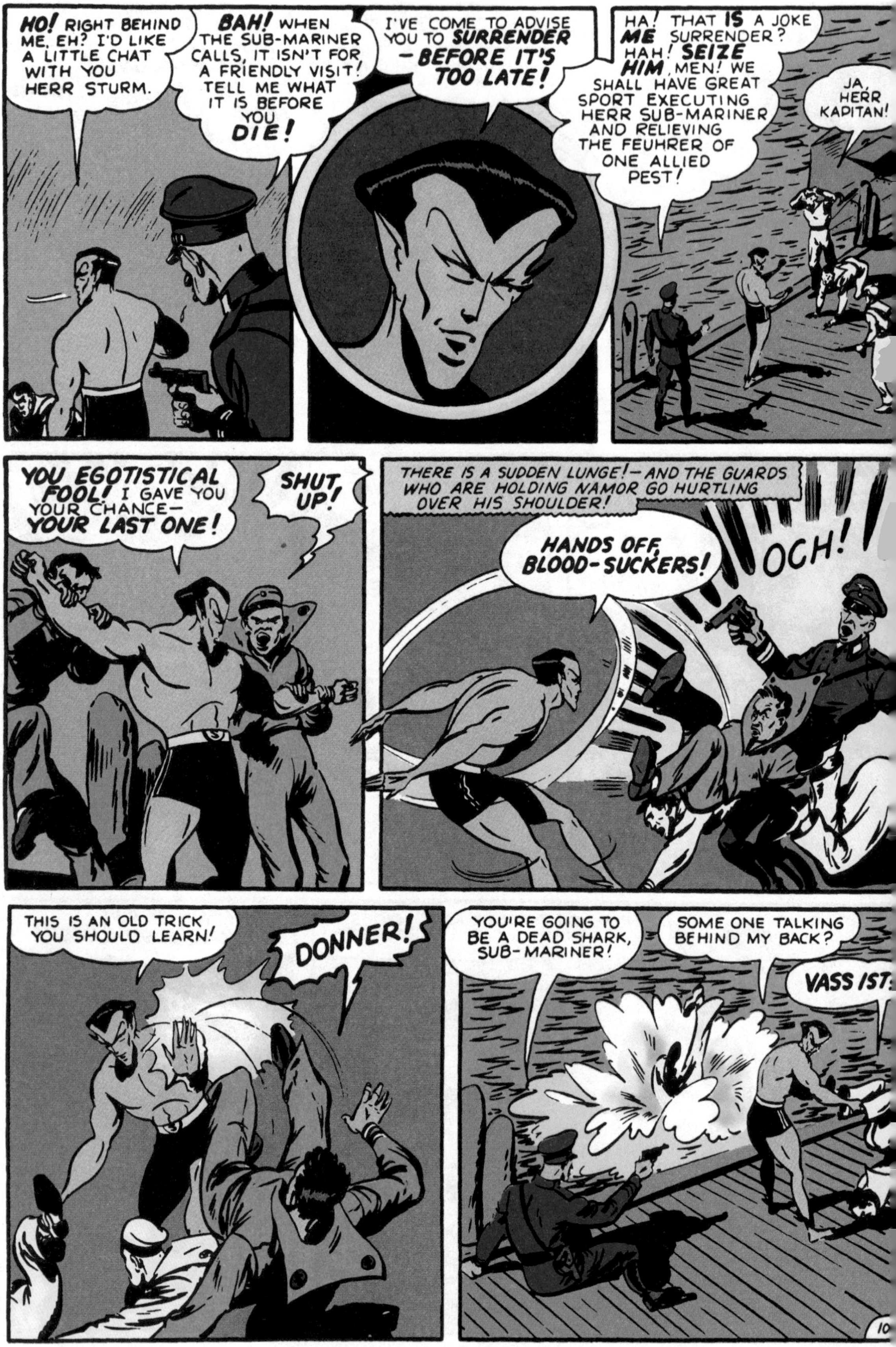
HO! RIGHT BEHIND ME, EH? I'D LIKE A LITTLE CHAT WITH YOU HERR STURM.
BAH! WHEN THE SUB-MARINER CALLS, IT ISN'T FOR A FRIENDLY VISIT! TELL ME WHAT IT IS BEFORE YOU DIE!
I'VE COME TO ADVISE YOU TO SURRENDER —BEFORE IT'S TOO LATE!
HA! THAT IS A JOKE ME SURRENDER? HAH! SEIZE HIM, MEN! WE SHALL HAVE GREAT SPORT EXECUTING HERR SUB-MARINER AND RELIEVING THE FEUHRER OF ONE ALLIED PEST!
JA, HERR KAPITAN!
YOU EGOTISTICAL FOOL! I GAVE YOU YOUR CHANCE— YOUR LAST ONE!
SHUT UP!
THERE IS A SUDDEN LUNGE!—AND THE GUARDS WHO ARE HOLDING NAMOR GO HURTLING OVER HIS SHOULDER!
HANDS OFF, BLOOD-SUCKERS!
OCH!
THIS IS AN OLD TRICK YOU SHOULD LEARN!
DONNER!
YOU'RE GOING TO BE A DEAD SHARK, SUB-MARINER!
SOME ONE TALKING BEHIND MY BACK?
VASS IST?
10

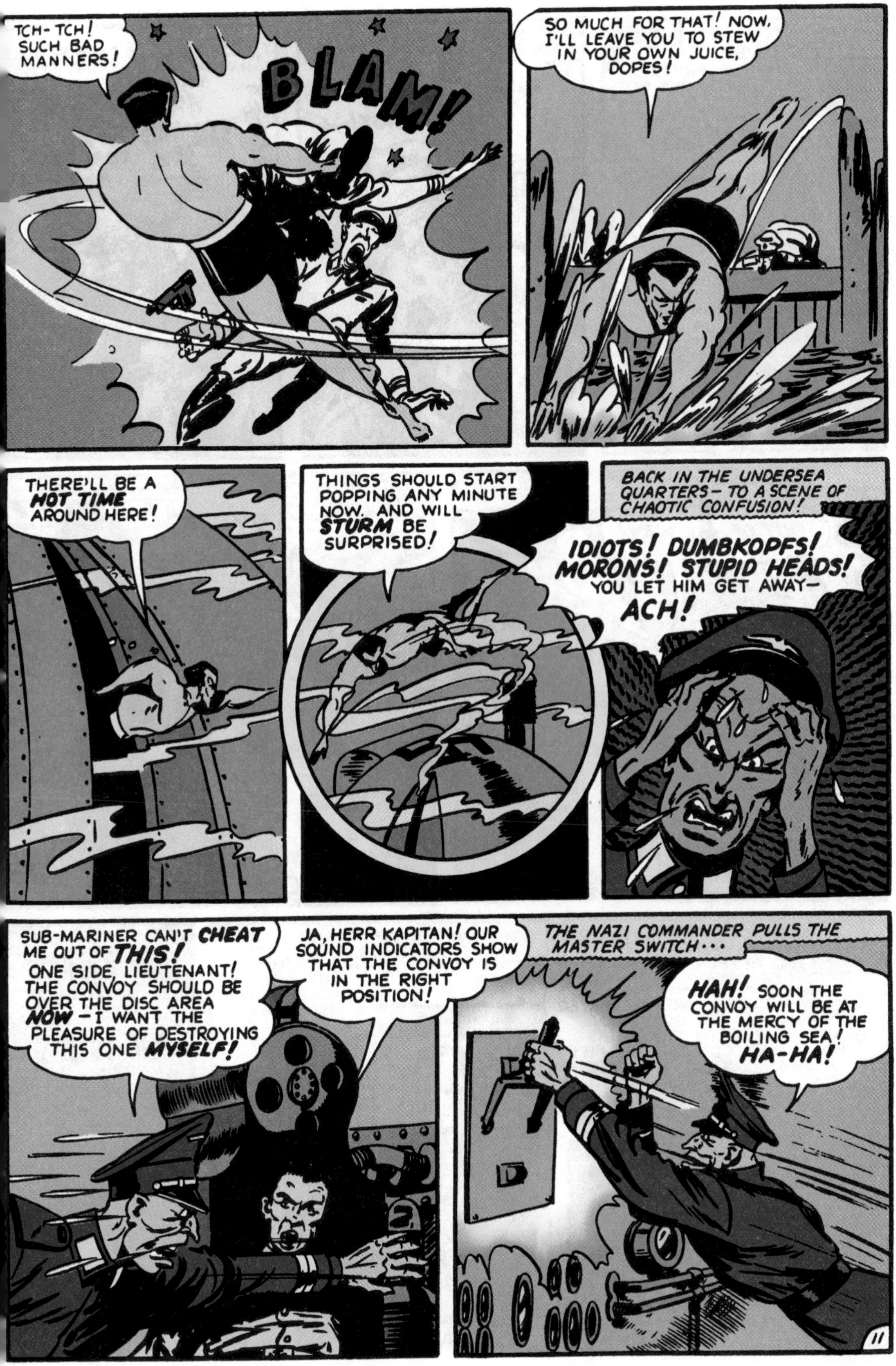
TCH-TCH! SUCH BAD MANNERS!
BLAM!
SO MUCH FOR THAT! NOW, I'LL LEAVE YOU TO STEW IN YOUR OWN JUICE, DOPES!
THERE'LL BE A HOT TIME AROUND HERE!
THINGS SHOULD START POPPING ANY MINUTE NOW. AND WILL STURM BE SURPRISED!
BACK IN THE UNDERSEA QUARTERS— TO A SCENE OF CHAOTIC CONFUSION!
IDIOTS! DUMBKOPFS! MORONS! STUPID HEADS! YOU LET HIM GET AWAY— ACH!
SUB-MARINER CAN'T CHEAT ME OUT OF THIS! ONE SIDE, LIEUTENANT! THE CONVOY SHOULD BE OVER THE DISC AREA NOW —I WANT THE PLEASURE OF DESTROYING THIS ONE MYSELF!
JA, HERR KAPITAN! OUR SOUND INDICATORS SHOW THAT THE CONVOY IS IN THE RIGHT POSITION!
THE NAZI COMMANDER PULLS THE MASTER SWITCH···
HAH! SOON THE CONVOY WILL BE AT THE MERCY OF THE BOILING SEA! HA-HA!
11

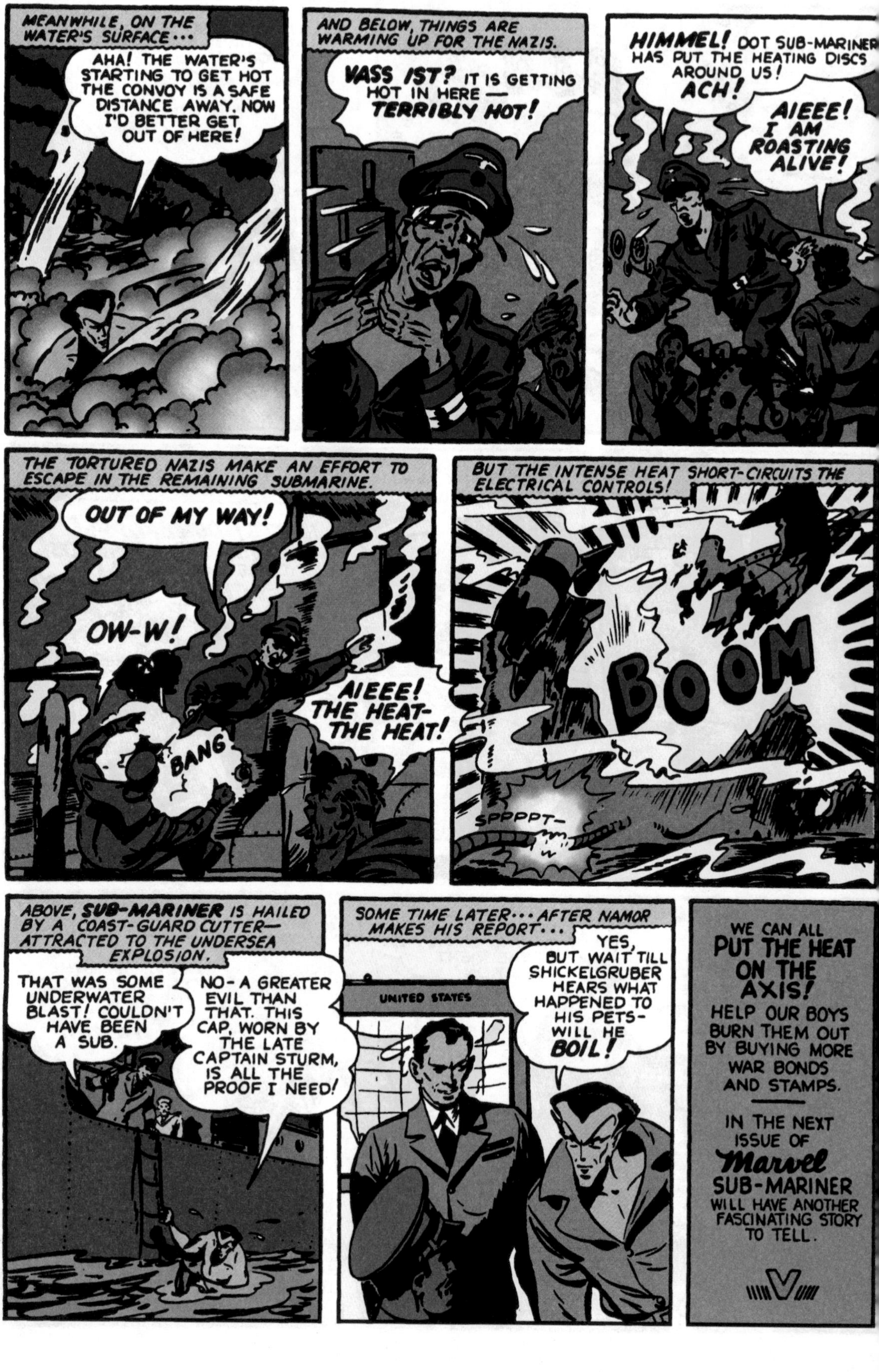
MEANWHILE, ON THE WATER'S SURFACE...
AHA! THE WATER'S STARTING TO GET HOT THE CONVOY IS A SAFE DISTANCE AWAY. NOW I'D BETTER GET OUT OF HERE!
AND BELOW, THINGS ARE WARMING UP FOR THE NAZIS.
VASS IST? IT IS GETTING HOT IN HERE — TERRIBLY HOT!
HIMMEL! DOT SUB-MARINER HAS PUT THE HEATING DISCS AROUND US! ACH!
AIEEE! I AM ROASTING ALIVE!
THE TORTURED NAZIS MAKE AN EFFORT TO ESCAPE IN THE REMAINING SUBMARINE.
OUT OF MY WAY!
OW-W!
AIEEE! THE HEAT- THE HEAT!
BANG
BUT THE INTENSE HEAT SHORT-CIRCUITS THE ELECTRICAL CONTROLS!
BOOM
SPPPPT-
ABOVE, SUB-MARINER IS HAILED BY A COAST-GUARD CUTTER— ATTRACTED TO THE UNDERSEA EXPLOSION.
THAT WAS SOME UNDERWATER BLAST! COULDN'T HAVE BEEN A SUB.
NO- A GREATER EVIL THAN THAT. THIS CAP, WORN BY THE LATE CAPTAIN STURM, IS ALL THE PROOF I NEED!
SOME TIME LATER... AFTER NAMOR MAKES HIS REPORT...
UNITED STATES
YES, BUT WAIT TILL SHICKELGRUBER HEARS WHAT HAPPENED TO HIS PETS- WILL HE BOIL!
WE CAN ALL PUT THE HEAT ON THE AXIS!
HELP OUR BOYS BURN THEM OUT BY BUYING MORE WAR BONDS AND STAMPS.
IN THE NEXT ISSUE OF Marvel SUB-MARINER WILL HAVE ANOTHER FASCINATING STORY TO TELL.

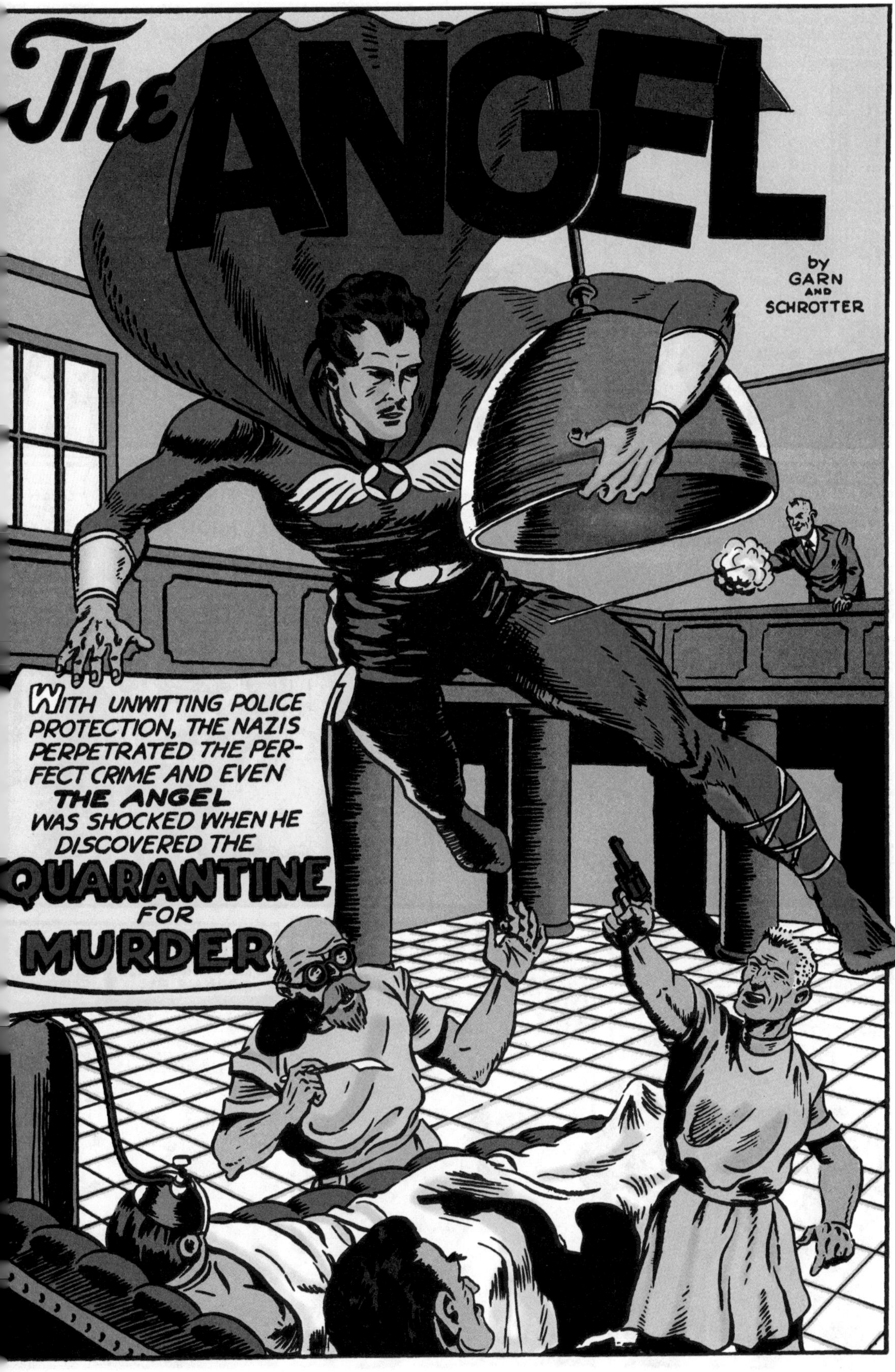

The ANGEL
by GARN AND SCHROTTER
WITH UNWITTING POLICE PROTECTION, THE NAZIS PERPETRATED THE PERFECT CRIME AND EVEN THE ANGEL WAS SHOCKED WHEN HE DISCOVERED THE
QUARANTINE FOR MURDER

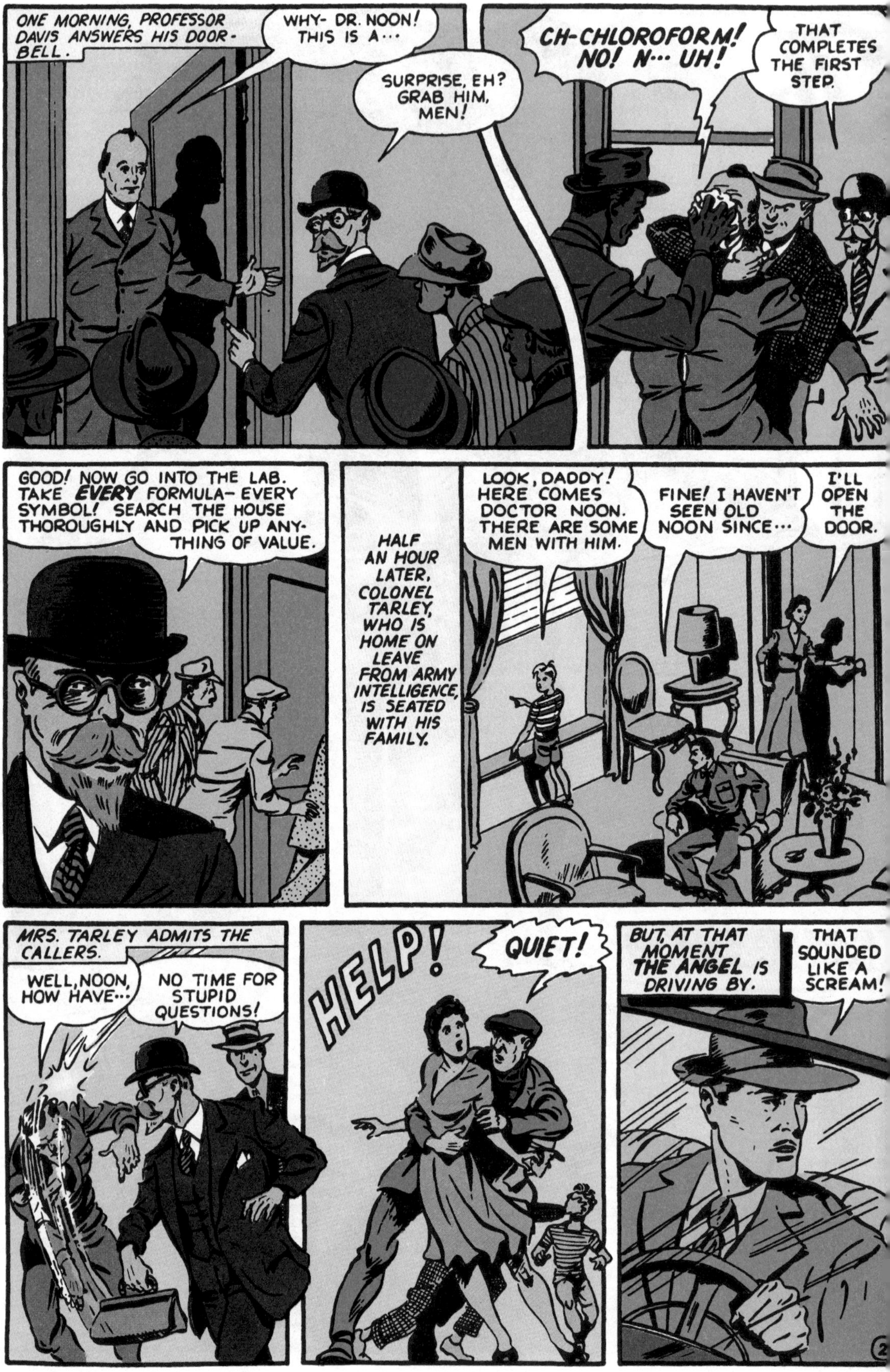
ONE MORNING, PROFESSOR DAVIS ANSWERS HIS DOOR-BELL.
WHY- DR. NOON! THIS IS A···
SURPRISE, EH? GRAB HIM, MEN!
CH-CHLOROFORM! NO! N··· UH!
THAT COMPLETES THE FIRST STEP.
GOOD! NOW GO INTO THE LAB. TAKE EVERY FORMULA- EVERY SYMBOL! SEARCH THE HOUSE THOROUGHLY AND PICK UP ANYTHING OF VALUE.
HALF AN HOUR LATER, COLONEL TARLEY, WHO IS HOME ON LEAVE FROM ARMY INTELLIGENCE, IS SEATED WITH HIS FAMILY.
LOOK, DADDY! HERE COMES DOCTOR NOON. THERE ARE SOME MEN WITH HIM.
FINE! I HAVEN'T SEEN OLD NOON SINCE···
I'LL OPEN THE DOOR.
MRS. TARLEY ADMITS THE CALLERS.
WELL, NOON, HOW HAVE···
NO TIME FOR STUPID QUESTIONS!
HELP!
QUIET!
BUT, AT THAT MOMENT THE ANGEL IS DRIVING BY.
THAT SOUNDED LIKE A SCREAM!
2

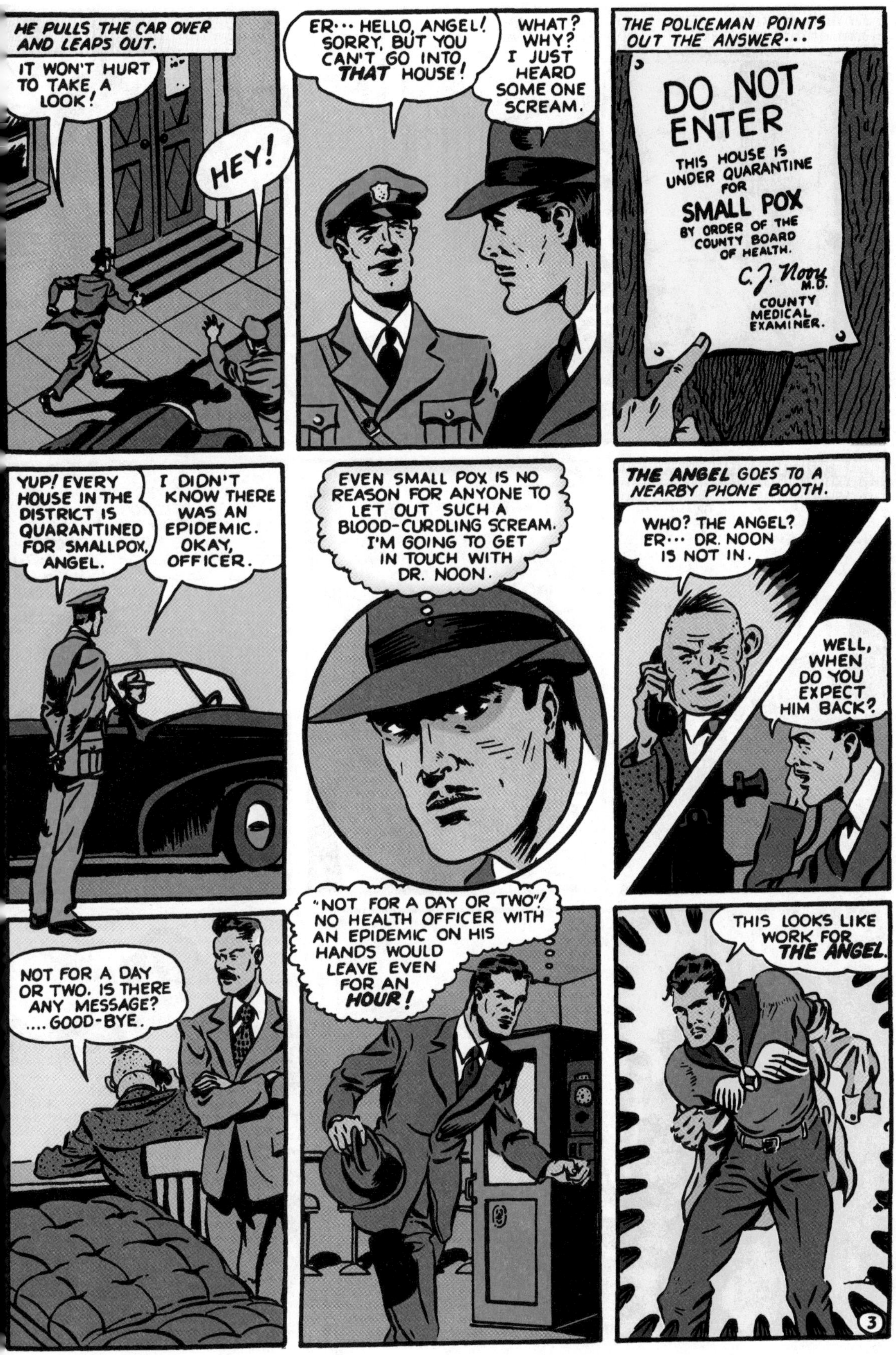
HE PULLS THE CAR OVER AND LEAPS OUT.
IT WON'T HURT TO TAKE A LOOK!
HEY!
ER... HELLO, ANGEL! SORRY, BUT YOU CAN'T GO INTO THAT HOUSE!
WHAT? WHY? I JUST HEARD SOME ONE SCREAM.
THE POLICEMAN POINTS OUT THE ANSWER...
DO NOT ENTER
THIS HOUSE IS UNDER QUARANTINE FOR
SMALL POX
BY ORDER OF THE COUNTY BOARD OF HEALTH.
C. J. Noon M.D.
COUNTY MEDICAL EXAMINER.
YUP! EVERY HOUSE IN THE DISTRICT IS QUARANTINED FOR SMALLPOX, ANGEL.
I DIDN'T KNOW THERE WAS AN EPIDEMIC. OKAY, OFFICER.
EVEN SMALL POX IS NO REASON FOR ANYONE TO LET OUT SUCH A BLOOD-CURDLING SCREAM. I'M GOING TO GET IN TOUCH WITH DR. NOON.
THE ANGEL GOES TO A NEARBY PHONE BOOTH.
WHO? THE ANGEL? ER... DR. NOON IS NOT IN.
WELL, WHEN DO YOU EXPECT HIM BACK?
NOT FOR A DAY OR TWO. IS THERE ANY MESSAGE? ....GOOD-BYE.
"NOT FOR A DAY OR TWO"! NO HEALTH OFFICER WITH AN EPIDEMIC ON HIS HANDS WOULD LEAVE EVEN FOR AN HOUR!
THIS LOOKS LIKE WORK FOR THE ANGEL.
3

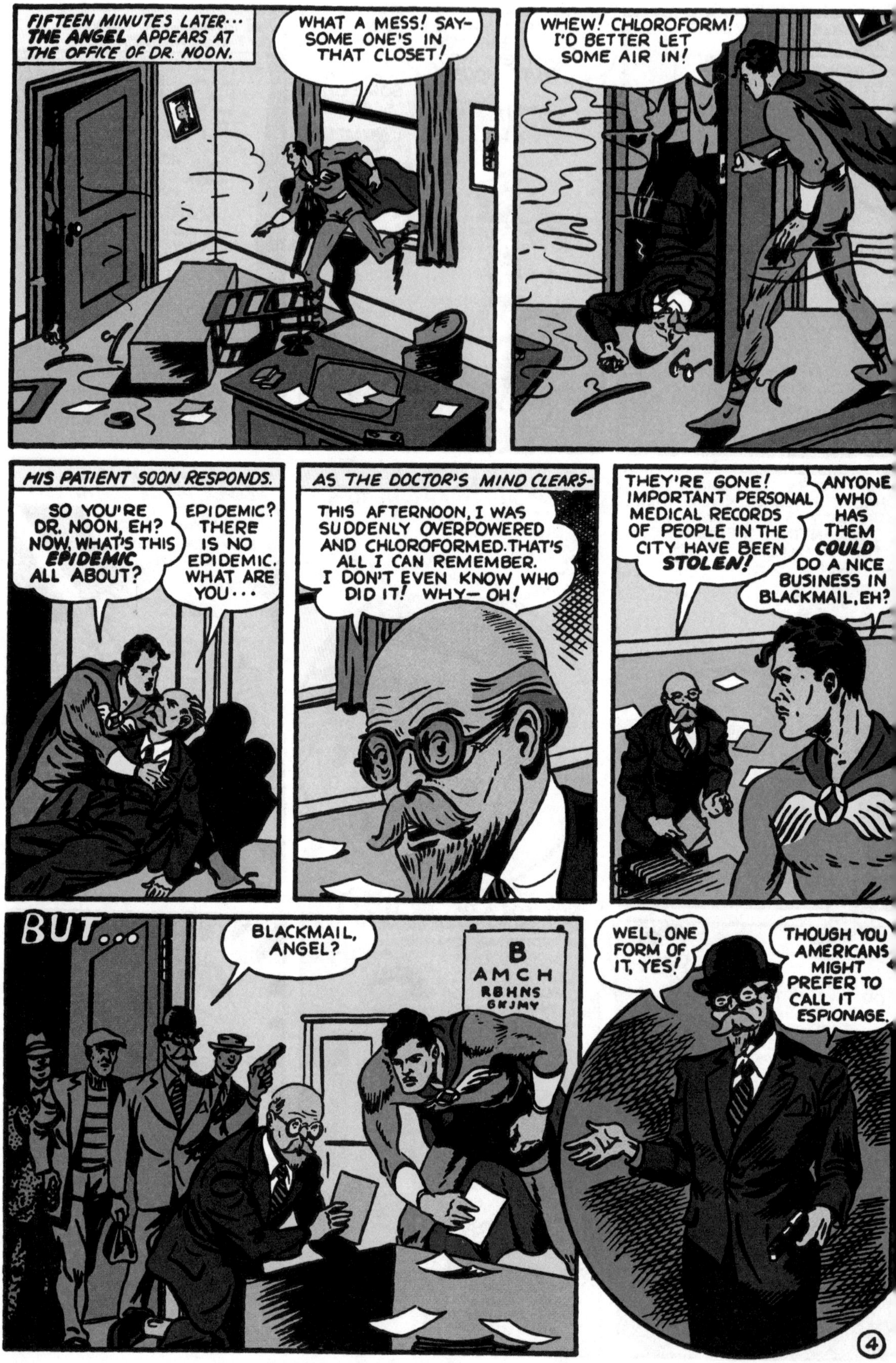

FIFTEEN MINUTES LATER... THE ANGEL APPEARS AT THE OFFICE OF DR. NOON.
WHAT A MESS! SAY-SOME ONE'S IN THAT CLOSET!
WHEW! CHLOROFORM! I'D BETTER LET SOME AIR IN!
HIS PATIENT SOON RESPONDS.
SO YOU'RE DR. NOON, EH? NOW, WHAT'S THIS EPIDEMIC ALL ABOUT?
EPIDEMIC? THERE IS NO EPIDEMIC. WHAT ARE YOU...
AS THE DOCTOR'S MIND CLEARS-
THIS AFTERNOON, I WAS SUDDENLY OVERPOWERED AND CHLOROFORMED. THAT'S ALL I CAN REMEMBER. I DON'T EVEN KNOW WHO DID IT! WHY-OH!
THEY'RE GONE! IMPORTANT PERSONAL MEDICAL RECORDS OF PEOPLE IN THE CITY HAVE BEEN STOLEN!
ANYONE WHO HAS THEM COULD DO A NICE BUSINESS IN BLACKMAIL, EH?
BUT...
BLACKMAIL, ANGEL?
B
AMCH
RBHNS
GKJMY
WELL, ONE FORM OF IT, YES!
THOUGH YOU AMERICANS MIGHT PREFER TO CALL IT ESPIONAGE.

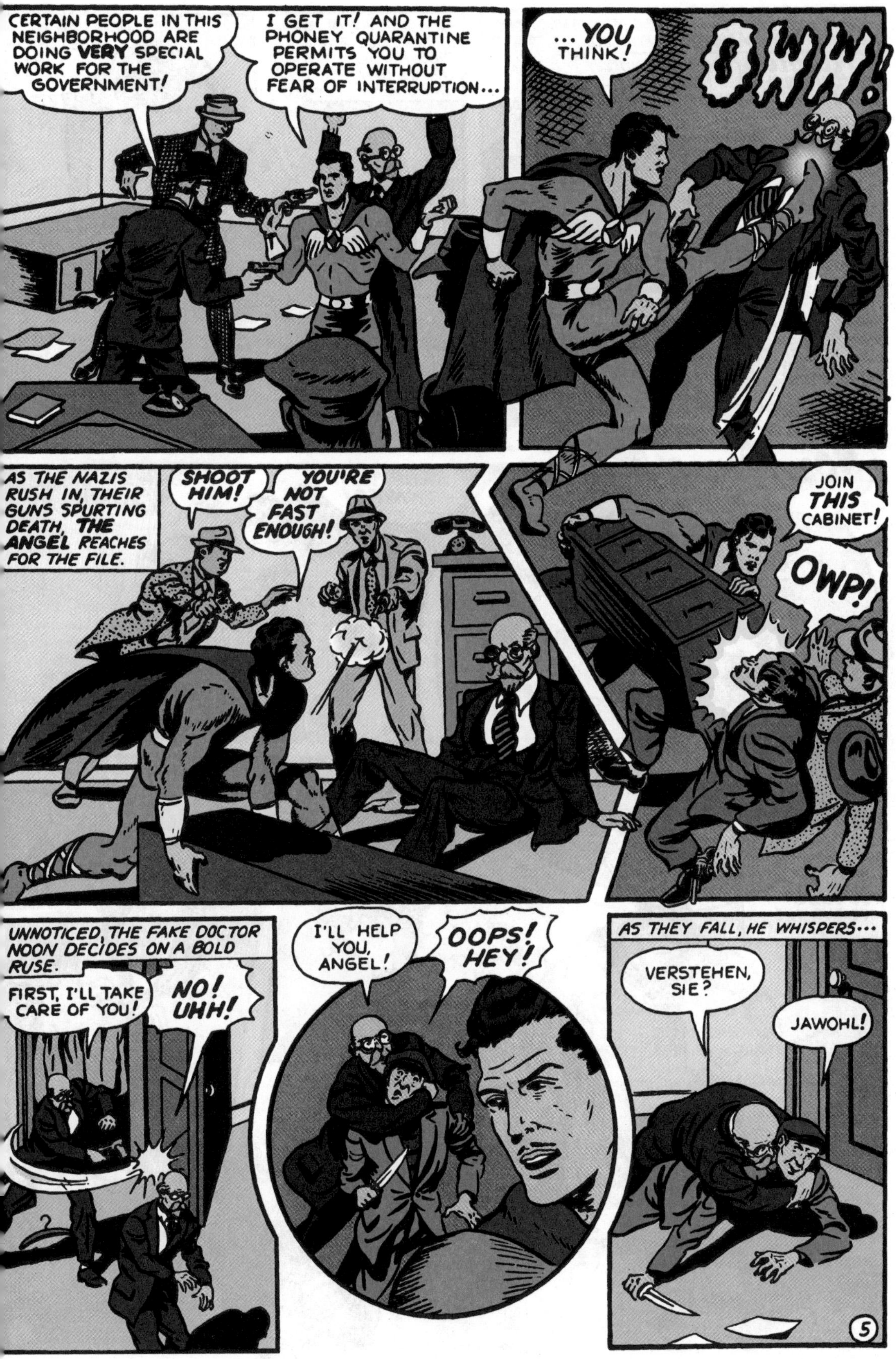
CERTAIN PEOPLE IN THIS NEIGHBORHOOD ARE DOING VERY SPECIAL WORK FOR THE GOVERNMENT!
I GET IT! AND THE PHONEY QUARANTINE PERMITS YOU TO OPERATE WITHOUT FEAR OF INTERRUPTION...
...YOU THINK!
OWW!
AS THE NAZIS RUSH IN, THEIR GUNS SPURTING DEATH, THE ANGEL REACHES FOR THE FILE.
SHOOT HIM!
YOU'RE NOT FAST ENOUGH!
JOIN THIS CABINET!
OWP!
UNNOTICED, THE FAKE DOCTOR NOON DECIDES ON A BOLD RUSE.
FIRST, I'LL TAKE CARE OF YOU!
NO! UHH!
I'LL HELP YOU, ANGEL!
OOPS! HEY!
AS THEY FALL, HE WHISPERS...
VERSTEHEN, SIE?
JAWOHL!
5

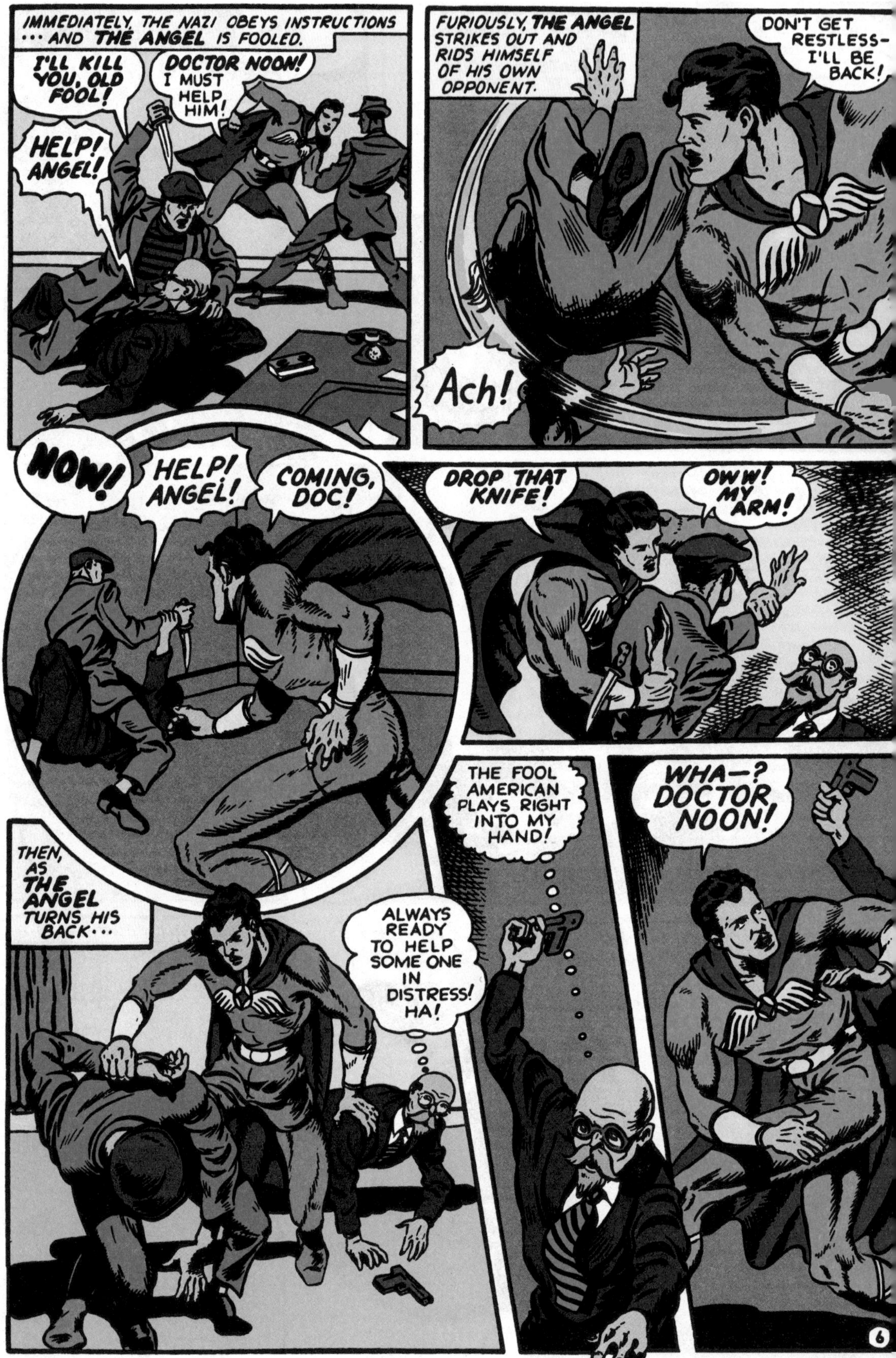
IMMEDIATELY, THE NAZI OBEYS INSTRUCTIONS ··· AND THE ANGEL IS FOOLED.
I'LL KILL YOU, OLD FOOL!
DOCTOR NOON! I MUST HELP HIM!
HELP! ANGEL!
FURIOUSLY, THE ANGEL STRIKES OUT AND RIDS HIMSELF OF HIS OWN OPPONENT.
DON'T GET RESTLESS-I'LL BE BACK!
Ach!
NOW!
HELP! ANGEL!
COMING, DOC!
DROP THAT KNIFE!
OWW! MY ARM!
THEN, AS THE ANGEL TURNS HIS BACK···
ALWAYS READY TO HELP SOME ONE IN DISTRESS! HA!
THE FOOL AMERICAN PLAYS RIGHT INTO MY HAND!
WHA—? DOCTOR NOON!

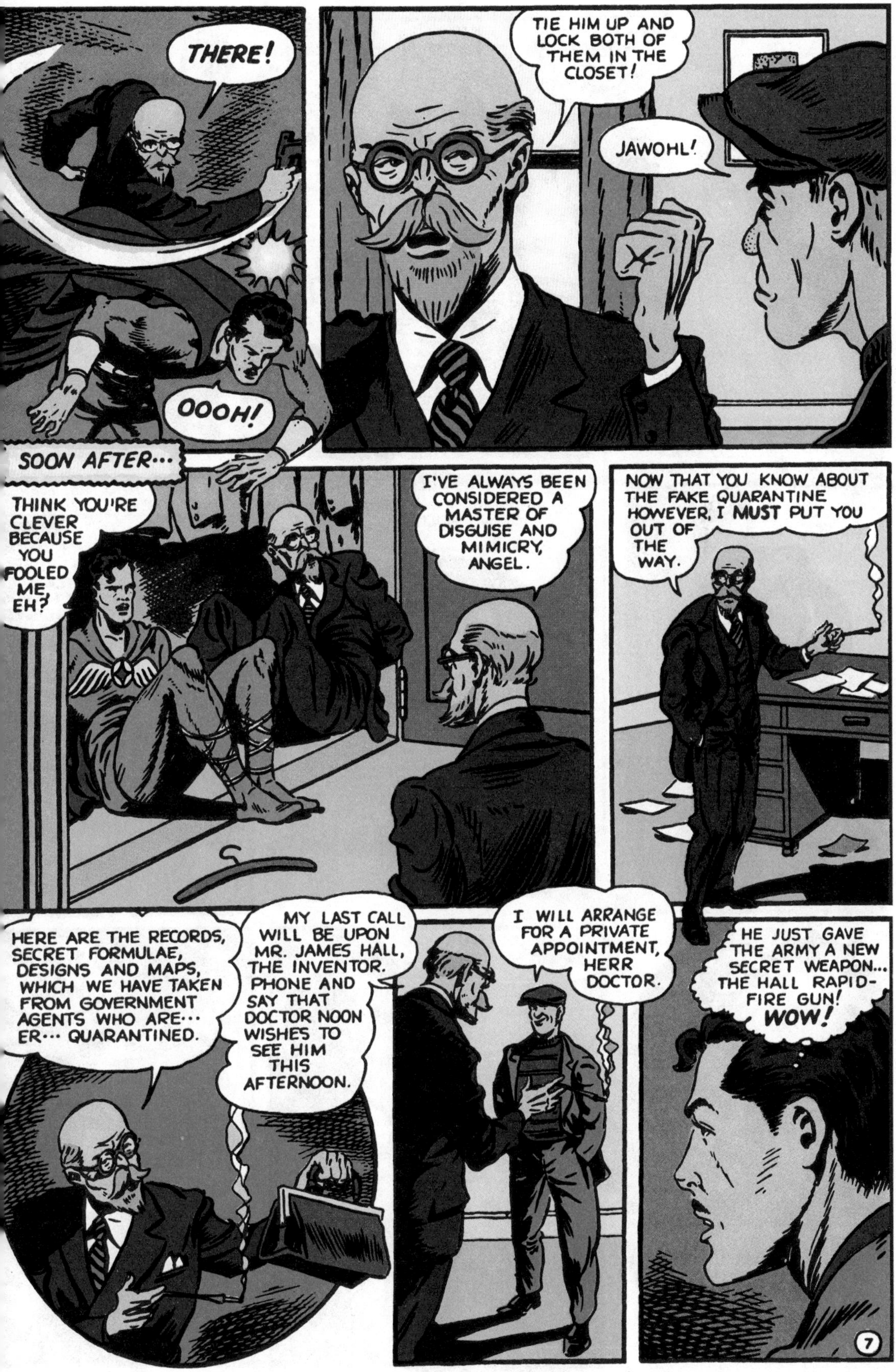

THERE!
OOOH!
TIE HIM UP AND LOCK BOTH OF THEM IN THE CLOSET!
JAWOHL!
SOON AFTER...
THINK YOU'RE CLEVER BECAUSE YOU FOOLED ME, EH?
I'VE ALWAYS BEEN CONSIDERED A MASTER OF DISGUISE AND MIMICRY, ANGEL.
NOW THAT YOU KNOW ABOUT THE FAKE QUARANTINE HOWEVER, I MUST PUT YOU OUT OF THE WAY.
HERE ARE THE RECORDS, SECRET FORMULAE, DESIGNS AND MAPS, WHICH WE HAVE TAKEN FROM GOVERNMENT AGENTS WHO ARE... ER... QUARANTINED.
MY LAST CALL WILL BE UPON MR. JAMES HALL, THE INVENTOR. PHONE AND SAY THAT DOCTOR NOON WISHES TO SEE HIM THIS AFTERNOON.
I WILL ARRANGE FOR A PRIVATE APPOINTMENT, HERR DOCTOR.
HE JUST GAVE THE ARMY A NEW SECRET WEAPON... THE HALL RAPID-FIRE GUN! WOW!

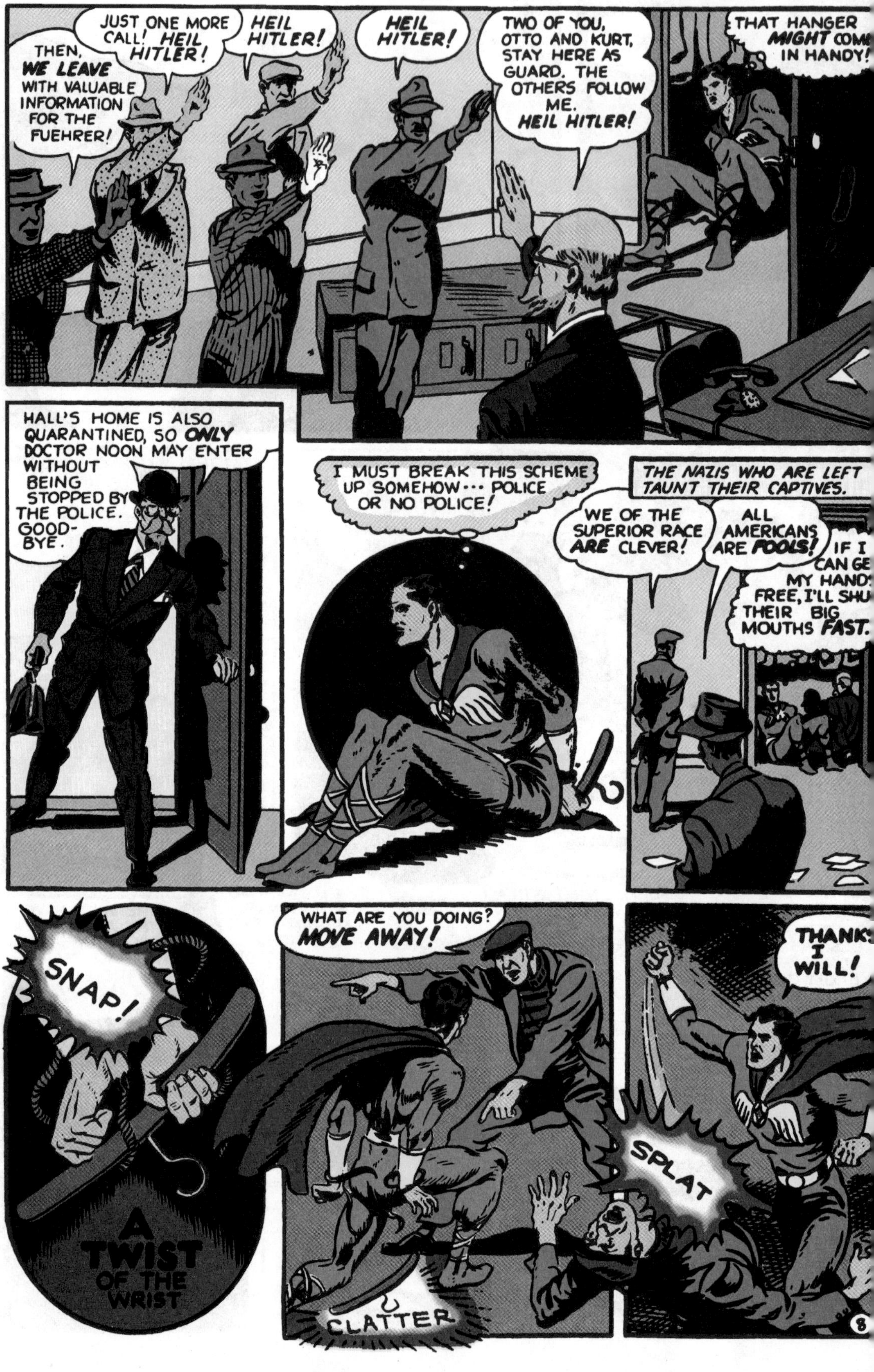

THEN, WE LEAVE WITH VALUABLE INFORMATION FOR THE FUEHRER!
JUST ONE MORE CALL! HEIL HITLER!
HEIL HITLER!
HEIL HITLER!
TWO OF YOU, OTTO AND KURT, STAY HERE AS GUARD. THE OTHERS FOLLOW ME. HEIL HITLER!
THAT HANGER MIGHT COME IN HANDY!
HALL'S HOME IS ALSO QUARANTINED, SO ONLY DOCTOR NOON MAY ENTER WITHOUT BEING STOPPED BY THE POLICE. GOOD-BYE.
I MUST BREAK THIS SCHEME UP SOMEHOW... POLICE OR NO POLICE!
THE NAZIS WHO ARE LEFT TAUNT THEIR CAPTIVES.
WE OF THE SUPERIOR RACE ARE CLEVER!
ALL AMERICANS ARE FOOLS!
IF I CAN GET MY HANDS FREE, I'LL SHUT THEIR BIG MOUTHS FAST.
SNAP!
A TWIST OF THE WRIST
WHAT ARE YOU DOING? MOVE AWAY!
CLATTER
THANKS I WILL!
SPLAT

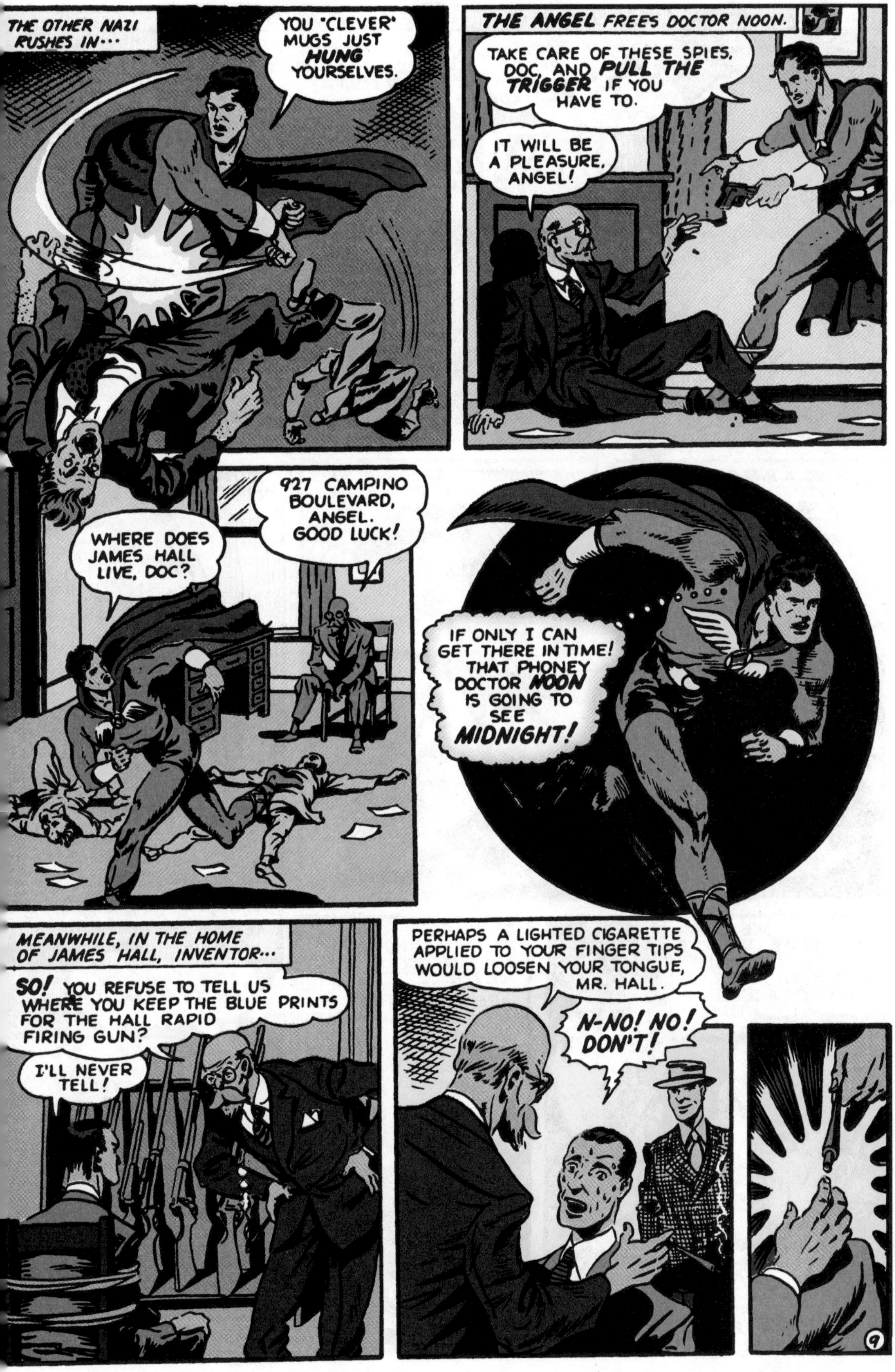
THE OTHER NAZI RUSHES IN...
YOU "CLEVER" MUGS JUST HUNG YOURSELVES.
THE ANGEL FREES DOCTOR NOON.
TAKE CARE OF THESE SPIES, DOC, AND PULL THE TRIGGER IF YOU HAVE TO.
IT WILL BE A PLEASURE, ANGEL!
WHERE DOES JAMES HALL LIVE, DOC?
927 CAMPINO BOULEVARD, ANGEL. GOOD LUCK!
IF ONLY I CAN GET THERE IN TIME! THAT PHONEY DOCTOR NOON IS GOING TO SEE MIDNIGHT!
MEANWHILE, IN THE HOME OF JAMES HALL, INVENTOR...
SO! YOU REFUSE TO TELL US WHERE YOU KEEP THE BLUE PRINTS FOR THE HALL RAPID FIRING GUN?
I'LL NEVER TELL!
PERHAPS A LIGHTED CIGARETTE APPLIED TO YOUR FINGER TIPS WOULD LOOSEN YOUR TONGUE, MR. HALL.
N-NO! NO! DON'T!
9

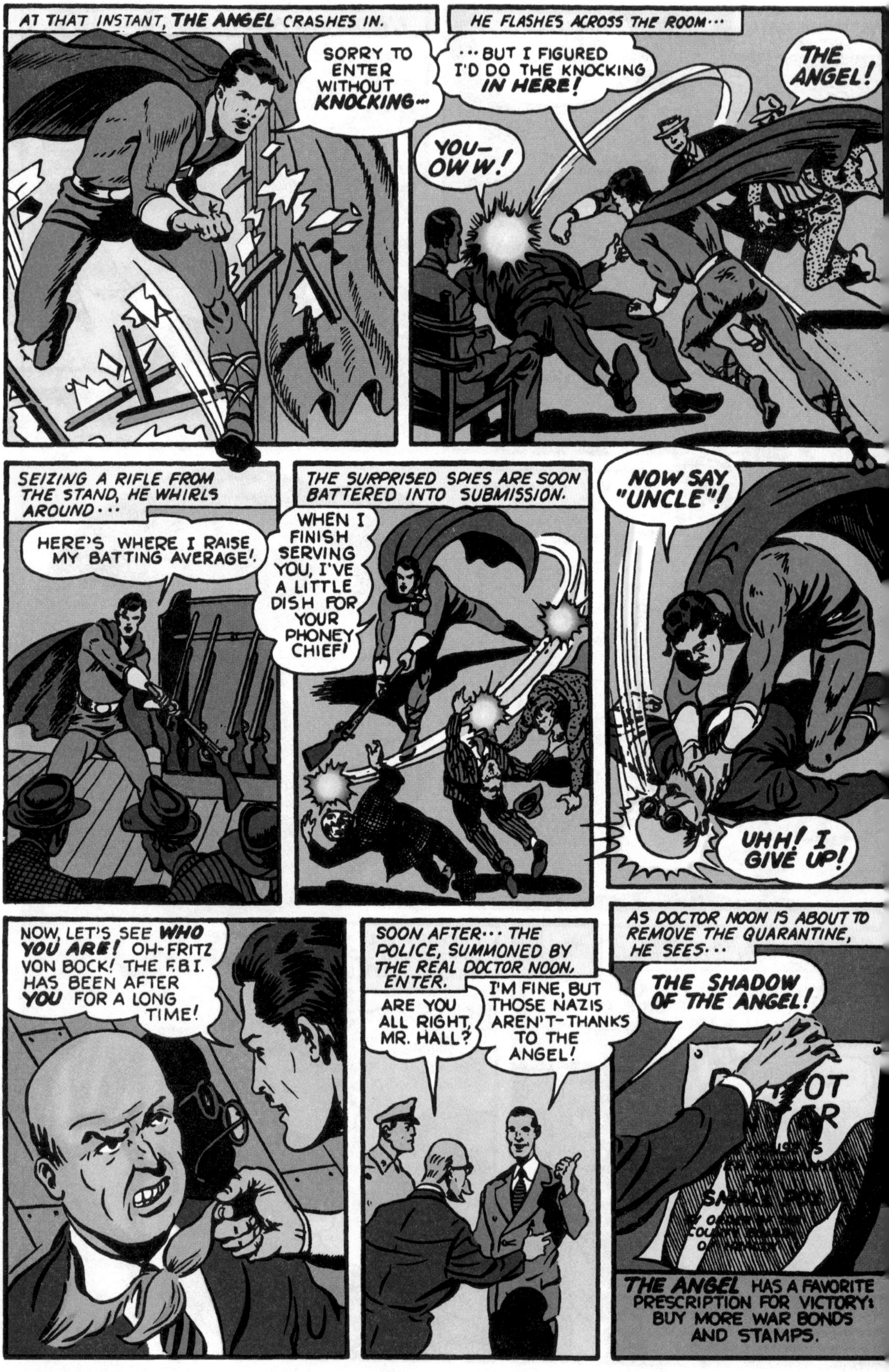
AT THAT INSTANT, THE ANGEL CRASHES IN.
SORRY TO ENTER WITHOUT KNOCKING...
HE FLASHES ACROSS THE ROOM...
...BUT I FIGURED I'D DO THE KNOCKING IN HERE!
THE ANGEL!
YOU-OWW!
SEIZING A RIFLE FROM THE STAND, HE WHIRLS AROUND...
HERE'S WHERE I RAISE MY BATTING AVERAGE!
THE SURPRISED SPIES ARE SOON BATTERED INTO SUBMISSION.
WHEN I FINISH SERVING YOU, I'VE A LITTLE DISH FOR YOUR PHONEY CHIEF!
NOW SAY "UNCLE"!
UHH! I GIVE UP!
NOW, LET'S SEE WHO YOU ARE! OH-FRITZ VON BOCK! THE F.B.I. HAS BEEN AFTER YOU FOR A LONG TIME!
SOON AFTER... THE POLICE, SUMMONED BY THE REAL DOCTOR NOON, ENTER.
ARE YOU ALL RIGHT, MR. HALL?
I'M FINE, BUT THOSE NAZIS AREN'T-THANKS TO THE ANGEL!
AS DOCTOR NOON IS ABOUT TO REMOVE THE QUARANTINE, HE SEES...
THE SHADOW OF THE ANGEL!
THE ANGEL HAS A FAVORITE PRESCRIPTION FOR VICTORY: BUY MORE WAR BONDS AND STAMPS.

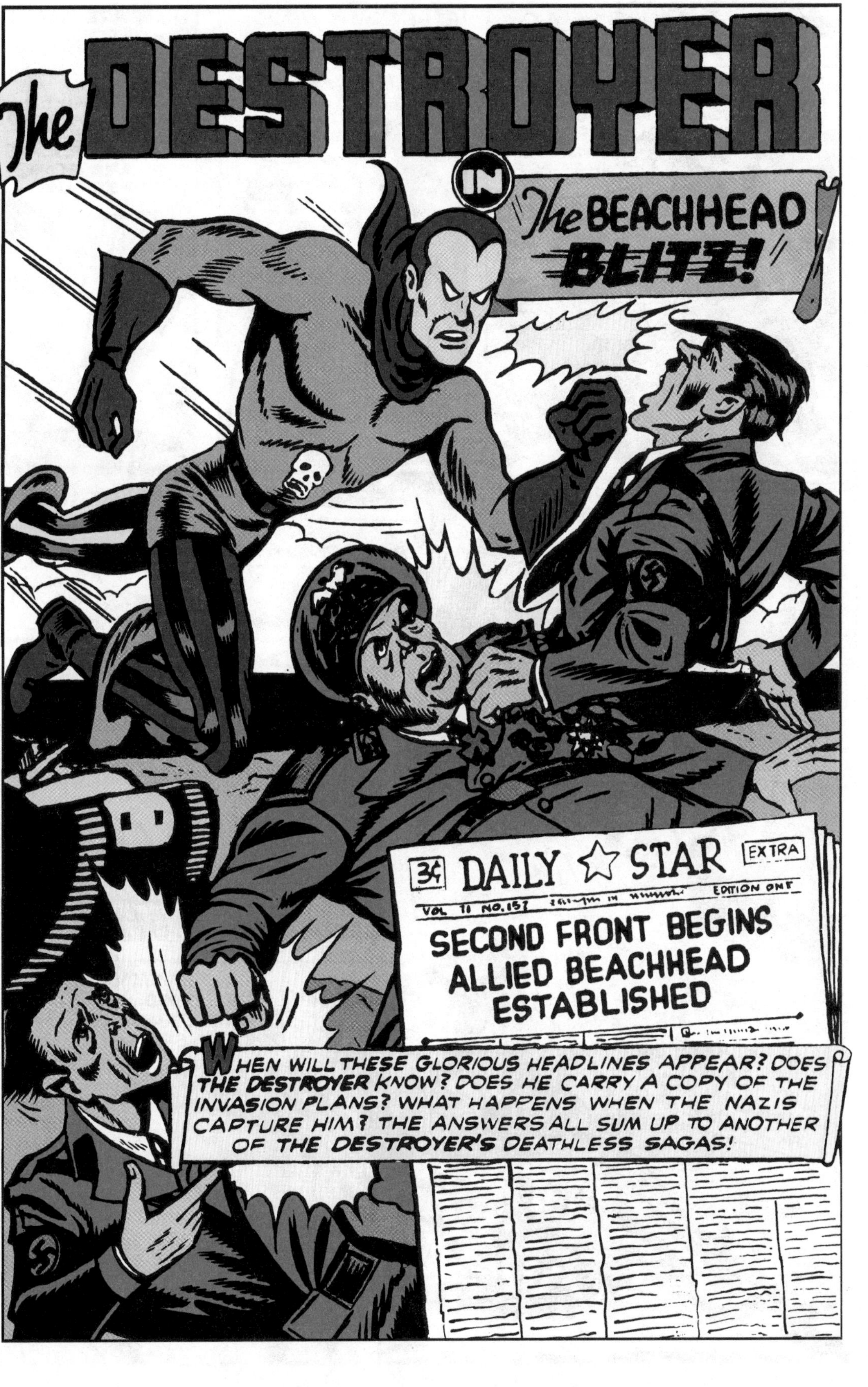
The DESTROYER
IN
The BEACHHEAD BLITZ!
3¢ DAILY ☆ STAR EXTRA
EDITION ONE
SECOND FRONT BEGINS
ALLIED BEACHHEAD
ESTABLISHED
WHEN WILL THESE GLORIOUS HEADLINES APPEAR? DOES THE DESTROYER KNOW? DOES HE CARRY A COPY OF THE INVASION PLANS? WHAT HAPPENS WHEN THE NAZIS CAPTURE HIM? THE ANSWERS ALL SUM UP TO ANOTHER OF THE DESTROYER'S DEATHLESS SAGAS!

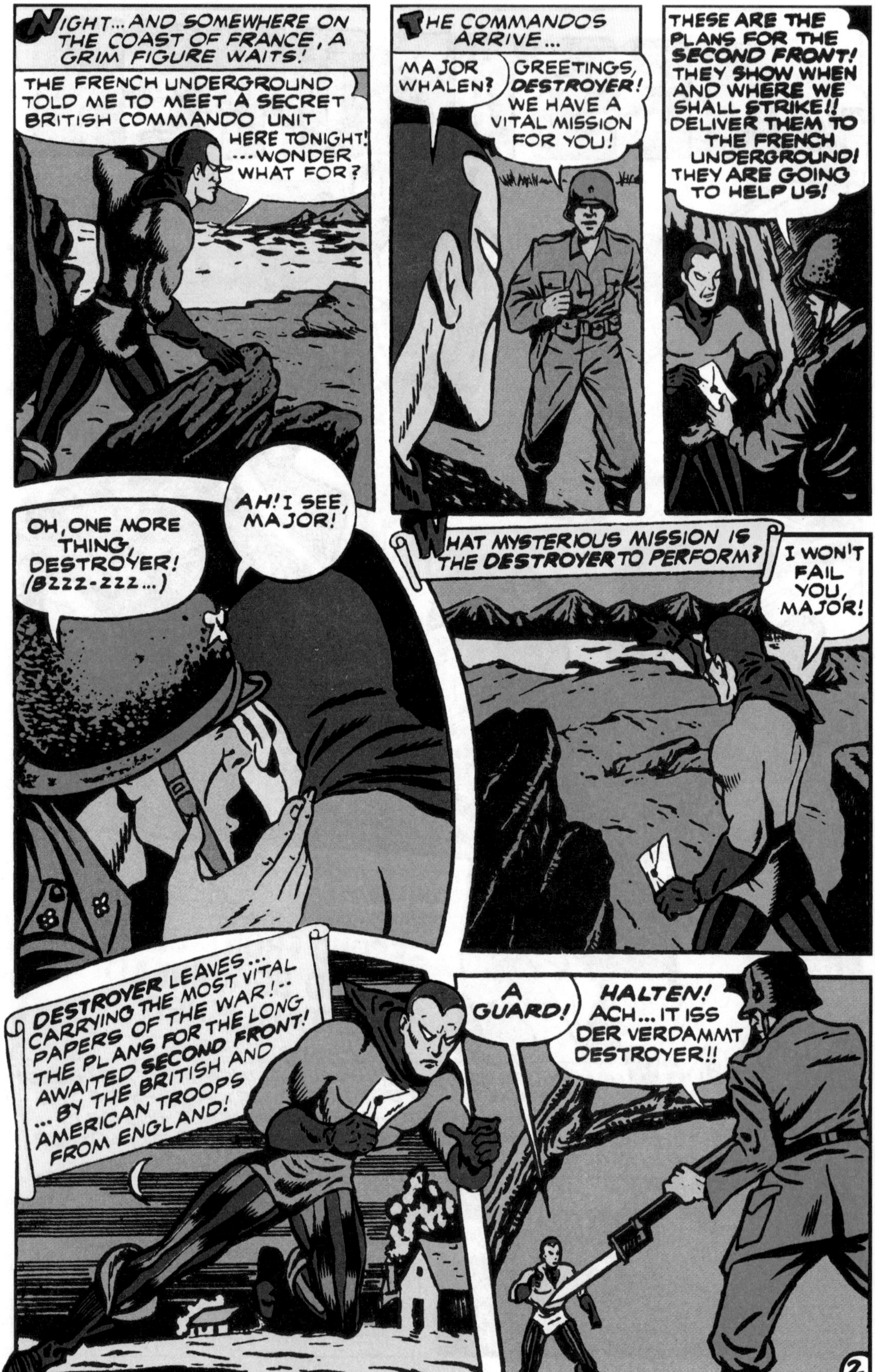
NIGHT... AND SOMEWHERE ON THE COAST OF FRANCE, A GRIM FIGURE WAITS!
THE FRENCH UNDERGROUND TOLD ME TO MEET A SECRET BRITISH COMMANDO UNIT HERE TONIGHT! ...WONDER WHAT FOR?
THE COMMANDOS ARRIVE...
MAJOR WHALEN?
GREETINGS, DESTROYER! WE HAVE A VITAL MISSION FOR YOU!
THESE ARE THE PLANS FOR THE SECOND FRONT! THEY SHOW WHEN AND WHERE WE SHALL STRIKE!! DELIVER THEM TO THE FRENCH UNDERGROUND! THEY ARE GOING TO HELP US!
OH, ONE MORE THING, DESTROYER! (BZZZ-ZZZ...)
AH! I SEE, MAJOR!
WHAT MYSTERIOUS MISSION IS THE DESTROYER TO PERFORM?
I WON'T FAIL YOU, MAJOR!
DESTROYER LEAVES... CARRYING THE MOST VITAL PAPERS OF THE WAR!-- THE PLANS FOR THE LONG AWAITED SECOND FRONT! ...BY THE BRITISH AND AMERICAN TROOPS FROM ENGLAND!
A GUARD!
HALTEN! ACH... IT ISS DER VERDAMMT DESTROYER!!
2

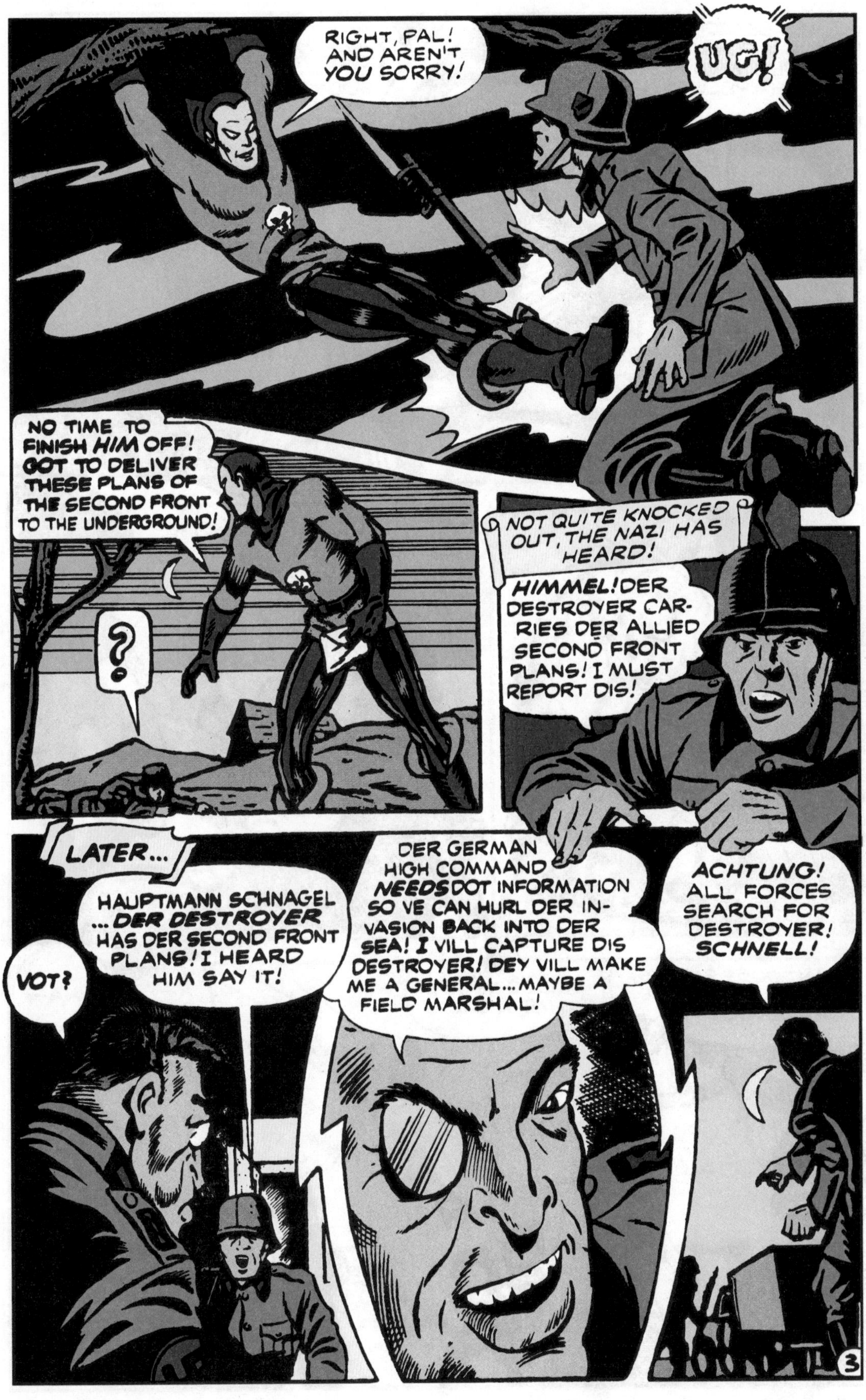
RIGHT, PAL! AND AREN'T YOU SORRY!
UG!
NO TIME TO FINISH HIM OFF! GOT TO DELIVER THESE PLANS OF THE SECOND FRONT TO THE UNDERGROUND!
?
NOT QUITE KNOCKED OUT, THE NAZI HAS HEARD!
HIMMEL! DER DESTROYER CARRIES DER ALLIED SECOND FRONT PLANS! I MUST REPORT DIS!
LATER...
HAUPTMANN SCHNAGEL ...DER DESTROYER HAS DER SECOND FRONT PLANS! I HEARD HIM SAY IT!
VOT?
DER GERMAN HIGH COMMAND NEEDS DOT INFORMATION SO VE CAN HURL DER INVASION BACK INTO DER SEA! I VILL CAPTURE DIS DESTROYER! DEY VILL MAKE ME A GENERAL... MAYBE A FIELD MARSHAL!
ACHTUNG! ALL FORCES SEARCH FOR DESTROYER! SCHNELL!
3

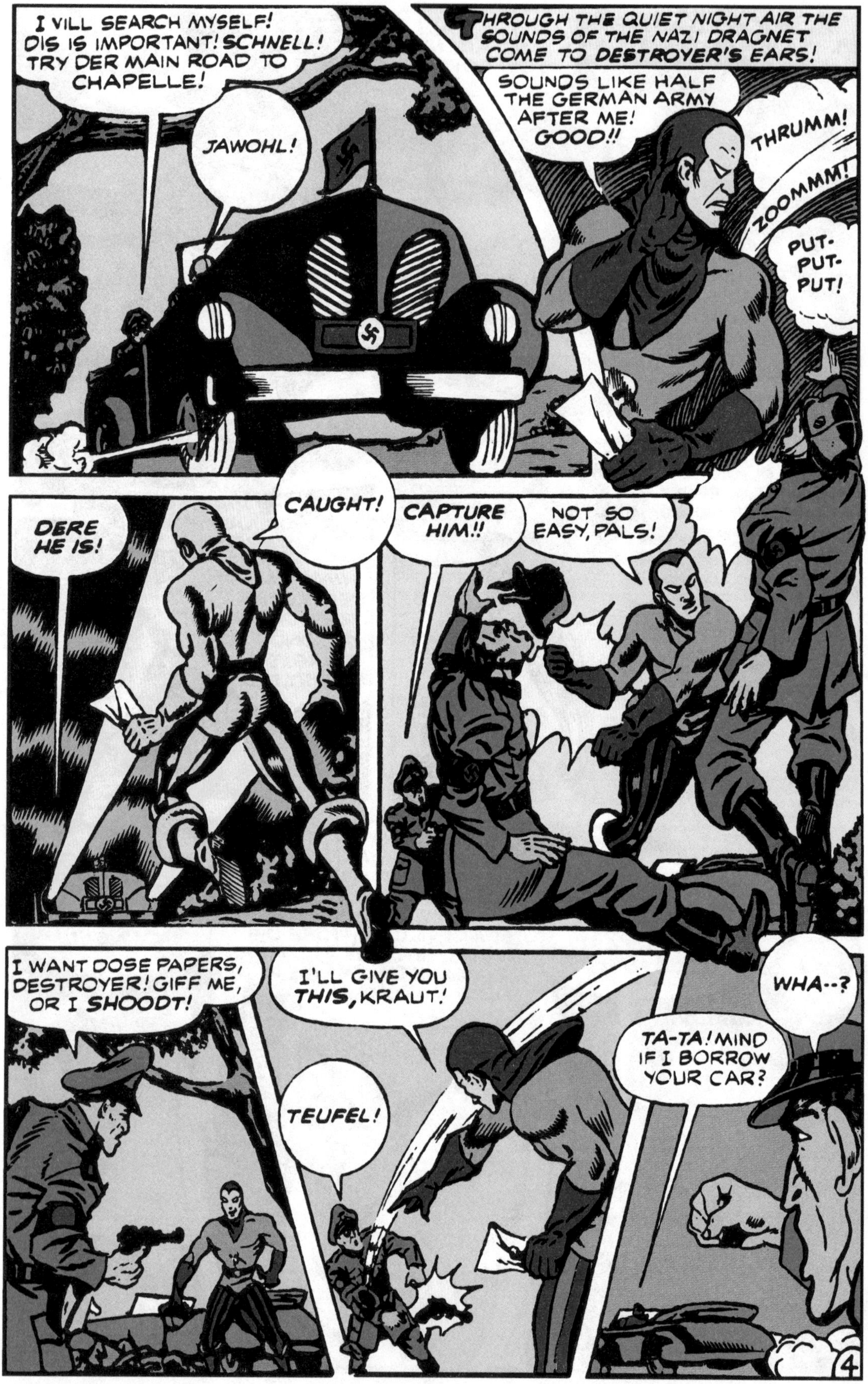
I VILL SEARCH MYSELF! DIS IS IMPORTANT! SCHNELL! TRY DER MAIN ROAD TO CHAPELLE!
JAWOHL!
THROUGH THE QUIET NIGHT AIR THE SOUNDS OF THE NAZI DRAGNET COME TO DESTROYER'S EARS!
SOUNDS LIKE HALF THE GERMAN ARMY AFTER ME! GOOD!!
THRUMM!
ZOOMMM!
PUT-PUT-PUT!
DERE HE IS!
CAUGHT!
CAPTURE HIM!!
NOT SO EASY, PALS!
I WANT DOSE PAPERS, DESTROYER! GIFF ME, OR I SHOODT!
I'LL GIVE YOU THIS, KRAUT!
TEUFEL!
WHA--?
TA-TA! MIND IF I BORROW YOUR CAR?
4

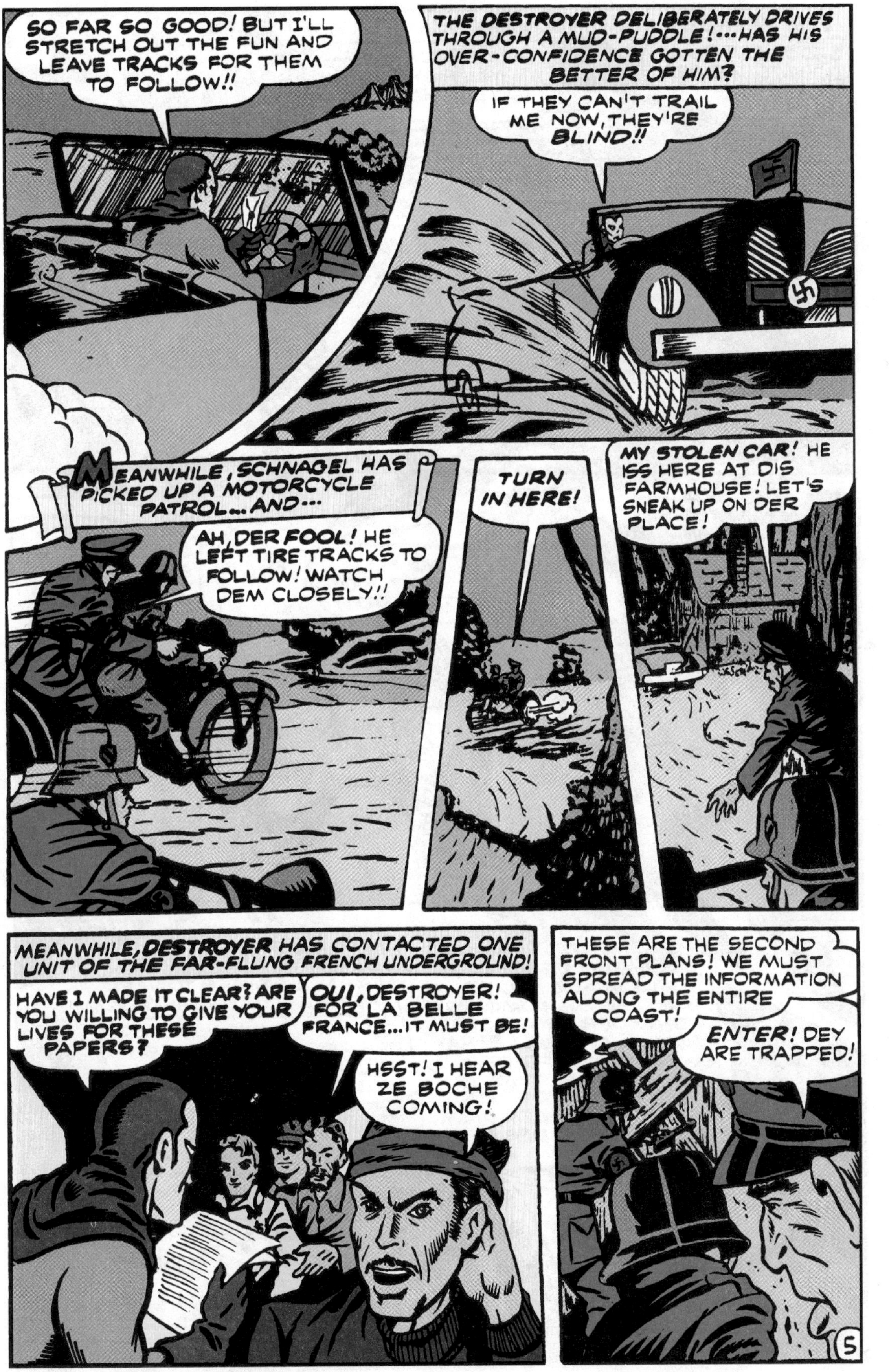
SO FAR SO GOOD! BUT I'LL STRETCH OUT THE FUN AND LEAVE TRACKS FOR THEM TO FOLLOW!!
THE DESTROYER DELIBERATELY DRIVES THROUGH A MUD-PUDDLE!...HAS HIS OVER-CONFIDENCE GOTTEN THE BETTER OF HIM?
IF THEY CAN'T TRAIL ME NOW, THEY'RE BLIND!!
MEANWHILE, SCHNAGEL HAS PICKED UP A MOTORCYCLE PATROL...AND...
AH, DER FOOL! HE LEFT TIRE TRACKS TO FOLLOW! WATCH DEM CLOSELY!!
TURN IN HERE!
MY STOLEN CAR! HE ISS HERE AT DIS FARMHOUSE! LET'S SNEAK UP ON DER PLACE!
MEANWHILE, DESTROYER HAS CONTACTED ONE UNIT OF THE FAR-FLUNG FRENCH UNDERGROUND!
HAVE I MADE IT CLEAR? ARE YOU WILLING TO GIVE YOUR LIVES FOR THESE PAPERS?
OUI, DESTROYER! FOR LA BELLE FRANCE...IT MUST BE!
HSST! I HEAR ZE BOCHE COMING!
THESE ARE THE SECOND FRONT PLANS! WE MUST SPREAD THE INFORMATION ALONG THE ENTIRE COAST!
ENTER! DEY ARE TRAPPED!
5

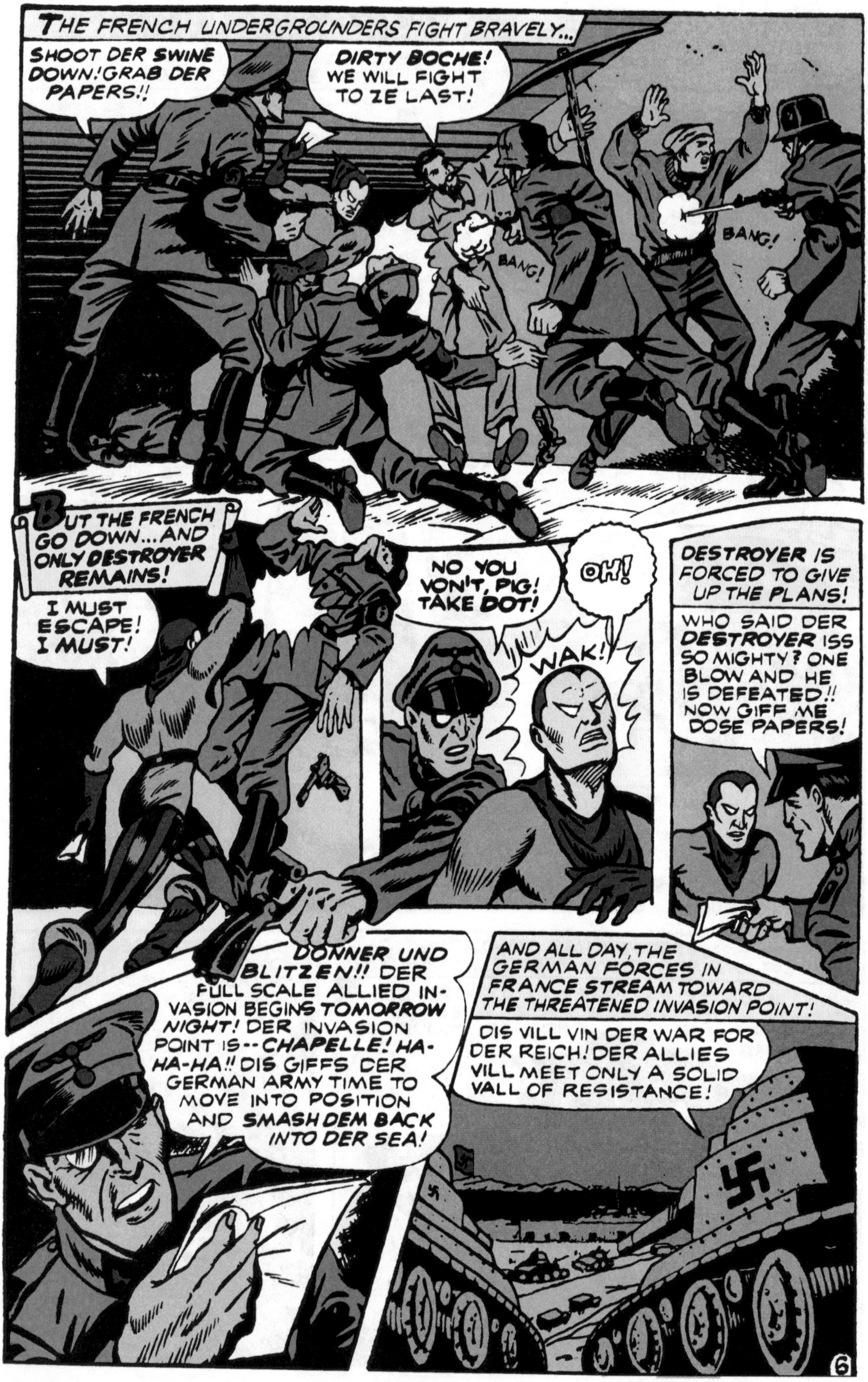
THE FRENCH UNDERGROUNDERS FIGHT BRAVELY...
SHOOT DER SWINE DOWN! GRAB DER PAPERS!!
DIRTY BOCHE! WE WILL FIGHT TO ZE LAST!
BANG!
BANG!
BUT THE FRENCH GO DOWN... AND ONLY DESTROYER REMAINS!
I MUST ESCAPE! I MUST!
NO YOU VON'T, PIG! TAKE DOT!
OH!
WAK!
DESTROYER IS FORCED TO GIVE UP THE PLANS!
WHO SAID DER DESTROYER ISS SO MIGHTY? ONE BLOW AND HE IS DEFEATED!! NOW GIFF ME DOSE PAPERS!
DONNER UND BLITZEN!! DER FULL SCALE ALLIED INVASION BEGINS TOMORROW NIGHT! DER INVASION POINT IS--CHAPELLE! HA-HA-HA!! DIS GIFFS DER GERMAN ARMY TIME TO MOVE INTO POSITION AND SMASH DEM BACK INTO DER SEA!
AND ALL DAY, THE GERMAN FORCES IN FRANCE STREAM TOWARD THE THREATENED INVASION POINT!
DIS VILL VIN DER WAR FOR DER REICH! DER ALLIES VILL MEET ONLY A SOLID VALL OF RESISTANCE!
6

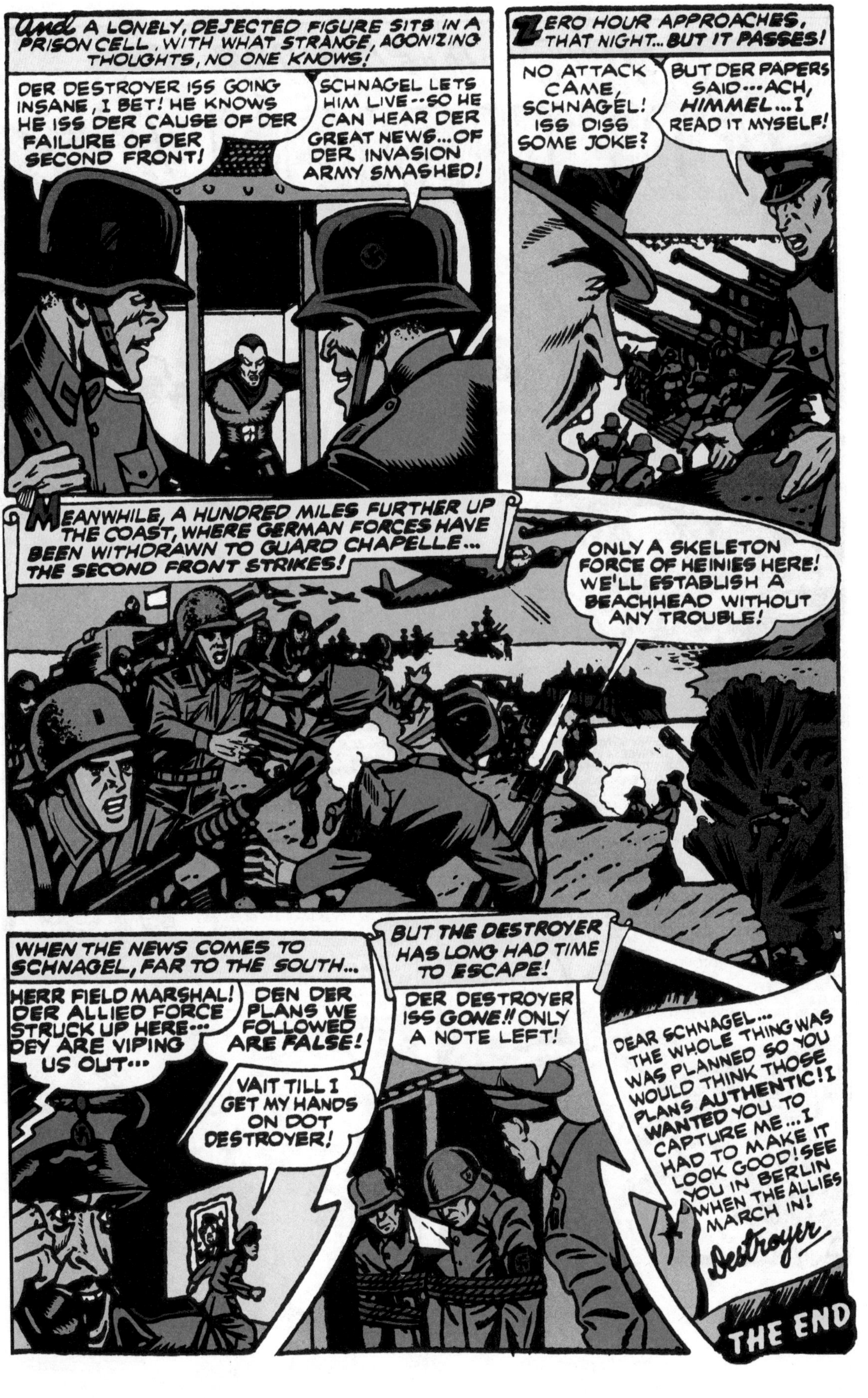
And A LONELY, DEJECTED FIGURE SITS IN A PRISON CELL, WITH WHAT STRANGE, AGONIZING THOUGHTS, NO ONE KNOWS!
DER DESTROYER ISS GOING INSANE, I BET! HE KNOWS HE ISS DER CAUSE OF DER FAILURE OF DER SECOND FRONT!
SCHNAGEL LETS HIM LIVE--SO HE CAN HEAR DER GREAT NEWS...OF DER INVASION ARMY SMASHED!
ZERO HOUR APPROACHES, THAT NIGHT...BUT IT PASSES!
NO ATTACK CAME, SCHNAGEL! ISS DISS SOME JOKE?
BUT DER PAPERS SAID---ACH, HIMMEL...I READ IT MYSELF!
MEANWHILE, A HUNDRED MILES FURTHER UP THE COAST, WHERE GERMAN FORCES HAVE BEEN WITHDRAWN TO GUARD CHAPELLE... THE SECOND FRONT STRIKES!
ONLY A SKELETON FORCE OF HEINIES HERE! WE'LL ESTABLISH A BEACHHEAD WITHOUT ANY TROUBLE!
WHEN THE NEWS COMES TO SCHNAGEL, FAR TO THE SOUTH...
HERR FIELD MARSHAL! DER ALLIED FORCE STRUCK UP HERE--- DEY ARE VIPING US OUT---
DEN DER PLANS WE FOLLOWED ARE FALSE!
VAIT TILL I GET MY HANDS ON DOT DESTROYER!
BUT THE DESTROYER HAS LONG HAD TIME TO ESCAPE!
DER DESTROYER ISS GONE!! ONLY A NOTE LEFT!
DEAR SCHNAGEL... THE WHOLE THING WAS PLANNED SO YOU WOULD THINK THOSE PLANS AUTHENTIC! I WANTED YOU TO CAPTURE ME...I HAD TO MAKE IT LOOK GOOD! SEE YOU IN BERLIN WHEN THE ALLIES MARCH IN!
Destroyer
THE END

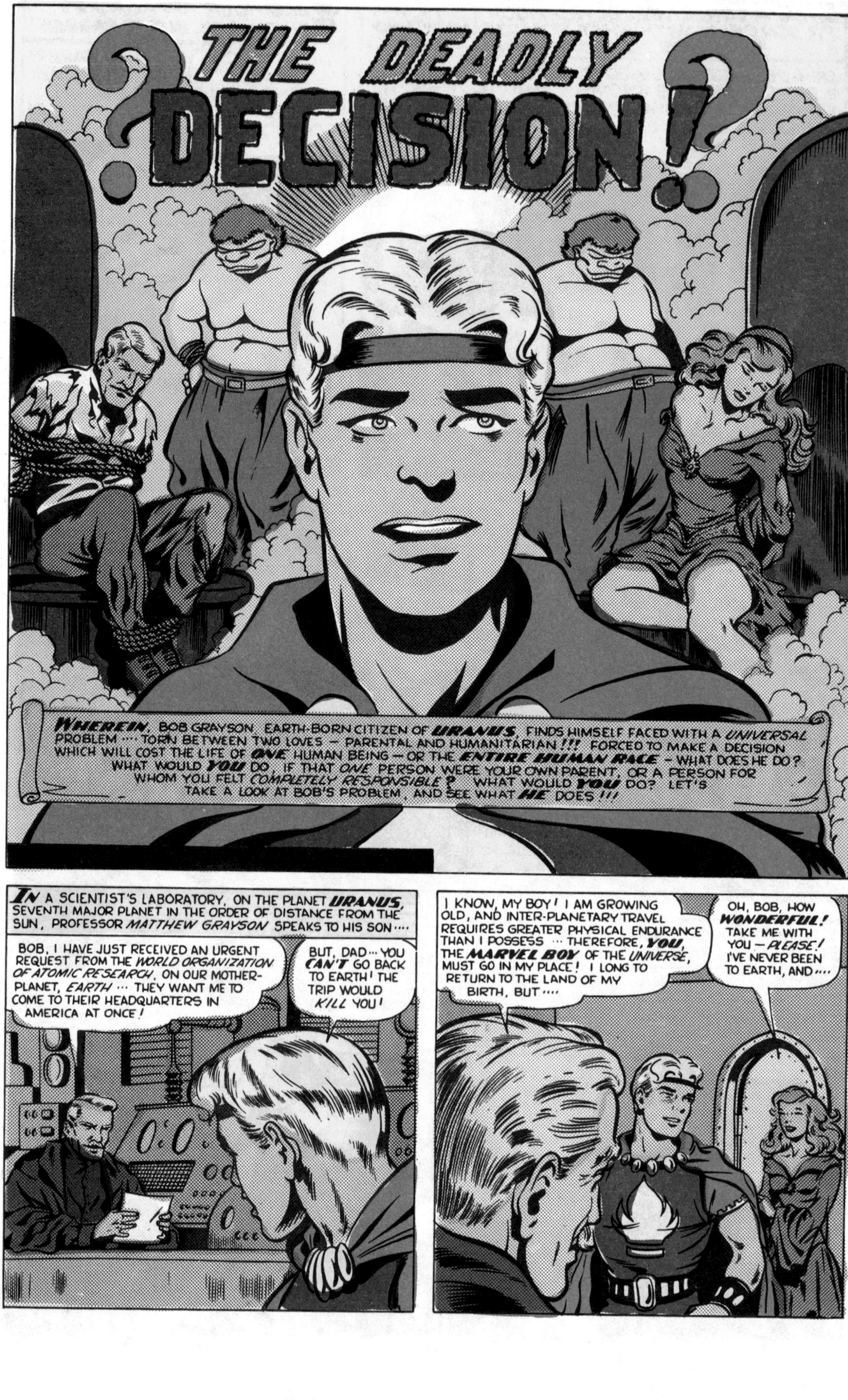
THE DEADLY DECISION!
WHEREIN, BOB GRAYSON, EARTH-BORN CITIZEN OF URANUS, FINDS HIMSELF FACED WITH A UNIVERSAL PROBLEM .... TORN BETWEEN TWO LOVES — PARENTAL AND HUMANITARIAN!!! FORCED TO MAKE A DECISION WHICH WILL COST THE LIFE OF ONE HUMAN BEING — OR THE ENTIRE HUMAN RACE — WHAT DOES HE DO? WHAT WOULD YOU DO, IF THAT ONE PERSON WERE YOUR OWN PARENT, OR A PERSON FOR WHOM YOU FELT COMPLETELY RESPONSIBLE? WHAT WOULD YOU DO? LET'S TAKE A LOOK AT BOB'S PROBLEM, AND SEE WHAT HE DOES!!!
IN A SCIENTIST'S LABORATORY, ON THE PLANET URANUS, SEVENTH MAJOR PLANET IN THE ORDER OF DISTANCE FROM THE SUN, PROFESSOR MATTHEW GRAYSON SPEAKS TO HIS SON....
BOB, I HAVE JUST RECEIVED AN URGENT REQUEST FROM THE WORLD ORGANIZATION OF ATOMIC RESEARCH, ON OUR MOTHER-PLANET, EARTH ... THEY WANT ME TO COME TO THEIR HEADQUARTERS IN AMERICA AT ONCE!
BUT, DAD... YOU CAN'T GO BACK TO EARTH! THE TRIP WOULD KILL YOU!
I KNOW, MY BOY! I AM GROWING OLD, AND INTER-PLANETARY TRAVEL REQUIRES GREATER PHYSICAL ENDURANCE THAN I POSSESS ... THEREFORE, YOU, THE MARVEL BOY OF THE UNIVERSE, MUST GO IN MY PLACE! I LONG TO RETURN TO THE LAND OF MY BIRTH, BUT....
OH, BOB, HOW WONDERFUL! TAKE ME WITH YOU — PLEASE! I'VE NEVER BEEN TO EARTH, AND....

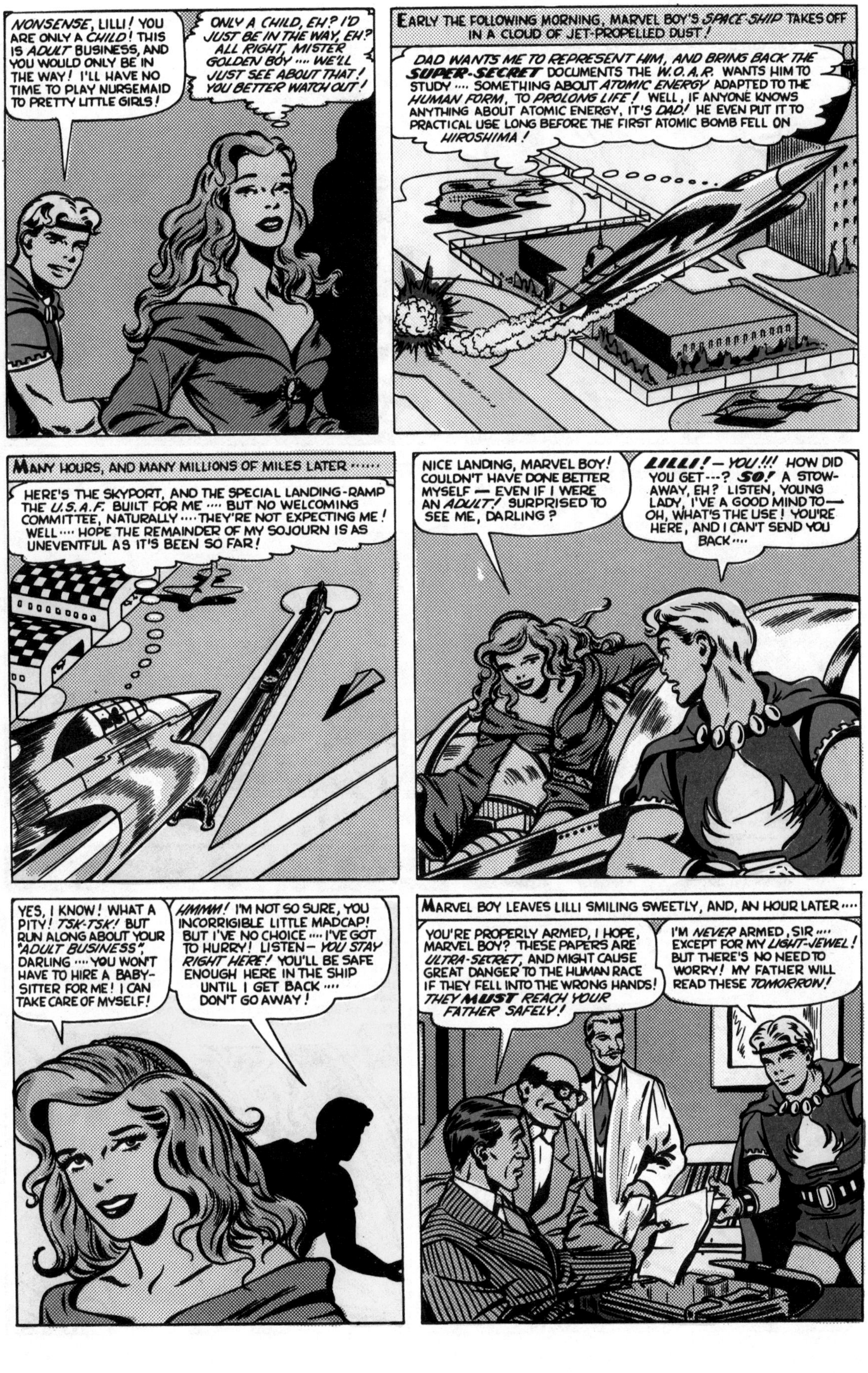
NONSENSE, LILLI! YOU ARE ONLY A CHILD! THIS IS ADULT BUSINESS, AND YOU WOULD ONLY BE IN THE WAY! I'LL HAVE NO TIME TO PLAY NURSEMAID TO PRETTY LITTLE GIRLS!
ONLY A CHILD, EH? I'D JUST BE IN THE WAY, EH? ALL RIGHT, MISTER GOLDEN BOY .... WE'LL JUST SEE ABOUT THAT! YOU BETTER WATCH OUT!
EARLY THE FOLLOWING MORNING, MARVEL BOY'S SPACE-SHIP TAKES OFF IN A CLOUD OF JET-PROPELLED DUST!
DAD WANTS ME TO REPRESENT HIM, AND BRING BACK THE SUPER-SECRET DOCUMENTS THE W.O.A.R. WANTS HIM TO STUDY .... SOMETHING ABOUT ATOMIC ENERGY ADAPTED TO THE HUMAN FORM, TO PROLONG LIFE! WELL, IF ANYONE KNOWS ANYTHING ABOUT ATOMIC ENERGY, IT'S DAD! HE EVEN PUT IT TO PRACTICAL USE LONG BEFORE THE FIRST ATOMIC BOMB FELL ON HIROSHIMA!
MANY HOURS, AND MANY MILLIONS OF MILES LATER ......
HERE'S THE SKYPORT, AND THE SPECIAL LANDING-RAMP THE U.S.A.F. BUILT FOR ME .... BUT NO WELCOMING COMMITTEE, NATURALLY .... THEY'RE NOT EXPECTING ME! WELL .... HOPE THE REMAINDER OF MY SOJOURN IS AS UNEVENTFUL AS IT'S BEEN SO FAR!
NICE LANDING, MARVEL BOY! COULDN'T HAVE DONE BETTER MYSELF — EVEN IF I WERE AN ADULT! SURPRISED TO SEE ME, DARLING?
LILLI! — YOU!!! HOW DID YOU GET ---? SO! A STOW-AWAY, EH? LISTEN, YOUNG LADY, I'VE A GOOD MIND TO— OH, WHAT'S THE USE! YOU'RE HERE, AND I CAN'T SEND YOU BACK ....
YES, I KNOW! WHAT A PITY! TSK-TSK! BUT RUN ALONG ABOUT YOUR "ADULT BUSINESS", DARLING .... YOU WON'T HAVE TO HIRE A BABY-SITTER FOR ME! I CAN TAKE CARE OF MYSELF!
HMMM! I'M NOT SO SURE, YOU INCORRIGIBLE LITTLE MADCAP! BUT I'VE NO CHOICE .... I'VE GOT TO HURRY! LISTEN— YOU STAY RIGHT HERE! YOU'LL BE SAFE ENOUGH HERE IN THE SHIP UNTIL I GET BACK .... DON'T GO AWAY!
MARVEL BOY LEAVES LILLI SMILING SWEETLY, AND, AN HOUR LATER ....
YOU'RE PROPERLY ARMED, I HOPE, MARVEL BOY? THESE PAPERS ARE ULTRA-SECRET, AND MIGHT CAUSE GREAT DANGER TO THE HUMAN RACE IF THEY FELL INTO THE WRONG HANDS! THEY MUST REACH YOUR FATHER SAFELY!
I'M NEVER ARMED, SIR .... EXCEPT FOR MY LIGHT-JEWEL! BUT THERE'S NO NEED TO WORRY! MY FATHER WILL READ THESE TOMORROW!

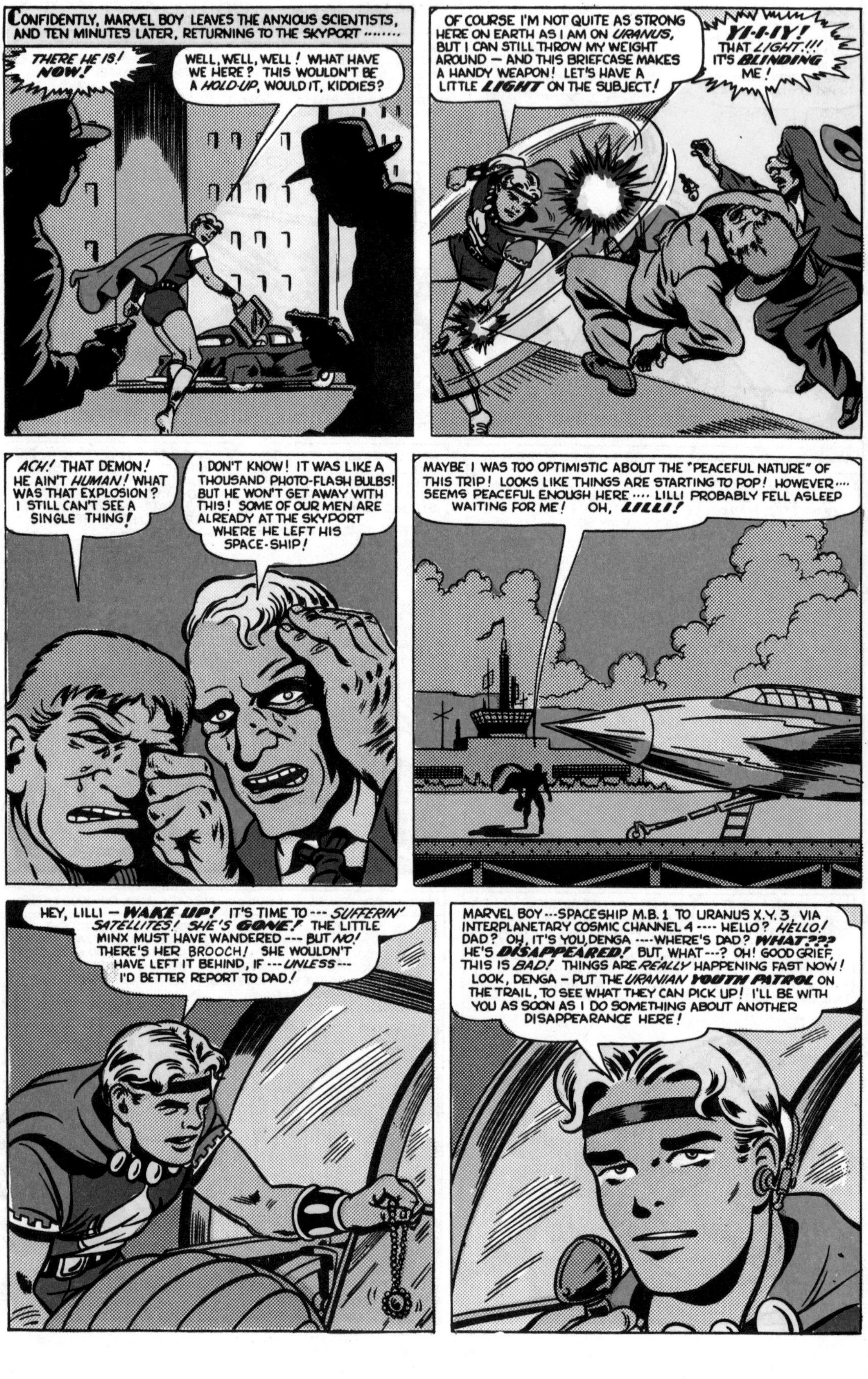
CONFIDENTLY, MARVEL BOY LEAVES THE ANXIOUS SCIENTISTS, AND TEN MINUTES LATER, RETURNING TO THE SKYPORT ....
THERE HE IS! NOW!
WELL, WELL, WELL! WHAT HAVE WE HERE? THIS WOULDN'T BE A HOLD-UP, WOULD IT, KIDDIES?
OF COURSE I'M NOT QUITE AS STRONG HERE ON EARTH AS I AM ON URANUS, BUT I CAN STILL THROW MY WEIGHT AROUND — AND THIS BRIEFCASE MAKES A HANDY WEAPON! LET'S HAVE A LITTLE LIGHT ON THE SUBJECT!
YI-I-IY! THAT LIGHT!!! IT'S BLINDING ME!
ACH! THAT DEMON! HE AIN'T HUMAN! WHAT WAS THAT EXPLOSION? I STILL CAN'T SEE A SINGLE THING!
I DON'T KNOW! IT WAS LIKE A THOUSAND PHOTO-FLASH BULBS! BUT HE WON'T GET AWAY WITH THIS! SOME OF OUR MEN ARE ALREADY AT THE SKYPORT WHERE HE LEFT HIS SPACE-SHIP!
MAYBE I WAS TOO OPTIMISTIC ABOUT THE "PEACEFUL NATURE" OF THIS TRIP! LOOKS LIKE THINGS ARE STARTING TO POP! HOWEVER.... SEEMS PEACEFUL ENOUGH HERE.... LILLI PROBABLY FELL ASLEEP WAITING FOR ME! OH, LILLI!
HEY, LILLI — WAKE UP! IT'S TIME TO --- SUFFERIN' SATELLITES! SHE'S GONE! THE LITTLE MINX MUST HAVE WANDERED --- BUT NO! THERE'S HER BROOCH! SHE WOULDN'T HAVE LEFT IT BEHIND, IF --- UNLESS --- I'D BETTER REPORT TO DAD!
MARVEL BOY --- SPACESHIP M.B. 1 TO URANUS X.Y. 3 VIA INTERPLANETARY COSMIC CHANNEL 4 ---- HELLO? HELLO! DAD? OH, IT'S YOU, DENGA ---- WHERE'S DAD? WHAT??? HE'S DISAPPEARED! BUT, WHAT ---? OH! GOOD GRIEF, THIS IS BAD! THINGS ARE REALLY HAPPENING FAST NOW! LOOK, DENGA — PUT THE URANIAN YOUTH PATROL ON THE TRAIL, TO SEE WHAT THEY CAN PICK UP! I'LL BE WITH YOU AS SOON AS I DO SOMETHING ABOUT ANOTHER DISAPPEARANCE HERE!

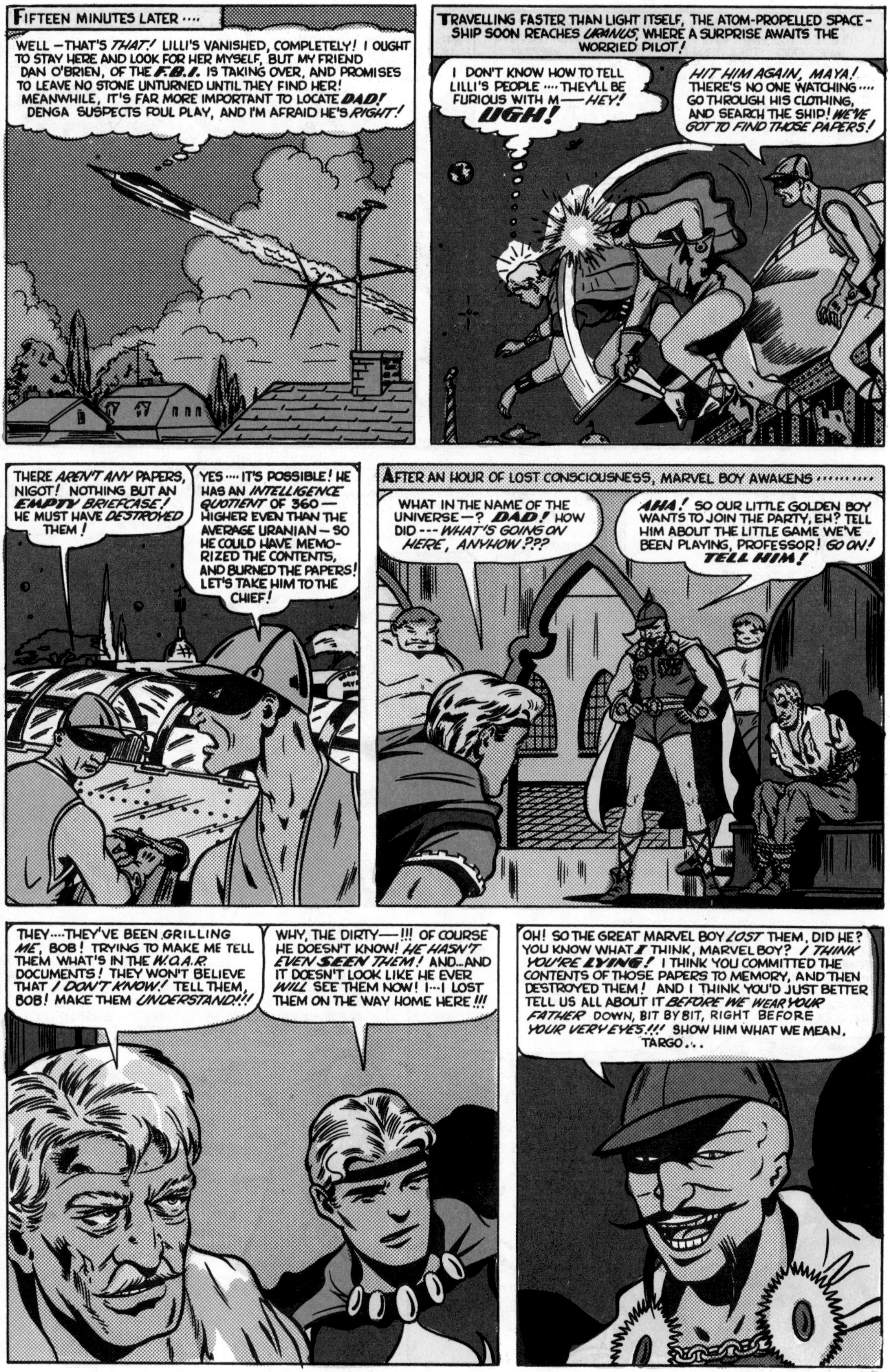
FIFTEEN MINUTES LATER ....
WELL — THAT'S THAT! LILLI'S VANISHED, COMPLETELY! I OUGHT TO STAY HERE AND LOOK FOR HER MYSELF, BUT MY FRIEND DAN O'BRIEN, OF THE F.B.I. IS TAKING OVER, AND PROMISES TO LEAVE NO STONE UNTURNED UNTIL THEY FIND HER! MEANWHILE, IT'S FAR MORE IMPORTANT TO LOCATE DAD! DENGA SUSPECTS FOUL PLAY, AND I'M AFRAID HE'S RIGHT!
TRAVELLING FASTER THAN LIGHT ITSELF, THE ATOM-PROPELLED SPACE-SHIP SOON REACHES URANUS, WHERE A SURPRISE AWAITS THE WORRIED PILOT!
I DON'T KNOW HOW TO TELL LILLI'S PEOPLE .... THEY'LL BE FURIOUS WITH M — HEY! UGH!
HIT HIM AGAIN, MAYA! THERE'S NO ONE WATCHING .... GO THROUGH HIS CLOTHING, AND SEARCH THE SHIP! WE'VE GOT TO FIND THOSE PAPERS!
THERE AREN'T ANY PAPERS, NIGOT! NOTHING BUT AN EMPTY BRIEFCASE! HE MUST HAVE DESTROYED THEM!
YES .... IT'S POSSIBLE! HE HAS AN INTELLIGENCE QUOTIENT OF 360 — HIGHER EVEN THAN THE AVERAGE URANIAN — SO HE COULD HAVE MEMORIZED THE CONTENTS, AND BURNED THE PAPERS! LET'S TAKE HIM TO THE CHIEF!
AFTER AN HOUR OF LOST CONSCIOUSNESS, MARVEL BOY AWAKENS ....
WHAT IN THE NAME OF THE UNIVERSE — ? DAD! HOW DID --- WHAT'S GOING ON HERE, ANYHOW ???
AHA! SO OUR LITTLE GOLDEN BOY WANTS TO JOIN THE PARTY, EH? TELL HIM ABOUT THE LITTLE GAME WE'VE BEEN PLAYING, PROFESSOR! GO ON! TELL HIM!
THEY .... THEY'VE BEEN GRILLING ME, BOB! TRYING TO MAKE ME TELL THEM WHAT'S IN THE W.O.A.R. DOCUMENTS! THEY WON'T BELIEVE THAT I DON'T KNOW! TELL THEM, BOB! MAKE THEM UNDERSTAND!!!
WHY, THE DIRTY — !!! OF COURSE HE DOESN'T KNOW! HE HASN'T EVEN SEEN THEM! AND...AND IT DOESN'T LOOK LIKE HE EVER WILL SEE THEM NOW! I---I LOST THEM ON THE WAY HOME HERE!!!
OH! SO THE GREAT MARVEL BOY LOST THEM, DID HE? YOU KNOW WHAT I THINK, MARVEL BOY? I THINK YOU'RE LYING! I THINK YOU COMMITTED THE CONTENTS OF THOSE PAPERS TO MEMORY, AND THEN DESTROYED THEM! AND I THINK YOU'D JUST BETTER TELL US ALL ABOUT IT BEFORE WE WEAR YOUR FATHER DOWN, BIT BY BIT, RIGHT BEFORE YOUR VERY EYES!!! SHOW HIM WHAT WE MEAN, TARGO...

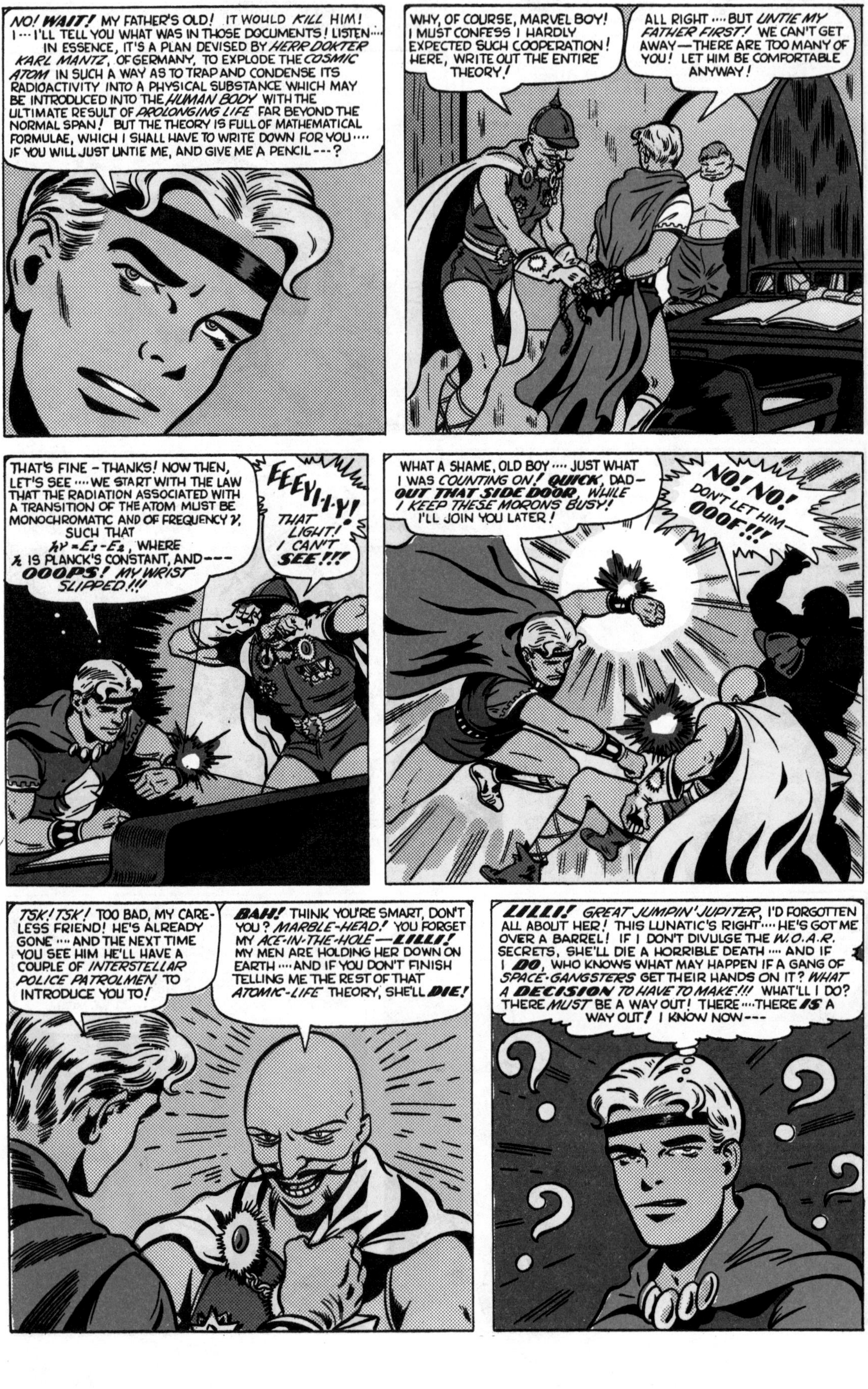
NO! WAIT! MY FATHER'S OLD! IT WOULD KILL HIM! I---I'LL TELL YOU WHAT WAS IN THOSE DOCUMENTS! LISTEN---- IN ESSENCE, IT'S A PLAN DEVISED BY HERR DOKTER KARL MANTZ, OF GERMANY, TO EXPLODE THE COSMIC ATOM IN SUCH A WAY AS TO TRAP AND CONDENSE ITS RADIOACTIVITY INTO A PHYSICAL SUBSTANCE WHICH MAY BE INTRODUCED INTO THE HUMAN BODY WITH THE ULTIMATE RESULT OF PROLONGING LIFE FAR BEYOND THE NORMAL SPAN! BUT THE THEORY IS FULL OF MATHEMATICAL FORMULAE, WHICH I SHALL HAVE TO WRITE DOWN FOR YOU---- IF YOU WILL JUST UNTIE ME, AND GIVE ME A PENCIL---?
WHY, OF COURSE, MARVEL BOY! I MUST CONFESS I HARDLY EXPECTED SUCH COOPERATION! HERE, WRITE OUT THE ENTIRE THEORY!
ALL RIGHT---- BUT UNTIE MY FATHER FIRST! WE CAN'T GET AWAY—THERE ARE TOO MANY OF YOU! LET HIM BE COMFORTABLE ANYWAY!
THAT'S FINE - THANKS! NOW THEN, LET'S SEE ---- WE START WITH THE LAW THAT THE RADIATION ASSOCIATED WITH A TRANSITION OF THE ATOM MUST BE MONOCHROMATIC AND OF FREQUENCY ν, SUCH THAT $h\nu = E_1 - E_2$, WHERE h IS PLANCK'S CONSTANT, AND--- OOOPS! MY WRIST SLIPPED!!!
EEEYI-I-Y! THAT LIGHT! I CAN'T SEE!!!
WHAT A SHAME, OLD BOY ---- JUST WHAT I WAS COUNTING ON! QUICK, DAD-OUT THAT SIDE DOOR, WHILE I KEEP THESE MORONS BUSY! I'LL JOIN YOU LATER!
NO! NO! DON'T LET HIM— OOOF!!!
TSK! TSK! TOO BAD, MY CARELESS FRIEND! HE'S ALREADY GONE ---- AND THE NEXT TIME YOU SEE HIM HE'LL HAVE A COUPLE OF INTERSTELLAR POLICE PATROLMEN TO INTRODUCE YOU TO!
BAH! THINK YOU'RE SMART, DON'T YOU? MARBLE-HEAD! YOU FORGET MY ACE-IN-THE-HOLE—LILLI! MY MEN ARE HOLDING HER DOWN ON EARTH ---- AND IF YOU DON'T FINISH TELLING ME THE REST OF THAT ATOMIC-LIFE THEORY, SHE'LL DIE!
LILLI! GREAT JUMPIN' JUPITER, I'D FORGOTTEN ALL ABOUT HER! THIS LUNATIC'S RIGHT ---- HE'S GOT ME OVER A BARREL! IF I DON'T DIVULGE THE W.O.A.R. SECRETS, SHE'LL DIE A HORRIBLE DEATH ---- AND IF I DO, WHO KNOWS WHAT MAY HAPPEN IF A GANG OF SPACE-GANGSTERS GET THEIR HANDS ON IT? WHAT A DECISION TO HAVE TO MAKE!!! WHAT'LL I DO? THERE MUST BE A WAY OUT! THERE ---- THERE IS A WAY OUT! I KNOW NOW---

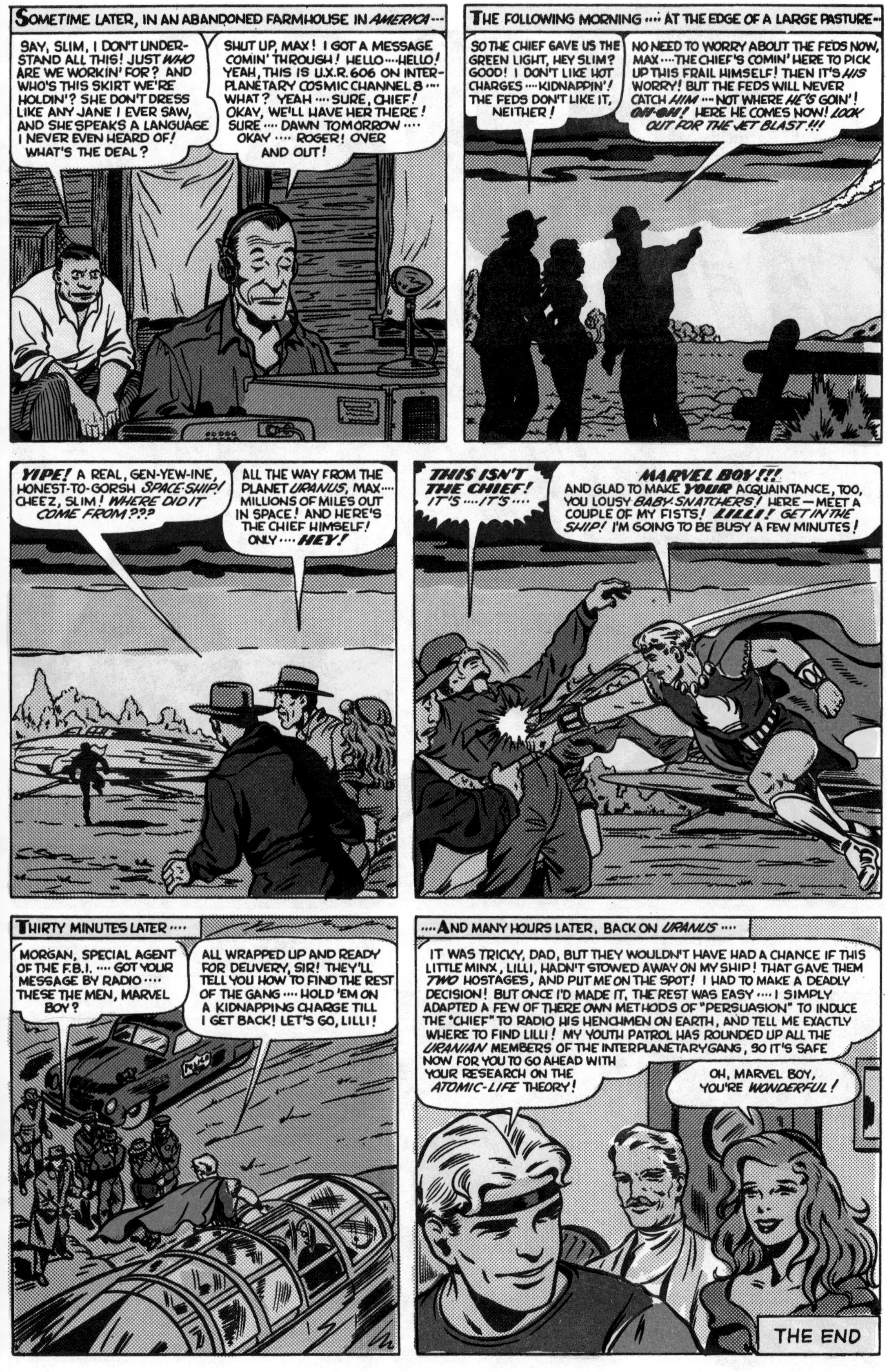

SOMETIME LATER, IN AN ABANDONED FARMHOUSE IN AMERICA ---
SAY, SLIM, I DON'T UNDERSTAND ALL THIS! JUST WHO ARE WE WORKIN' FOR? AND WHO'S THIS SKIRT WE'RE HOLDIN'? SHE DON'T DRESS LIKE ANY JANE I EVER SAW, AND SHE SPEAKS A LANGUAGE I NEVER EVEN HEARD OF! WHAT'S THE DEAL?
SHUT UP, MAX! I GOT A MESSAGE COMIN' THROUGH! HELLO .... HELLO! YEAH, THIS IS U.X.R. 606 ON INTER-PLANETARY COSMIC CHANNEL 8 .... WHAT? YEAH .... SURE, CHIEF! OKAY, WE'LL HAVE HER THERE! SURE .... DAWN TOMORROW .... OKAY .... ROGER! OVER AND OUT!
THE FOLLOWING MORNING .... AT THE EDGE OF A LARGE PASTURE --
SO THE CHIEF GAVE US THE GREEN LIGHT, HEY SLIM? GOOD! I DON'T LIKE HOT CHARGES .... KIDNAPPIN'! THE FEDS DON'T LIKE IT, NEITHER!
NO NEED TO WORRY ABOUT THE FEDS NOW, MAX .... THE CHIEF'S COMIN' HERE TO PICK UP THIS FRAIL HIMSELF! THEN IT'S HIS WORRY! BUT THE FEDS WILL NEVER CATCH HIM .... NOT WHERE HE'S GOIN'! OH-OH! HERE HE COMES NOW! LOOK OUT FOR THE JET BLAST!!!
YIPE! A REAL, GEN-YEW-INE, HONEST-TO-GORSH SPACE-SHIP! CHEEZ, SLIM! WHERE DID IT COME FROM???
ALL THE WAY FROM THE PLANET URANUS, MAX .... MILLIONS OF MILES OUT IN SPACE! AND HERE'S THE CHIEF HIMSELF! ONLY .... HEY!
THIS ISN'T THE CHIEF! IT'S .... IT'S ....
MARVEL BOY!!! AND GLAD TO MAKE YOUR ACQUAINTANCE, TOO, YOU LOUSY BABY-SNATCHERS! HERE — MEET A COUPLE OF MY FISTS! LILLI! GET IN THE SHIP! I'M GOING TO BE BUSY A FEW MINUTES!
THIRTY MINUTES LATER ....
MORGAN, SPECIAL AGENT OF THE F.B.I. .... GOT YOUR MESSAGE BY RADIO .... THESE THE MEN, MARVEL BOY?
ALL WRAPPED UP AND READY FOR DELIVERY, SIR! THEY'LL TELL YOU HOW TO FIND THE REST OF THE GANG .... HOLD 'EM ON A KIDNAPPING CHARGE TILL I GET BACK! LET'S GO, LILLI!
.... AND MANY HOURS LATER, BACK ON URANUS ....
IT WAS TRICKY, DAD, BUT THEY WOULDN'T HAVE HAD A CHANCE IF THIS LITTLE MINX, LILLI, HADN'T STOWED AWAY ON MY SHIP! THAT GAVE THEM TWO HOSTAGES, AND PUT ME ON THE SPOT! I HAD TO MAKE A DEADLY DECISION! BUT ONCE I'D MADE IT, THE REST WAS EASY .... I SIMPLY ADAPTED A FEW OF THERE OWN METHODS OF "PERSUASION" TO INDUCE THE "CHIEF" TO RADIO HIS HENCHMEN ON EARTH, AND TELL ME EXACTLY WHERE TO FIND LILLI! MY YOUTH PATROL HAS ROUNDED UP ALL THE URANIAN MEMBERS OF THE INTERPLANETARY GANG, SO IT'S SAFE NOW FOR YOU TO GO AHEAD WITH YOUR RESEARCH ON THE ATOMIC-LIFE THEORY!
OH, MARVEL BOY, YOU'RE WONDERFUL!
THE END

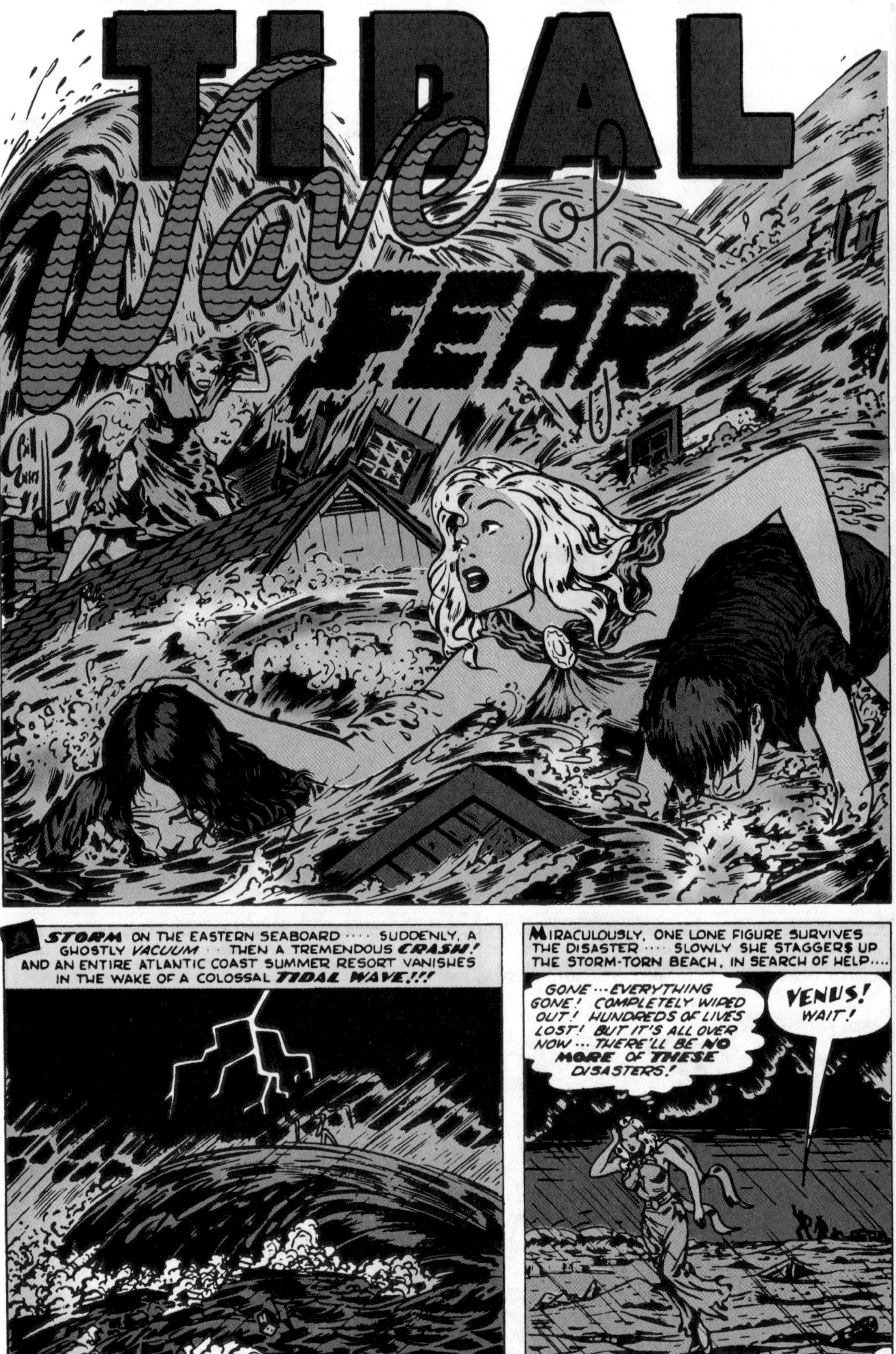
TIDAL
Wave of
FEAR
A STORM ON THE EASTERN SEABOARD .... SUDDENLY, A GHOSTLY VACUUM .. THEN A TREMENDOUS CRASH! AND AN ENTIRE ATLANTIC COAST SUMMER RESORT VANISHES IN THE WAKE OF A COLOSSAL TIDAL WAVE!!!
MIRACULOUSLY, ONE LONE FIGURE SURVIVES THE DISASTER .... SLOWLY SHE STAGGERS UP THE STORM-TORN BEACH, IN SEARCH OF HELP....
GONE ... EVERYTHING GONE! COMPLETELY WIPED OUT! HUNDREDS OF LIVES LOST! BUT IT'S ALL OVER NOW ... THERE'LL BE NO MORE OF THESE DISASTERS!
VENUS! WAIT!
1

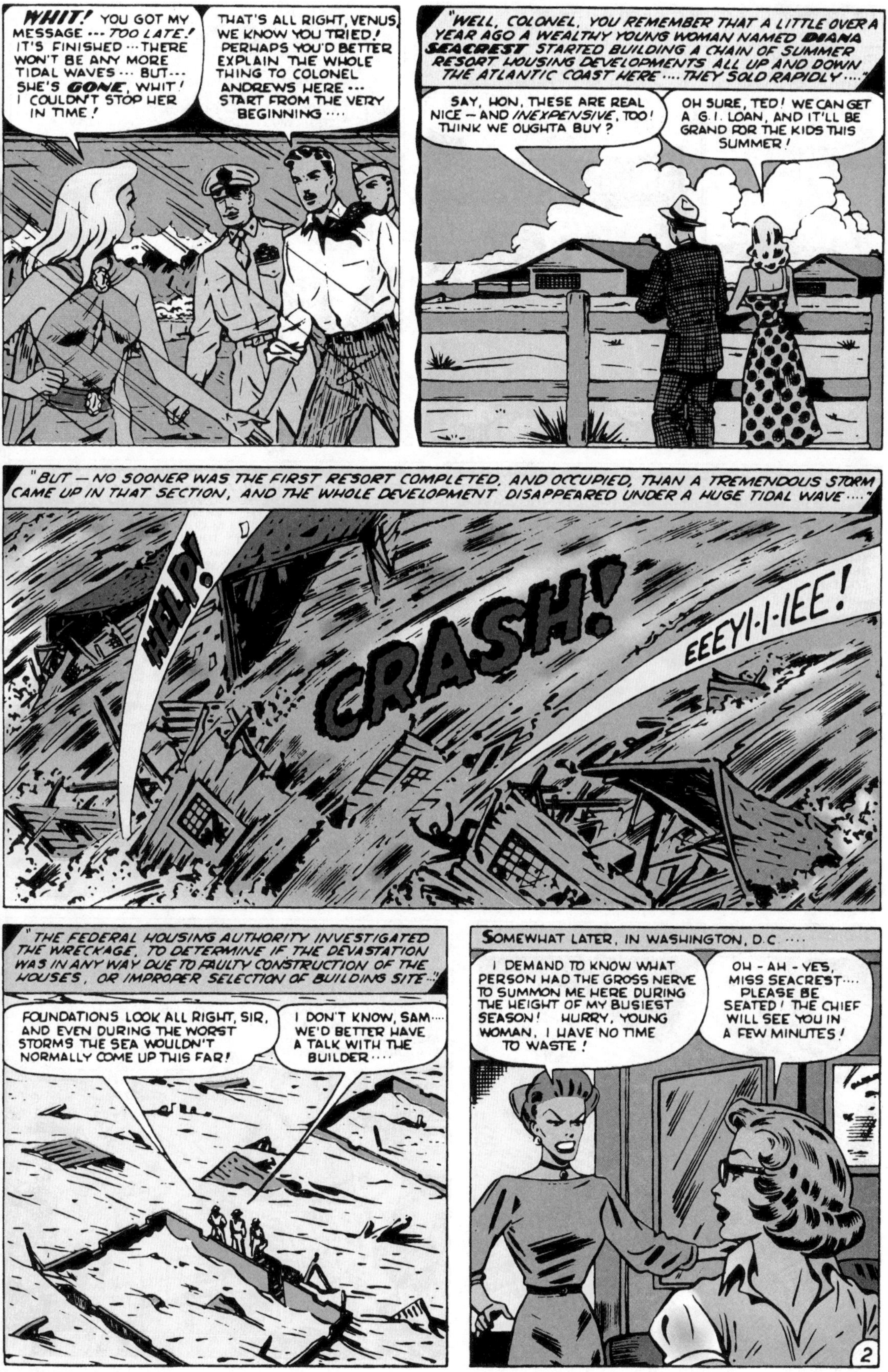
WHIT! YOU GOT MY MESSAGE --- TOO LATE! IT'S FINISHED --- THERE WON'T BE ANY MORE TIDAL WAVES --- BUT --- SHE'S GONE, WHIT! I COULDN'T STOP HER IN TIME!
THAT'S ALL RIGHT, VENUS, WE KNOW YOU TRIED! PERHAPS YOU'D BETTER EXPLAIN THE WHOLE THING TO COLONEL ANDREWS HERE --- START FROM THE VERY BEGINNING ....
"WELL, COLONEL, YOU REMEMBER THAT A LITTLE OVER A YEAR AGO A WEALTHY YOUNG WOMAN NAMED DIANA SEACREST STARTED BUILDING A CHAIN OF SUMMER RESORT HOUSING DEVELOPMENTS ALL UP AND DOWN THE ATLANTIC COAST HERE .... THEY SOLD RAPIDLY ...."
SAY, HON, THESE ARE REAL NICE — AND INEXPENSIVE, TOO! THINK WE OUGHTA BUY?
OH SURE, TED! WE CAN GET A G. I. LOAN, AND IT'LL BE GRAND FOR THE KIDS THIS SUMMER!
"BUT — NO SOONER WAS THE FIRST RESORT COMPLETED, AND OCCUPIED, THAN A TREMENDOUS STORM CAME UP IN THAT SECTION, AND THE WHOLE DEVELOPMENT DISAPPEARED UNDER A HUGE TIDAL WAVE ...."
HELP!
CRASH!
EEEYI-I-IEE!
"THE FEDERAL HOUSING AUTHORITY INVESTIGATED THE WRECKAGE, TO DETERMINE IF THE DEVASTATION WAS IN ANY WAY DUE TO FAULTY CONSTRUCTION OF THE HOUSES, OR IMPROPER SELECTION OF BUILDING SITE ..."
FOUNDATIONS LOOK ALL RIGHT, SIR, AND EVEN DURING THE WORST STORMS THE SEA WOULDN'T NORMALLY COME UP THIS FAR!
I DON'T KNOW, SAM .... WE'D BETTER HAVE A TALK WITH THE BUILDER ....
SOMEWHAT LATER, IN WASHINGTON, D.C ....
I DEMAND TO KNOW WHAT PERSON HAD THE GROSS NERVE TO SUMMON ME HERE DURING THE HEIGHT OF MY BUSIEST SEASON! HURRY, YOUNG WOMAN, I HAVE NO TIME TO WASTE!
OH - AH - YES, MISS SEACREST .... PLEASE BE SEATED! THE CHIEF WILL SEE YOU IN A FEW MINUTES!
2

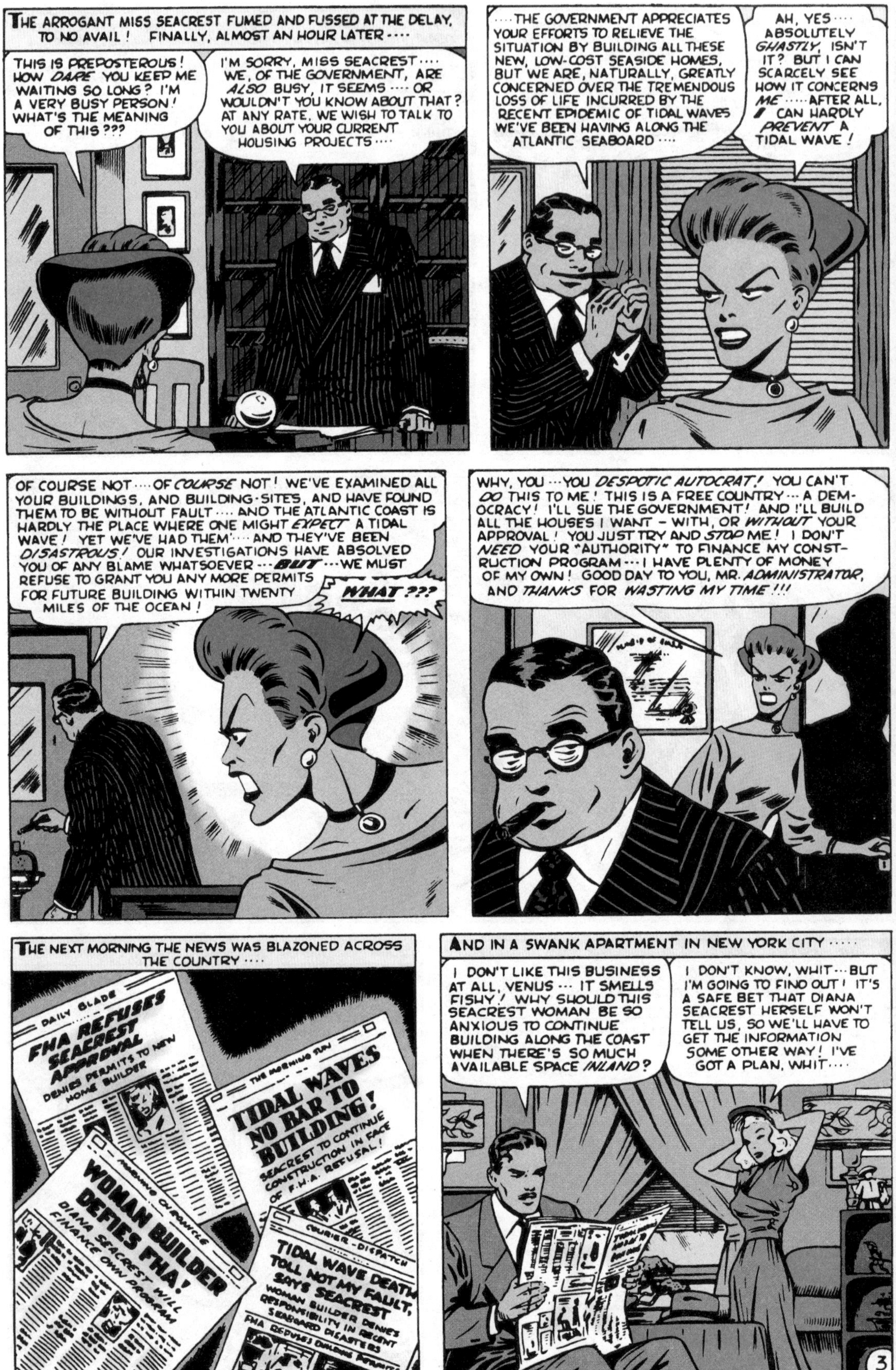
THE ARROGANT MISS SEACREST FUMED AND FUSSED AT THE DELAY, TO NO AVAIL! FINALLY, ALMOST AN HOUR LATER....
THIS IS PREPOSTEROUS! HOW DARE YOU KEEP ME WAITING SO LONG? I'M A VERY BUSY PERSON! WHAT'S THE MEANING OF THIS???
I'M SORRY, MISS SEACREST.... WE, OF THE GOVERNMENT, ARE ALSO BUSY, IT SEEMS.... OR WOULDN'T YOU KNOW ABOUT THAT? AT ANY RATE, WE WISH TO TALK TO YOU ABOUT YOUR CURRENT HOUSING PROJECTS....
....THE GOVERNMENT APPRECIATES YOUR EFFORTS TO RELIEVE THE SITUATION BY BUILDING ALL THESE NEW, LOW-COST SEASIDE HOMES, BUT WE ARE, NATURALLY, GREATLY CONCERNED OVER THE TREMENDOUS LOSS OF LIFE INCURRED BY THE RECENT EPIDEMIC OF TIDAL WAVES WE'VE BEEN HAVING ALONG THE ATLANTIC SEABOARD....
AH, YES.... ABSOLUTELY GHASTLY, ISN'T IT? BUT I CAN SCARCELY SEE HOW IT CONCERNS ME.... AFTER ALL, I CAN HARDLY PREVENT A TIDAL WAVE!
OF COURSE NOT.... OF COURSE NOT! WE'VE EXAMINED ALL YOUR BUILDINGS, AND BUILDING-SITES, AND HAVE FOUND THEM TO BE WITHOUT FAULT.... AND THE ATLANTIC COAST IS HARDLY THE PLACE WHERE ONE MIGHT EXPECT A TIDAL WAVE! YET WE'VE HAD THEM.... AND THEY'VE BEEN DISASTROUS! OUR INVESTIGATIONS HAVE ABSOLVED YOU OF ANY BLAME WHATSOEVER... BUT... WE MUST REFUSE TO GRANT YOU ANY MORE PERMITS FOR FUTURE BUILDING WITHIN TWENTY MILES OF THE OCEAN!
WHAT???
WHY, YOU... YOU DESPOTIC AUTOCRAT! YOU CAN'T DO THIS TO ME! THIS IS A FREE COUNTRY... A DEMOCRACY! I'LL SUE THE GOVERNMENT! AND I'LL BUILD ALL THE HOUSES I WANT - WITH, OR WITHOUT YOUR APPROVAL! YOU JUST TRY AND STOP ME! I DON'T NEED YOUR "AUTHORITY" TO FINANCE MY CONSTRUCTION PROGRAM... I HAVE PLENTY OF MONEY OF MY OWN! GOOD DAY TO YOU, MR. ADMINISTRATOR, AND THANKS FOR WASTING MY TIME!!!
THE NEXT MORNING THE NEWS WAS BLAZONED ACROSS THE COUNTRY....
DAILY BLADE
FHA REFUSES SEACREST APPROVAL
DENIES PERMITS TO NEW HOME BUILDER
THE MORNING SUN
TIDAL WAVES NO BAR TO BUILDING!
SEACREST TO CONTINUE CONSTRUCTION IN FACE OF F.H.A. REFUSAL!
MORNING CHRONICLE
WOMAN BUILDER DEFIES FHA!
DIANA SEACREST WILL FINANCE OWN PROGRAM
COURIER-DISPATCH
TIDAL WAVE DEATH TOLL NOT MY FAULT, SAYS SEACREST
WOMAN BUILDER DENIES RESPONSIBILITY IN RECENT SEABOARD DISASTERS
AND IN A SWANK APARTMENT IN NEW YORK CITY....
I DON'T LIKE THIS BUSINESS AT ALL, VENUS... IT SMELLS FISHY! WHY SHOULD THIS SEACREST WOMAN BE SO ANXIOUS TO CONTINUE BUILDING ALONG THE COAST WHEN THERE'S SO MUCH AVAILABLE SPACE INLAND?
I DON'T KNOW, WHIT... BUT I'M GOING TO FIND OUT! IT'S A SAFE BET THAT DIANA SEACREST HERSELF WON'T TELL US, SO WE'LL HAVE TO GET THE INFORMATION SOME OTHER WAY! I'VE GOT A PLAN, WHIT....

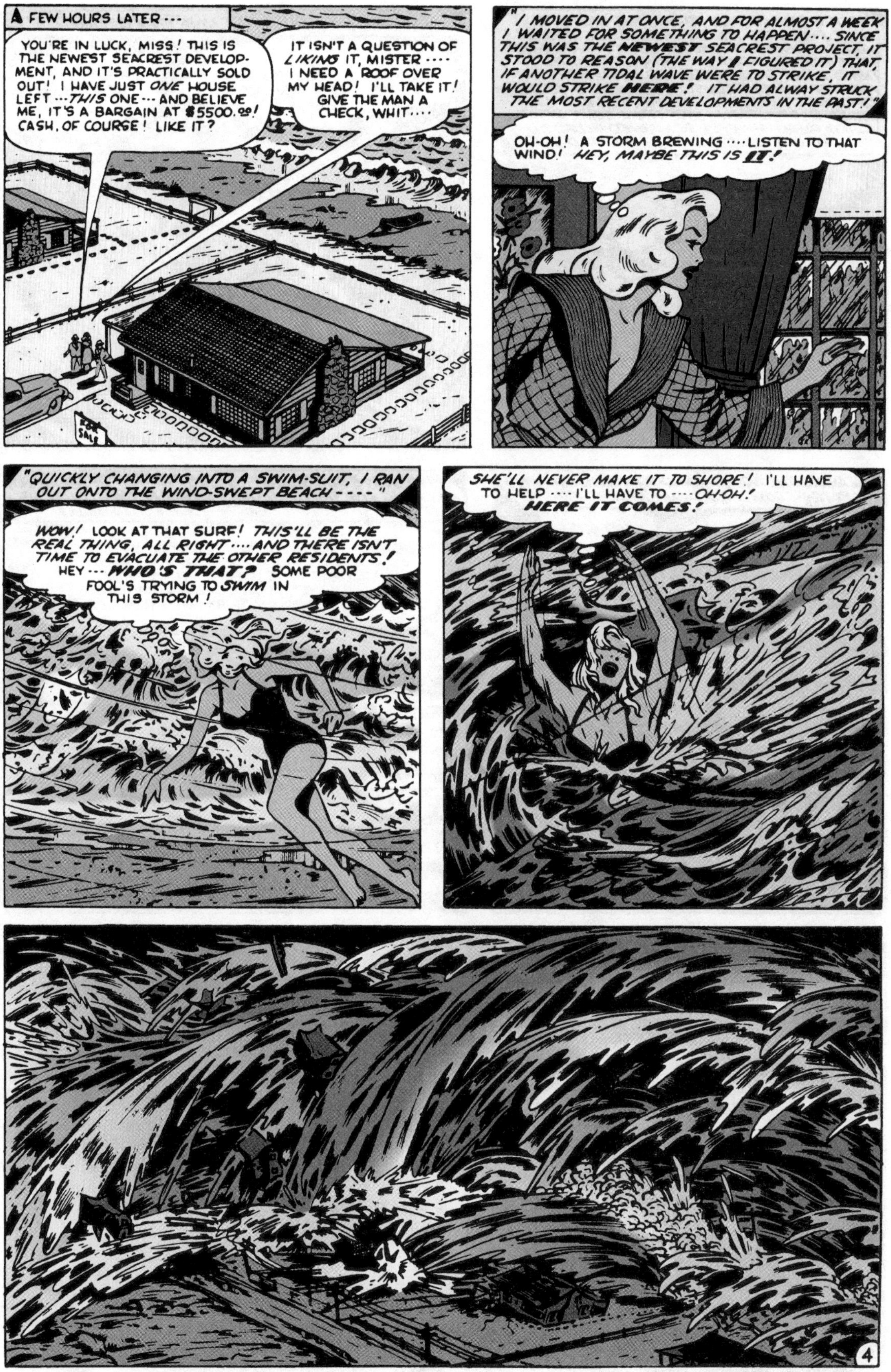
A FEW HOURS LATER ---
YOU'RE IN LUCK, MISS! THIS IS THE NEWEST SEACREST DEVELOPMENT, AND IT'S PRACTICALLY SOLD OUT! I HAVE JUST ONE HOUSE LEFT ---THIS ONE--- AND BELIEVE ME, IT'S A BARGAIN AT $5500.00! CASH, OF COURSE! LIKE IT?
IT ISN'T A QUESTION OF LIKING IT, MISTER ···· I NEED A ROOF OVER MY HEAD! I'LL TAKE IT! GIVE THE MAN A CHECK, WHIT····
FOR SALE
"I MOVED IN AT ONCE, AND FOR ALMOST A WEEK I WAITED FOR SOMETHING TO HAPPEN···· SINCE THIS WAS THE NEWEST SEACREST PROJECT, IT STOOD TO REASON (THE WAY I FIGURED IT) THAT, IF ANOTHER TIDAL WAVE WERE TO STRIKE, IT WOULD STRIKE HERE! IT HAD ALWAY STRUCK THE MOST RECENT DEVELOPMENTS IN THE PAST!"
OH-OH! A STORM BREWING ···· LISTEN TO THAT WIND! HEY, MAYBE THIS IS IT!
"QUICKLY CHANGING INTO A SWIM-SUIT, I RAN OUT ONTO THE WIND-SWEPT BEACH----"
WOW! LOOK AT THAT SURF! THIS'LL BE THE REAL THING, ALL RIGHT···· AND THERE ISN'T TIME TO EVACUATE THE OTHER RESIDENTS! HEY--- WHO'S THAT? SOME POOR FOOL'S TRYING TO SWIM IN THIS STORM!
SHE'LL NEVER MAKE IT TO SHORE! I'LL HAVE TO HELP ···· I'LL HAVE TO ···· OH-OH! HERE IT COMES!

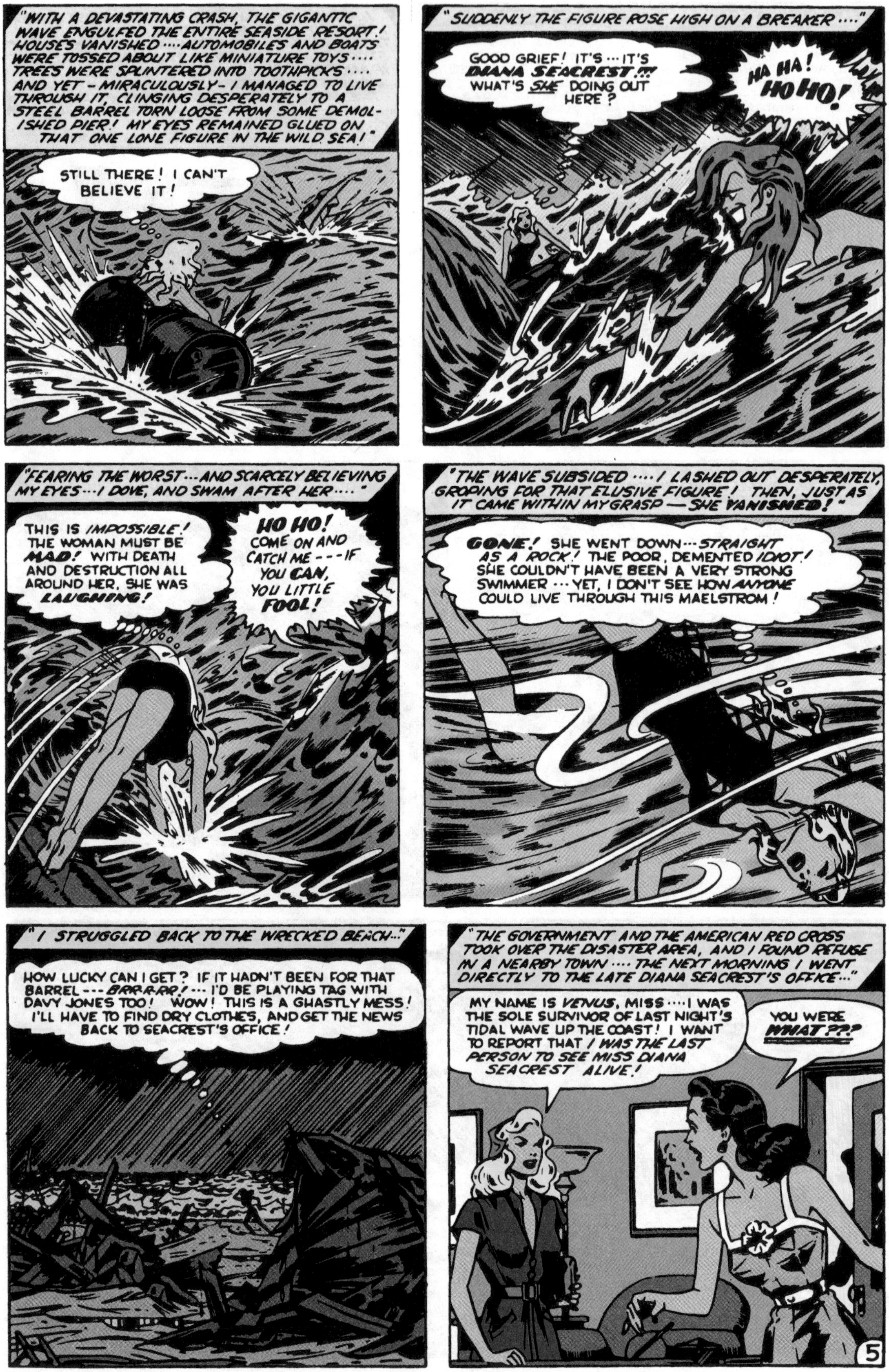
"WITH A DEVASTATING CRASH, THE GIGANTIC WAVE ENGULFED THE ENTIRE SEASIDE RESORT! HOUSES VANISHED .... AUTOMOBILES AND BOATS WERE TOSSED ABOUT LIKE MINIATURE TOYS .... TREES WERE SPLINTERED INTO TOOTHPICKS .... AND YET - MIRACULOUSLY - I MANAGED TO LIVE THROUGH IT, CLINGING DESPERATELY TO A STEEL BARREL TORN LOOSE FROM SOME DEMOLISHED PIER! MY EYES REMAINED GLUED ON THAT ONE LONE FIGURE IN THE WILD SEA!"
STILL THERE! I CAN'T BELIEVE IT!
"SUDDENLY THE FIGURE ROSE HIGH ON A BREAKER ...."
GOOD GRIEF! IT'S ... IT'S DIANA SEACREST!?! WHAT'S SHE DOING OUT HERE?
HA HA! HO HO!
"FEARING THE WORST ... AND SCARCELY BELIEVING MY EYES ... I DOVE, AND SWAM AFTER HER ...."
THIS IS IMPOSSIBLE! THE WOMAN MUST BE MAD! WITH DEATH AND DESTRUCTION ALL AROUND HER, SHE WAS LAUGHING!
HO HO! COME ON AND CATCH ME --- IF YOU CAN, YOU LITTLE FOOL!
"THE WAVE SUBSIDED .... I LASHED OUT DESPERATELY, GROPING FOR THAT ELUSIVE FIGURE! THEN, JUST AS IT CAME WITHIN MY GRASP — SHE VANISHED!"
GONE! SHE WENT DOWN ... STRAIGHT AS A ROCK! THE POOR, DEMENTED IDIOT! SHE COULDN'T HAVE BEEN A VERY STRONG SWIMMER ... YET, I DON'T SEE HOW ANYONE COULD LIVE THROUGH THIS MAELSTROM!
"I STRUGGLED BACK TO THE WRECKED BEACH..."
HOW LUCKY CAN I GET? IF IT HADN'T BEEN FOR THAT BARREL --- BRRRRR! ... I'D BE PLAYING TAG WITH DAVY JONES TOO! WOW! THIS IS A GHASTLY MESS! I'LL HAVE TO FIND DRY CLOTHES, AND GET THE NEWS BACK TO SEACREST'S OFFICE!
"THE GOVERNMENT AND THE AMERICAN RED CROSS TOOK OVER THE DISASTER AREA, AND I FOUND REFUGE IN A NEARBY TOWN .... THE NEXT MORNING I WENT DIRECTLY TO THE LATE DIANA SEACREST'S OFFICE..."
MY NAME IS VENUS, MISS .... I WAS THE SOLE SURVIVOR OF LAST NIGHT'S TIDAL WAVE UP THE COAST! I WANT TO REPORT THAT I WAS THE LAST PERSON TO SEE MISS DIANA SEACREST ALIVE!
YOU WERE WHAT???
5

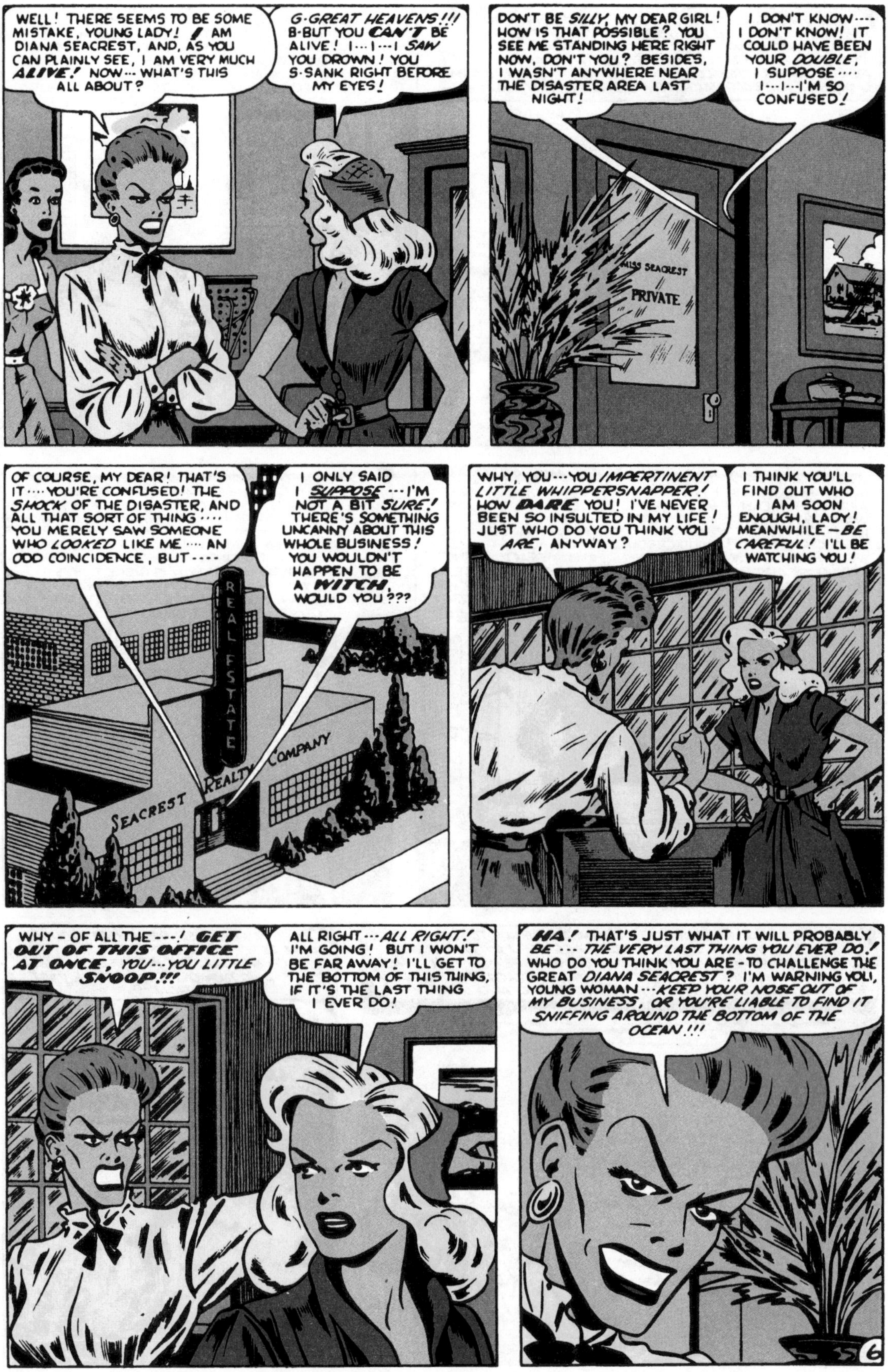
WELL! THERE SEEMS TO BE SOME MISTAKE, YOUNG LADY! I AM DIANA SEACREST, AND, AS YOU CAN PLAINLY SEE, I AM VERY MUCH ALIVE! NOW... WHAT'S THIS ALL ABOUT?
G-GREAT HEAVENS!!! B-BUT YOU CAN'T BE ALIVE! I...I...I SAW YOU DROWN! YOU S-SANK RIGHT BEFORE MY EYES!
DON'T BE SILLY, MY DEAR GIRL! HOW IS THAT POSSIBLE? YOU SEE ME STANDING HERE RIGHT NOW, DON'T YOU? BESIDES, I WASN'T ANYWHERE NEAR THE DISASTER AREA LAST NIGHT!
I DON'T KNOW.... I DON'T KNOW! IT COULD HAVE BEEN YOUR DOUBLE, I SUPPOSE.... I...I...I'M SO CONFUSED!
MISS SEACREST
PRIVATE
OF COURSE, MY DEAR! THAT'S IT....YOU'RE CONFUSED! THE SHOCK OF THE DISASTER, AND ALL THAT SORT OF THING.... YOU MERELY SAW SOMEONE WHO LOOKED LIKE ME.... AN ODD COINCIDENCE, BUT....
I ONLY SAID I SUPPOSE...I'M NOT A BIT SURE! THERE'S SOMETHING UNCANNY ABOUT THIS WHOLE BUSINESS! YOU WOULDN'T HAPPEN TO BE A WITCH, WOULD YOU???
REAL ESTATE
SEACREST REALTY COMPANY
WHY, YOU...YOU IMPERTINENT LITTLE WHIPPERSNAPPER! HOW DARE YOU! I'VE NEVER BEEN SO INSULTED IN MY LIFE! JUST WHO DO YOU THINK YOU ARE, ANYWAY?
I THINK YOU'LL FIND OUT WHO I AM SOON ENOUGH, LADY! MEANWHILE—BE CAREFUL! I'LL BE WATCHING YOU!
WHY—OF ALL THE...! GET OUT OF THIS OFFICE AT ONCE, YOU...YOU LITTLE SNOOP!!!
ALL RIGHT...ALL RIGHT! I'M GOING! BUT I WON'T BE FAR AWAY! I'LL GET TO THE BOTTOM OF THIS THING, IF IT'S THE LAST THING I EVER DO!
HA! THAT'S JUST WHAT IT WILL PROBABLY BE...THE VERY LAST THING YOU EVER DO! WHO DO YOU THINK YOU ARE—TO CHALLENGE THE GREAT DIANA SEACREST? I'M WARNING YOU, YOUNG WOMAN...KEEP YOUR NOSE OUT OF MY BUSINESS, OR YOU'RE LIABLE TO FIND IT SNIFFING AROUND THE BOTTOM OF THE OCEAN!!!
6

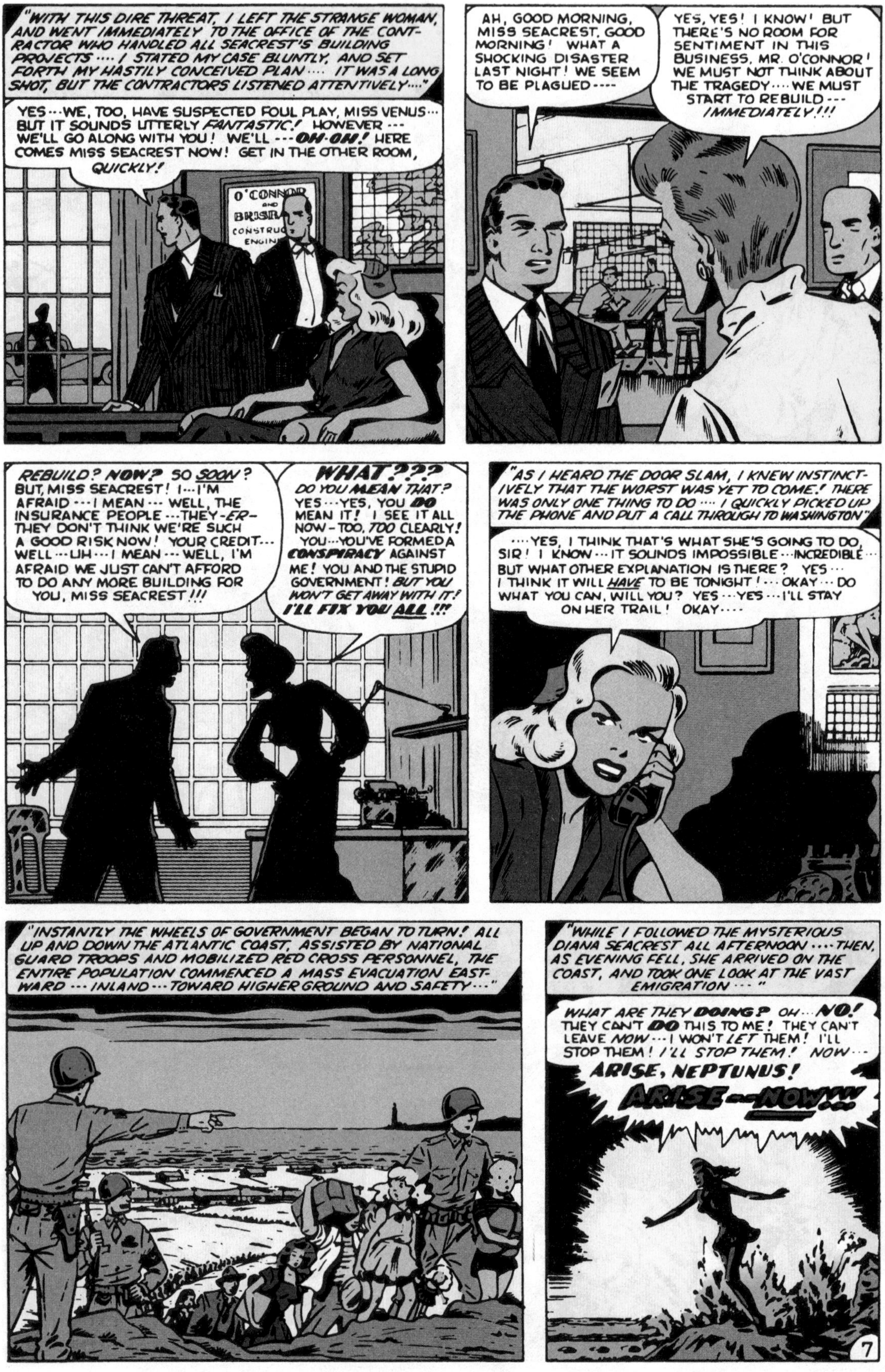
"WITH THIS DIRE THREAT, I LEFT THE STRANGE WOMAN, AND WENT IMMEDIATELY TO THE OFFICE OF THE CONTRACTOR WHO HANDLED ALL SEACREST'S BUILDING PROJECTS .... I STATED MY CASE BLUNTLY, AND SET FORTH MY HASTILY CONCEIVED PLAN .... IT WAS A LONG SHOT, BUT THE CONTRACTORS LISTENED ATTENTIVELY...."
YES --- WE, TOO, HAVE SUSPECTED FOUL PLAY, MISS VENUS --- BUT IT SOUNDS UTTERLY FANTASTIC! HOWEVER --- WE'LL GO ALONG WITH YOU! WE'LL --- OH-OH! HERE COMES MISS SEACREST NOW! GET IN THE OTHER ROOM, QUICKLY!
AH, GOOD MORNING, MISS SEACREST, GOOD MORNING! WHAT A SHOCKING DISASTER LAST NIGHT! WE SEEM TO BE PLAGUED ----
YES, YES! I KNOW! BUT THERE'S NO ROOM FOR SENTIMENT IN THIS BUSINESS, MR. O'CONNOR! WE MUST NOT THINK ABOUT THE TRAGEDY .... WE MUST START TO REBUILD --- IMMEDIATELY!!!
REBUILD? NOW? SO SOON? BUT, MISS SEACREST! I --- I'M AFRAID --- I MEAN --- WELL, THE INSURANCE PEOPLE --- THEY - ER - THEY DON'T THINK WE'RE SUCH A GOOD RISK NOW! YOUR CREDIT --- WELL --- UH --- I MEAN --- WELL, I'M AFRAID WE JUST CAN'T AFFORD TO DO ANY MORE BUILDING FOR YOU, MISS SEACREST!!!
WHAT??? DO YOU MEAN THAT? YES --- YES, YOU DO MEAN IT! I SEE IT ALL NOW - TOO, TOO CLEARLY! YOU --- YOU'VE FORMED A CONSPIRACY AGAINST ME! YOU AND THE STUPID GOVERNMENT! BUT YOU WON'T GET AWAY WITH IT! I'LL FIX YOU ALL!!!
"AS I HEARD THE DOOR SLAM, I KNEW INSTINCTIVELY THAT THE WORST WAS YET TO COME! THERE WAS ONLY ONE THING TO DO .... I QUICKLY PICKED UP THE PHONE AND PUT A CALL THROUGH TO WASHINGTON"
.... YES, I THINK THAT'S WHAT SHE'S GOING TO DO, SIR! I KNOW --- IT SOUNDS IMPOSSIBLE --- INCREDIBLE --- BUT WHAT OTHER EXPLANATION IS THERE? YES --- I THINK IT WILL HAVE TO BE TONIGHT! --- OKAY --- DO WHAT YOU CAN, WILL YOU? YES --- YES --- I'LL STAY ON HER TRAIL! OKAY ----
"INSTANTLY THE WHEELS OF GOVERNMENT BEGAN TO TURN! ALL UP AND DOWN THE ATLANTIC COAST, ASSISTED BY NATIONAL GUARD TROOPS AND MOBILIZED RED CROSS PERSONNEL, THE ENTIRE POPULATION COMMENCED A MASS EVACUATION EASTWARD --- INLAND --- TOWARD HIGHER GROUND AND SAFETY ---"
"WHILE I FOLLOWED THE MYSTERIOUS DIANA SEACREST ALL AFTERNOON .... THEN, AS EVENING FELL, SHE ARRIVED ON THE COAST, AND TOOK ONE LOOK AT THE VAST EMIGRATION --- "
WHAT ARE THEY DOING? OH --- NO! THEY CAN'T DO THIS TO ME! THEY CAN'T LEAVE NOW --- I WON'T LET THEM! I'LL STOP THEM! I'LL STOP THEM! NOW --- ARISE, NEPTUNUS!
ARISE -- NOW!!!
7

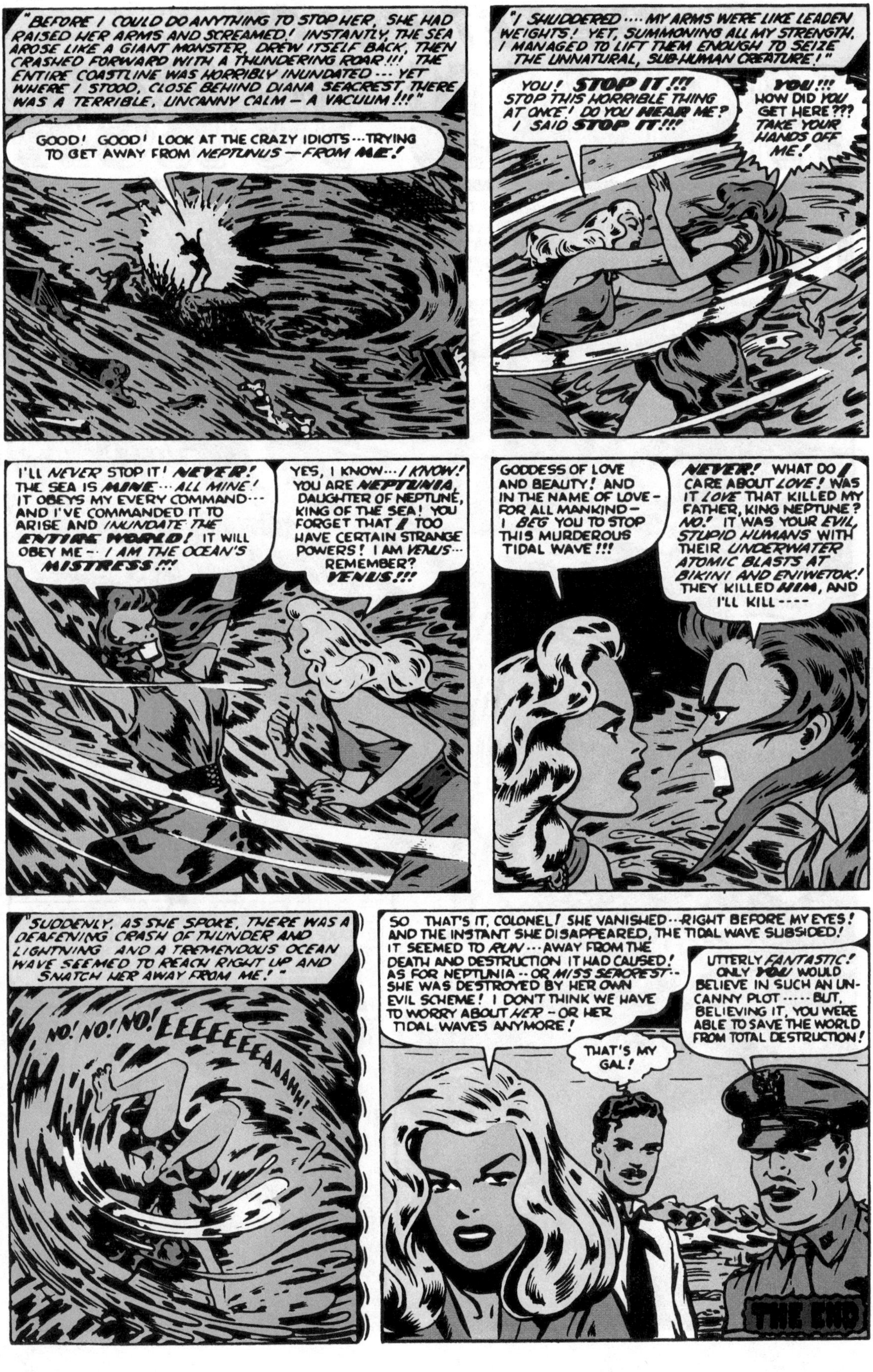
"BEFORE I COULD DO ANYTHING TO STOP HER, SHE HAD RAISED HER ARMS AND SCREAMED! INSTANTLY, THE SEA AROSE LIKE A GIANT MONSTER, DREW ITSELF BACK, THEN CRASHED FORWARD WITH A THUNDERING ROAR!!! THE ENTIRE COASTLINE WAS HORRIBLY INUNDATED --- YET WHERE I STOOD, CLOSE BEHIND DIANA SEACREST THERE WAS A TERRIBLE, UNCANNY CALM — A VACUUM!!!"
GOOD! GOOD! LOOK AT THE CRAZY IDIOTS --- TRYING TO GET AWAY FROM NEPTUNUS — FROM ME!
"I SHUDDERED .... MY ARMS WERE LIKE LEADEN WEIGHTS! YET, SUMMONING ALL MY STRENGTH, I MANAGED TO LIFT THEM ENOUGH TO SEIZE THE UNNATURAL, SUB-HUMAN CREATURE!"
YOU! STOP IT!!! STOP THIS HORRIBLE THING AT ONCE! DO YOU HEAR ME? I SAID STOP IT!!!
YOU!!! HOW DID YOU GET HERE??? TAKE YOUR HANDS OFF ME!
I'LL NEVER STOP IT! NEVER! THE SEA IS MINE --- ALL MINE! IT OBEYS MY EVERY COMMAND --- AND I'VE COMMANDED IT TO ARISE AND INUNDATE THE ENTIRE WORLD! IT WILL OBEY ME -- I AM THE OCEAN'S MISTRESS!!!
YES, I KNOW --- I KNOW! YOU ARE NEPTUNIA, DAUGHTER OF NEPTUNE, KING OF THE SEA! YOU FORGET THAT I TOO HAVE CERTAIN STRANGE POWERS! I AM VENUS --- REMEMBER? VENUS!!!
GODDESS OF LOVE AND BEAUTY! AND IN THE NAME OF LOVE — FOR ALL MANKIND — I BEG YOU TO STOP THIS MURDEROUS TIDAL WAVE!!!
NEVER! WHAT DO I CARE ABOUT LOVE! WAS IT LOVE THAT KILLED MY FATHER, KING NEPTUNE? NO! IT WAS YOUR EVIL, STUPID HUMANS WITH THEIR UNDERWATER ATOMIC BLASTS AT BIKINI AND ENIWETOK! THEY KILLED HIM, AND I'LL KILL ----
"SUDDENLY, AS SHE SPOKE, THERE WAS A DEAFENING CRASH OF THUNDER AND LIGHTNING AND A TREMENDOUS OCEAN WAVE SEEMED TO REACH RIGHT UP AND SNATCH HER AWAY FROM ME!"
NO! NO! NO! EEEEEEEAAAAHH!
SO THAT'S IT, COLONEL! SHE VANISHED --- RIGHT BEFORE MY EYES! AND THE INSTANT SHE DISAPPEARED, THE TIDAL WAVE SUBSIDED! IT SEEMED TO RUN --- AWAY FROM THE DEATH AND DESTRUCTION IT HAD CAUSED! AS FOR NEPTUNIA -- OR MISS SEACREST -- SHE WAS DESTROYED BY HER OWN EVIL SCHEME! I DON'T THINK WE HAVE TO WORRY ABOUT HER — OR HER TIDAL WAVES ANYMORE!
THAT'S MY GAL!
UTTERLY FANTASTIC! ONLY YOU WOULD BELIEVE IN SUCH AN UNCANNY PLOT ----- BUT, BELIEVING IT, YOU WERE ABLE TO SAVE THE WORLD FROM TOTAL DESTRUCTION!
THE END

THE RETURN OF...
THE HUMAN TORCH

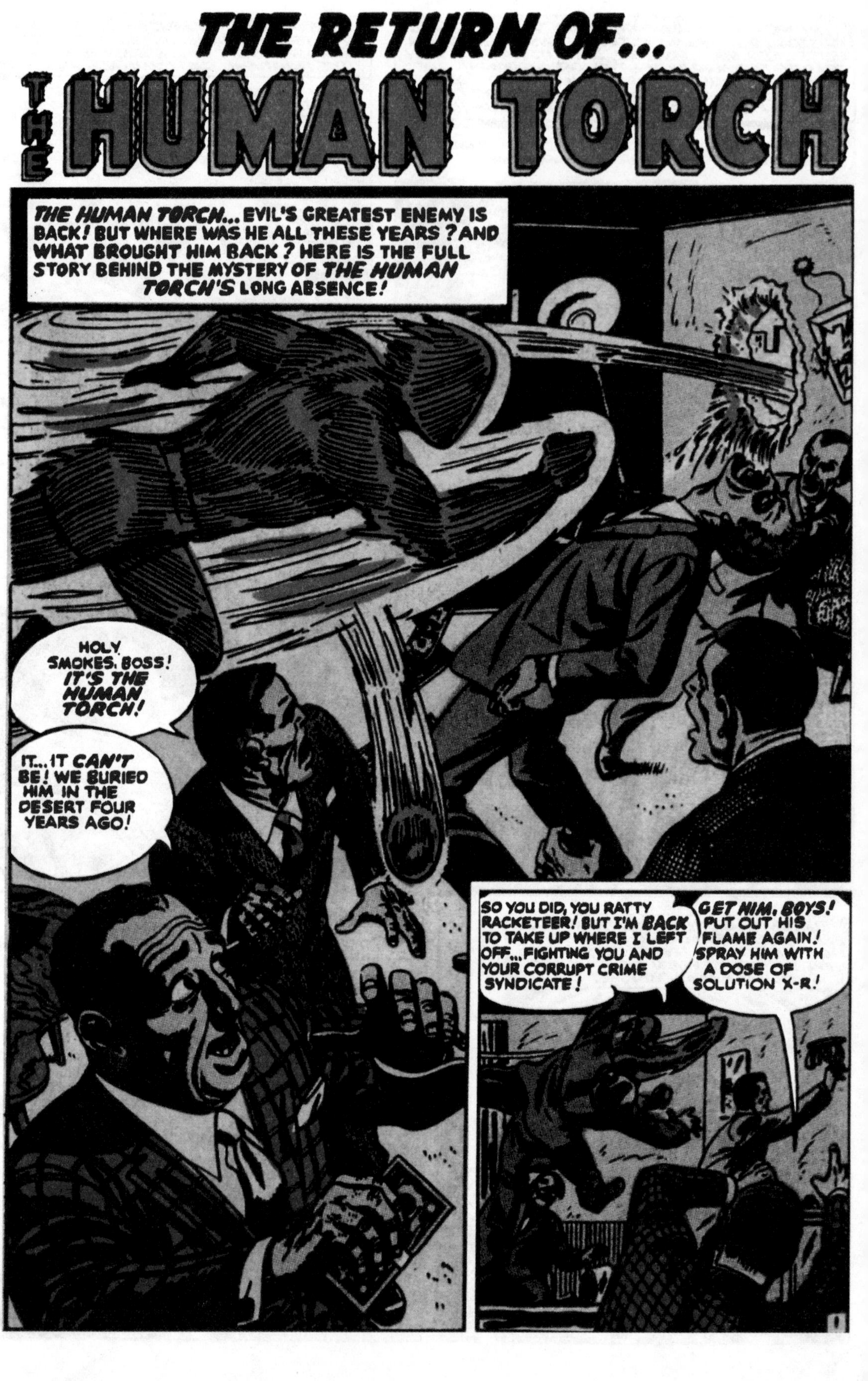
THE HUMAN TORCH... EVIL'S GREATEST ENEMY IS BACK! BUT WHERE WAS HE ALL THESE YEARS? AND WHAT BROUGHT HIM BACK? HERE IS THE FULL STORY BEHIND THE MYSTERY OF THE HUMAN TORCH'S LONG ABSENCE!
HOLY SMOKES, BOSS! IT'S THE HUMAN TORCH!
IT... IT CAN'T BE! WE BURIED HIM IN THE DESERT FOUR YEARS AGO!
SO YOU DID, YOU RATTY RACKETEER! BUT I'M BACK TO TAKE UP WHERE I LEFT OFF... FIGHTING YOU AND YOUR CORRUPT CRIME SYNDICATE!
GET HIM, BOYS! PUT OUT HIS FLAME AGAIN! SPRAY HIM WITH A DOSE OF SOLUTION X-R!

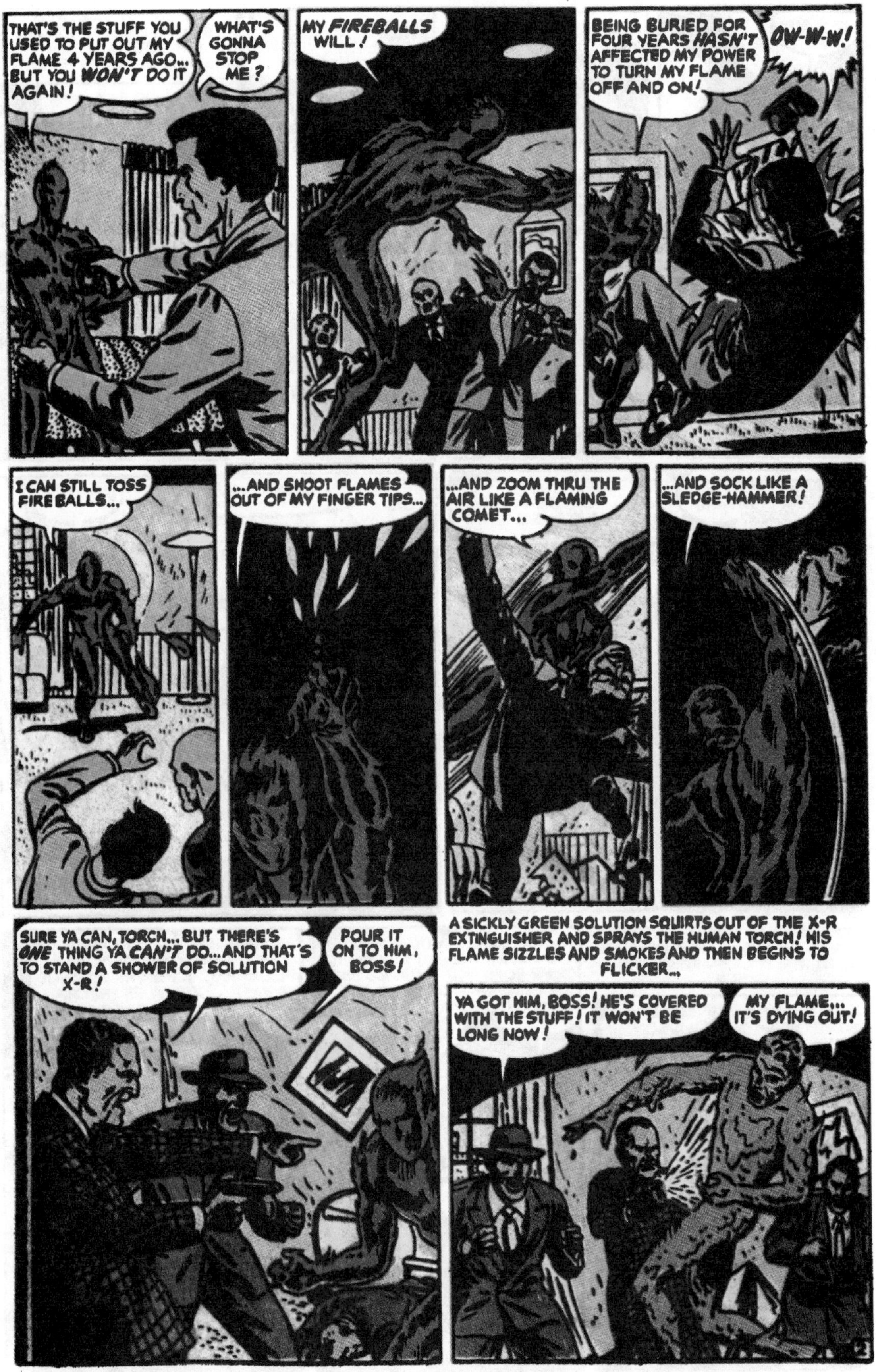
THAT'S THE STUFF YOU USED TO PUT OUT MY FLAME 4 YEARS AGO... BUT YOU WON'T DO IT AGAIN!
WHAT'S GONNA STOP ME?
MY FIREBALLS WILL!
BEING BURIED FOR FOUR YEARS HASN'T AFFECTED MY POWER TO TURN MY FLAME OFF AND ON!
OW-W-W!
I CAN STILL TOSS FIRE BALLS...
...AND SHOOT FLAMES OUT OF MY FINGER TIPS...
...AND ZOOM THRU THE AIR LIKE A FLAMING COMET...
...AND SOCK LIKE A SLEDGE-HAMMER!
SURE YA CAN, TORCH... BUT THERE'S ONE THING YA CAN'T DO...AND THAT'S TO STAND A SHOWER OF SOLUTION X-R!
POUR IT ON TO HIM, BOSS!
A SICKLY GREEN SOLUTION SQUIRTS OUT OF THE X-R EXTINGUISHER AND SPRAYS THE HUMAN TORCH! HIS FLAME SIZZLES AND SMOKES AND THEN BEGINS TO FLICKER...
YA GOT HIM, BOSS! HE'S COVERED WITH THE STUFF! IT WON'T BE LONG NOW!
MY FLAME... IT'S DYING OUT!

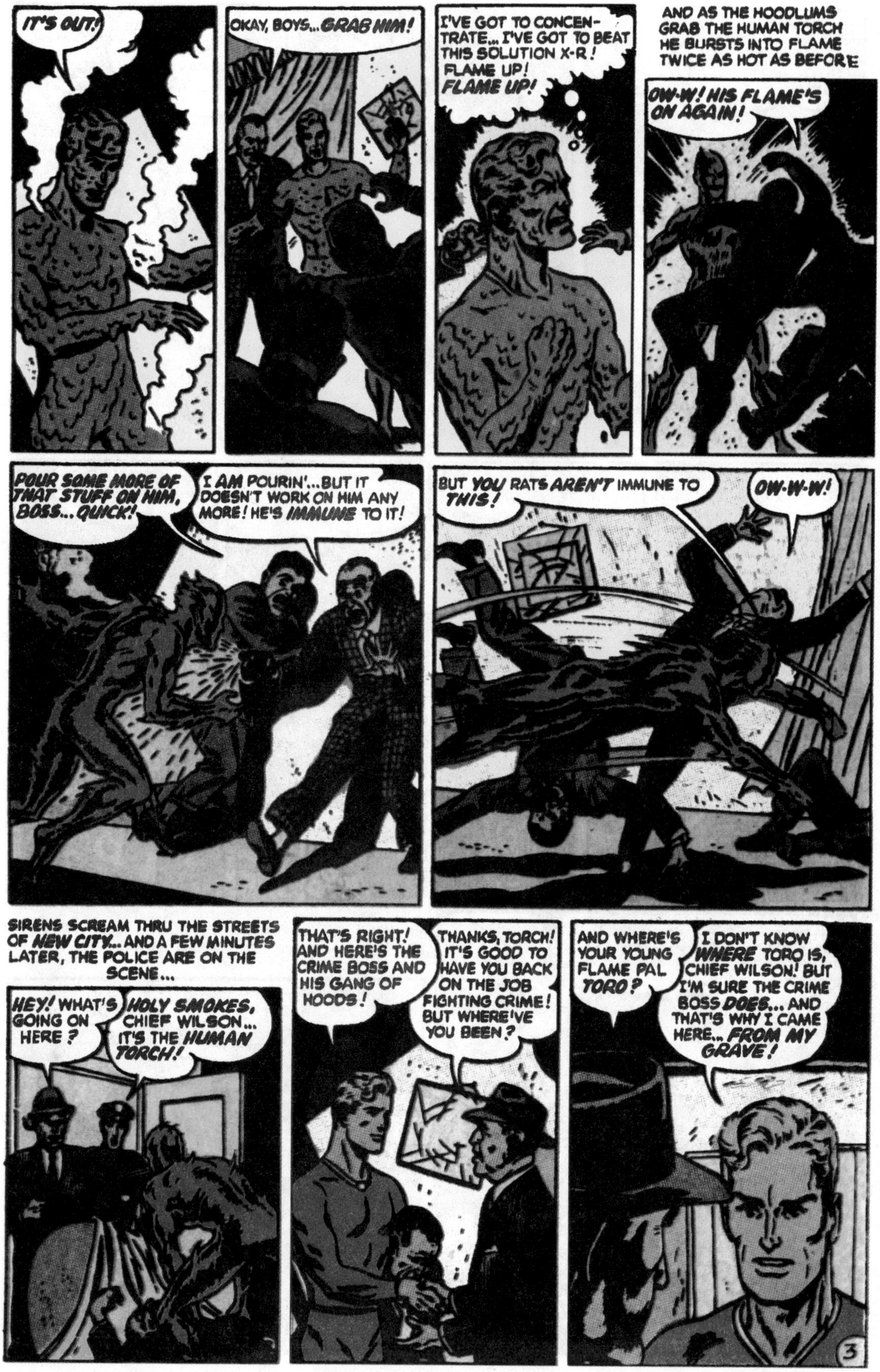
IT'S OUT!
OKAY, BOYS... GRAB HIM!
I'VE GOT TO CONCENTRATE... I'VE GOT TO BEAT THIS SOLUTION X-R! FLAME UP! FLAME UP!
AND AS THE HOODLUMS GRAB THE HUMAN TORCH HE BURSTS INTO FLAME TWICE AS HOT AS BEFORE
OW-W! HIS FLAME'S ON AGAIN!
POUR SOME MORE OF THAT STUFF ON HIM, BOSS... QUICK!
I AM POURIN'... BUT IT DOESN'T WORK ON HIM ANY MORE! HE'S IMMUNE TO IT!
BUT YOU RATS AREN'T IMMUNE TO THIS!
OW-W-W!
SIRENS SCREAM THRU THE STREETS OF NEW CITY... AND A FEW MINUTES LATER, THE POLICE ARE ON THE SCENE...
HEY! WHAT'S GOING ON HERE?
HOLY SMOKES, CHIEF WILSON... IT'S THE HUMAN TORCH!
THAT'S RIGHT! AND HERE'S THE CRIME BOSS AND HIS GANG OF HOODS!
THANKS, TORCH! IT'S GOOD TO HAVE YOU BACK ON THE JOB FIGHTING CRIME! BUT WHERE'VE YOU BEEN?
AND WHERE'S YOUR YOUNG FLAME PAL TORO?
I DON'T KNOW WHERE TORO IS, CHIEF WILSON! BUT I'M SURE THE CRIME BOSS DOES... AND THAT'S WHY I CAME HERE... FROM MY GRAVE!
3

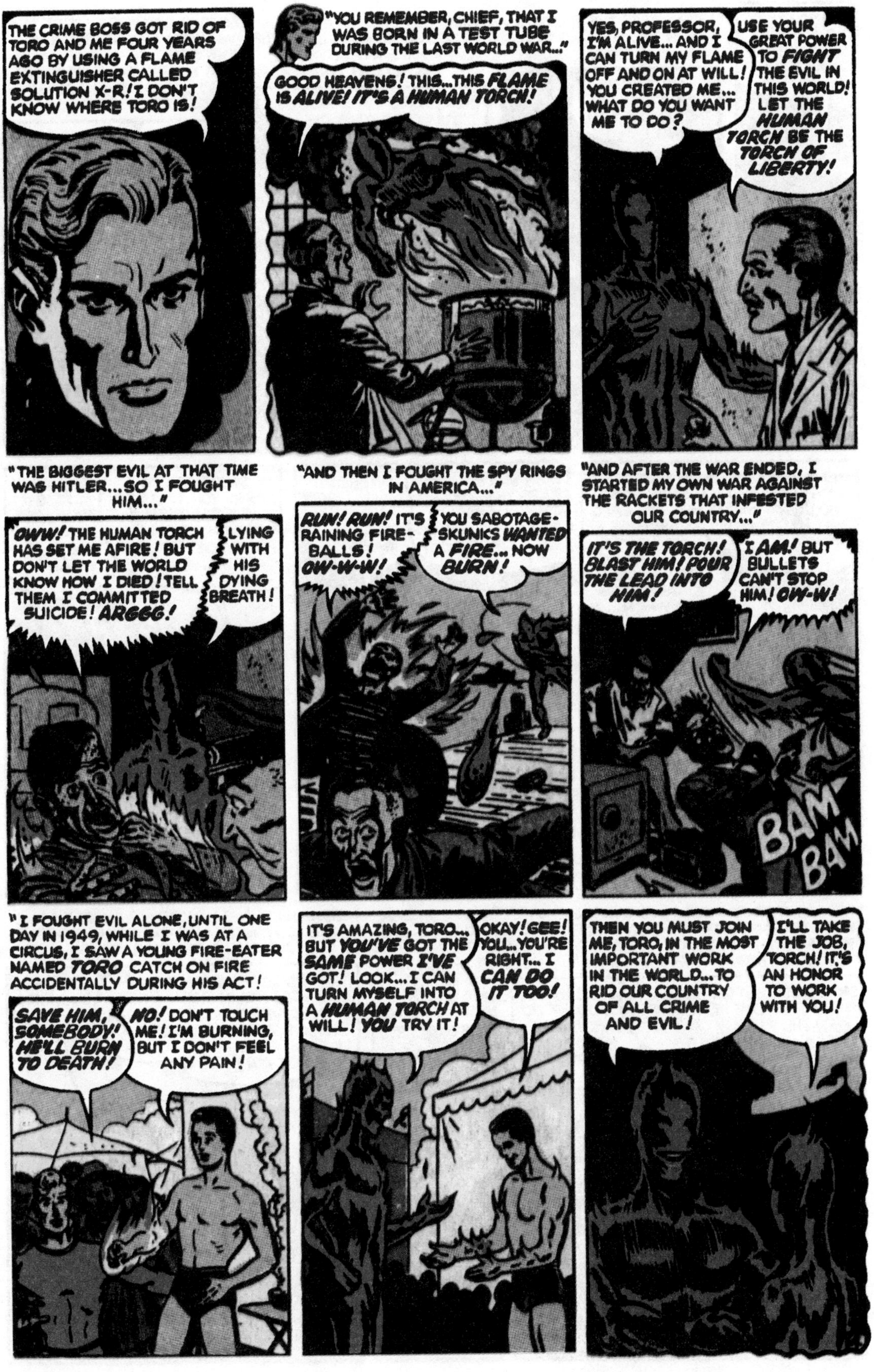
THE CRIME BOSS GOT RID OF TORO AND ME FOUR YEARS AGO BY USING A FLAME EXTINGUISHER CALLED SOLUTION X-R! I DON'T KNOW WHERE TORO IS!
"YOU REMEMBER, CHIEF, THAT I WAS BORN IN A TEST TUBE DURING THE LAST WORLD WAR..."
GOOD HEAVENS! THIS...THIS FLAME IS ALIVE! IT'S A HUMAN TORCH!
YES, PROFESSOR, I'M ALIVE... AND I CAN TURN MY FLAME OFF AND ON AT WILL! YOU CREATED ME... WHAT DO YOU WANT ME TO DO?
USE YOUR GREAT POWER TO FIGHT THE EVIL IN THIS WORLD! LET THE HUMAN TORCH BE THE TORCH OF LIBERTY!
"THE BIGGEST EVIL AT THAT TIME WAS HITLER...SO I FOUGHT HIM..."
OWW! THE HUMAN TORCH HAS SET ME AFIRE! BUT DON'T LET THE WORLD KNOW HOW I DIED! TELL THEM I COMMITTED SUICIDE! ARGGG!
LYING WITH HIS DYING BREATH!
"AND THEN I FOUGHT THE SPY RINGS IN AMERICA..."
RUN! RUN! IT'S RAINING FIRE-BALLS! OW-W-W!
YOU SABOTAGE-SKUNKS WANTED A FIRE... NOW BURN!
"AND AFTER THE WAR ENDED, I STARTED MY OWN WAR AGAINST THE RACKETS THAT INFESTED OUR COUNTRY..."
IT'S THE TORCH! BLAST HIM! POUR THE LEAD INTO HIM!
I AM! BUT BULLETS CAN'T STOP HIM! OW-W!
BAM
BAM
"I FOUGHT EVIL ALONE, UNTIL ONE DAY IN 1949, WHILE I WAS AT A CIRCUS, I SAW A YOUNG FIRE-EATER NAMED TORO CATCH ON FIRE ACCIDENTALLY DURING HIS ACT!
SAVE HIM, SOMEBODY! HE'LL BURN TO DEATH!
NO! DON'T TOUCH ME! I'M BURNING, BUT I DON'T FEEL ANY PAIN!
IT'S AMAZING, TORO... BUT YOU'VE GOT THE SAME POWER I'VE GOT! LOOK...I CAN TURN MYSELF INTO A HUMAN TORCH AT WILL! YOU TRY IT!
OKAY! GEE! YOU...YOU'RE RIGHT... I CAN DO IT TOO!
THEN YOU MUST JOIN ME, TORO, IN THE MOST IMPORTANT WORK IN THE WORLD...TO RID OUR COUNTRY OF ALL CRIME AND EVIL!
I'LL TAKE THE JOB, TORCH! IT'S AN HONOR TO WORK WITH YOU!

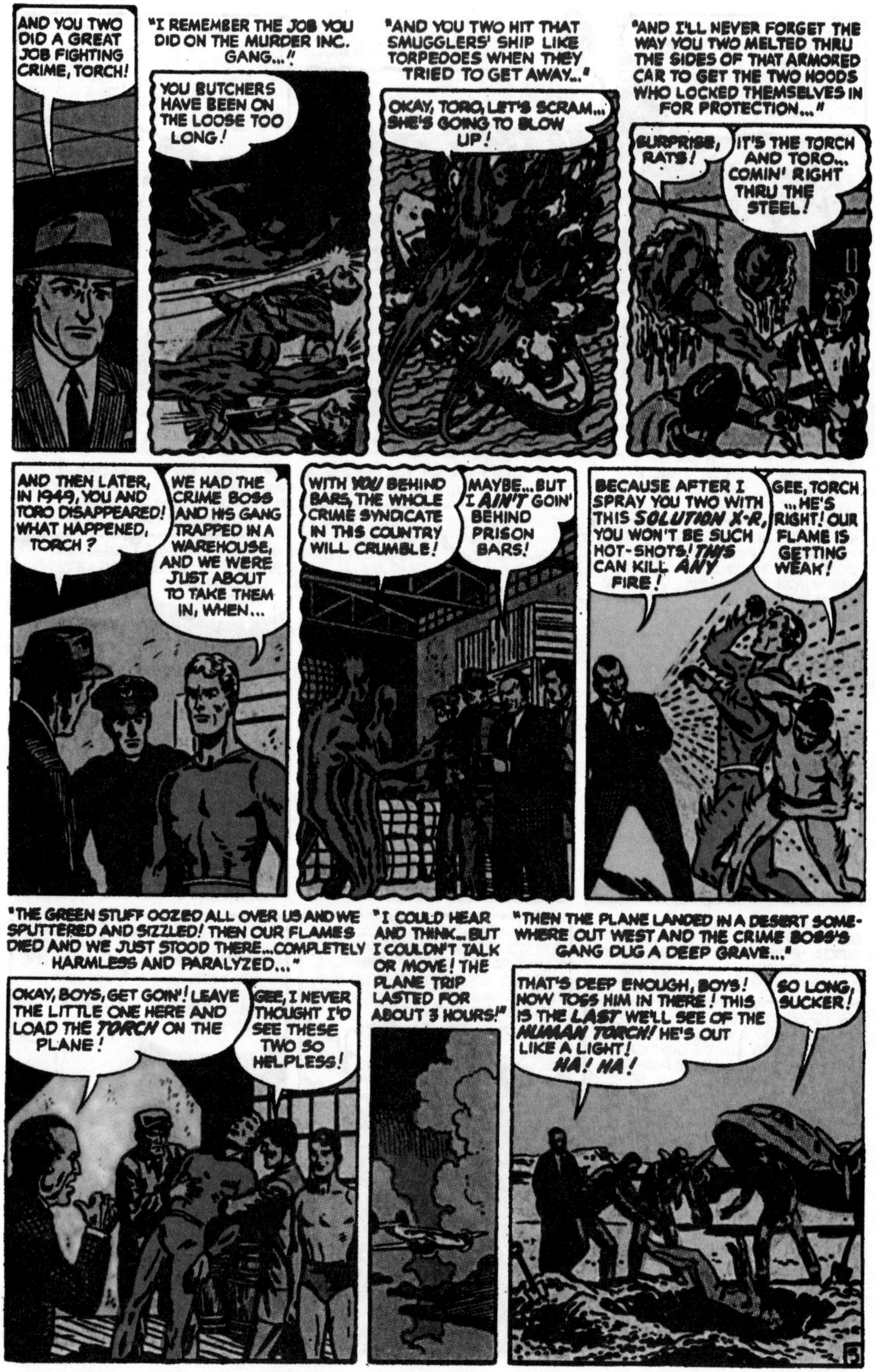
AND YOU TWO DID A GREAT JOB FIGHTING CRIME, TORCH!
"I REMEMBER THE JOB YOU DID ON THE MURDER INC. GANG...!
YOU BUTCHERS HAVE BEEN ON THE LOOSE TOO LONG!
"AND YOU TWO HIT THAT SMUGGLERS' SHIP LIKE TORPEDOES WHEN THEY TRIED TO GET AWAY..."
OKAY, TORO, LET'S SCRAM... SHE'S GOING TO BLOW UP!
"AND I'LL NEVER FORGET THE WAY YOU TWO MELTED THRU THE SIDES OF THAT ARMORED CAR TO GET THE TWO HOODS WHO LOCKED THEMSELVES IN FOR PROTECTION..."
SURPRISE, RATS!
IT'S THE TORCH AND TORO... COMIN' RIGHT THRU THE STEEL!
AND THEN LATER, IN 1949, YOU AND TORO DISAPPEARED! WHAT HAPPENED, TORCH?
WE HAD THE CRIME BOSS AND HIS GANG TRAPPED IN A WAREHOUSE, AND WE WERE JUST ABOUT TO TAKE THEM IN, WHEN...
WITH YOU BEHIND BARS, THE WHOLE CRIME SYNDICATE IN THIS COUNTRY WILL CRUMBLE!
MAYBE... BUT I AIN'T GOIN' BEHIND PRISON BARS!
BECAUSE AFTER I SPRAY YOU TWO WITH THIS SOLUTION X-R, YOU WON'T BE SUCH HOT-SHOTS! THIS CAN KILL ANY FIRE!
GEE, TORCH ...HE'S RIGHT! OUR FLAME IS GETTING WEAK!
"THE GREEN STUFF OOZED ALL OVER US AND WE SPUTTERED AND SIZZLED! THEN OUR FLAMES DIED AND WE JUST STOOD THERE...COMPLETELY HARMLESS AND PARALYZED..."
OKAY, BOYS, GET GOIN'! LEAVE THE LITTLE ONE HERE AND LOAD THE TORCH ON THE PLANE!
GEE, I NEVER THOUGHT I'D SEE THESE TWO SO HELPLESS!
"I COULD HEAR AND THINK... BUT I COULDN'T TALK OR MOVE! THE PLANE TRIP LASTED FOR ABOUT 3 HOURS!"
"THEN THE PLANE LANDED IN A DESERT SOMEWHERE OUT WEST AND THE CRIME BOSS'S GANG DUG A DEEP GRAVE..."
THAT'S DEEP ENOUGH, BOYS! NOW TOSS HIM IN THERE! THIS IS THE LAST WE'LL SEE OF THE HUMAN TORCH! HE'S OUT LIKE A LIGHT! HA! HA!
SO LONG, SUCKER!
5

"THEY BURIED ME AND WENT AWAY! I DIDN'T DIE... I JUST LAY THERE FOR A LONG TIME, SMOLDERING... "

"YEARS PASSED, AND THEN ONE DAY A TERRIFIC EXPLOSION SHOOK THE GROUND AROUND ME..."

"I FELT A PECULIAR SENSATION SWEEP THRU ME! THEN SUDDENLY I BURST INTO FLAME AGAIN!"

"I TRIED MY POWERS AND THEY WORKED... SO I BLASTED AND BURNED MY WAY OUT OF MY GRAVE!"

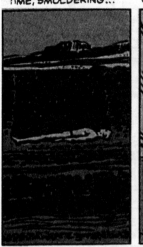

"THAT TERRIFIC BLAST GAVE ME A GREATER POWER THAN I HAD BEFORE! I COULDN'T UNDERSTAND HOW OR WHY... NOT UNTIL I LOOKED BACK AS I BLAZED THRU THE SKY AND SAW A GIANT MUSHROOM CLOUD RISING FROM THE SPOT WHERE I HAD BEEN BURIED!"

GREAT SCOTT, TORCH! THAT WAS AN ATOMIC EXPLOSION! YOU WERE BURIED IN YUCCA FLAT IN NEVADA... THE GOVERNMENT TESTING GROUNDS FOR THE ATOMIC EXPLOSIONS!

YES, CHIEF WILSON... AND NOW MY ENTIRE BODY IS RADIOACTIVATED GIVING ME A POWER MUCH GREATER THAN I POSSESSED BEFORE! EVEN THE SOLUTION X-R DOESN'T HAVE AN EFFECT ON ME NOW!

I CAME STRAIGHT TO THIS PLACE FROM MY GRAVE! I KNEW I'D FIND THE CRIME BOSS IN HIS FAVORITE HOLE!

NOW THERE'S ONLY ONE THING I'D LIKE TO KNOW... WHAT DID YOU DO WITH TORO? TALK, YOU VULTURE, OR I'LL BURN YOU TO CINDERS!

NO! NOT THAT! TURN OFF YOUR FIRE! I'LL TALK!

WE...WE GAVE TORO TO A COUNTRY BEHIND THE IRON CURTAIN IN EXCHANGE FOR SOLUTION X-R, PREPARED FOR US BY THEIR SCIENTISTS! THAT WAS THE DEAL, TORCH!

WHY, YOU DIRTY TRAITOR! YOU'RE EVEN LOWER THAN I THOUGHT!

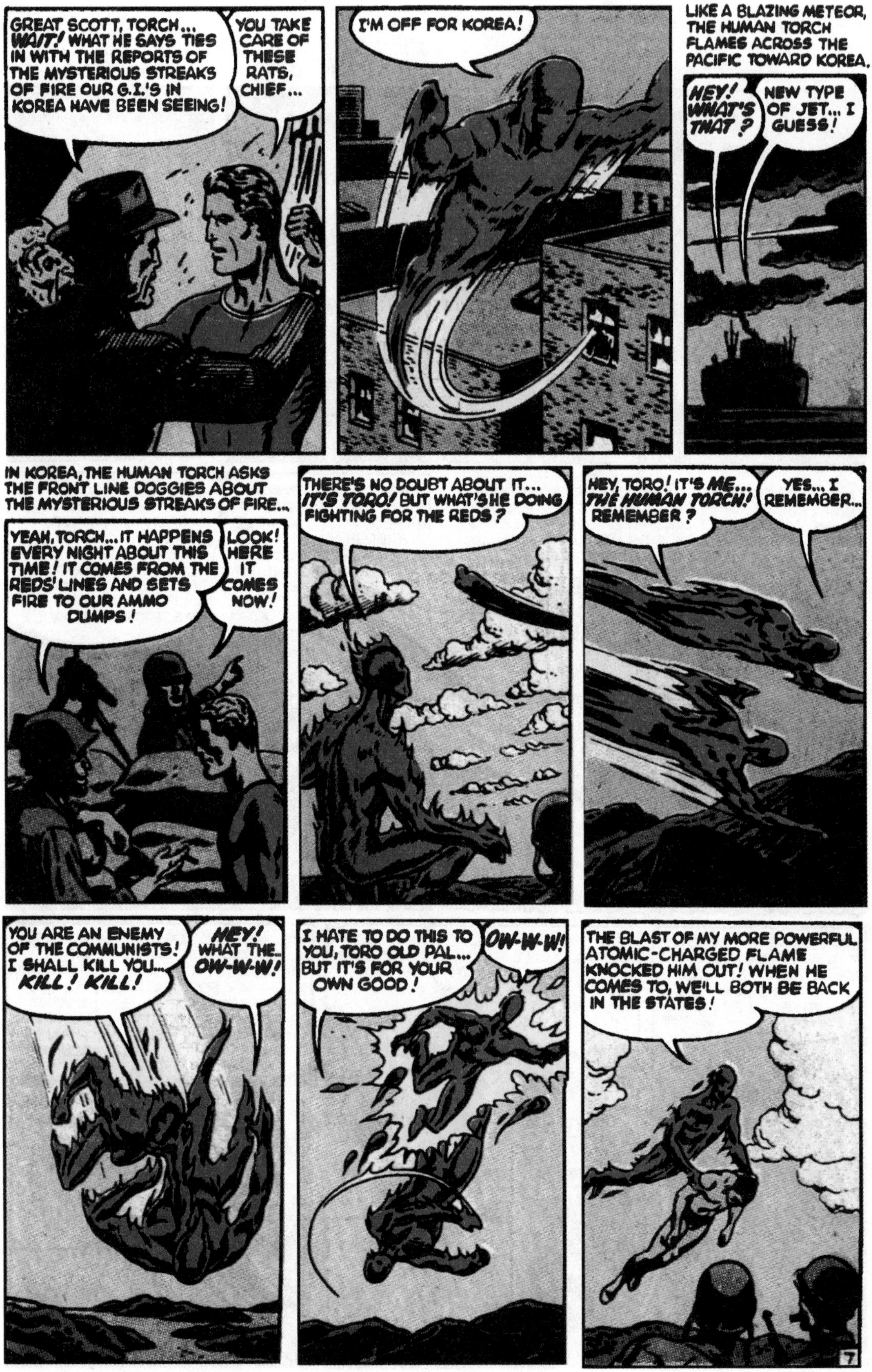
GREAT SCOTT, TORCH... WAIT! WHAT HE SAYS TIES IN WITH THE REPORTS OF THE MYSTERIOUS STREAKS OF FIRE OUR G.I.'S IN KOREA HAVE BEEN SEEING!
YOU TAKE CARE OF THESE RATS, CHIEF...
I'M OFF FOR KOREA!
LIKE A BLAZING METEOR, THE HUMAN TORCH FLAMES ACROSS THE PACIFIC TOWARD KOREA.
HEY! WHAT'S THAT?
NEW TYPE OF JET... I GUESS!
IN KOREA, THE HUMAN TORCH ASKS THE FRONT LINE DOGGIES ABOUT THE MYSTERIOUS STREAKS OF FIRE...
YEAH, TORCH... IT HAPPENS EVERY NIGHT ABOUT THIS TIME! IT COMES FROM THE REDS' LINES AND SETS FIRE TO OUR AMMO DUMPS!
LOOK! HERE IT COMES NOW!
THERE'S NO DOUBT ABOUT IT... IT'S TORO! BUT WHAT'S HE DOING FIGHTING FOR THE REDS?
HEY, TORO! IT'S ME... THE HUMAN TORCH! REMEMBER?
YES... I REMEMBER...
YOU ARE AN ENEMY OF THE COMMUNISTS! I SHALL KILL YOU... KILL! KILL!
HEY! WHAT THE.. OW-W-W!
I HATE TO DO THIS TO YOU, TORO OLD PAL... BUT IT'S FOR YOUR OWN GOOD!
OW-W-W!
THE BLAST OF MY MORE POWERFUL ATOMIC-CHARGED FLAME KNOCKED HIM OUT! WHEN HE COMES TO, WE'LL BOTH BE BACK IN THE STATES!
7

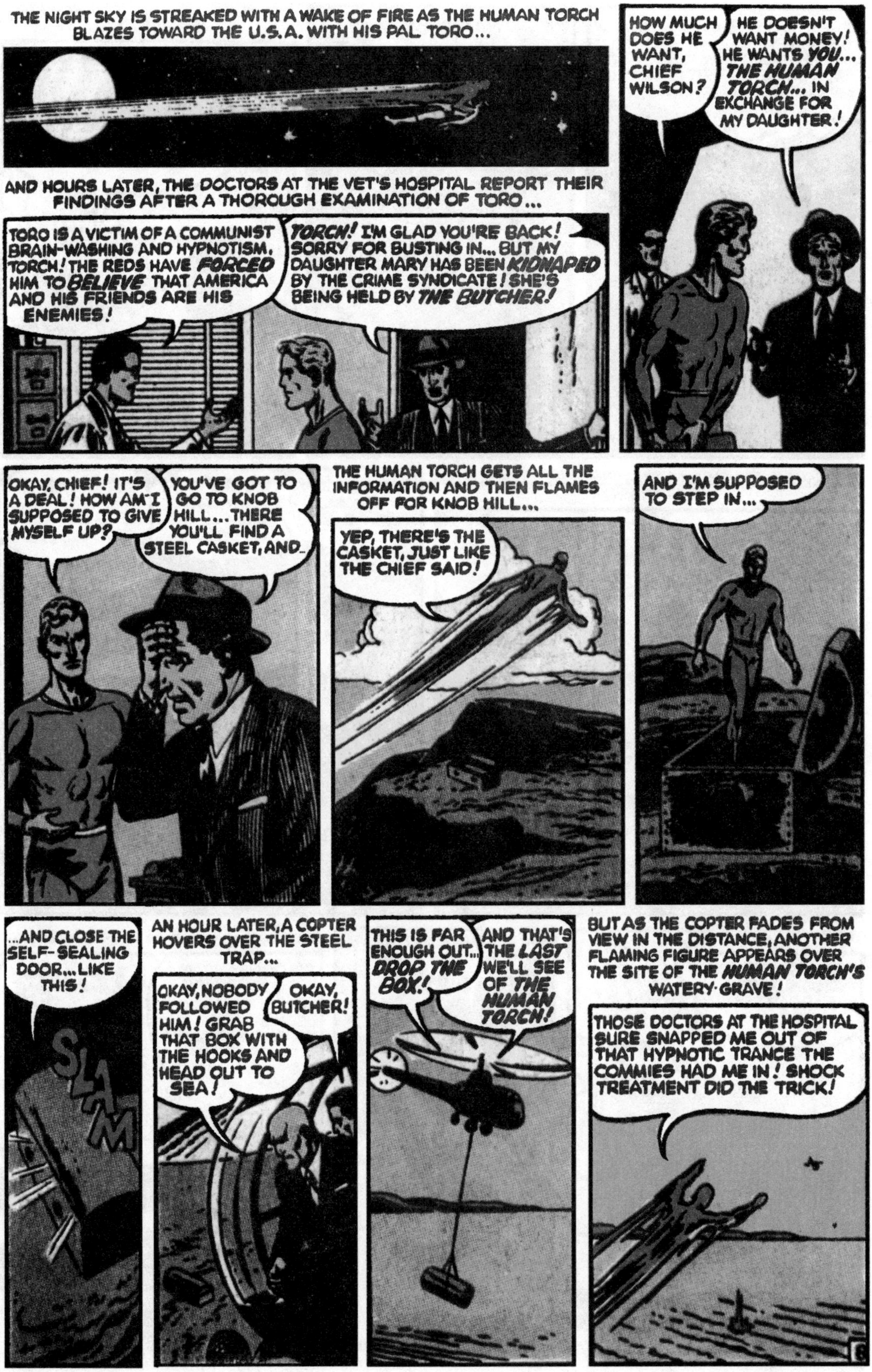
THE NIGHT SKY IS STREAKED WITH A WAKE OF FIRE AS THE HUMAN TORCH BLAZES TOWARD THE U.S.A. WITH HIS PAL TORO...
AND HOURS LATER, THE DOCTORS AT THE VET'S HOSPITAL REPORT THEIR FINDINGS AFTER A THOROUGH EXAMINATION OF TORO...
TORO IS A VICTIM OF A COMMUNIST BRAIN-WASHING AND HYPNOTISM, TORCH! THE REDS HAVE FORCED HIM TO BELIEVE THAT AMERICA AND HIS FRIENDS ARE HIS ENEMIES!
TORCH! I'M GLAD YOU'RE BACK! SORRY FOR BUSTING IN... BUT MY DAUGHTER MARY HAS BEEN KIDNAPED BY THE CRIME SYNDICATE! SHE'S BEING HELD BY THE BUTCHER!
HOW MUCH DOES HE WANT, CHIEF WILSON?
HE DOESN'T WANT MONEY! HE WANTS YOU... THE HUMAN TORCH... IN EXCHANGE FOR MY DAUGHTER!
OKAY, CHIEF! IT'S A DEAL! HOW AM I SUPPOSED TO GIVE MYSELF UP?
YOU'VE GOT TO GO TO KNOB HILL... THERE YOU'LL FIND A STEEL CASKET, AND...
THE HUMAN TORCH GETS ALL THE INFORMATION AND THEN FLAMES OFF FOR KNOB HILL...
YEP, THERE'S THE CASKET, JUST LIKE THE CHIEF SAID!
AND I'M SUPPOSED TO STEP IN...
...AND CLOSE THE SELF-SEALING DOOR... LIKE THIS!
SLAM
AN HOUR LATER, A COPTER HOVERS OVER THE STEEL TRAP...
OKAY, NOBODY FOLLOWED HIM! GRAB THAT BOX WITH THE HOOKS AND HEAD OUT TO SEA!
OKAY, BUTCHER!
THIS IS FAR ENOUGH OUT... DROP THE BOX!
AND THAT'S THE LAST WE'LL SEE OF THE HUMAN TORCH!
BUT AS THE COPTER FADES FROM VIEW IN THE DISTANCE, ANOTHER FLAMING FIGURE APPEARS OVER THE SITE OF THE HUMAN TORCH'S WATERY GRAVE!
THOSE DOCTORS AT THE HOSPITAL SURE SNAPPED ME OUT OF THAT HYPNOTIC TRANCE THE COMMIES HAD ME IN! SHOCK TREATMENT DID THE TRICK!

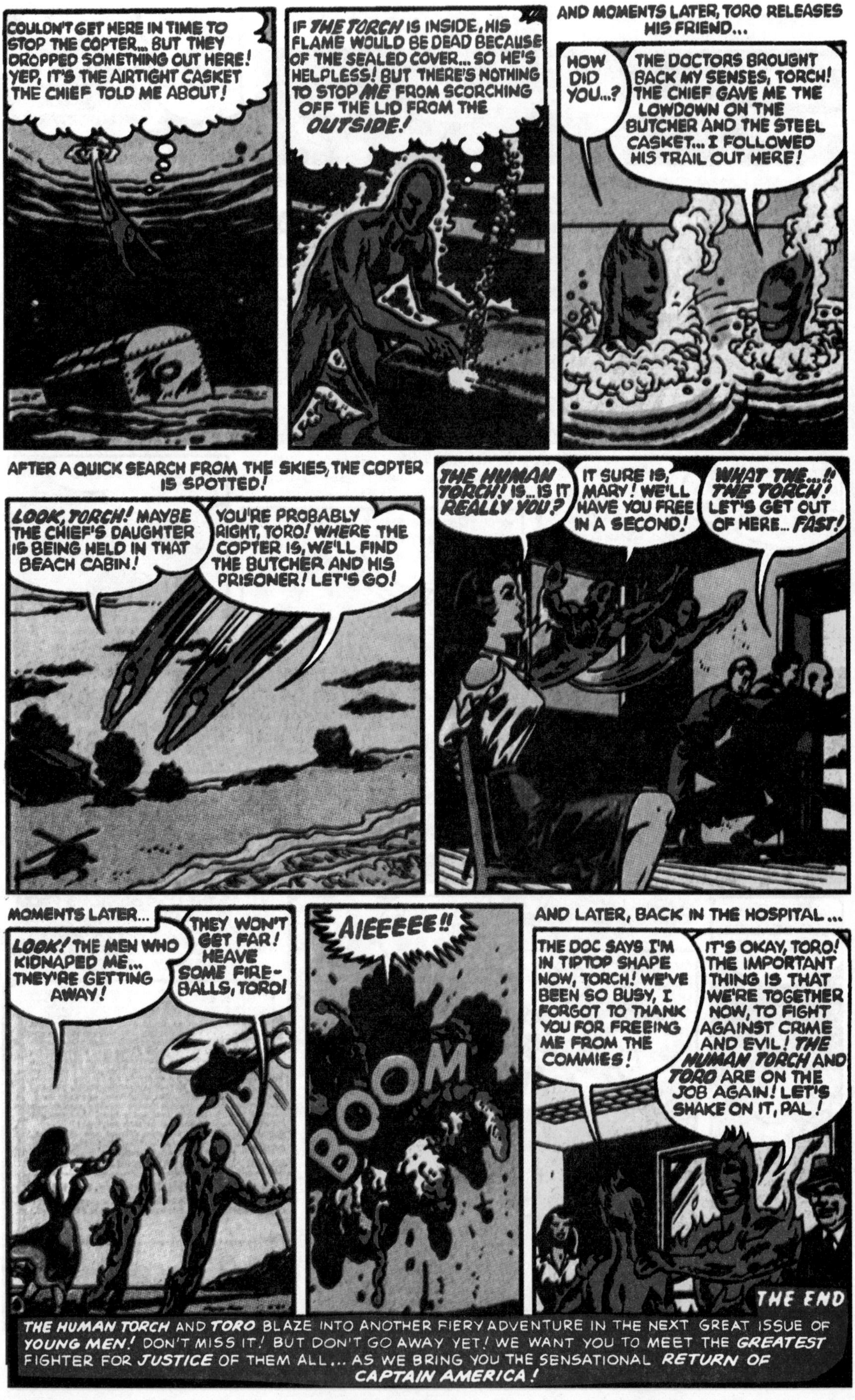
COULDN'T GET HERE IN TIME TO STOP THE COPTER... BUT THEY DROPPED SOMETHING OUT HERE! YEP, IT'S THE AIRTIGHT CASKET THE CHIEF TOLD ME ABOUT!
IF THE TORCH IS INSIDE, HIS FLAME WOULD BE DEAD BECAUSE OF THE SEALED COVER... SO HE'S HELPLESS! BUT THERE'S NOTHING TO STOP ME FROM SCORCHING OFF THE LID FROM THE OUTSIDE!
AND MOMENTS LATER, TORO RELEASES HIS FRIEND...
HOW DID YOU...?
THE DOCTORS BROUGHT BACK MY SENSES, TORCH! THE CHIEF GAVE ME THE LOWDOWN ON THE BUTCHER AND THE STEEL CASKET... I FOLLOWED HIS TRAIL OUT HERE!
AFTER A QUICK SEARCH FROM THE SKIES, THE COPTER IS SPOTTED!
LOOK, TORCH! MAYBE THE CHIEF'S DAUGHTER IS BEING HELD IN THAT BEACH CABIN!
YOU'RE PROBABLY RIGHT, TORO! WHERE THE COPTER IS, WE'LL FIND THE BUTCHER AND HIS PRISONER! LET'S GO!
THE HUMAN TORCH! IS...IS IT REALLY YOU?
IT SURE IS, MARY! WE'LL HAVE YOU FREE IN A SECOND!
WHAT THE...!! THE TORCH! LET'S GET OUT OF HERE... FAST!
MOMENTS LATER...
LOOK! THE MEN WHO KIDNAPED ME... THEY'RE GETTING AWAY!
THEY WON'T GET FAR! HEAVE SOME FIRE-BALLS, TORO!
AIEEEEE!!
BOOM
AND LATER, BACK IN THE HOSPITAL...
THE DOC SAYS I'M IN TIPTOP SHAPE NOW, TORCH! WE'VE BEEN SO BUSY, I FORGOT TO THANK YOU FOR FREEING ME FROM THE COMMIES!
IT'S OKAY, TORO! THE IMPORTANT THING IS THAT WE'RE TOGETHER NOW, TO FIGHT AGAINST CRIME AND EVIL! THE HUMAN TORCH AND TORO ARE ON THE JOB AGAIN! LET'S SHAKE ON IT, PAL!
THE END
THE HUMAN TORCH AND TORO BLAZE INTO ANOTHER FIERY ADVENTURE IN THE NEXT GREAT ISSUE OF YOUNG MEN! DON'T MISS IT! BUT DON'T GO AWAY YET! WE WANT YOU TO MEET THE GREATEST FIGHTER FOR JUSTICE OF THEM ALL... AS WE BRING YOU THE SENSATIONAL RETURN OF CAPTAIN AMERICA!

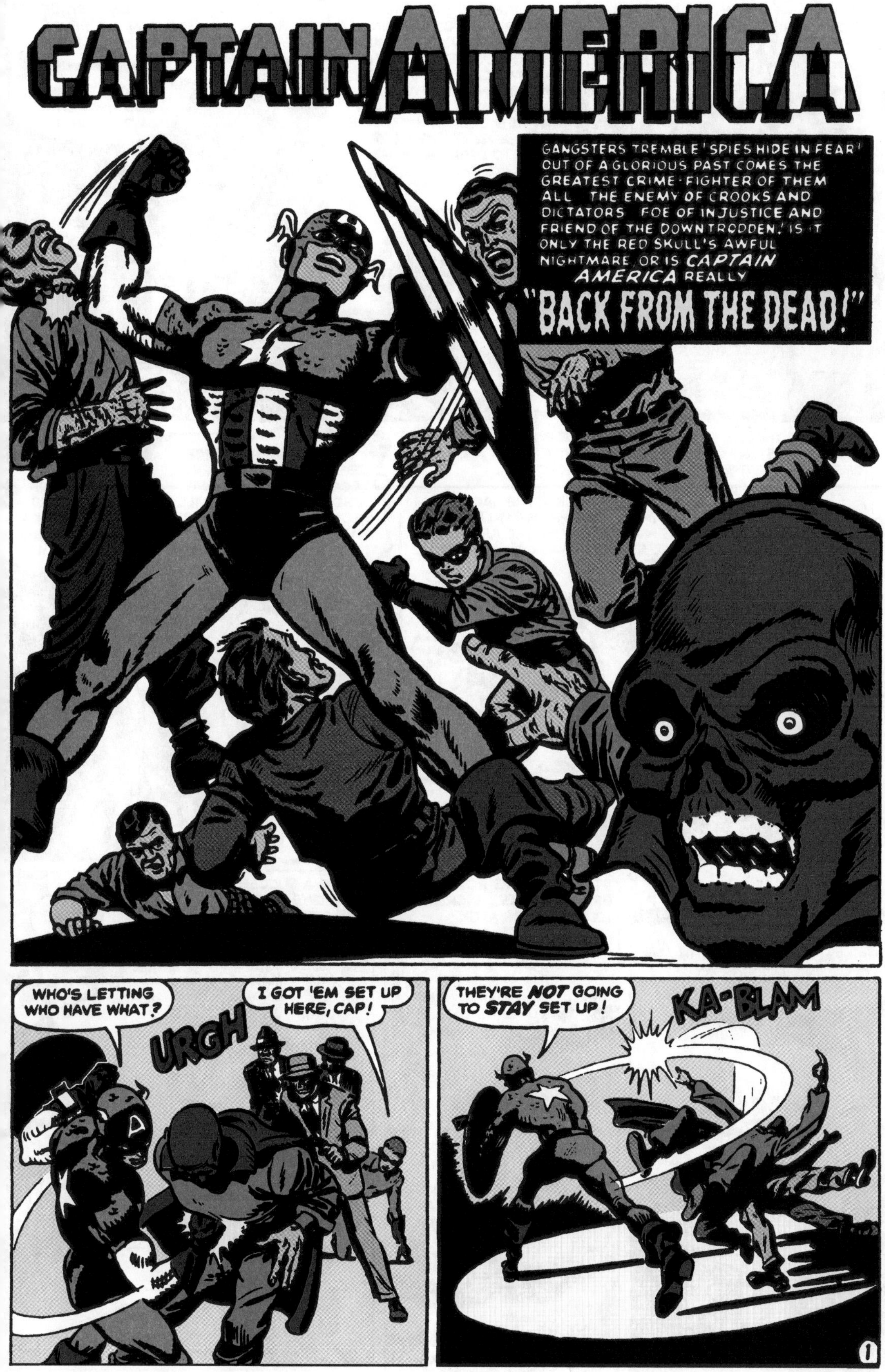
CAPTAIN AMERICA
GANGSTERS TREMBLE! SPIES HIDE IN FEAR! OUT OF A GLORIOUS PAST COMES THE GREATEST CRIME-FIGHTER OF THEM ALL THE ENEMY OF CROOKS AND DICTATORS FOE OF INJUSTICE AND FRIEND OF THE DOWNTRODDEN! IS IT ONLY THE RED SKULL'S AWFUL NIGHTMARE, OR IS CAPTAIN AMERICA REALLY
"BACK FROM THE DEAD!"
WHO'S LETTING WHO HAVE WHAT?
I GOT 'EM SET UP HERE, CAP!
URGH
THEY'RE NOT GOING TO STAY SET UP!
KA-BLAM
1

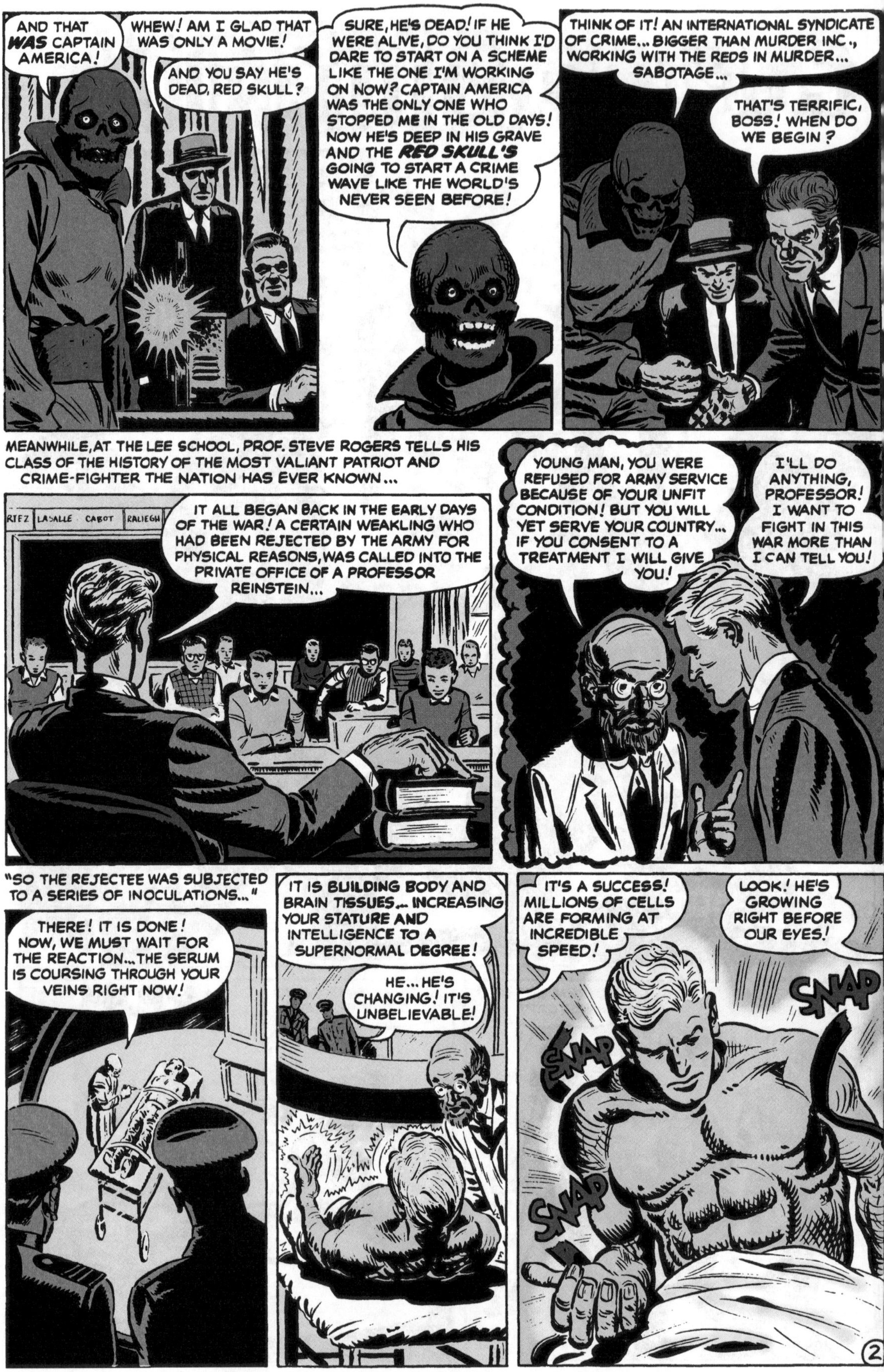

AND THAT WAS CAPTAIN AMERICA!
WHEW! AM I GLAD THAT WAS ONLY A MOVIE!
AND YOU SAY HE'S DEAD, RED SKULL?
SURE, HE'S DEAD! IF HE WERE ALIVE, DO YOU THINK I'D DARE TO START ON A SCHEME LIKE THE ONE I'M WORKING ON NOW? CAPTAIN AMERICA WAS THE ONLY ONE WHO STOPPED ME IN THE OLD DAYS! NOW HE'S DEEP IN HIS GRAVE AND THE RED SKULL'S GOING TO START A CRIME WAVE LIKE THE WORLD'S NEVER SEEN BEFORE!
THINK OF IT! AN INTERNATIONAL SYNDICATE OF CRIME... BIGGER THAN MURDER INC., WORKING WITH THE REDS IN MURDER... SABOTAGE...
THAT'S TERRIFIC, BOSS! WHEN DO WE BEGIN?
MEANWHILE, AT THE LEE SCHOOL, PROF. STEVE ROGERS TELLS HIS CLASS OF THE HISTORY OF THE MOST VALIANT PATRIOT AND CRIME-FIGHTER THE NATION HAS EVER KNOWN...
RIEZ LASALLE CABOT RALIEGH
IT ALL BEGAN BACK IN THE EARLY DAYS OF THE WAR! A CERTAIN WEAKLING WHO HAD BEEN REJECTED BY THE ARMY FOR PHYSICAL REASONS, WAS CALLED INTO THE PRIVATE OFFICE OF A PROFESSOR REINSTEIN...
YOUNG MAN, YOU WERE REFUSED FOR ARMY SERVICE BECAUSE OF YOUR UNFIT CONDITION! BUT YOU WILL YET SERVE YOUR COUNTRY... IF YOU CONSENT TO A TREATMENT I WILL GIVE YOU!
I'LL DO ANYTHING, PROFESSOR! I WANT TO FIGHT IN THIS WAR MORE THAN I CAN TELL YOU!
"SO THE REJECTEE WAS SUBJECTED TO A SERIES OF INOCULATIONS..."
THERE! IT IS DONE! NOW, WE MUST WAIT FOR THE REACTION... THE SERUM IS COURSING THROUGH YOUR VEINS RIGHT NOW!
IT IS BUILDING BODY AND BRAIN TISSUES... INCREASING YOUR STATURE AND INTELLIGENCE TO A SUPERNORMAL DEGREE!
HE... HE'S CHANGING! IT'S UNBELIEVABLE!
IT'S A SUCCESS! MILLIONS OF CELLS ARE FORMING AT INCREDIBLE SPEED!
LOOK! HE'S GROWING RIGHT BEFORE OUR EYES!
SNAP
SNAP
SNAP

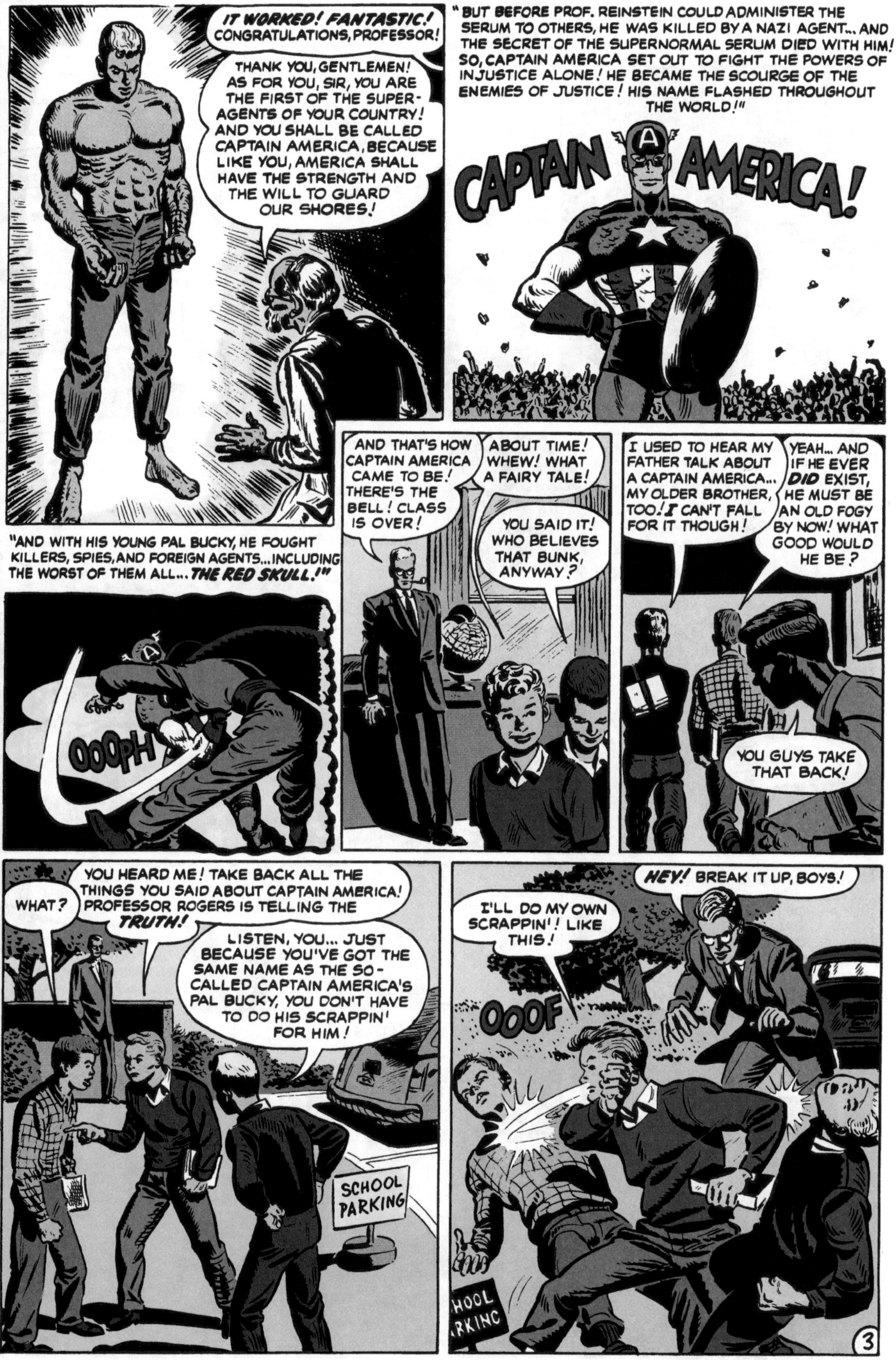

IT WORKED! FANTASTIC! CONGRATULATIONS, PROFESSOR!
THANK YOU, GENTLEMEN! AS FOR YOU, SIR, YOU ARE THE FIRST OF THE SUPER-AGENTS OF YOUR COUNTRY! AND YOU SHALL BE CALLED CAPTAIN AMERICA, BECAUSE LIKE YOU, AMERICA SHALL HAVE THE STRENGTH AND THE WILL TO GUARD OUR SHORES!
"BUT BEFORE PROF. REINSTEIN COULD ADMINISTER THE SERUM TO OTHERS, HE WAS KILLED BY A NAZI AGENT... AND THE SECRET OF THE SUPERNORMAL SERUM DIED WITH HIM! SO, CAPTAIN AMERICA SET OUT TO FIGHT THE POWERS OF INJUSTICE ALONE! HE BECAME THE SCOURGE OF THE ENEMIES OF JUSTICE! HIS NAME FLASHED THROUGHOUT THE WORLD!"
CAPTAIN AMERICA!
"AND WITH HIS YOUNG PAL BUCKY, HE FOUGHT KILLERS, SPIES, AND FOREIGN AGENTS... INCLUDING THE WORST OF THEM ALL... THE RED SKULL!"
OOOPH
AND THAT'S HOW CAPTAIN AMERICA CAME TO BE! THERE'S THE BELL! CLASS IS OVER!
ABOUT TIME! WHEW! WHAT A FAIRY TALE!
YOU SAID IT! WHO BELIEVES THAT BUNK, ANYWAY?
I USED TO HEAR MY FATHER TALK ABOUT A CAPTAIN AMERICA... MY OLDER BROTHER, TOO! I CAN'T FALL FOR IT THOUGH!
YEAH... AND IF HE EVER DID EXIST, HE MUST BE AN OLD FOGY BY NOW! WHAT GOOD WOULD HE BE?
YOU GUYS TAKE THAT BACK!
WHAT?
YOU HEARD ME! TAKE BACK ALL THE THINGS YOU SAID ABOUT CAPTAIN AMERICA! PROFESSOR ROGERS IS TELLING THE TRUTH!
LISTEN, YOU... JUST BECAUSE YOU'VE GOT THE SAME NAME AS THE SO-CALLED CAPTAIN AMERICA'S PAL BUCKY, YOU DON'T HAVE TO DO HIS SCRAPPIN' FOR HIM!
SCHOOL PARKING
HEY! BREAK IT UP, BOYS!
I'LL DO MY OWN SCRAPPIN'! LIKE THIS!
OOOF
HOOL
RKING
3

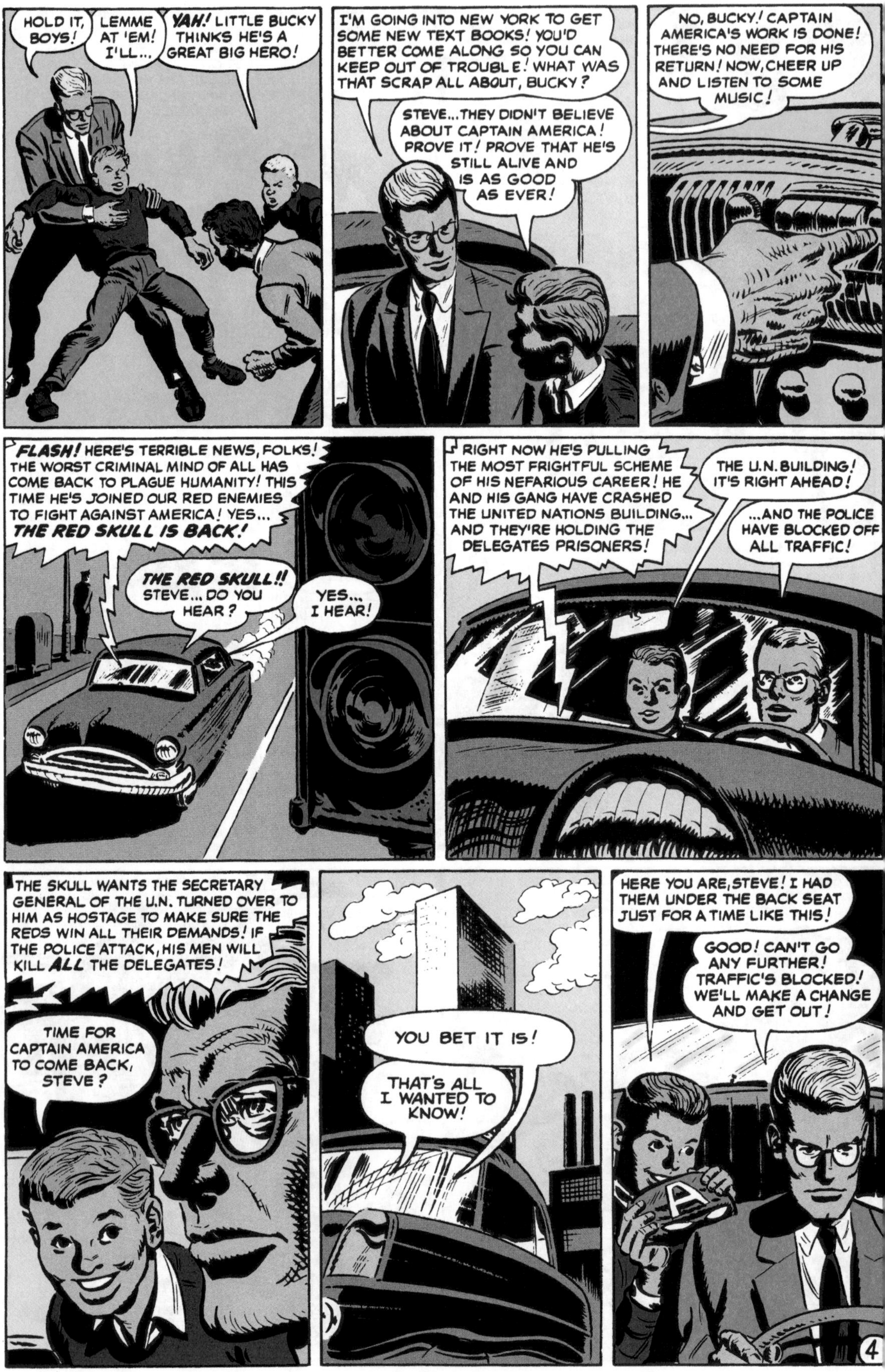
HOLD IT, BOYS!
LEMME AT 'EM! I'LL...
YAH! LITTLE BUCKY THINKS HE'S A GREAT BIG HERO!
I'M GOING INTO NEW YORK TO GET SOME NEW TEXT BOOKS! YOU'D BETTER COME ALONG SO YOU CAN KEEP OUT OF TROUBLE! WHAT WAS THAT SCRAP ALL ABOUT, BUCKY?
STEVE...THEY DIDN'T BELIEVE ABOUT CAPTAIN AMERICA! PROVE IT! PROVE THAT HE'S STILL ALIVE AND IS AS GOOD AS EVER!
NO, BUCKY! CAPTAIN AMERICA'S WORK IS DONE! THERE'S NO NEED FOR HIS RETURN! NOW, CHEER UP AND LISTEN TO SOME MUSIC!
FLASH! HERE'S TERRIBLE NEWS, FOLKS! THE WORST CRIMINAL MIND OF ALL HAS COME BACK TO PLAGUE HUMANITY! THIS TIME HE'S JOINED OUR RED ENEMIES TO FIGHT AGAINST AMERICA! YES... THE RED SKULL IS BACK!
THE RED SKULL!! STEVE... DO YOU HEAR?
YES... I HEAR!
RIGHT NOW HE'S PULLING THE MOST FRIGHTFUL SCHEME OF HIS NEFARIOUS CAREER! HE AND HIS GANG HAVE CRASHED THE UNITED NATIONS BUILDING... AND THEY'RE HOLDING THE DELEGATES PRISONERS!
THE U.N. BUILDING! IT'S RIGHT AHEAD!
...AND THE POLICE HAVE BLOCKED OFF ALL TRAFFIC!
THE SKULL WANTS THE SECRETARY GENERAL OF THE U.N. TURNED OVER TO HIM AS HOSTAGE TO MAKE SURE THE REDS WIN ALL THEIR DEMANDS! IF THE POLICE ATTACK, HIS MEN WILL KILL ALL THE DELEGATES!
TIME FOR CAPTAIN AMERICA TO COME BACK, STEVE?
YOU BET IT IS!
THAT'S ALL I WANTED TO KNOW!
HERE YOU ARE, STEVE! I HAD THEM UNDER THE BACK SEAT JUST FOR A TIME LIKE THIS!
GOOD! CAN'T GO ANY FURTHER! TRAFFIC'S BLOCKED! WE'LL MAKE A CHANGE AND GET OUT!
A
4

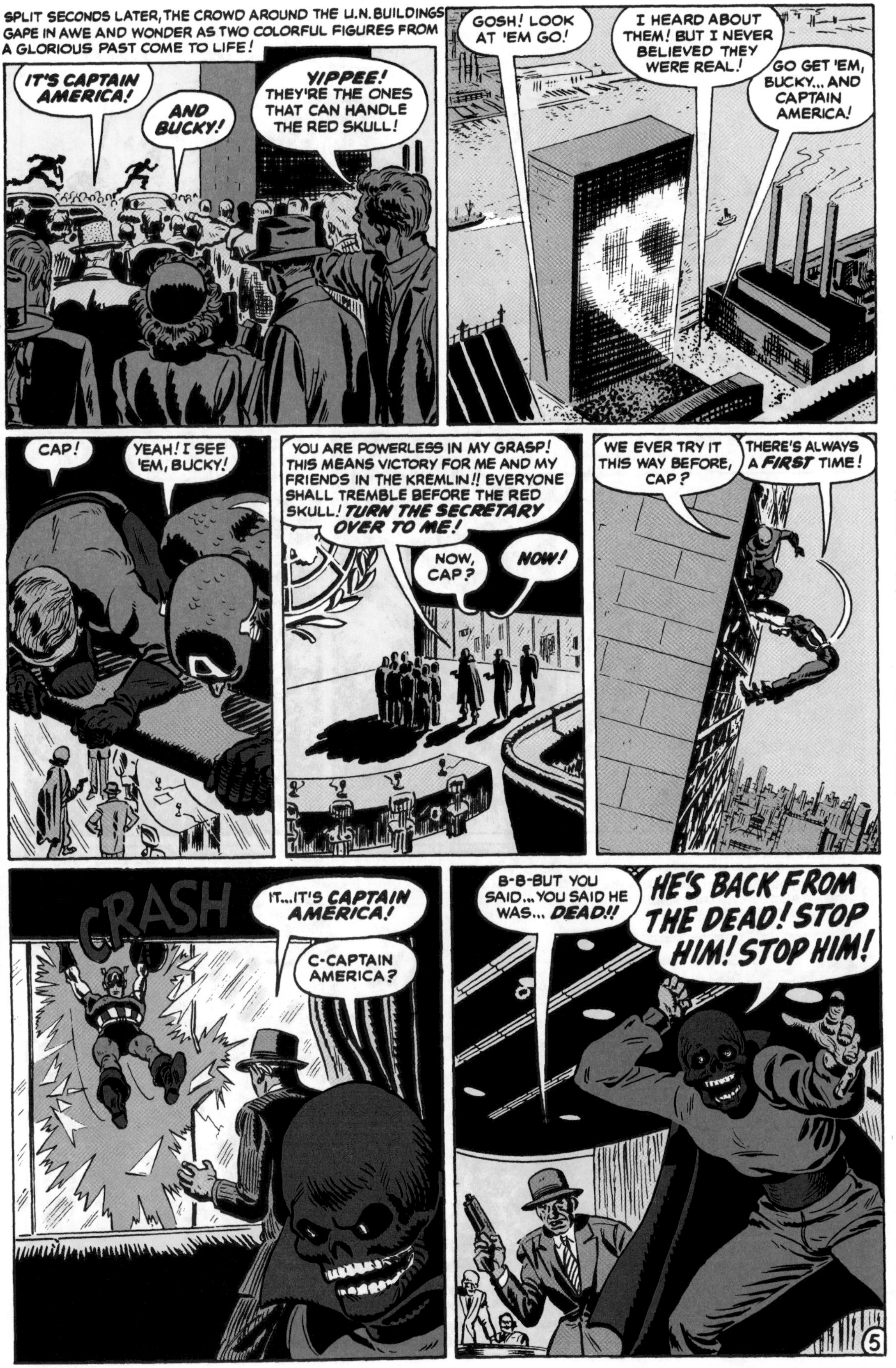

SPLIT SECONDS LATER, THE CROWD AROUND THE U.N. BUILDINGS GAPE IN AWE AND WONDER AS TWO COLORFUL FIGURES FROM A GLORIOUS PAST COME TO LIFE!
IT'S CAPTAIN AMERICA!
AND BUCKY!
YIPPEE! THEY'RE THE ONES THAT CAN HANDLE THE RED SKULL!
GOSH! LOOK AT 'EM GO!
I HEARD ABOUT THEM! BUT I NEVER BELIEVED THEY WERE REAL!
GO GET 'EM, BUCKY... AND CAPTAIN AMERICA!
CAP!
YEAH! I SEE 'EM, BUCKY!
YOU ARE POWERLESS IN MY GRASP! THIS MEANS VICTORY FOR ME AND MY FRIENDS IN THE KREMLIN!! EVERYONE SHALL TREMBLE BEFORE THE RED SKULL! TURN THE SECRETARY OVER TO ME!
NOW, CAP?
NOW!
WE EVER TRY IT THIS WAY BEFORE, CAP?
THERE'S ALWAYS A FIRST TIME!
CRASH
IT...IT'S CAPTAIN AMERICA!
C-CAPTAIN AMERICA?
B-B-BUT YOU SAID... YOU SAID HE WAS... DEAD!!
HE'S BACK FROM THE DEAD! STOP HIM! STOP HIM!
5

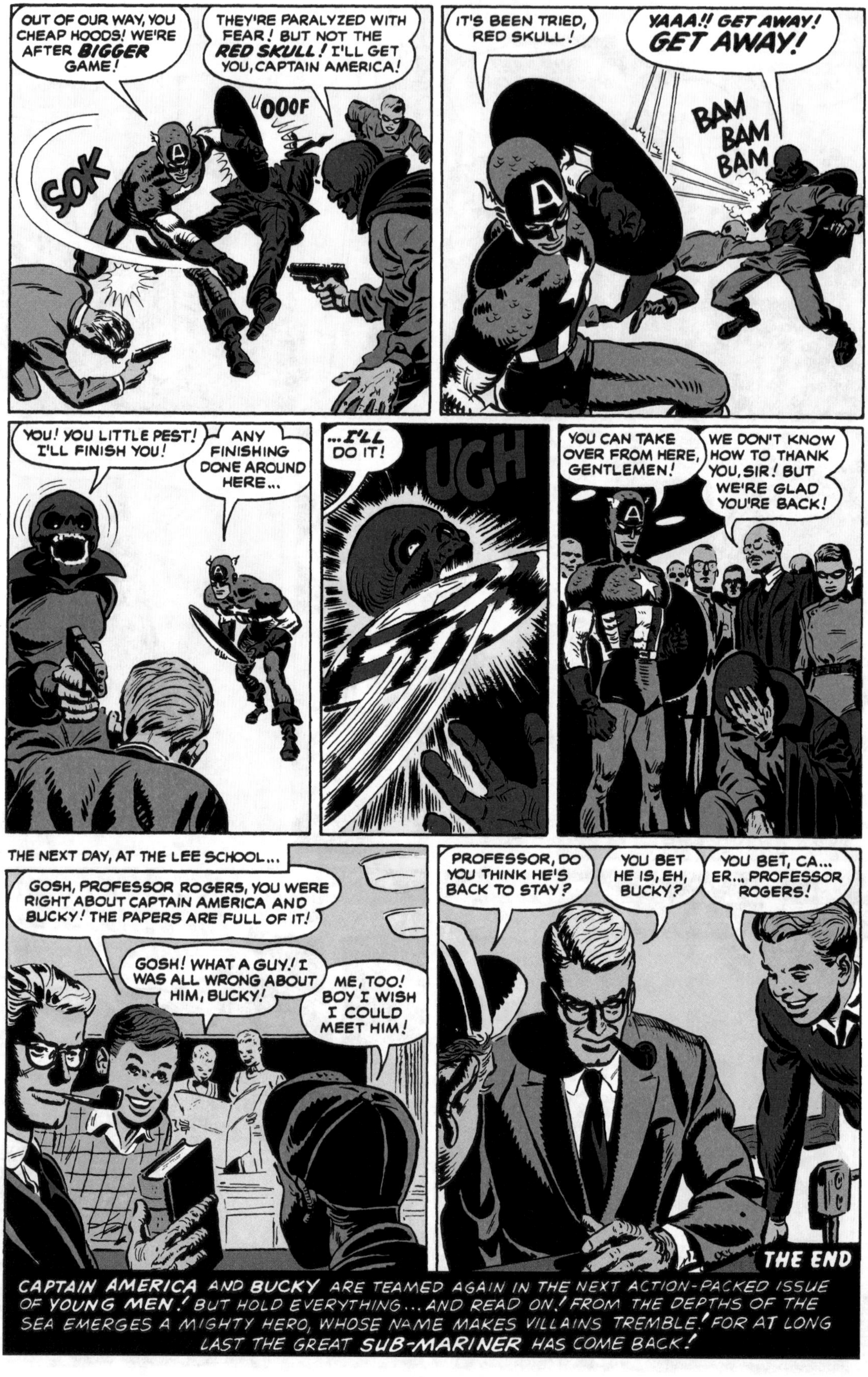
OUT OF OUR WAY, YOU CHEAP HOODS! WE'RE AFTER BIGGER GAME!
THEY'RE PARALYZED WITH FEAR! BUT NOT THE RED SKULL! I'LL GET YOU, CAPTAIN AMERICA!
SOK
OOOF
IT'S BEEN TRIED, RED SKULL!
YAAA!! GET AWAY! GET AWAY!
BAM BAM BAM
YOU! YOU LITTLE PEST! I'LL FINISH YOU!
ANY FINISHING DONE AROUND HERE...
...I'LL DO IT!
UGH
YOU CAN TAKE OVER FROM HERE, GENTLEMEN!
WE DON'T KNOW HOW TO THANK YOU, SIR! BUT WE'RE GLAD YOU'RE BACK!
THE NEXT DAY, AT THE LEE SCHOOL...
GOSH, PROFESSOR ROGERS, YOU WERE RIGHT ABOUT CAPTAIN AMERICA AND BUCKY! THE PAPERS ARE FULL OF IT!
GOSH! WHAT A GUY! I WAS ALL WRONG ABOUT HIM, BUCKY!
ME, TOO! BOY I WISH I COULD MEET HIM!
PROFESSOR, DO YOU THINK HE'S BACK TO STAY?
YOU BET HE IS, EH, BUCKY?
YOU BET, CA... ER... PROFESSOR ROGERS!
THE END
CAPTAIN AMERICA AND BUCKY ARE TEAMED AGAIN IN THE NEXT ACTION-PACKED ISSUE OF YOUNG MEN! BUT HOLD EVERYTHING... AND READ ON! FROM THE DEPTHS OF THE SEA EMERGES A MIGHTY HERO, WHOSE NAME MAKES VILLAINS TREMBLE! FOR AT LONG LAST THE GREAT SUB-MARINER HAS COME BACK!

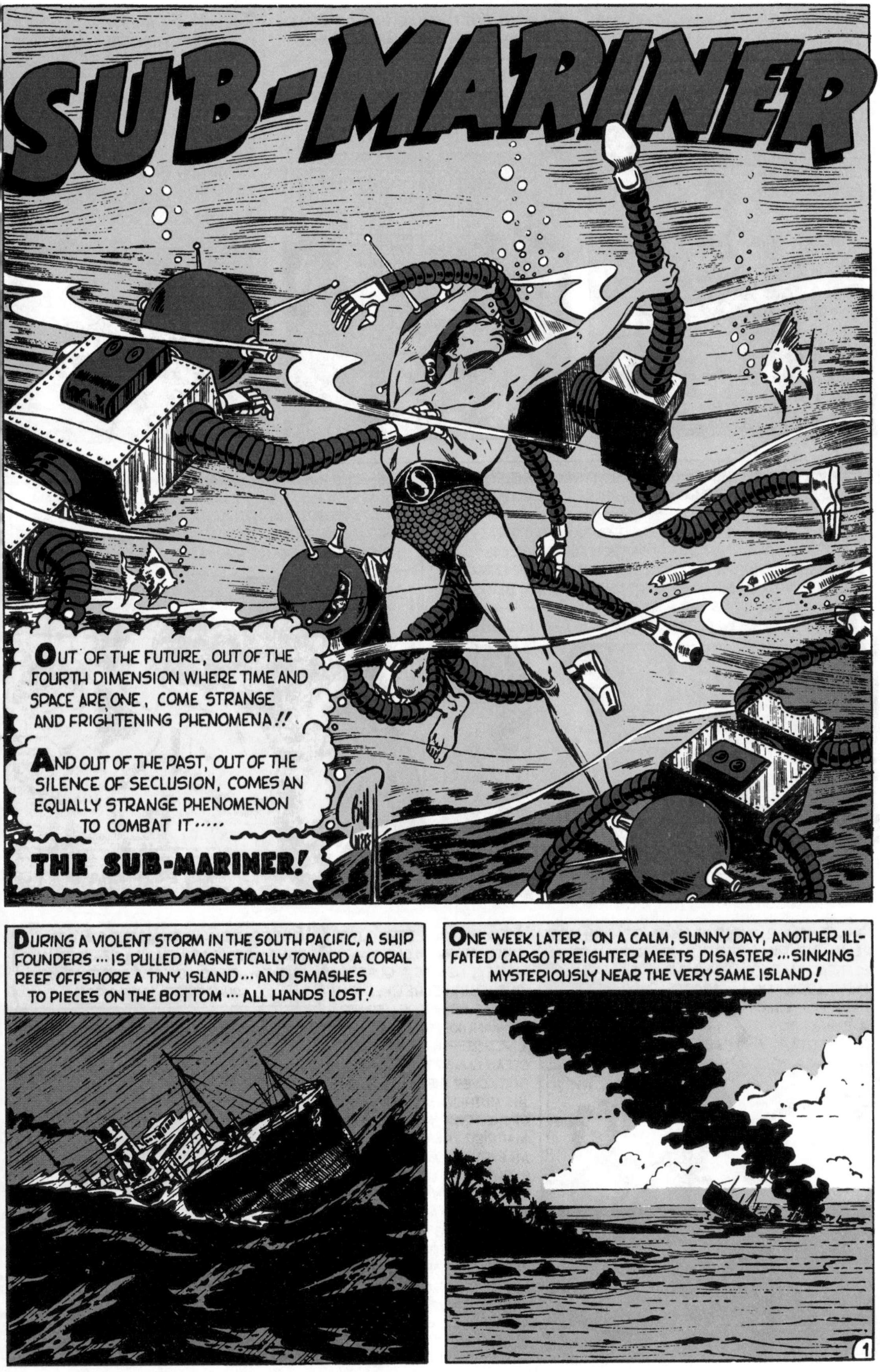
SUB-MARINER
OUT OF THE FUTURE, OUT OF THE FOURTH DIMENSION WHERE TIME AND SPACE ARE ONE, COME STRANGE AND FRIGHTENING PHENOMENA!!
AND OUT OF THE PAST, OUT OF THE SILENCE OF SECLUSION, COMES AN EQUALLY STRANGE PHENOMENON TO COMBAT IT.....
THE SUB-MARINER!
DURING A VIOLENT STORM IN THE SOUTH PACIFIC, A SHIP FOUNDERS ... IS PULLED MAGNETICALLY TOWARD A CORAL REEF OFFSHORE A TINY ISLAND ... AND SMASHES TO PIECES ON THE BOTTOM ... ALL HANDS LOST!
ONE WEEK LATER, ON A CALM, SUNNY DAY, ANOTHER ILL-FATED CARGO FREIGHTER MEETS DISASTER ... SINKING MYSTERIOUSLY NEAR THE VERY SAME ISLAND!
1

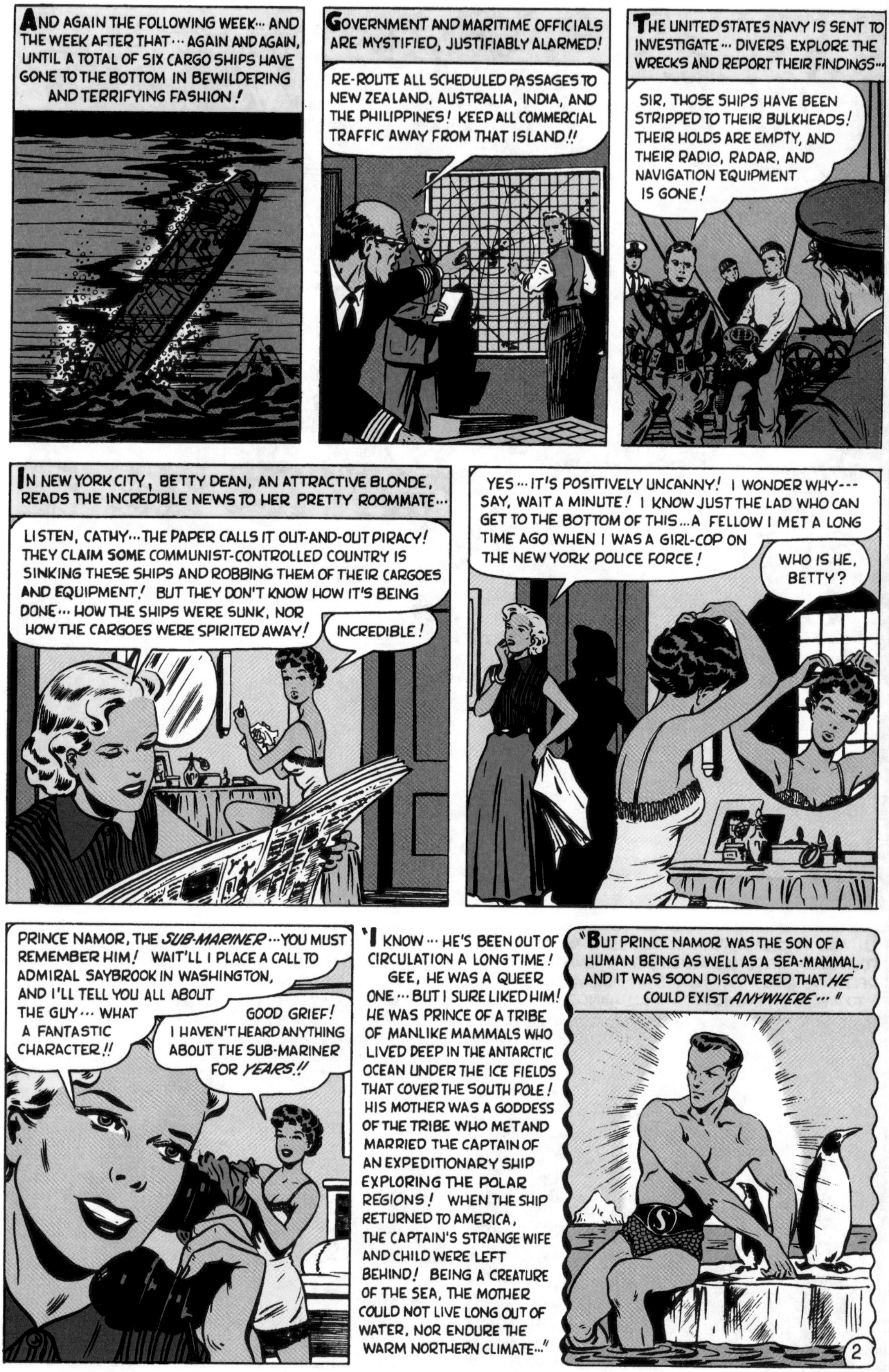

AND AGAIN THE FOLLOWING WEEK... AND THE WEEK AFTER THAT... AGAIN AND AGAIN, UNTIL A TOTAL OF SIX CARGO SHIPS HAVE GONE TO THE BOTTOM IN BEWILDERING AND TERRIFYING FASHION!
GOVERNMENT AND MARITIME OFFICIALS ARE MYSTIFIED, JUSTIFIABLY ALARMED!
RE-ROUTE ALL SCHEDULED PASSAGES TO NEW ZEALAND, AUSTRALIA, INDIA, AND THE PHILIPPINES! KEEP ALL COMMERCIAL TRAFFIC AWAY FROM THAT ISLAND!!
THE UNITED STATES NAVY IS SENT TO INVESTIGATE... DIVERS EXPLORE THE WRECKS AND REPORT THEIR FINDINGS...
SIR, THOSE SHIPS HAVE BEEN STRIPPED TO THEIR BULKHEADS! THEIR HOLDS ARE EMPTY, AND THEIR RADIO, RADAR, AND NAVIGATION EQUIPMENT IS GONE!
IN NEW YORK CITY, BETTY DEAN, AN ATTRACTIVE BLONDE, READS THE INCREDIBLE NEWS TO HER PRETTY ROOMMATE...
LISTEN, CATHY... THE PAPER CALLS IT OUT-AND-OUT PIRACY! THEY CLAIM SOME COMMUNIST-CONTROLLED COUNTRY IS SINKING THESE SHIPS AND ROBBING THEM OF THEIR CARGOES AND EQUIPMENT! BUT THEY DON'T KNOW HOW IT'S BEING DONE... HOW THE SHIPS WERE SUNK, NOR HOW THE CARGOES WERE SPIRITED AWAY!
INCREDIBLE!
YES... IT'S POSITIVELY UNCANNY! I WONDER WHY--- SAY, WAIT A MINUTE! I KNOW JUST THE LAD WHO CAN GET TO THE BOTTOM OF THIS... A FELLOW I MET A LONG TIME AGO WHEN I WAS A GIRL-COP ON THE NEW YORK POLICE FORCE!
WHO IS HE, BETTY?
PRINCE NAMOR, THE *SUB-MARINER*... YOU MUST REMEMBER HIM! WAIT'LL I PLACE A CALL TO ADMIRAL SAYBROOK IN WASHINGTON, AND I'LL TELL YOU ALL ABOUT THE GUY... WHAT A FANTASTIC CHARACTER!!
GOOD GRIEF! I HAVEN'T HEARD ANYTHING ABOUT THE SUB-MARINER FOR *YEARS!!*
"I KNOW... HE'S BEEN OUT OF CIRCULATION A LONG TIME! GEE, HE WAS A QUEER ONE... BUT I SURE LIKED HIM! HE WAS PRINCE OF A TRIBE OF MANLIKE MAMMALS WHO LIVED DEEP IN THE ANTARCTIC OCEAN UNDER THE ICE FIELDS THAT COVER THE SOUTH POLE! HIS MOTHER WAS A GODDESS OF THE TRIBE WHO MET AND MARRIED THE CAPTAIN OF AN EXPEDITIONARY SHIP EXPLORING THE POLAR REGIONS! WHEN THE SHIP RETURNED TO AMERICA, THE CAPTAIN'S STRANGE WIFE AND CHILD WERE LEFT BEHIND! BEING A CREATURE OF THE SEA, THE MOTHER COULD NOT LIVE LONG OUT OF WATER, NOR ENDURE THE WARM NORTHERN CLIMATE..."
"BUT PRINCE NAMOR WAS THE SON OF A HUMAN BEING AS WELL AS A SEA-MAMMAL, AND IT WAS SOON DISCOVERED THAT *HE* COULD EXIST *ANYWHERE*..."

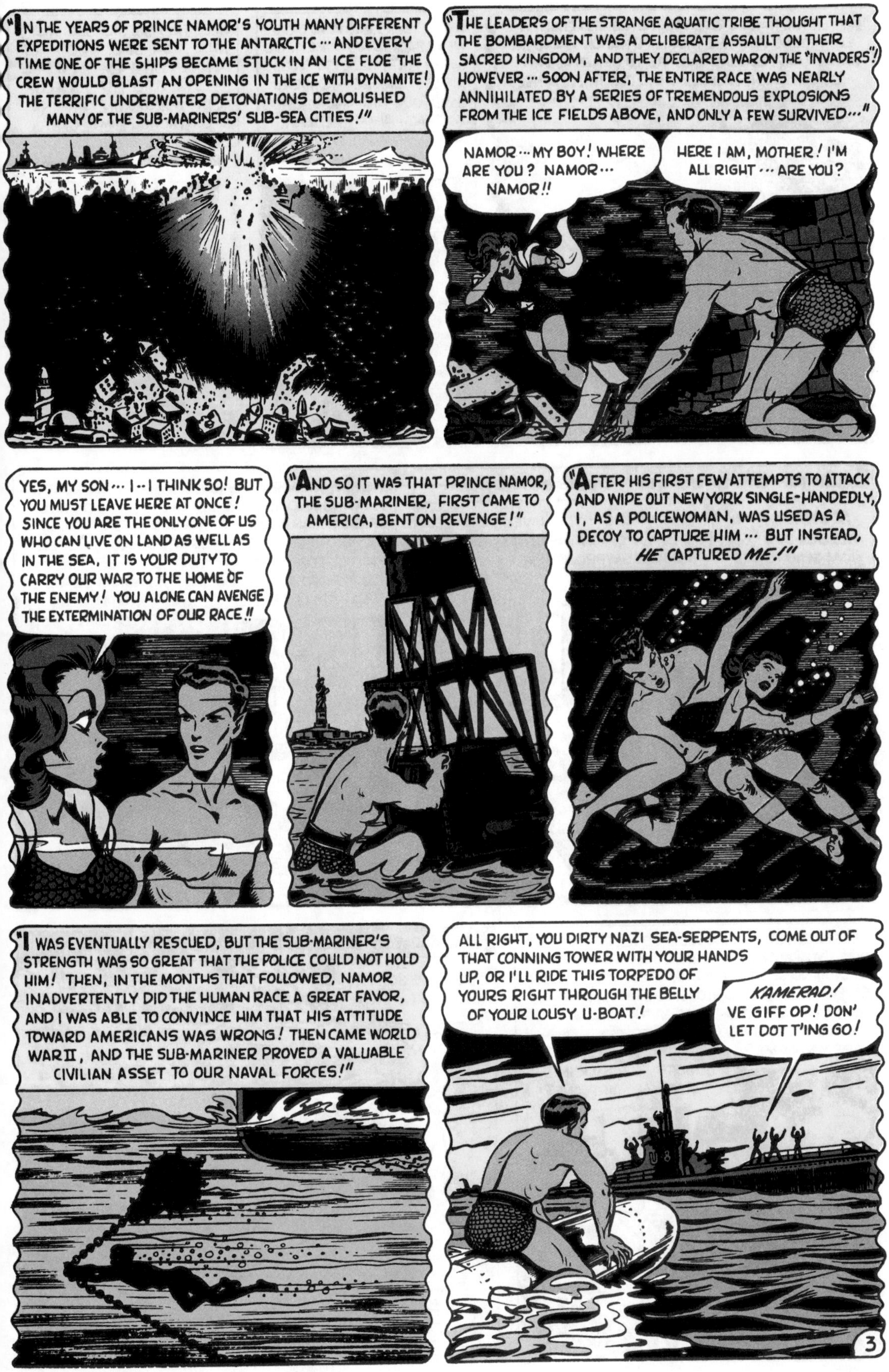
"IN THE YEARS OF PRINCE NAMOR'S YOUTH MANY DIFFERENT EXPEDITIONS WERE SENT TO THE ANTARCTIC ... AND EVERY TIME ONE OF THE SHIPS BECAME STUCK IN AN ICE FLOE THE CREW WOULD BLAST AN OPENING IN THE ICE WITH DYNAMITE! THE TERRIFIC UNDERWATER DETONATIONS DEMOLISHED MANY OF THE SUB-MARINERS' SUB-SEA CITIES!"
"THE LEADERS OF THE STRANGE AQUATIC TRIBE THOUGHT THAT THE BOMBARDMENT WAS A DELIBERATE ASSAULT ON THEIR SACRED KINGDOM, AND THEY DECLARED WAR ON THE "INVADERS"! HOWEVER ... SOON AFTER, THE ENTIRE RACE WAS NEARLY ANNIHILATED BY A SERIES OF TREMENDOUS EXPLOSIONS FROM THE ICE FIELDS ABOVE, AND ONLY A FEW SURVIVED..."
NAMOR ... MY BOY! WHERE ARE YOU? NAMOR ... NAMOR!!
HERE I AM, MOTHER! I'M ALL RIGHT ... ARE YOU?
YES, MY SON ... I -- I THINK SO! BUT YOU MUST LEAVE HERE AT ONCE! SINCE YOU ARE THE ONLY ONE OF US WHO CAN LIVE ON LAND AS WELL AS IN THE SEA, IT IS YOUR DUTY TO CARRY OUR WAR TO THE HOME OF THE ENEMY! YOU ALONE CAN AVENGE THE EXTERMINATION OF OUR RACE!!
"AND SO IT WAS THAT PRINCE NAMOR, THE SUB-MARINER, FIRST CAME TO AMERICA, BENT ON REVENGE!"
"AFTER HIS FIRST FEW ATTEMPTS TO ATTACK AND WIPE OUT NEW YORK SINGLE-HANDEDLY, I, AS A POLICEWOMAN, WAS USED AS A DECOY TO CAPTURE HIM ... BUT INSTEAD, HE CAPTURED ME!"
"I WAS EVENTUALLY RESCUED, BUT THE SUB-MARINER'S STRENGTH WAS SO GREAT THAT THE POLICE COULD NOT HOLD HIM! THEN, IN THE MONTHS THAT FOLLOWED, NAMOR INADVERTENTLY DID THE HUMAN RACE A GREAT FAVOR, AND I WAS ABLE TO CONVINCE HIM THAT HIS ATTITUDE TOWARD AMERICANS WAS WRONG! THEN CAME WORLD WAR II, AND THE SUB-MARINER PROVED A VALUABLE CIVILIAN ASSET TO OUR NAVAL FORCES!"
ALL RIGHT, YOU DIRTY NAZI SEA-SERPENTS, COME OUT OF THAT CONNING TOWER WITH YOUR HANDS UP, OR I'LL RIDE THIS TORPEDO OF YOURS RIGHT THROUGH THE BELLY OF YOUR LOUSY U-BOAT!
KAMERAD! VE GIFF OP! DON' LET DOT T'ING GO!
U-8

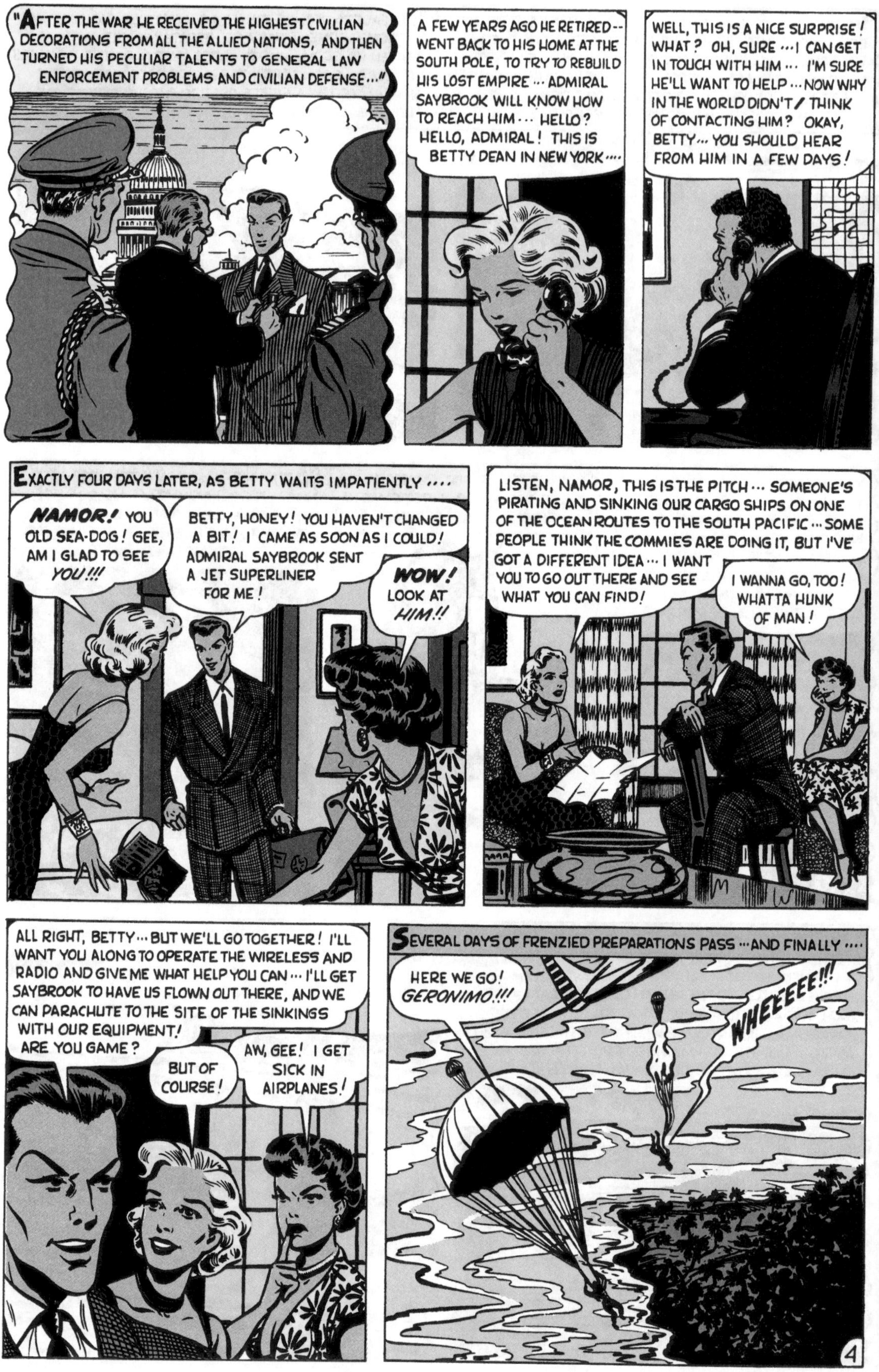
"AFTER THE WAR HE RECEIVED THE HIGHEST CIVILIAN DECORATIONS FROM ALL THE ALLIED NATIONS, AND THEN TURNED HIS PECULIAR TALENTS TO GENERAL LAW ENFORCEMENT PROBLEMS AND CIVILIAN DEFENSE..."
A FEW YEARS AGO HE RETIRED -- WENT BACK TO HIS HOME AT THE SOUTH POLE, TO TRY TO REBUILD HIS LOST EMPIRE ... ADMIRAL SAYBROOK WILL KNOW HOW TO REACH HIM ... HELLO? HELLO, ADMIRAL! THIS IS BETTY DEAN IN NEW YORK....
WELL, THIS IS A NICE SURPRISE! WHAT? OH, SURE ... I CAN GET IN TOUCH WITH HIM ... I'M SURE HE'LL WANT TO HELP ... NOW WHY IN THE WORLD DIDN'T I THINK OF CONTACTING HIM? OKAY, BETTY... YOU SHOULD HEAR FROM HIM IN A FEW DAYS!
EXACTLY FOUR DAYS LATER, AS BETTY WAITS IMPATIENTLY ....
NAMOR! YOU OLD SEA-DOG! GEE, AM I GLAD TO SEE YOU!!!
BETTY, HONEY! YOU HAVEN'T CHANGED A BIT! I CAME AS SOON AS I COULD! ADMIRAL SAYBROOK SENT A JET SUPERLINER FOR ME!
WOW! LOOK AT HIM!!
LISTEN, NAMOR, THIS IS THE PITCH ... SOMEONE'S PIRATING AND SINKING OUR CARGO SHIPS ON ONE OF THE OCEAN ROUTES TO THE SOUTH PACIFIC ... SOME PEOPLE THINK THE COMMIES ARE DOING IT, BUT I'VE GOT A DIFFERENT IDEA ... I WANT YOU TO GO OUT THERE AND SEE WHAT YOU CAN FIND!
I WANNA GO, TOO! WHATTA HUNK OF MAN!
ALL RIGHT, BETTY ... BUT WE'LL GO TOGETHER! I'LL WANT YOU ALONG TO OPERATE THE WIRELESS AND RADIO AND GIVE ME WHAT HELP YOU CAN ... I'LL GET SAYBROOK TO HAVE US FLOWN OUT THERE, AND WE CAN PARACHUTE TO THE SITE OF THE SINKINGS WITH OUR EQUIPMENT! ARE YOU GAME?
BUT OF COURSE!
AW, GEE! I GET SICK IN AIRPLANES!
SEVERAL DAYS OF FRENZIED PREPARATIONS PASS ... AND FINALLY ....
HERE WE GO! GERONIMO!!!
WHEEEEEE!!!
4

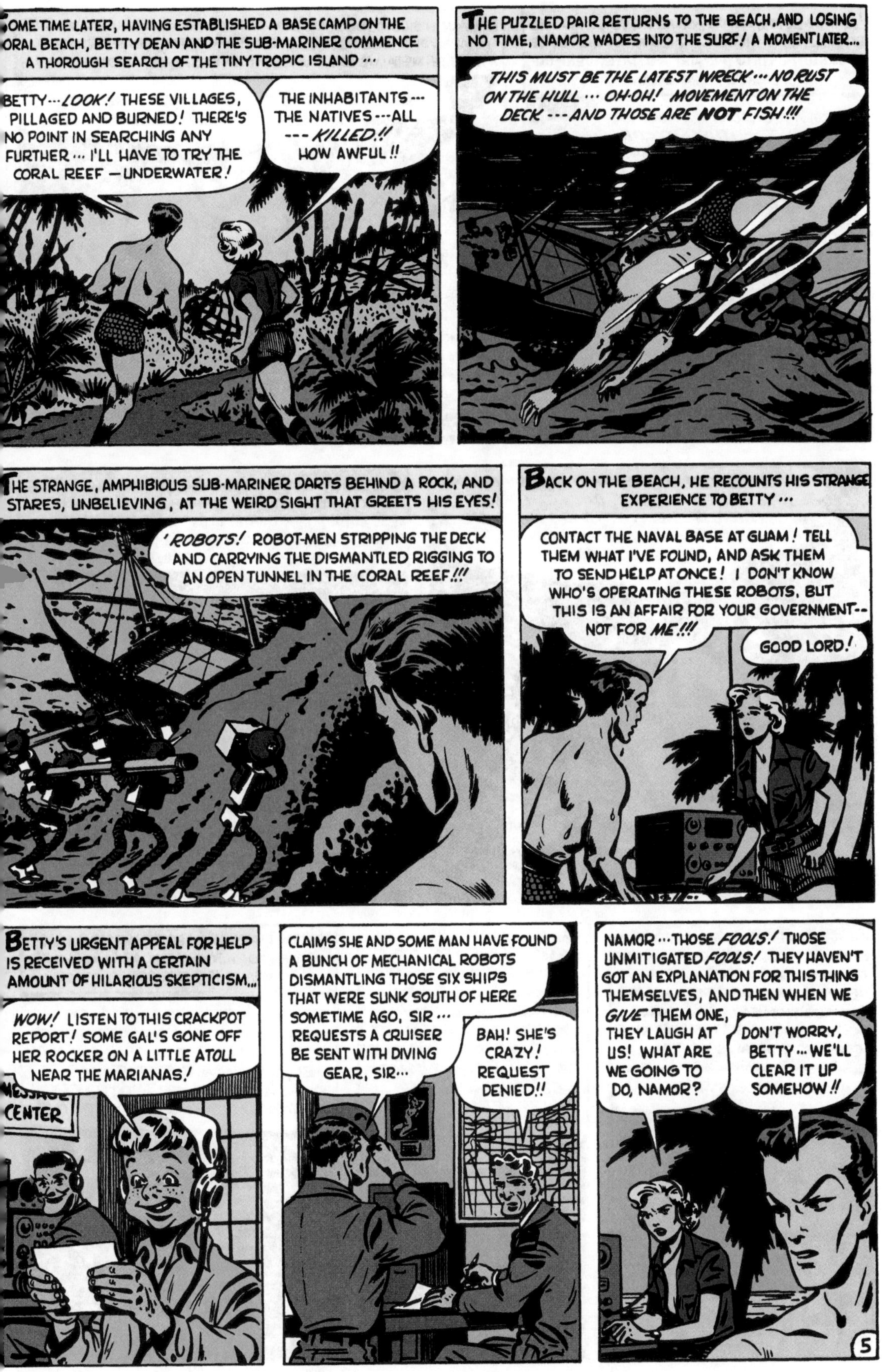
SOME TIME LATER, HAVING ESTABLISHED A BASE CAMP ON THE CORAL BEACH, BETTY DEAN AND THE SUB-MARINER COMMENCE A THOROUGH SEARCH OF THE TINY TROPIC ISLAND ...
BETTY... LOOK! THESE VILLAGES, PILLAGED AND BURNED! THERE'S NO POINT IN SEARCHING ANY FURTHER ... I'LL HAVE TO TRY THE CORAL REEF — UNDERWATER!
THE INHABITANTS --- THE NATIVES --- ALL --- KILLED!! HOW AWFUL!!
THE PUZZLED PAIR RETURNS TO THE BEACH, AND LOSING NO TIME, NAMOR WADES INTO THE SURF! A MOMENT LATER...
THIS MUST BE THE LATEST WRECK ... NO RUST ON THE HULL ... OH-OH! MOVEMENT ON THE DECK --- AND THOSE ARE NOT FISH!!!
THE STRANGE, AMPHIBIOUS SUB-MARINER DARTS BEHIND A ROCK, AND STARES, UNBELIEVING, AT THE WEIRD SIGHT THAT GREETS HIS EYES!
'ROBOTS! ROBOT-MEN STRIPPING THE DECK AND CARRYING THE DISMANTLED RIGGING TO AN OPEN TUNNEL IN THE CORAL REEF!!!
BACK ON THE BEACH, HE RECOUNTS HIS STRANGE EXPERIENCE TO BETTY ...
CONTACT THE NAVAL BASE AT GUAM! TELL THEM WHAT I'VE FOUND, AND ASK THEM TO SEND HELP AT ONCE! I DON'T KNOW WHO'S OPERATING THESE ROBOTS, BUT THIS IS AN AFFAIR FOR YOUR GOVERNMENT-- NOT FOR ME!!!
GOOD LORD!
BETTY'S URGENT APPEAL FOR HELP IS RECEIVED WITH A CERTAIN AMOUNT OF HILARIOUS SKEPTICISM...
WOW! LISTEN TO THIS CRACKPOT REPORT! SOME GAL'S GONE OFF HER ROCKER ON A LITTLE ATOLL NEAR THE MARIANAS!
CENTER
CLAIMS SHE AND SOME MAN HAVE FOUND A BUNCH OF MECHANICAL ROBOTS DISMANTLING THOSE SIX SHIPS THAT WERE SUNK SOUTH OF HERE SOMETIME AGO, SIR ... REQUESTS A CRUISER BE SENT WITH DIVING GEAR, SIR...
BAH! SHE'S CRAZY! REQUEST DENIED!!
NAMOR ... THOSE FOOLS! THOSE UNMITIGATED FOOLS! THEY HAVEN'T GOT AN EXPLANATION FOR THIS THING THEMSELVES, AND THEN WHEN WE GIVE THEM ONE, THEY LAUGH AT US! WHAT ARE WE GOING TO DO, NAMOR?
DON'T WORRY, BETTY ... WE'LL CLEAR IT UP SOMEHOW!!
5

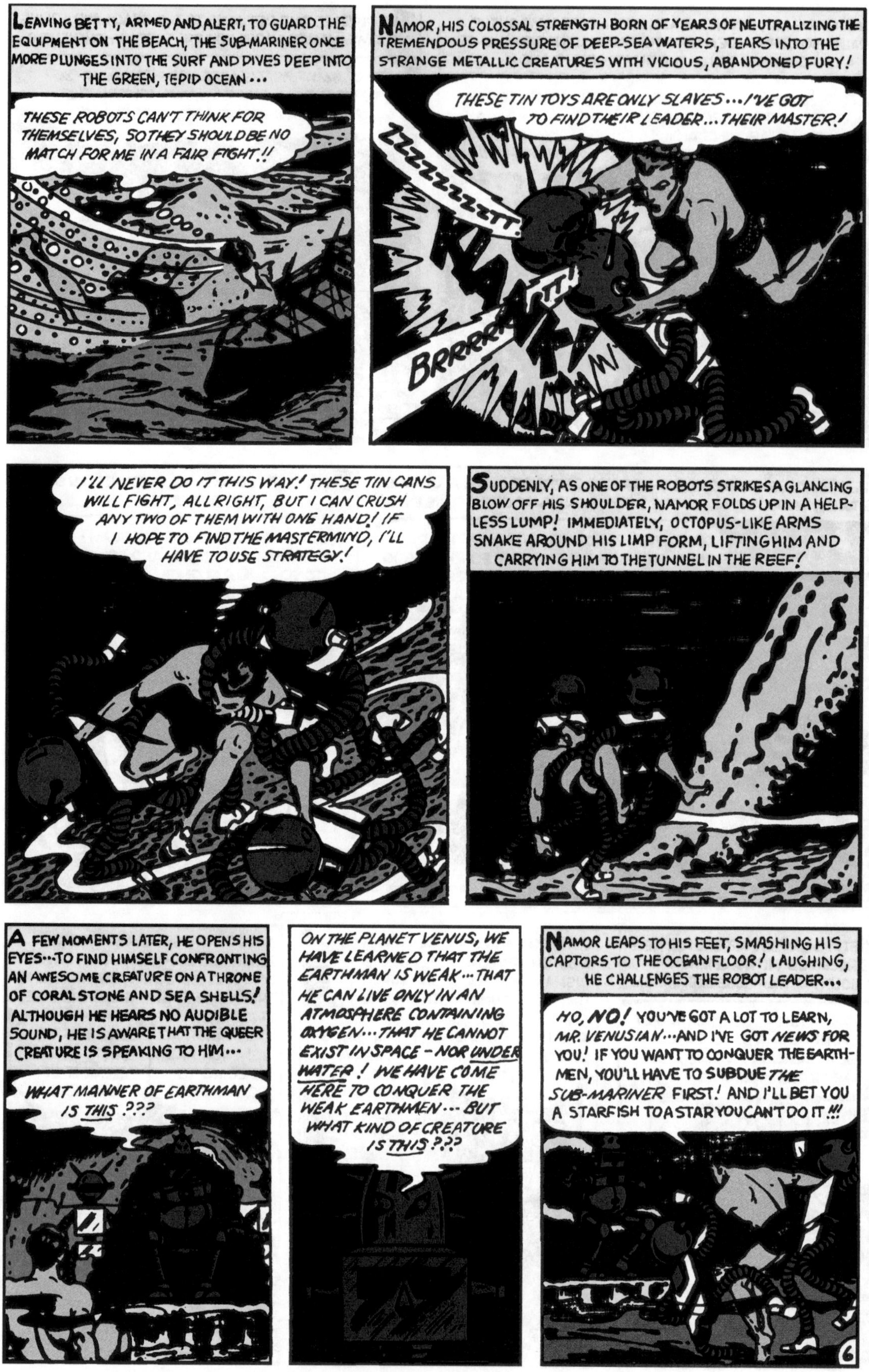
LEAVING BETTY, ARMED AND ALERT, TO GUARD THE EQUIPMENT ON THE BEACH, THE SUB-MARINER ONCE MORE PLUNGES INTO THE SURF AND DIVES DEEP INTO THE GREEN, TEPID OCEAN...
THESE ROBOTS CAN'T THINK FOR THEMSELVES, SO THEY SHOULD BE NO MATCH FOR ME IN A FAIR FIGHT!!
NAMOR, HIS COLOSSAL STRENGTH BORN OF YEARS OF NEUTRALIZING THE TREMENDOUS PRESSURE OF DEEP-SEA WATERS, TEARS INTO THE STRANGE METALLIC CREATURES WITH VICIOUS, ABANDONED FURY!
THESE TIN TOYS ARE ONLY SLAVES...I'VE GOT TO FIND THEIR LEADER...THEIR MASTER!
ZZZZZZZZZZTT!
BRRRRAKTTT!
I'LL NEVER DO IT THIS WAY! THESE TIN CANS WILL FIGHT, ALL RIGHT, BUT I CAN CRUSH ANY TWO OF THEM WITH ONE HAND! IF I HOPE TO FIND THE MASTERMIND, I'LL HAVE TO USE STRATEGY!
SUDDENLY, AS ONE OF THE ROBOTS STRIKES A GLANCING BLOW OFF HIS SHOULDER, NAMOR FOLDS UP IN A HELPLESS LUMP! IMMEDIATELY, OCTOPUS-LIKE ARMS SNAKE AROUND HIS LIMP FORM, LIFTING HIM AND CARRYING HIM TO THE TUNNEL IN THE REEF!
A FEW MOMENTS LATER, HE OPENS HIS EYES...TO FIND HIMSELF CONFRONTING AN AWESOME CREATURE ON A THRONE OF CORAL STONE AND SEA SHELLS! ALTHOUGH HE HEARS NO AUDIBLE SOUND, HE IS AWARE THAT THE QUEER CREATURE IS SPEAKING TO HIM...
WHAT MANNER OF EARTHMAN IS THIS ???
ON THE PLANET VENUS, WE HAVE LEARNED THAT THE EARTHMAN IS WEAK...THAT HE CAN LIVE ONLY IN AN ATMOSPHERE CONTAINING OXYGEN...THAT HE CANNOT EXIST IN SPACE - NOR UNDER WATER! WE HAVE COME HERE TO CONQUER THE WEAK EARTHMEN...BUT WHAT KIND OF CREATURE IS THIS ???
NAMOR LEAPS TO HIS FEET, SMASHING HIS CAPTORS TO THE OCEAN FLOOR! LAUGHING, HE CHALLENGES THE ROBOT LEADER...
HO, NO! YOU'VE GOT A LOT TO LEARN, MR. VENUSIAN...AND I'VE GOT NEWS FOR YOU! IF YOU WANT TO CONQUER THE EARTHMEN, YOU'LL HAVE TO SUBDUE THE SUB-MARINER FIRST! AND I'LL BET YOU A STARFISH TO A STAR YOU CAN'T DO IT!!!
6

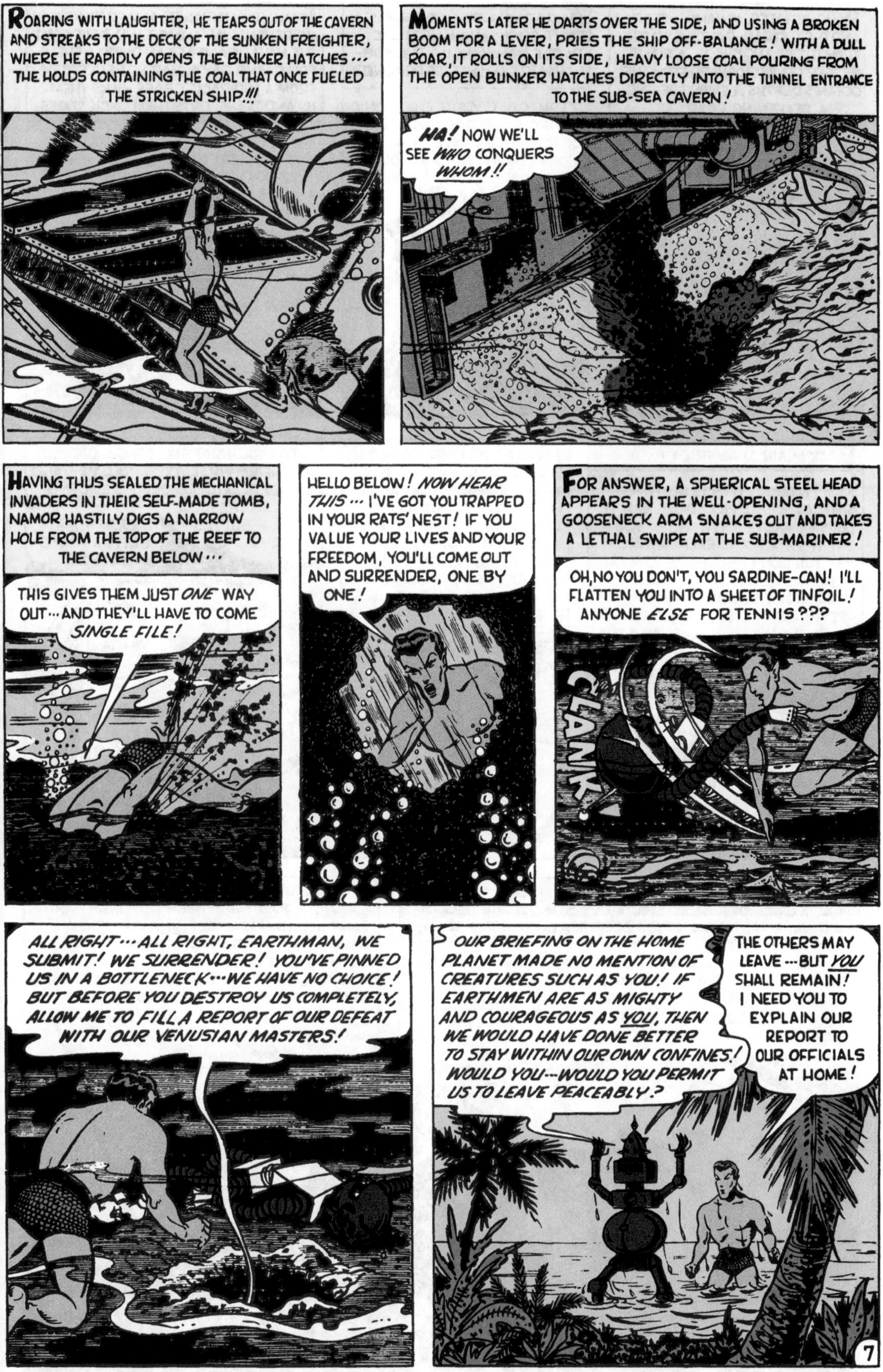
ROARING WITH LAUGHTER, HE TEARS OUT OF THE CAVERN AND STREAKS TO THE DECK OF THE SUNKEN FREIGHTER, WHERE HE RAPIDLY OPENS THE BUNKER HATCHES ... THE HOLDS CONTAINING THE COAL THAT ONCE FUELED THE STRICKEN SHIP!!!
MOMENTS LATER HE DARTS OVER THE SIDE, AND USING A BROKEN BOOM FOR A LEVER, PRIES THE SHIP OFF-BALANCE! WITH A DULL ROAR, IT ROLLS ON ITS SIDE, HEAVY LOOSE COAL POURING FROM THE OPEN BUNKER HATCHES DIRECTLY INTO THE TUNNEL ENTRANCE TO THE SUB-SEA CAVERN!
HA! NOW WE'LL SEE WHO CONQUERS WHOM!!
HAVING THUS SEALED THE MECHANICAL INVADERS IN THEIR SELF-MADE TOMB, NAMOR HASTILY DIGS A NARROW HOLE FROM THE TOP OF THE REEF TO THE CAVERN BELOW...
THIS GIVES THEM JUST ONE WAY OUT... AND THEY'LL HAVE TO COME SINGLE FILE!
HELLO BELOW! NOW HEAR THIS ... I'VE GOT YOU TRAPPED IN YOUR RATS' NEST! IF YOU VALUE YOUR LIVES AND YOUR FREEDOM, YOU'LL COME OUT AND SURRENDER, ONE BY ONE!
FOR ANSWER, A SPHERICAL STEEL HEAD APPEARS IN THE WELL-OPENING, AND A GOOSENECK ARM SNAKES OUT AND TAKES A LETHAL SWIPE AT THE SUB-MARINER!
OH, NO YOU DON'T, YOU SARDINE-CAN! I'LL FLATTEN YOU INTO A SHEET OF TINFOIL! ANYONE ELSE FOR TENNIS???
CLANK
ALL RIGHT ... ALL RIGHT, EARTHMAN, WE SUBMIT! WE SURRENDER! YOU'VE PINNED US IN A BOTTLENECK ... WE HAVE NO CHOICE! BUT BEFORE YOU DESTROY US COMPLETELY, ALLOW ME TO FILL A REPORT OF OUR DEFEAT WITH OUR VENUSIAN MASTERS!
OUR BRIEFING ON THE HOME PLANET MADE NO MENTION OF CREATURES SUCH AS YOU! IF EARTHMEN ARE AS MIGHTY AND COURAGEOUS AS YOU, THEN WE WOULD HAVE DONE BETTER TO STAY WITHIN OUR OWN CONFINES! WOULD YOU---WOULD YOU PERMIT US TO LEAVE PEACEABLY?
THE OTHERS MAY LEAVE --- BUT YOU SHALL REMAIN! I NEED YOU TO EXPLAIN OUR REPORT TO OUR OFFICIALS AT HOME!

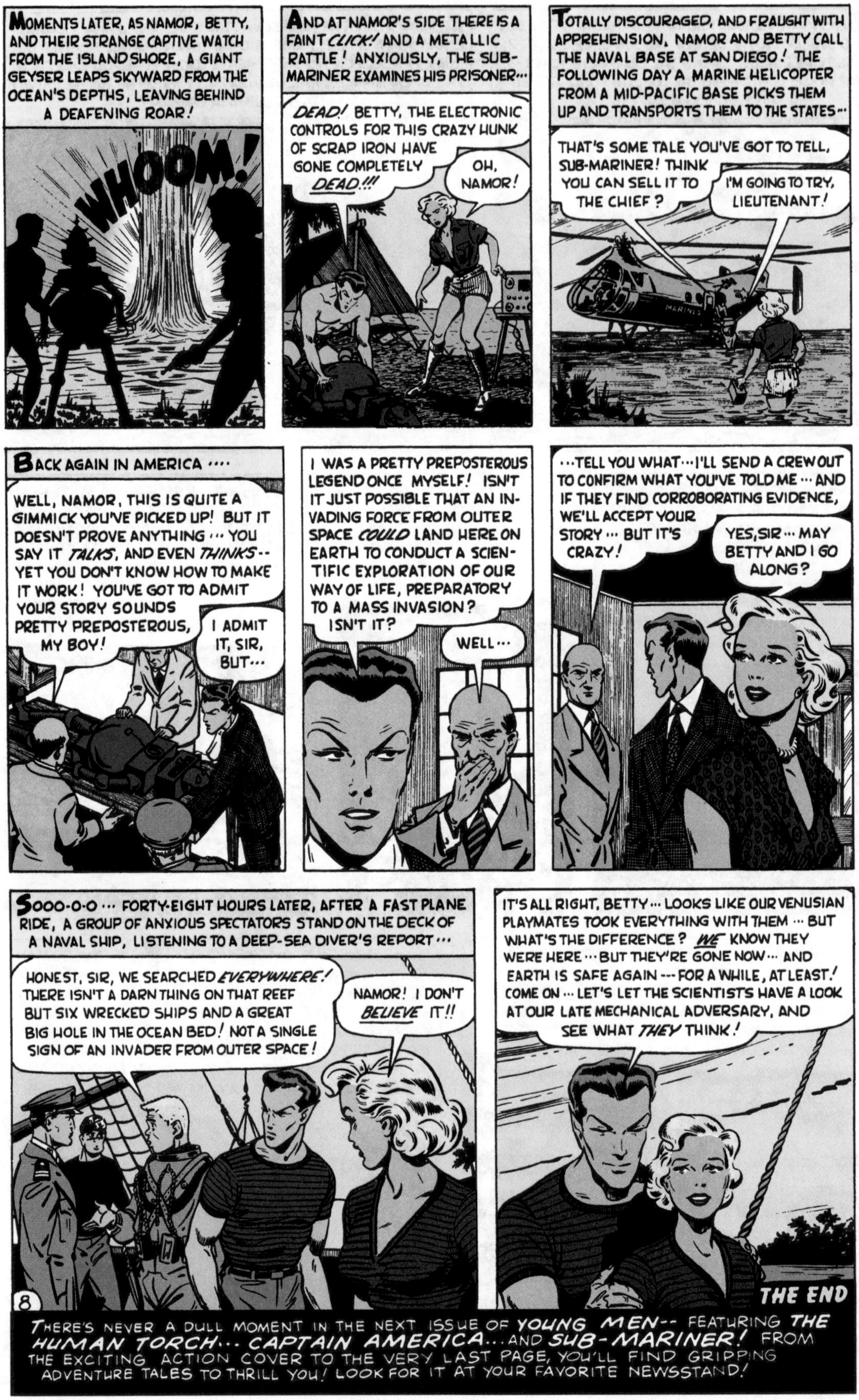
MOMENTS LATER, AS NAMOR, BETTY, AND THEIR STRANGE CAPTIVE WATCH FROM THE ISLAND SHORE, A GIANT GEYSER LEAPS SKYWARD FROM THE OCEAN'S DEPTHS, LEAVING BEHIND A DEAFENING ROAR!
WHOOM!
AND AT NAMOR'S SIDE THERE IS A FAINT CLICK! AND A METALLIC RATTLE! ANXIOUSLY, THE SUB-MARINER EXAMINES HIS PRISONER...
DEAD! BETTY, THE ELECTRONIC CONTROLS FOR THIS CRAZY HUNK OF SCRAP IRON HAVE GONE COMPLETELY DEAD!!!
OH, NAMOR!
TOTALLY DISCOURAGED, AND FRAUGHT WITH APPREHENSION, NAMOR AND BETTY CALL THE NAVAL BASE AT SAN DIEGO! THE FOLLOWING DAY A MARINE HELICOPTER FROM A MID-PACIFIC BASE PICKS THEM UP AND TRANSPORTS THEM TO THE STATES...
THAT'S SOME TALE YOU'VE GOT TO TELL, SUB-MARINER! THINK YOU CAN SELL IT TO THE CHIEF?
I'M GOING TO TRY, LIEUTENANT!
MARINES
BACK AGAIN IN AMERICA ....
WELL, NAMOR, THIS IS QUITE A GIMMICK YOU'VE PICKED UP! BUT IT DOESN'T PROVE ANYTHING ... YOU SAY IT TALKS, AND EVEN THINKS -- YET YOU DON'T KNOW HOW TO MAKE IT WORK! YOU'VE GOT TO ADMIT YOUR STORY SOUNDS PRETTY PREPOSTEROUS, MY BOY!
I ADMIT IT, SIR, BUT...
I WAS A PRETTY PREPOSTEROUS LEGEND ONCE MYSELF! ISN'T IT JUST POSSIBLE THAT AN INVADING FORCE FROM OUTER SPACE COULD LAND HERE ON EARTH TO CONDUCT A SCIENTIFIC EXPLORATION OF OUR WAY OF LIFE, PREPARATORY TO A MASS INVASION? ISN'T IT?
WELL...
...TELL YOU WHAT...I'LL SEND A CREW OUT TO CONFIRM WHAT YOU'VE TOLD ME ... AND IF THEY FIND CORROBORATING EVIDENCE, WE'LL ACCEPT YOUR STORY ... BUT IT'S CRAZY!
YES, SIR ... MAY BETTY AND I GO ALONG?
SOOO-O-O ... FORTY-EIGHT HOURS LATER, AFTER A FAST PLANE RIDE, A GROUP OF ANXIOUS SPECTATORS STAND ON THE DECK OF A NAVAL SHIP, LISTENING TO A DEEP-SEA DIVER'S REPORT...
HONEST, SIR, WE SEARCHED EVERYWHERE! THERE ISN'T A DARN THING ON THAT REEF BUT SIX WRECKED SHIPS AND A GREAT BIG HOLE IN THE OCEAN BED! NOT A SINGLE SIGN OF AN INVADER FROM OUTER SPACE!
NAMOR! I DON'T BELIEVE IT!!
8
IT'S ALL RIGHT, BETTY ... LOOKS LIKE OUR VENUSIAN PLAYMATES TOOK EVERYTHING WITH THEM ... BUT WHAT'S THE DIFFERENCE? WE KNOW THEY WERE HERE ... BUT THEY'RE GONE NOW ... AND EARTH IS SAFE AGAIN --- FOR A WHILE, AT LEAST! COME ON ... LET'S LET THE SCIENTISTS HAVE A LOOK AT OUR LATE MECHANICAL ADVERSARY, AND SEE WHAT THEY THINK!
THE END
THERE'S NEVER A DULL MOMENT IN THE NEXT ISSUE OF YOUNG MEN-- FEATURING THE HUMAN TORCH... CAPTAIN AMERICA... AND SUB-MARINER! FROM THE EXCITING ACTION COVER TO THE VERY LAST PAGE, YOU'LL FIND GRIPPING ADVENTURE TALES TO THRILL YOU! LOOK FOR IT AT YOUR FAVORITE NEWSSTAND!

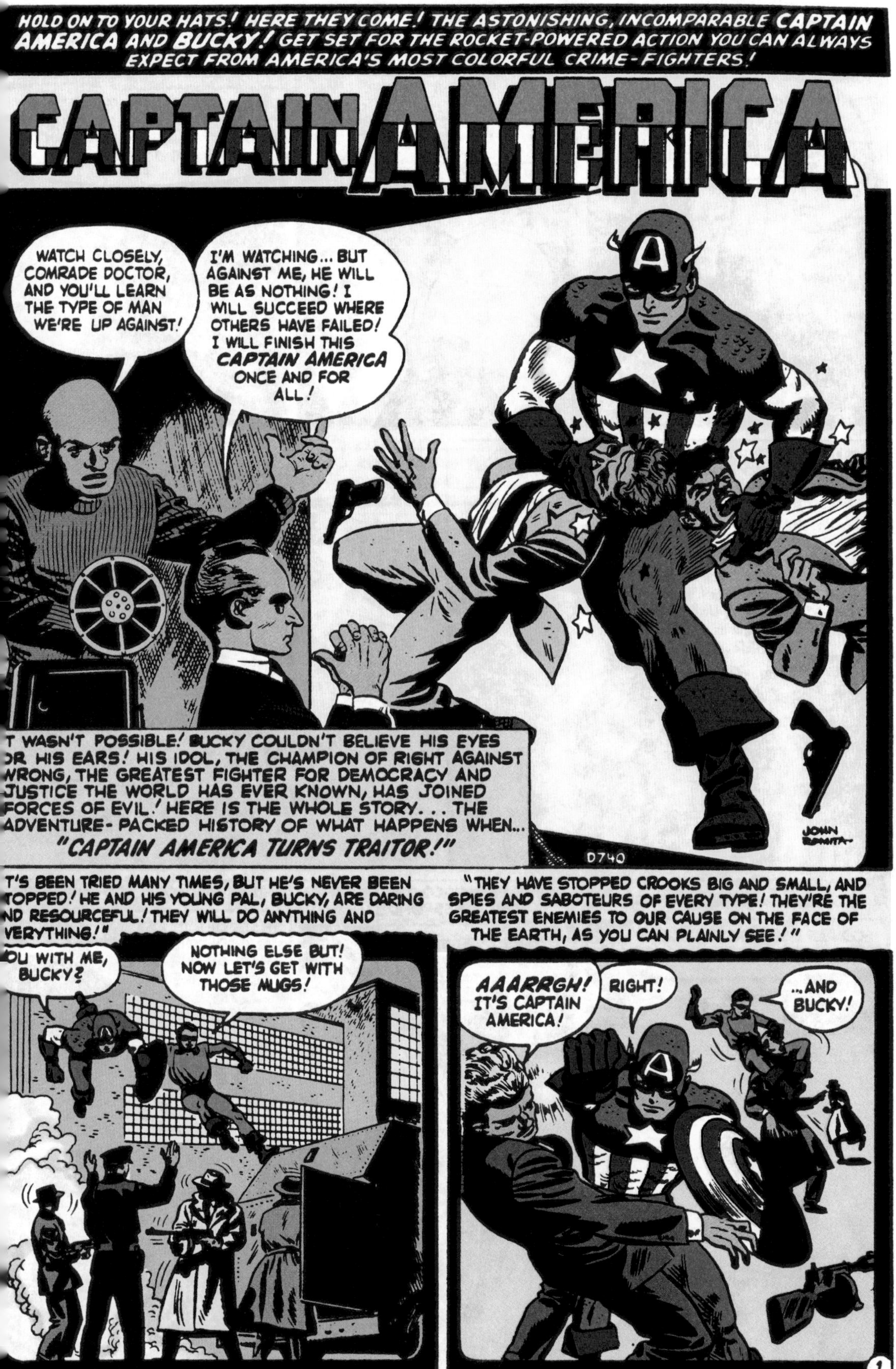
HOLD ON TO YOUR HATS! HERE THEY COME! THE ASTONISHING, INCOMPARABLE CAPTAIN AMERICA AND BUCKY! GET SET FOR THE ROCKET-POWERED ACTION YOU CAN ALWAYS EXPECT FROM AMERICA'S MOST COLORFUL CRIME-FIGHTERS!
CAPTAIN AMERICA
WATCH CLOSELY, COMRADE DOCTOR, AND YOU'LL LEARN THE TYPE OF MAN WE'RE UP AGAINST!
I'M WATCHING... BUT AGAINST ME, HE WILL BE AS NOTHING! I WILL SUCCEED WHERE OTHERS HAVE FAILED! I WILL FINISH THIS CAPTAIN AMERICA ONCE AND FOR ALL!
T WASN'T POSSIBLE! BUCKY COULDN'T BELIEVE HIS EYES OR HIS EARS! HIS IDOL, THE CHAMPION OF RIGHT AGAINST WRONG, THE GREATEST FIGHTER FOR DEMOCRACY AND JUSTICE THE WORLD HAS EVER KNOWN, HAS JOINED FORCES OF EVIL! HERE IS THE WHOLE STORY... THE ADVENTURE-PACKED HISTORY OF WHAT HAPPENS WHEN...
"CAPTAIN AMERICA TURNS TRAITOR!"
JOHN ROMITA
D740
T'S BEEN TRIED MANY TIMES, BUT HE'S NEVER BEEN TOPPED! HE AND HIS YOUNG PAL, BUCKY, ARE DARING ND RESOURCEFUL! THEY WILL DO ANYTHING AND VERYTHING!"
OU WITH ME, BUCKY?
NOTHING ELSE BUT! NOW LET'S GET WITH THOSE MUGS!
"THEY HAVE STOPPED CROOKS BIG AND SMALL, AND SPIES AND SABOTEURS OF EVERY TYPE! THEY'RE THE GREATEST ENEMIES TO OUR CAUSE ON THE FACE OF THE EARTH, AS YOU CAN PLAINLY SEE!"
AAARRGH! IT'S CAPTAIN AMERICA!
RIGHT!
...AND BUCKY!

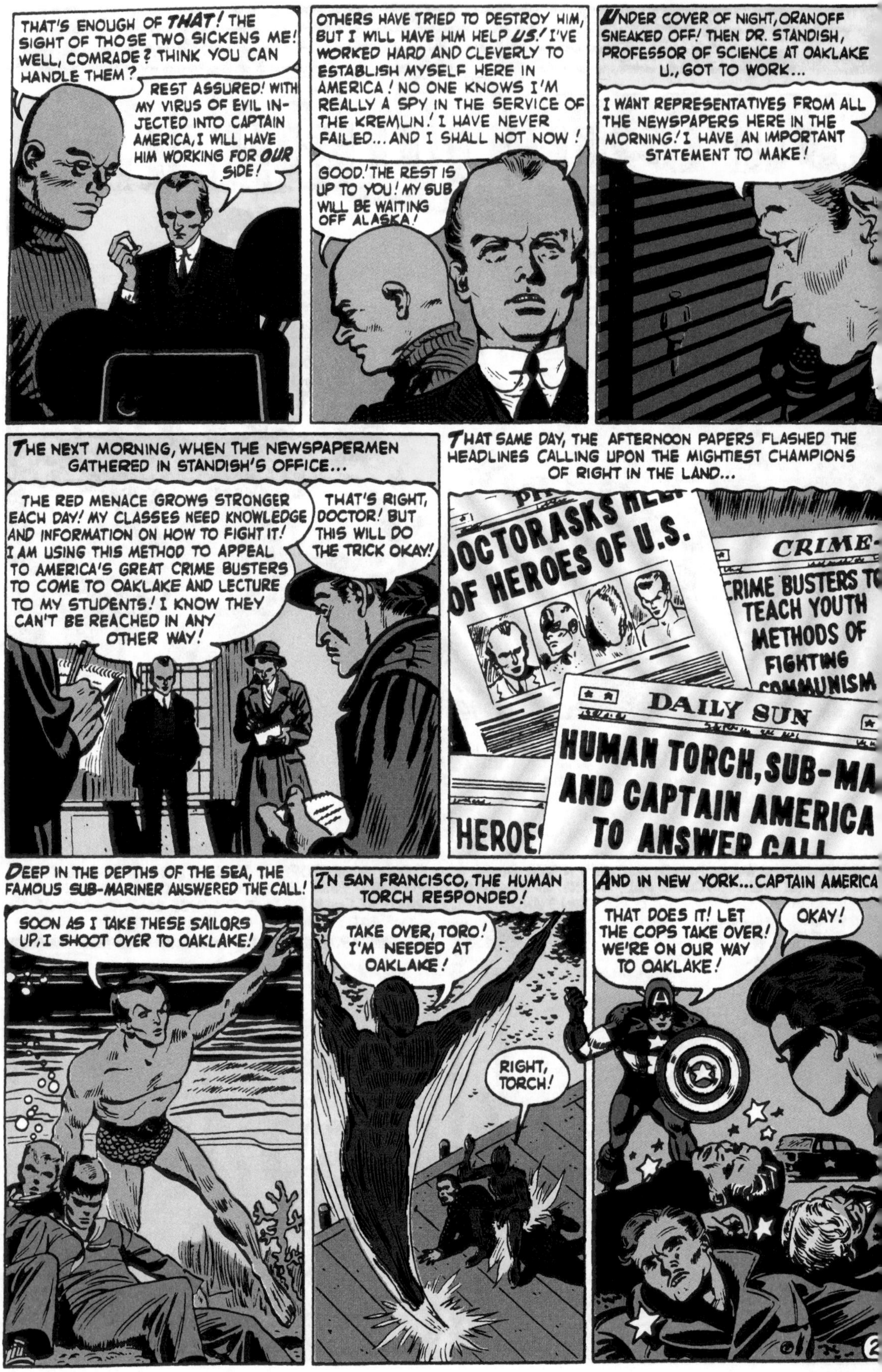
THAT'S ENOUGH OF THAT! THE SIGHT OF THOSE TWO SICKENS ME! WELL, COMRADE? THINK YOU CAN HANDLE THEM?
REST ASSURED! WITH MY VIRUS OF EVIL INJECTED INTO CAPTAIN AMERICA, I WILL HAVE HIM WORKING FOR OUR SIDE!
OTHERS HAVE TRIED TO DESTROY HIM, BUT I WILL HAVE HIM HELP US! I'VE WORKED HARD AND CLEVERLY TO ESTABLISH MYSELF HERE IN AMERICA! NO ONE KNOWS I'M REALLY A SPY IN THE SERVICE OF THE KREMLIN! I HAVE NEVER FAILED... AND I SHALL NOT NOW!
GOOD! THE REST IS UP TO YOU! MY SUB WILL BE WAITING OFF ALASKA!
UNDER COVER OF NIGHT, ORANOFF SNEAKED OFF! THEN DR. STANDISH, PROFESSOR OF SCIENCE AT OAKLAKE U., GOT TO WORK...
I WANT REPRESENTATIVES FROM ALL THE NEWSPAPERS HERE IN THE MORNING! I HAVE AN IMPORTANT STATEMENT TO MAKE!
THE NEXT MORNING, WHEN THE NEWSPAPERMEN GATHERED IN STANDISH'S OFFICE...
THE RED MENACE GROWS STRONGER EACH DAY! MY CLASSES NEED KNOWLEDGE AND INFORMATION ON HOW TO FIGHT IT! I AM USING THIS METHOD TO APPEAL TO AMERICA'S GREAT CRIME BUSTERS TO COME TO OAKLAKE AND LECTURE TO MY STUDENTS! I KNOW THEY CAN'T BE REACHED IN ANY OTHER WAY!
THAT'S RIGHT, DOCTOR! BUT THIS WILL DO THE TRICK OKAY!
THAT SAME DAY, THE AFTERNOON PAPERS FLASHED THE HEADLINES CALLING UPON THE MIGHTIEST CHAMPIONS OF RIGHT IN THE LAND...
DOCTOR ASKS HEL
OF HEROES OF U.S.
CRIME-
CRIME BUSTERS TO TEACH YOUTH METHODS OF FIGHTING COMMUNISM
DAILY SUN
HUMAN TORCH, SUB-MA AND CAPTAIN AMERICA TO ANSWER CALL
HEROES
DEEP IN THE DEPTHS OF THE SEA, THE FAMOUS SUB-MARINER ANSWERED THE CALL!
SOON AS I TAKE THESE SAILORS UP, I SHOOT OVER TO OAKLAKE!
IN SAN FRANCISCO, THE HUMAN TORCH RESPONDED!
TAKE OVER, TORO! I'M NEEDED AT OAKLAKE!
RIGHT, TORCH!
AND IN NEW YORK... CAPTAIN AMERICA
THAT DOES IT! LET THE COPS TAKE OVER! WE'RE ON OUR WAY TO OAKLAKE!
OKAY!
2

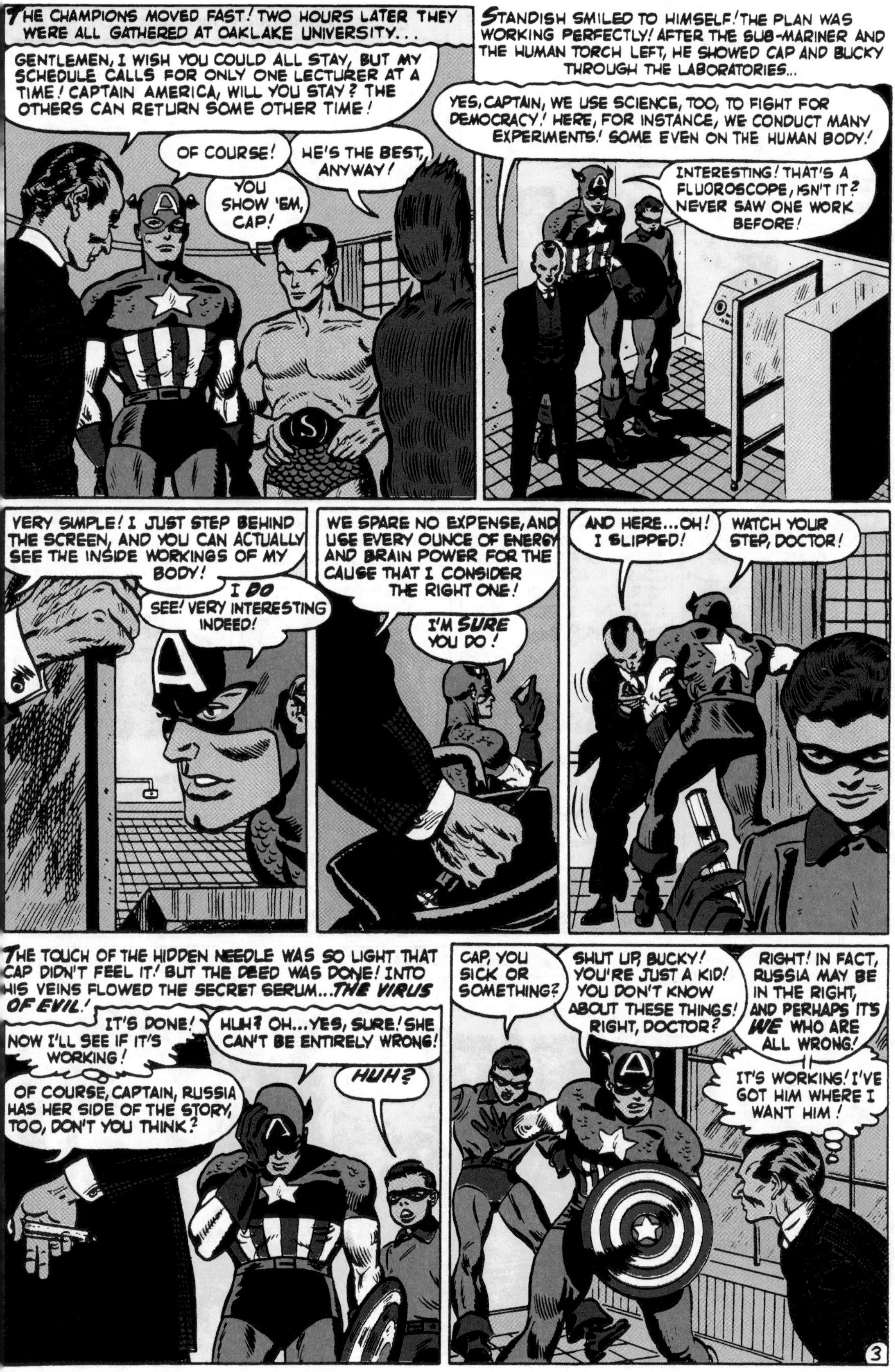
THE CHAMPIONS MOVED FAST! TWO HOURS LATER THEY WERE ALL GATHERED AT OAKLAKE UNIVERSITY...
GENTLEMEN, I WISH YOU COULD ALL STAY, BUT MY SCHEDULE CALLS FOR ONLY ONE LECTURER AT A TIME! CAPTAIN AMERICA, WILL YOU STAY? THE OTHERS CAN RETURN SOME OTHER TIME!
OF COURSE!
YOU SHOW 'EM, CAP!
HE'S THE BEST, ANYWAY!
STANDISH SMILED TO HIMSELF! THE PLAN WAS WORKING PERFECTLY! AFTER THE SUB-MARINER AND THE HUMAN TORCH LEFT, HE SHOWED CAP AND BUCKY THROUGH THE LABORATORIES...
YES, CAPTAIN, WE USE SCIENCE, TOO, TO FIGHT FOR DEMOCRACY! HERE, FOR INSTANCE, WE CONDUCT MANY EXPERIMENTS! SOME EVEN ON THE HUMAN BODY!
INTERESTING! THAT'S A FLUOROSCOPE, ISN'T IT? NEVER SAW ONE WORK BEFORE!
VERY SIMPLE! I JUST STEP BEHIND THE SCREEN, AND YOU CAN ACTUALLY SEE THE INSIDE WORKINGS OF MY BODY!
I DO SEE! VERY INTERESTING INDEED!
WE SPARE NO EXPENSE, AND USE EVERY OUNCE OF ENERGY AND BRAIN POWER FOR THE CAUSE THAT I CONSIDER THE RIGHT ONE!
I'M SURE YOU DO!
AND HERE...OH! I SLIPPED!
WATCH YOUR STEP, DOCTOR!
THE TOUCH OF THE HIDDEN NEEDLE WAS SO LIGHT THAT CAP DIDN'T FEEL IT! BUT THE DEED WAS DONE! INTO HIS VEINS FLOWED THE SECRET SERUM...THE VIRUS OF EVIL!
IT'S DONE! NOW I'LL SEE IF IT'S WORKING!
HUH? OH...YES, SURE! SHE CAN'T BE ENTIRELY WRONG!
OF COURSE, CAPTAIN, RUSSIA HAS HER SIDE OF THE STORY, TOO, DON'T YOU THINK?
HUH?
CAP, YOU SICK OR SOMETHING?
SHUT UP, BUCKY! YOU'RE JUST A KID! YOU DON'T KNOW ABOUT THESE THINGS! RIGHT, DOCTOR?
RIGHT! IN FACT, RUSSIA MAY BE IN THE RIGHT, AND PERHAPS IT'S WE WHO ARE ALL WRONG!
IT'S WORKING! I'VE GOT HIM WHERE I WANT HIM!
3

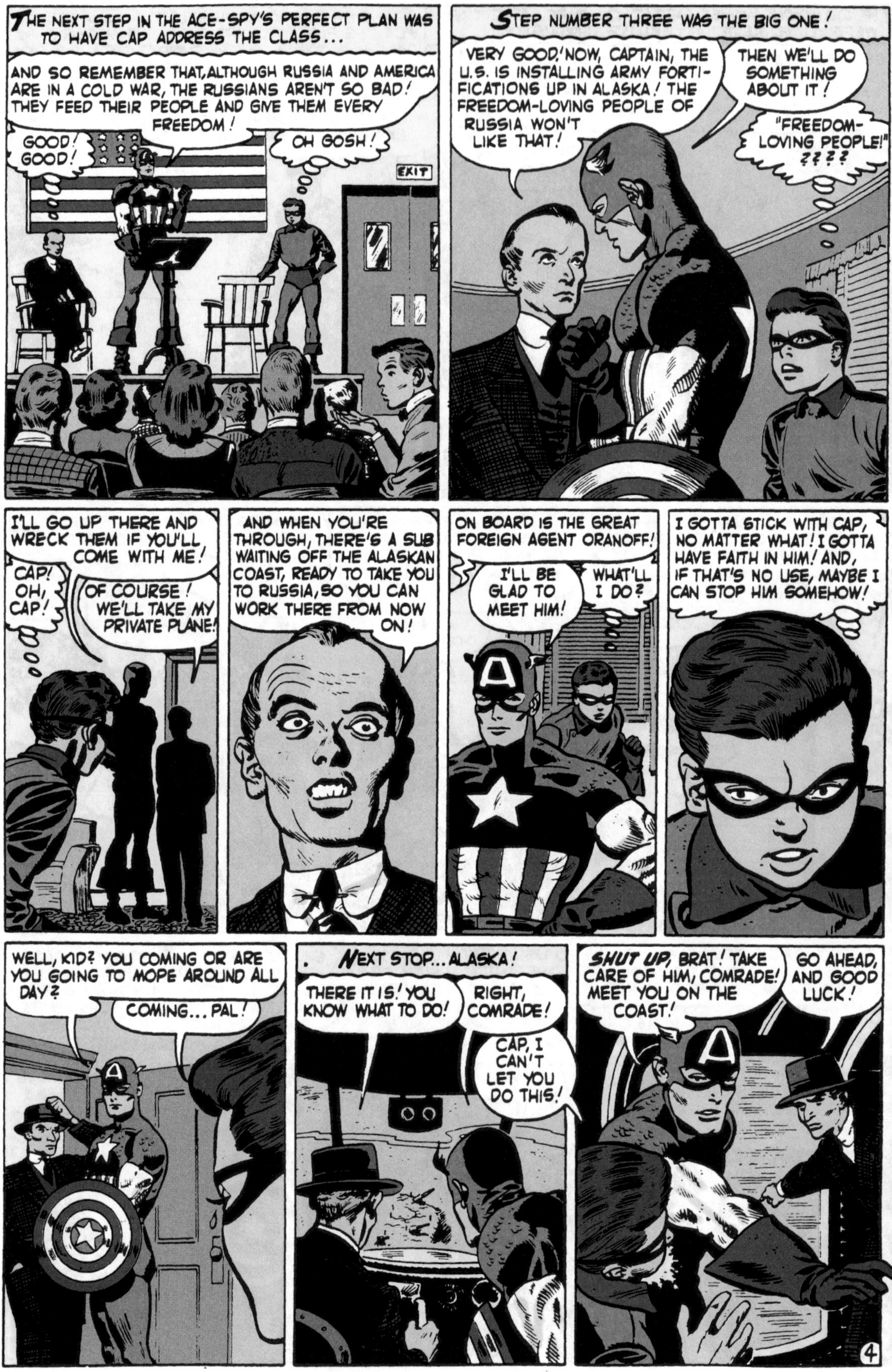
THE NEXT STEP IN THE ACE-SPY'S PERFECT PLAN WAS TO HAVE CAP ADDRESS THE CLASS...
AND SO REMEMBER THAT, ALTHOUGH RUSSIA AND AMERICA ARE IN A COLD WAR, THE RUSSIANS AREN'T SO BAD! THEY FEED THEIR PEOPLE AND GIVE THEM EVERY FREEDOM!
GOOD! GOOD!
OH GOSH!
EXIT
STEP NUMBER THREE WAS THE BIG ONE!
VERY GOOD! NOW, CAPTAIN, THE U.S. IS INSTALLING ARMY FORTIFICATIONS UP IN ALASKA! THE FREEDOM-LOVING PEOPLE OF RUSSIA WON'T LIKE THAT!
THEN WE'LL DO SOMETHING ABOUT IT!
"FREEDOM-LOVING PEOPLE!" ????
I'LL GO UP THERE AND WRECK THEM IF YOU'LL COME WITH ME!
CAP! OH, CAP!
OF COURSE! WE'LL TAKE MY PRIVATE PLANE!
AND WHEN YOU'RE THROUGH, THERE'S A SUB WAITING OFF THE ALASKAN COAST, READY TO TAKE YOU TO RUSSIA, SO YOU CAN WORK THERE FROM NOW ON!
ON BOARD IS THE GREAT FOREIGN AGENT ORANOFF!
I'LL BE GLAD TO MEET HIM!
WHAT'LL I DO?
I GOTTA STICK WITH CAP, NO MATTER WHAT! I GOTTA HAVE FAITH IN HIM! AND, IF THAT'S NO USE, MAYBE I CAN STOP HIM SOMEHOW!
WELL, KID? YOU COMING OR ARE YOU GOING TO MOPE AROUND ALL DAY?
COMING... PAL!
NEXT STOP... ALASKA!
THERE IT IS! YOU KNOW WHAT TO DO!
RIGHT, COMRADE!
CAP, I CAN'T LET YOU DO THIS!
SHUT UP, BRAT! TAKE CARE OF HIM, COMRADE! MEET YOU ON THE COAST!
GO AHEAD, AND GOOD LUCK!

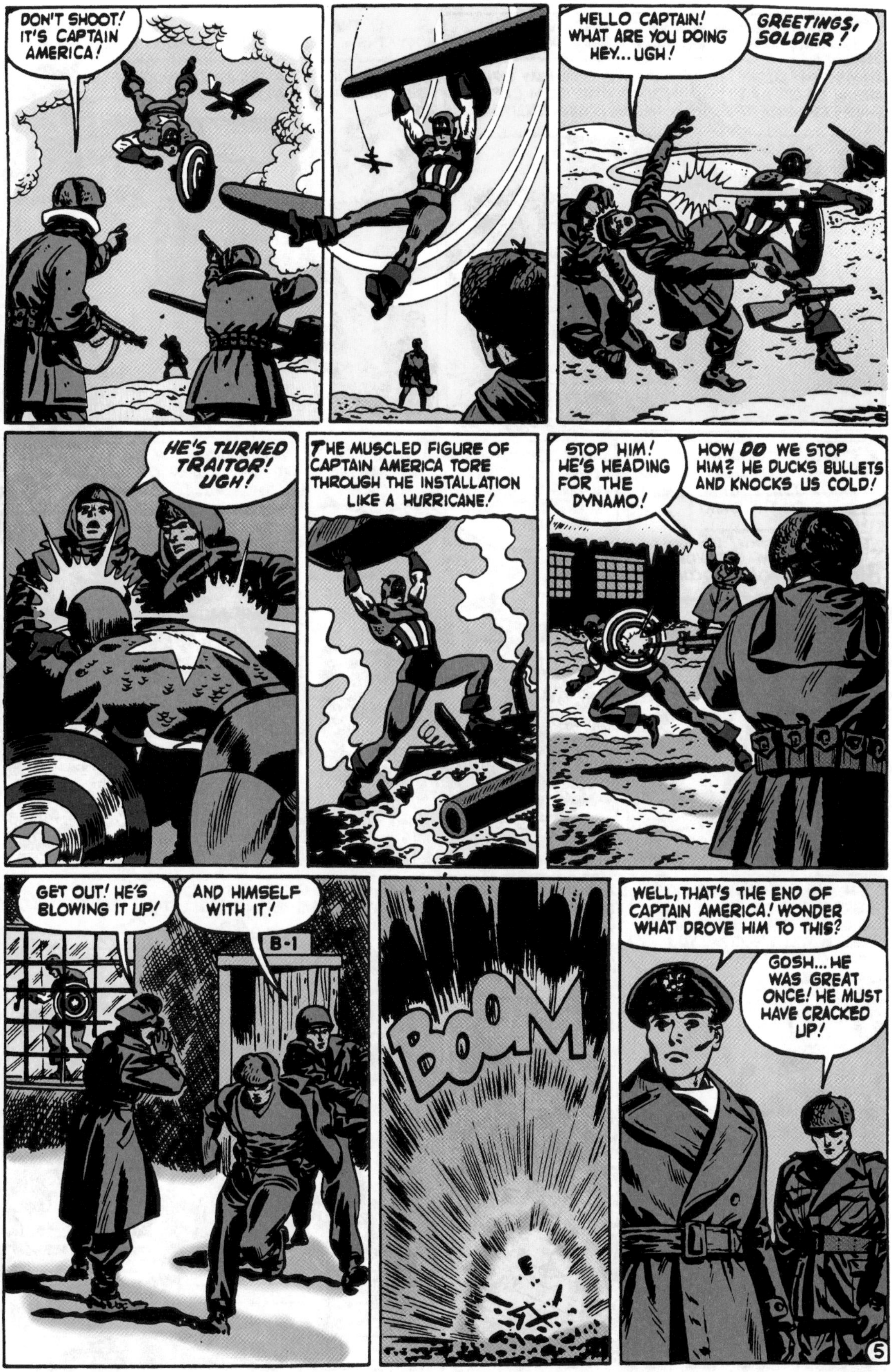
DON'T SHOOT! IT'S CAPTAIN AMERICA!
HELLO CAPTAIN! WHAT ARE YOU DOING HEY... UGH!
GREETINGS, SOLDIER!
HE'S TURNED TRAITOR! UGH!
THE MUSCLED FIGURE OF CAPTAIN AMERICA TORE THROUGH THE INSTALLATION LIKE A HURRICANE!
STOP HIM! HE'S HEADING FOR THE DYNAMO!
HOW DO WE STOP HIM? HE DUCKS BULLETS AND KNOCKS US COLD!
GET OUT! HE'S BLOWING IT UP!
AND HIMSELF WITH IT!
B-1
BOOM
WELL, THAT'S THE END OF CAPTAIN AMERICA! WONDER WHAT DROVE HIM TO THIS?
GOSH... HE WAS GREAT ONCE! HE MUST HAVE CRACKED UP!
5

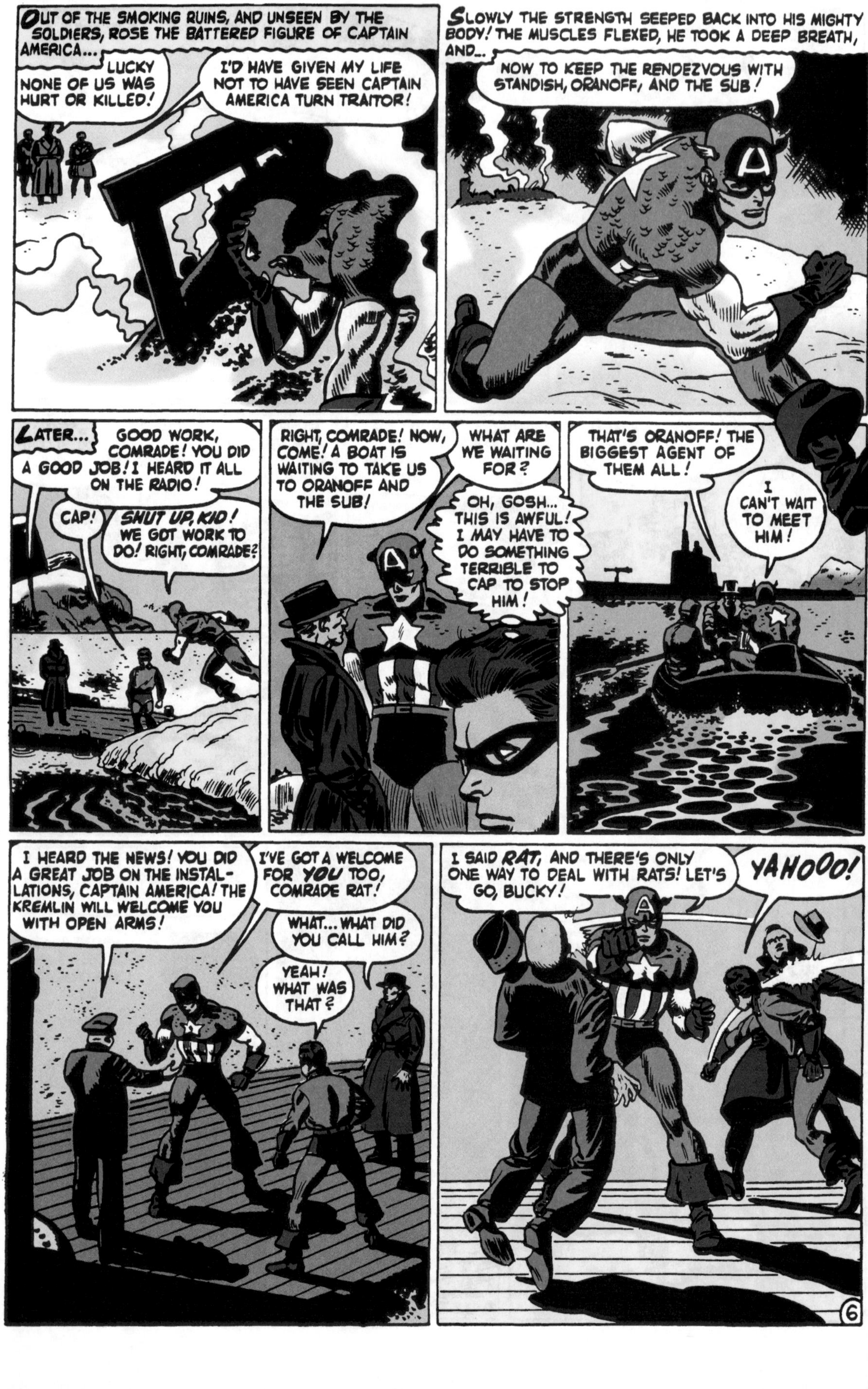
OUT OF THE SMOKING RUINS, AND UNSEEN BY THE SOLDIERS, ROSE THE BATTERED FIGURE OF CAPTAIN AMERICA...
LUCKY NONE OF US WAS HURT OR KILLED!
I'D HAVE GIVEN MY LIFE NOT TO HAVE SEEN CAPTAIN AMERICA TURN TRAITOR!
SLOWLY THE STRENGTH SEEPED BACK INTO HIS MIGHTY BODY! THE MUSCLES FLEXED, HE TOOK A DEEP BREATH, AND...
NOW TO KEEP THE RENDEZVOUS WITH STANDISH, ORANOFF, AND THE SUB!
LATER...
GOOD WORK, COMRADE! YOU DID A GOOD JOB! I HEARD IT ALL ON THE RADIO!
CAP!
SHUT UP, KID! WE GOT WORK TO DO! RIGHT, COMRADE?
RIGHT, COMRADE! NOW, COME! A BOAT IS WAITING TO TAKE US TO ORANOFF AND THE SUB!
WHAT ARE WE WAITING FOR?
OH, GOSH... THIS IS AWFUL! I MAY HAVE TO DO SOMETHING TERRIBLE TO CAP TO STOP HIM!
THAT'S ORANOFF! THE BIGGEST AGENT OF THEM ALL!
I CAN'T WAIT TO MEET HIM!
I HEARD THE NEWS! YOU DID A GREAT JOB ON THE INSTALLATIONS, CAPTAIN AMERICA! THE KREMLIN WILL WELCOME YOU WITH OPEN ARMS!
I'VE GOT A WELCOME FOR YOU TOO, COMRADE RAT!
WHAT... WHAT DID YOU CALL HIM?
YEAH! WHAT WAS THAT?
I SAID RAT, AND THERE'S ONLY ONE WAY TO DEAL WITH RATS! LET'S GO, BUCKY!
YAHOOO!
6

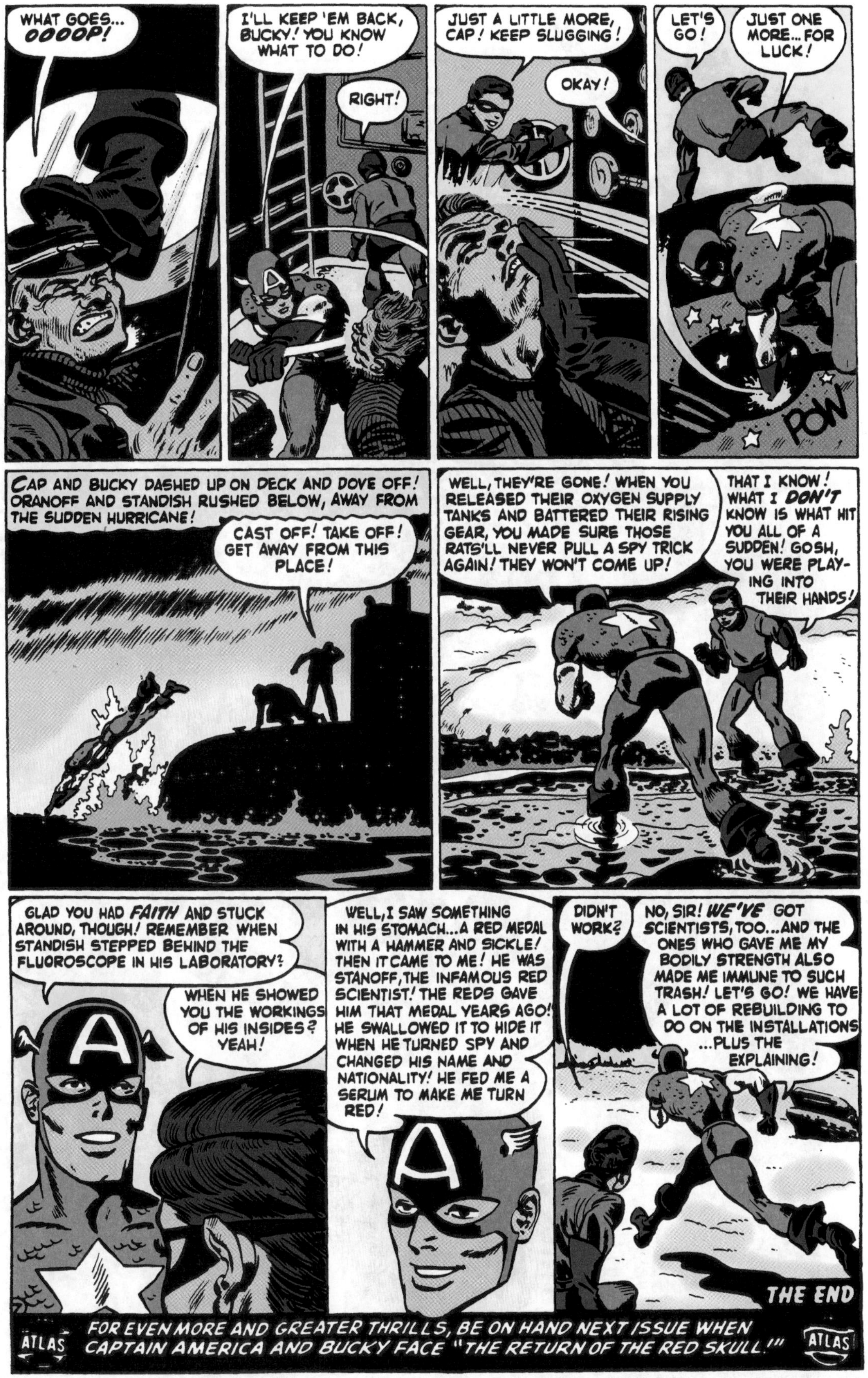
WHAT GOES... OOOOP!
I'LL KEEP 'EM BACK, BUCKY! YOU KNOW WHAT TO DO!
RIGHT!
JUST A LITTLE MORE, CAP! KEEP SLUGGING!
OKAY!
LET'S GO!
JUST ONE MORE... FOR LUCK!
POW
CAP AND BUCKY DASHED UP ON DECK AND DOVE OFF! ORANOFF AND STANDISH RUSHED BELOW, AWAY FROM THE SUDDEN HURRICANE!
CAST OFF! TAKE OFF! GET AWAY FROM THIS PLACE!
WELL, THEY'RE GONE! WHEN YOU RELEASED THEIR OXYGEN SUPPLY TANKS AND BATTERED THEIR RISING GEAR, YOU MADE SURE THOSE RATS'LL NEVER PULL A SPY TRICK AGAIN! THEY WON'T COME UP!
THAT I KNOW! WHAT I DON'T KNOW IS WHAT HIT YOU ALL OF A SUDDEN! GOSH, YOU WERE PLAYING INTO THEIR HANDS!
GLAD YOU HAD FAITH AND STUCK AROUND, THOUGH! REMEMBER WHEN STANDISH STEPPED BEHIND THE FLUOROSCOPE IN HIS LABORATORY?
WHEN HE SHOWED YOU THE WORKINGS OF HIS INSIDES? YEAH!
WELL, I SAW SOMETHING IN HIS STOMACH... A RED MEDAL WITH A HAMMER AND SICKLE! THEN IT CAME TO ME! HE WAS STANOFF, THE INFAMOUS RED SCIENTIST! THE REDS GAVE HIM THAT MEDAL YEARS AGO! HE SWALLOWED IT TO HIDE IT WHEN HE TURNED SPY AND CHANGED HIS NAME AND NATIONALITY! HE FED ME A SERUM TO MAKE ME TURN RED!
DIDN'T WORK?
NO, SIR! WE'VE GOT SCIENTISTS, TOO... AND THE ONES WHO GAVE ME MY BODILY STRENGTH ALSO MADE ME IMMUNE TO SUCH TRASH! LET'S GO! WE HAVE A LOT OF REBUILDING TO DO ON THE INSTALLATIONS ...PLUS THE EXPLAINING!
THE END
ATLAS
FOR EVEN MORE AND GREATER THRILLS, BE ON HAND NEXT ISSUE WHEN CAPTAIN AMERICA AND BUCKY FACE "THE RETURN OF THE RED SKULL."
ATLAS

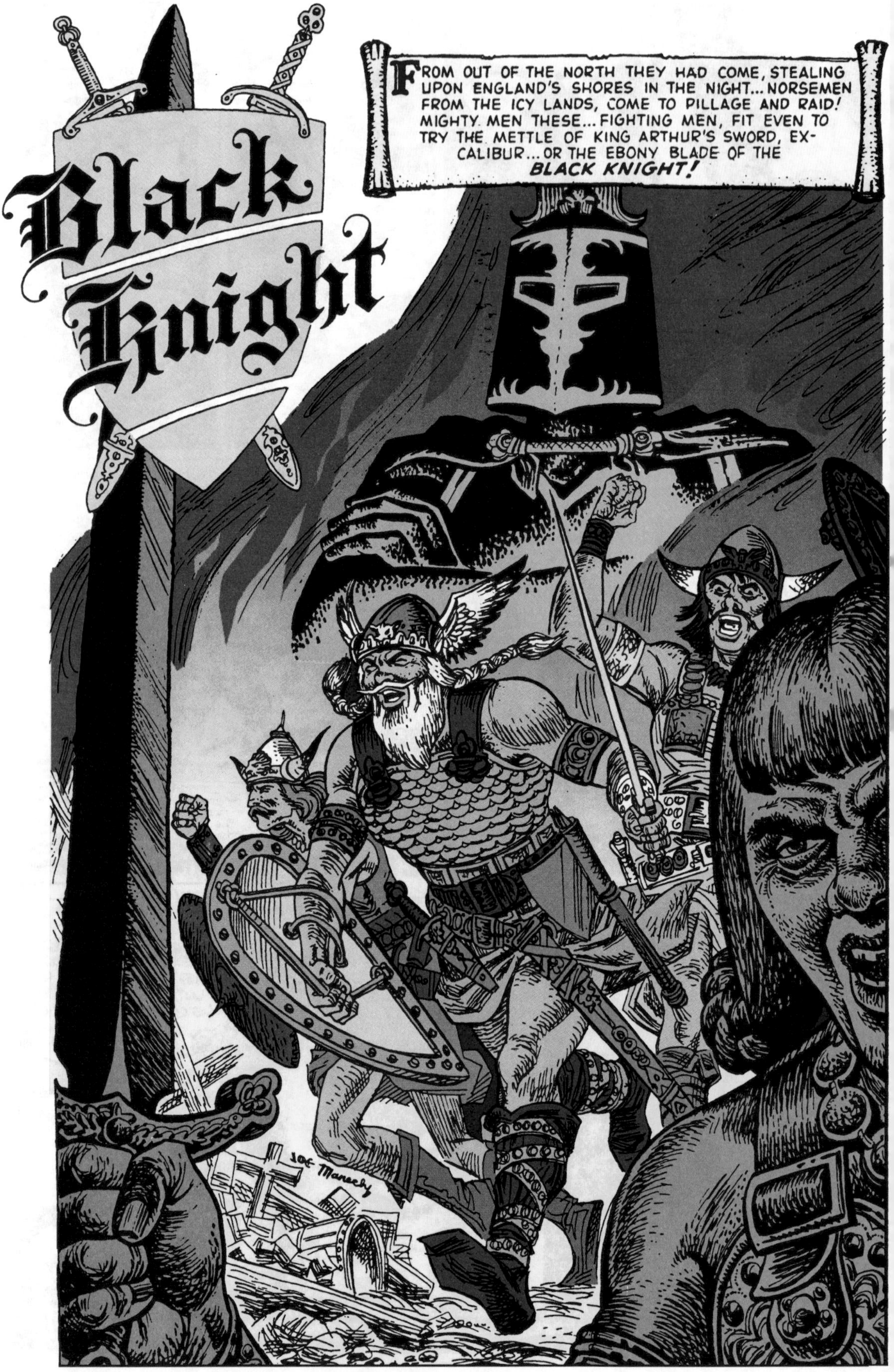
Black Knight
FROM OUT OF THE NORTH THEY HAD COME, STEALING UPON ENGLAND'S SHORES IN THE NIGHT... NORSEMEN FROM THE ICY LANDS, COME TO PILLAGE AND RAID! MIGHTY MEN THESE... FIGHTING MEN, FIT EVEN TO TRY THE METTLE OF KING ARTHUR'S SWORD, EX-CALIBUR... OR THE EBONY BLADE OF THE BLACK KNIGHT!
JOE Maneely

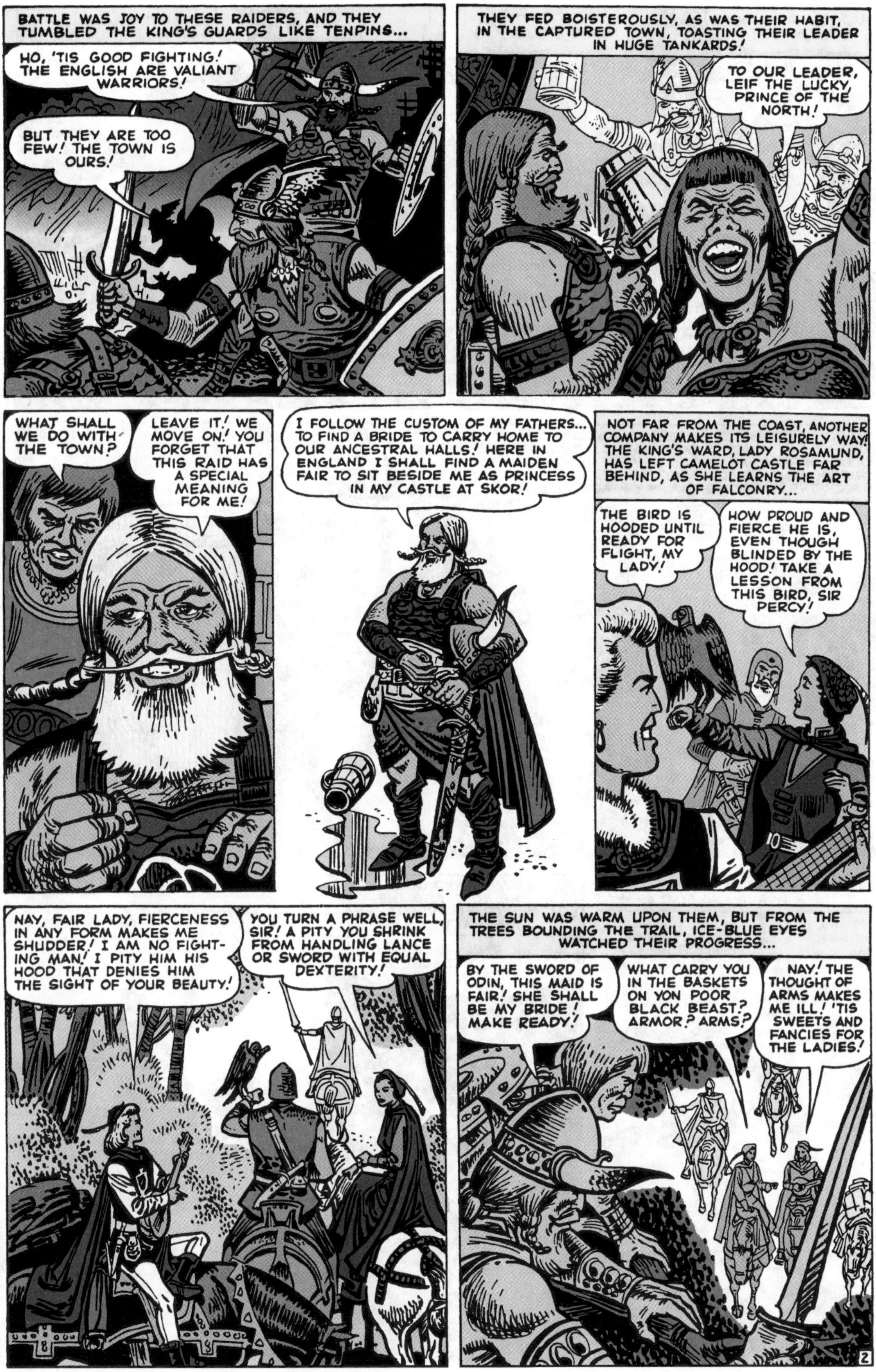
BATTLE WAS JOY TO THESE RAIDERS, AND THEY TUMBLED THE KING'S GUARDS LIKE TENPINS...
HO, 'TIS GOOD FIGHTING! THE ENGLISH ARE VALIANT WARRIORS!
BUT THEY ARE TOO FEW! THE TOWN IS OURS!
THEY FED BOISTEROUSLY, AS WAS THEIR HABIT, IN THE CAPTURED TOWN, TOASTING THEIR LEADER IN HUGE TANKARDS!
TO OUR LEADER, LEIF THE LUCKY, PRINCE OF THE NORTH!
WHAT SHALL WE DO WITH THE TOWN?
LEAVE IT! WE MOVE ON! YOU FORGET THAT THIS RAID HAS A SPECIAL MEANING FOR ME!
I FOLLOW THE CUSTOM OF MY FATHERS... TO FIND A BRIDE TO CARRY HOME TO OUR ANCESTRAL HALLS! HERE IN ENGLAND I SHALL FIND A MAIDEN FAIR TO SIT BESIDE ME AS PRINCESS IN MY CASTLE AT SKOR!
NOT FAR FROM THE COAST, ANOTHER COMPANY MAKES ITS LEISURELY WAY! THE KING'S WARD, LADY ROSAMUND, HAS LEFT CAMELOT CASTLE FAR BEHIND, AS SHE LEARNS THE ART OF FALCONRY...
THE BIRD IS HOODED UNTIL READY FOR FLIGHT, MY LADY!
HOW PROUD AND FIERCE HE IS, EVEN THOUGH BLINDED BY THE HOOD! TAKE A LESSON FROM THIS BIRD, SIR PERCY!
NAY, FAIR LADY, FIERCENESS IN ANY FORM MAKES ME SHUDDER! I AM NO FIGHTING MAN! I PITY HIM HIS HOOD THAT DENIES HIM THE SIGHT OF YOUR BEAUTY!
YOU TURN A PHRASE WELL, SIR! A PITY YOU SHRINK FROM HANDLING LANCE OR SWORD WITH EQUAL DEXTERITY!
THE SUN WAS WARM UPON THEM, BUT FROM THE TREES BOUNDING THE TRAIL, ICE-BLUE EYES WATCHED THEIR PROGRESS...
BY THE SWORD OF ODIN, THIS MAID IS FAIR! SHE SHALL BE MY BRIDE! MAKE READY!
WHAT CARRY YOU IN THE BASKETS ON YON POOR BLACK BEAST? ARMOR? ARMS?
NAY! THE THOUGHT OF ARMS MAKES ME ILL! 'TIS SWEETS AND FANCIES FOR THE LADIES!
2

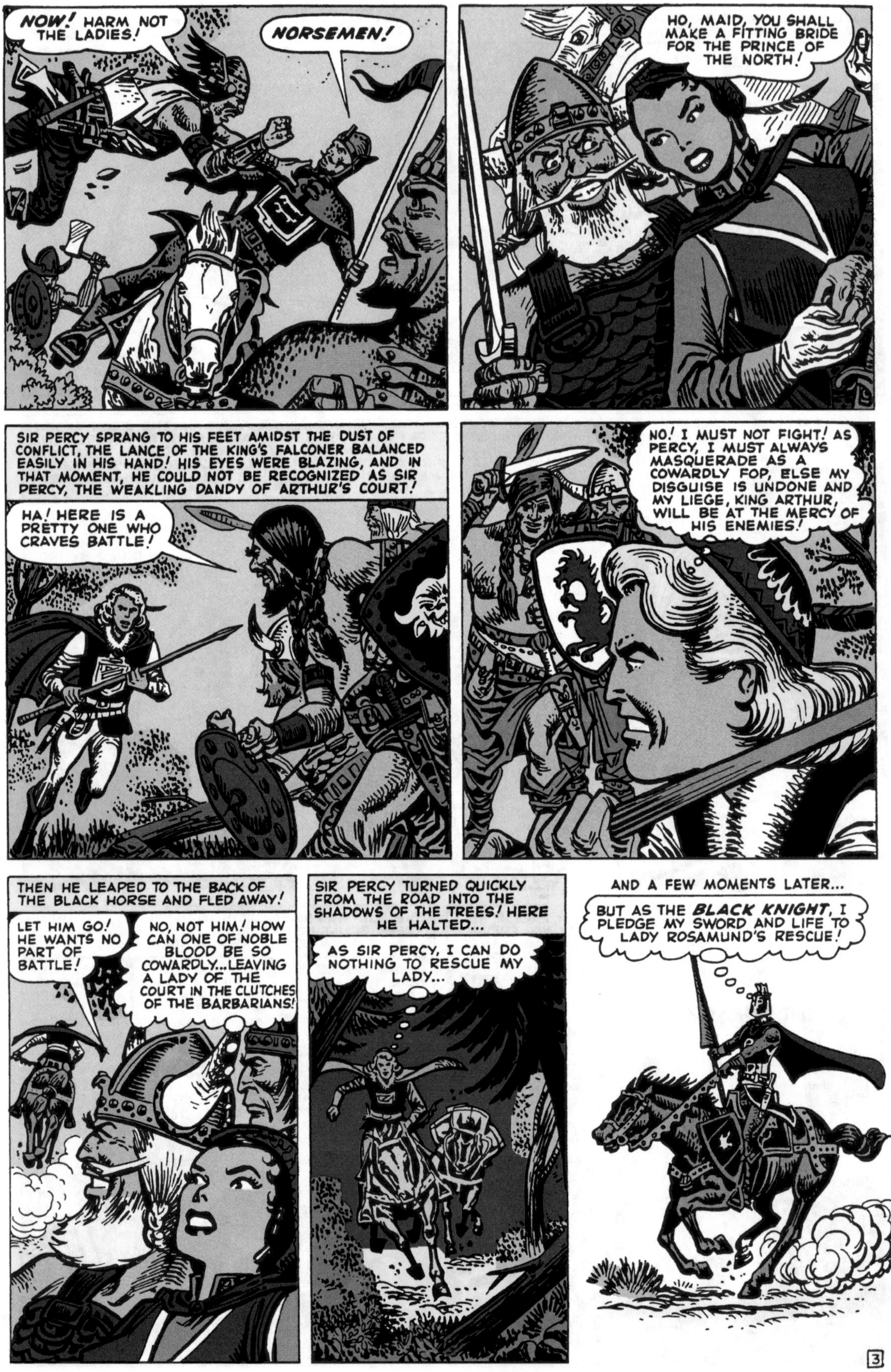
NOW! HARM NOT THE LADIES!
NORSEMEN!
HO, MAID, YOU SHALL MAKE A FITTING BRIDE FOR THE PRINCE OF THE NORTH!
SIR PERCY SPRANG TO HIS FEET AMIDST THE DUST OF CONFLICT, THE LANCE OF THE KING'S FALCONER BALANCED EASILY IN HIS HAND! HIS EYES WERE BLAZING, AND IN THAT MOMENT, HE COULD NOT BE RECOGNIZED AS SIR PERCY, THE WEAKLING DANDY OF ARTHUR'S COURT!
HA! HERE IS A PRETTY ONE WHO CRAVES BATTLE!
NO! I MUST NOT FIGHT! AS PERCY, I MUST ALWAYS MASQUERADE AS A COWARDLY FOP, ELSE MY DISGUISE IS UNDONE AND MY LIEGE, KING ARTHUR, WILL BE AT THE MERCY OF HIS ENEMIES!
THEN HE LEAPED TO THE BACK OF THE BLACK HORSE AND FLED AWAY!
LET HIM GO! HE WANTS NO PART OF BATTLE!
NO, NOT HIM! HOW CAN ONE OF NOBLE BLOOD BE SO COWARDLY...LEAVING A LADY OF THE COURT IN THE CLUTCHES OF THE BARBARIANS!
SIR PERCY TURNED QUICKLY FROM THE ROAD INTO THE SHADOWS OF THE TREES! HERE HE HALTED...
AS SIR PERCY, I CAN DO NOTHING TO RESCUE MY LADY...
AND A FEW MOMENTS LATER...
BUT AS THE BLACK KNIGHT, I PLEDGE MY SWORD AND LIFE TO LADY ROSAMUND'S RESCUE!

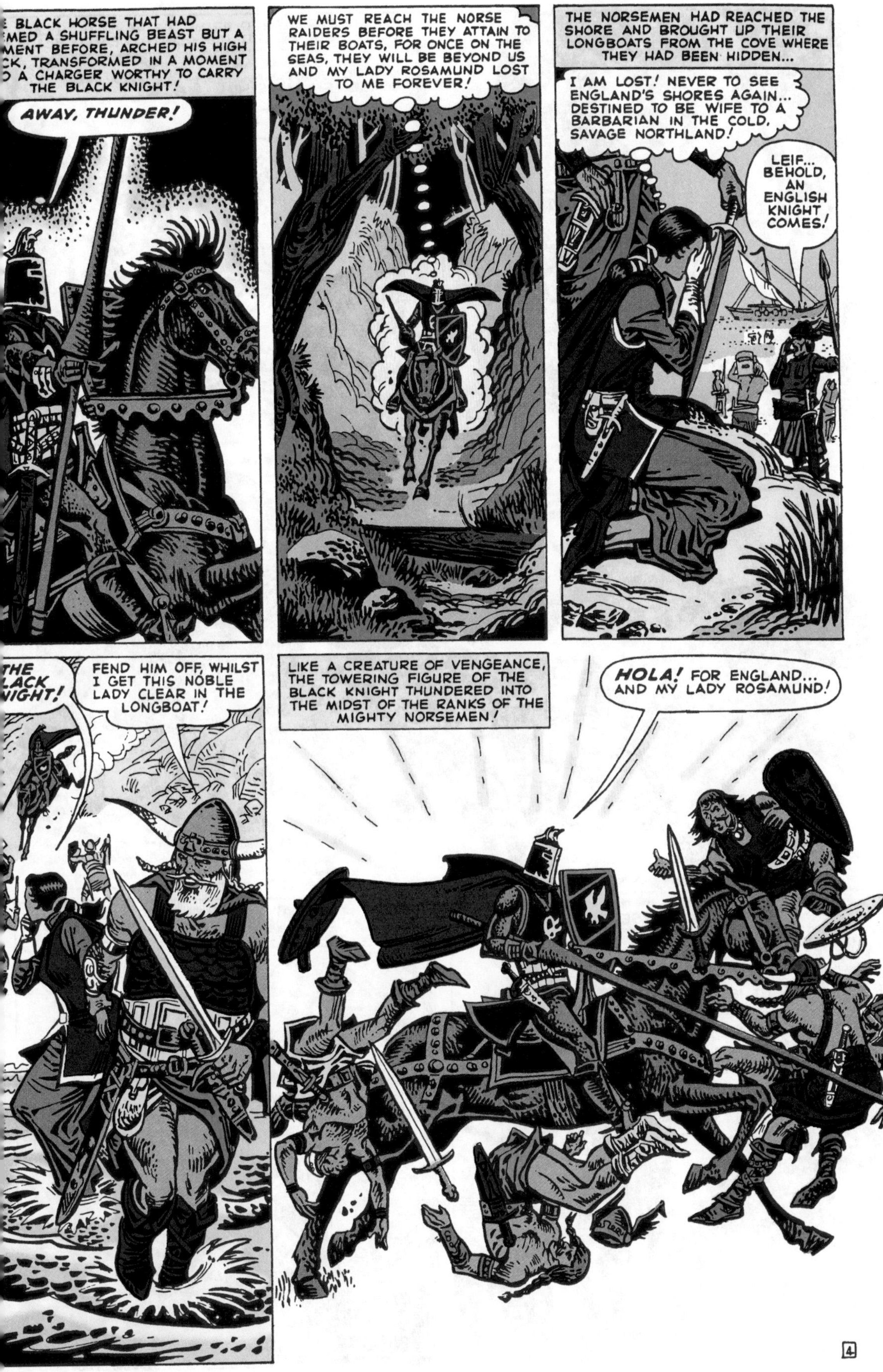

E BLACK HORSE THAT HAD
EMED A SHUFFLING BEAST BUT A
MENT BEFORE, ARCHED HIS HIGH
CK, TRANSFORMED IN A MOMENT
O A CHARGER WORTHY TO CARRY
THE BLACK KNIGHT!
AWAY, THUNDER!
WE MUST REACH THE NORSE RAIDERS BEFORE THEY ATTAIN TO THEIR BOATS, FOR ONCE ON THE SEAS, THEY WILL BE BEYOND US AND MY LADY ROSAMUND LOST TO ME FOREVER!
THE NORSEMEN HAD REACHED THE SHORE AND BROUGHT UP THEIR LONGBOATS FROM THE COVE WHERE THEY HAD BEEN HIDDEN...
I AM LOST! NEVER TO SEE ENGLAND'S SHORES AGAIN... DESTINED TO BE WIFE TO A BARBARIAN IN THE COLD, SAVAGE NORTHLAND!
LEIF... BEHOLD, AN ENGLISH KNIGHT COMES!
THE LACK NIGHT!
FEND HIM OFF, WHILST I GET THIS NOBLE LADY CLEAR IN THE LONGBOAT!
LIKE A CREATURE OF VENGEANCE, THE TOWERING FIGURE OF THE BLACK KNIGHT THUNDERED INTO THE MIDST OF THE RANKS OF THE MIGHTY NORSEMEN!
HOLA! FOR ENGLAND... AND MY LADY ROSAMUND!

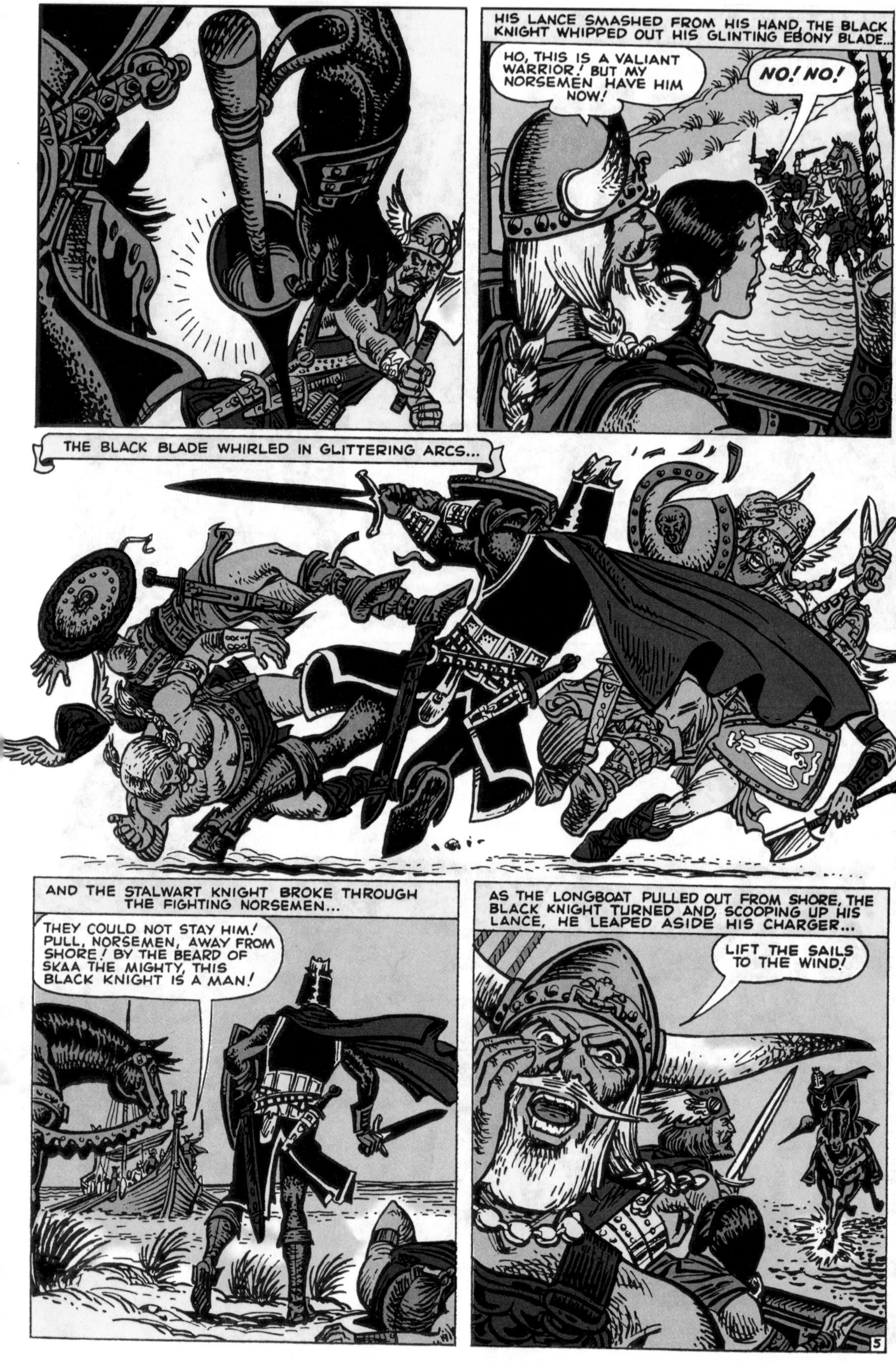
HIS LANCE SMASHED FROM HIS HAND, THE BLACK KNIGHT WHIPPED OUT HIS GLINTING EBONY BLADE...
HO, THIS IS A VALIANT WARRIOR! BUT MY NORSEMEN HAVE HIM NOW!
NO! NO!
THE BLACK BLADE WHIRLED IN GLITTERING ARCS...
AND THE STALWART KNIGHT BROKE THROUGH THE FIGHTING NORSEMEN...
THEY COULD NOT STAY HIM! PULL, NORSEMEN, AWAY FROM SHORE! BY THE BEARD OF SKAA THE MIGHTY, THIS BLACK KNIGHT IS A MAN!
AS THE LONGBOAT PULLED OUT FROM SHORE, THE BLACK KNIGHT TURNED AND, SCOOPING UP HIS LANCE, HE LEAPED ASIDE HIS CHARGER...
LIFT THE SAILS TO THE WIND!
5

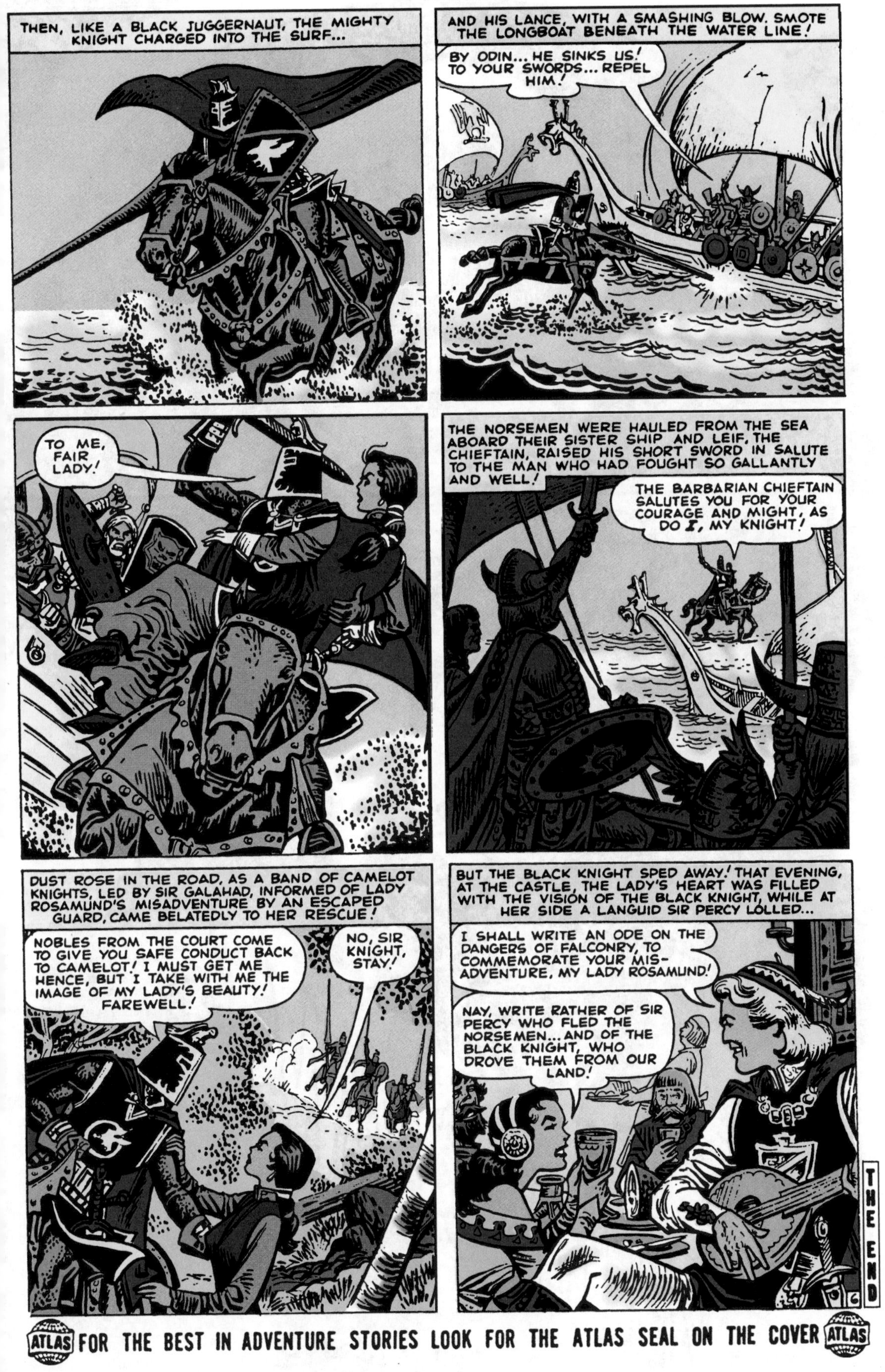
THEN, LIKE A BLACK JUGGERNAUT, THE MIGHTY KNIGHT CHARGED INTO THE SURF...
AND HIS LANCE, WITH A SMASHING BLOW. SMOTE THE LONGBOAT BENEATH THE WATER LINE!
BY ODIN... HE SINKS US! TO YOUR SWORDS... REPEL HIM!
TO ME, FAIR LADY!
THE NORSEMEN WERE HAULED FROM THE SEA ABOARD THEIR SISTER SHIP AND LEIF, THE CHIEFTAIN, RAISED HIS SHORT SWORD IN SALUTE TO THE MAN WHO HAD FOUGHT SO GALLANTLY AND WELL!
THE BARBARIAN CHIEFTAIN SALUTES YOU FOR YOUR COURAGE AND MIGHT, AS DO I, MY KNIGHT!
DUST ROSE IN THE ROAD, AS A BAND OF CAMELOT KNIGHTS, LED BY SIR GALAHAD, INFORMED OF LADY ROSAMUND'S MISADVENTURE BY AN ESCAPED GUARD, CAME BELATEDLY TO HER RESCUE!
NOBLES FROM THE COURT COME TO GIVE YOU SAFE CONDUCT BACK TO CAMELOT! I MUST GET ME HENCE, BUT I TAKE WITH ME THE IMAGE OF MY LADY'S BEAUTY! FAREWELL!
NO, SIR KNIGHT, STAY!
BUT THE BLACK KNIGHT SPED AWAY! THAT EVENING, AT THE CASTLE, THE LADY'S HEART WAS FILLED WITH THE VISION OF THE BLACK KNIGHT, WHILE AT HER SIDE A LANGUID SIR PERCY LOLLED...
I SHALL WRITE AN ODE ON THE DANGERS OF FALCONRY, TO COMMEMORATE YOUR MIS-ADVENTURE, MY LADY ROSAMUND!
NAY, WRITE RATHER OF SIR PERCY WHO FLED THE NORSEMEN... AND OF THE BLACK KNIGHT, WHO DROVE THEM FROM OUR LAND!
THE END
6

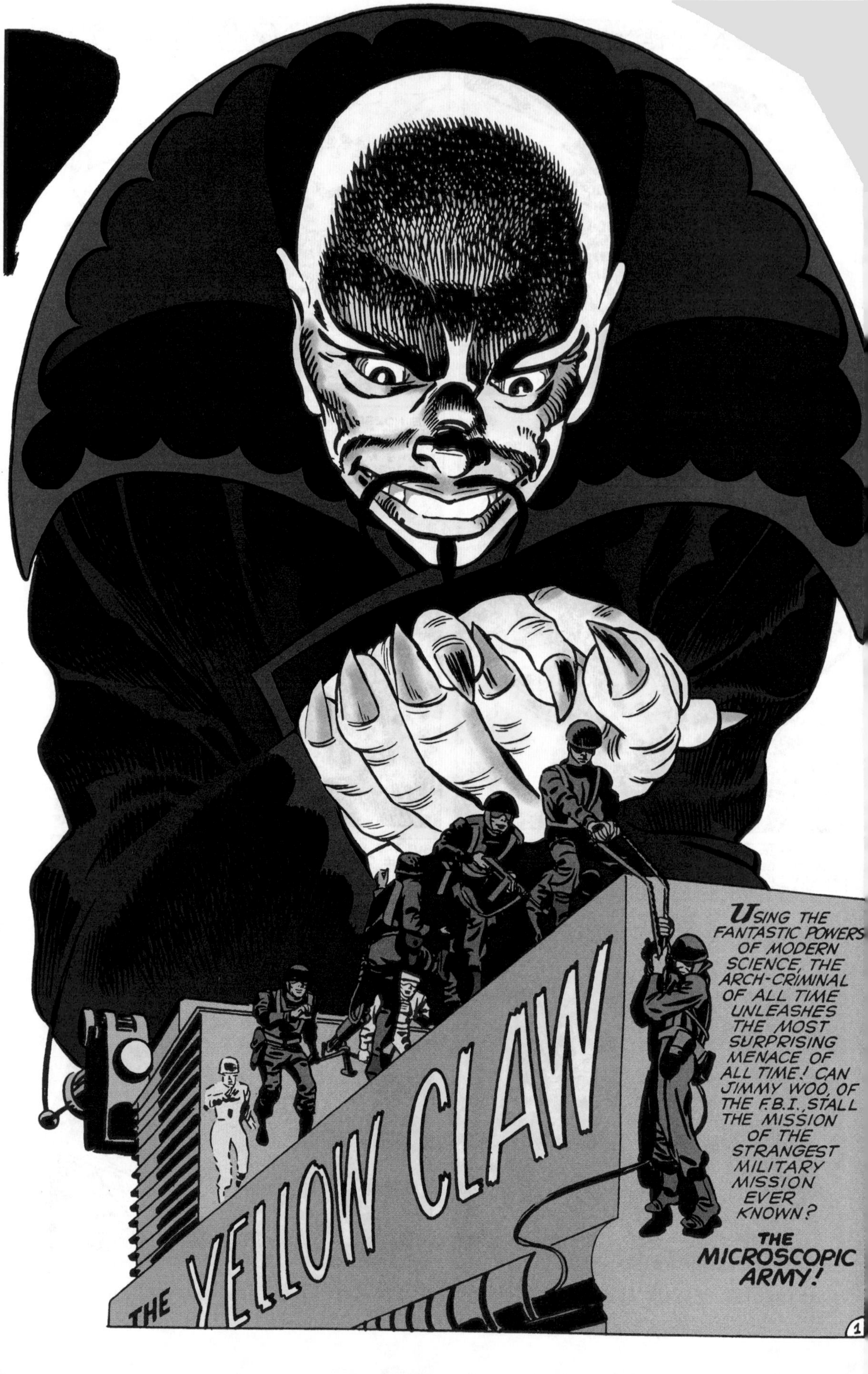
USING THE FANTASTIC POWERS OF MODERN SCIENCE, THE ARCH-CRIMINAL OF ALL TIME UNLEASHES THE MOST SURPRISING MENACE OF ALL TIME! CAN JIMMY WOO, OF THE F.B.I. STALL THE MISSION OF THE STRANGEST MILITARY MISSION EVER KNOWN?
THE YELLOW CLAW
THE MICROSCOPIC ARMY!
1

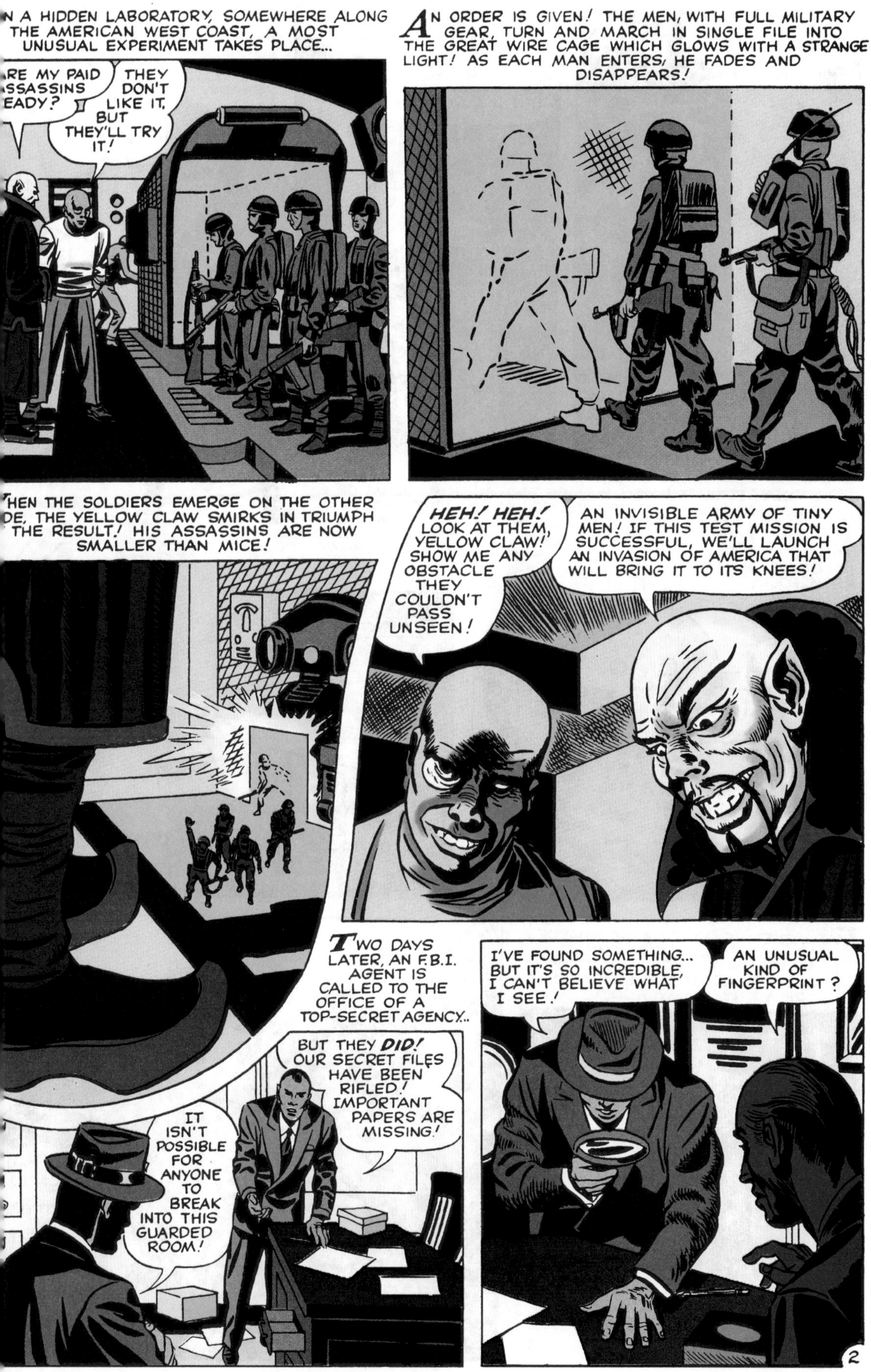
N A HIDDEN LABORATORY, SOMEWHERE ALONG THE AMERICAN WEST COAST, A MOST UNUSUAL EXPERIMENT TAKES PLACE...
RE MY PAID SSASSINS EADY?
THEY DON'T LIKE IT, BUT THEY'LL TRY IT!
AN ORDER IS GIVEN! THE MEN, WITH FULL MILITARY GEAR, TURN AND MARCH IN SINGLE FILE INTO THE GREAT WIRE CAGE WHICH GLOWS WITH A STRANGE LIGHT! AS EACH MAN ENTERS, HE FADES AND DISAPPEARS!
HEN THE SOLDIERS EMERGE ON THE OTHER DE, THE YELLOW CLAW SMIRKS IN TRIUMPH THE RESULT! HIS ASSASSINS ARE NOW SMALLER THAN MICE!
HEH! HEH! LOOK AT THEM, YELLOW CLAW! SHOW ME ANY OBSTACLE THEY COULDN'T PASS UNSEEN!
AN INVISIBLE ARMY OF TINY MEN! IF THIS TEST MISSION IS SUCCESSFUL, WE'LL LAUNCH AN INVASION OF AMERICA THAT WILL BRING IT TO ITS KNEES!
TWO DAYS LATER, AN F.B.I. AGENT IS CALLED TO THE OFFICE OF A TOP-SECRET AGENCY...
IT ISN'T POSSIBLE FOR ANYONE TO BREAK INTO THIS GUARDED ROOM!
BUT THEY DID! OUR SECRET FILES HAVE BEEN RIFLED! IMPORTANT PAPERS ARE MISSING!
I'VE FOUND SOMETHING... BUT IT'S SO INCREDIBLE, I CAN'T BELIEVE WHAT I SEE!
AN UNUSUAL KIND OF FINGERPRINT?

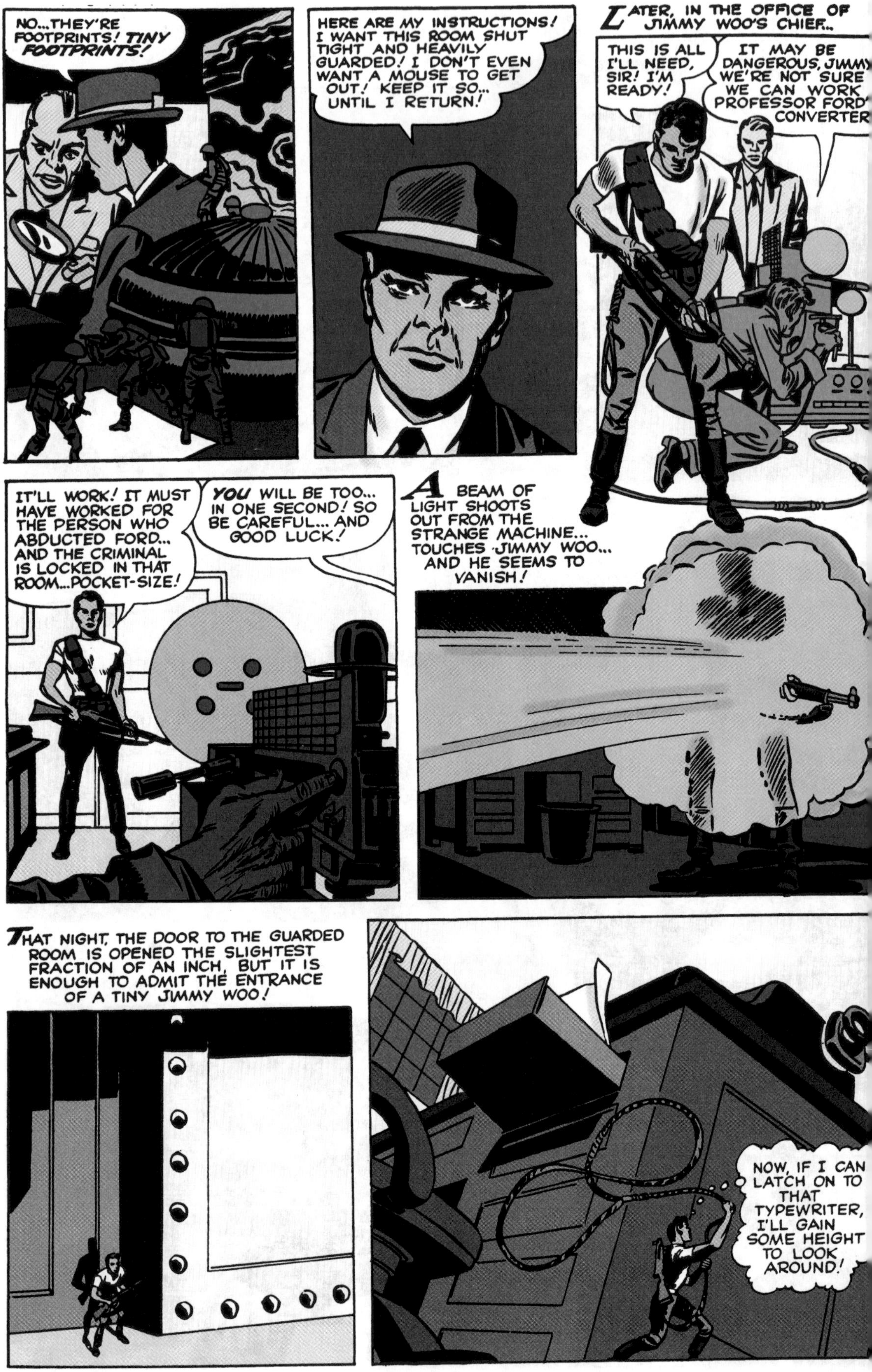
NO...THEY'RE FOOTPRINTS! TINY FOOTPRINTS!
HERE ARE MY INSTRUCTIONS! I WANT THIS ROOM SHUT TIGHT AND HEAVILY GUARDED! I DON'T EVEN WANT A MOUSE TO GET OUT! KEEP IT SO... UNTIL I RETURN!
LATER, IN THE OFFICE OF JIMMY WOO'S CHIEF..
THIS IS ALL I'LL NEED, SIR! I'M READY!
IT MAY BE DANGEROUS, JIMMY WE'RE NOT SURE WE CAN WORK PROFESSOR FORD' CONVERTER
IT'LL WORK! IT MUST HAVE WORKED FOR THE PERSON WHO ABDUCTED FORD... AND THE CRIMINAL IS LOCKED IN THAT ROOM...POCKET-SIZE!
YOU WILL BE TOO... IN ONE SECOND! SO BE CAREFUL... AND GOOD LUCK!
A BEAM OF LIGHT SHOOTS OUT FROM THE STRANGE MACHINE... TOUCHES JIMMY WOO... AND HE SEEMS TO VANISH!
THAT NIGHT, THE DOOR TO THE GUARDED ROOM IS OPENED THE SLIGHTEST FRACTION OF AN INCH, BUT IT IS ENOUGH TO ADMIT THE ENTRANCE OF A TINY JIMMY WOO!
NOW, IF I CAN LATCH ON TO THAT TYPEWRITER, I'LL GAIN SOME HEIGHT TO LOOK AROUND!

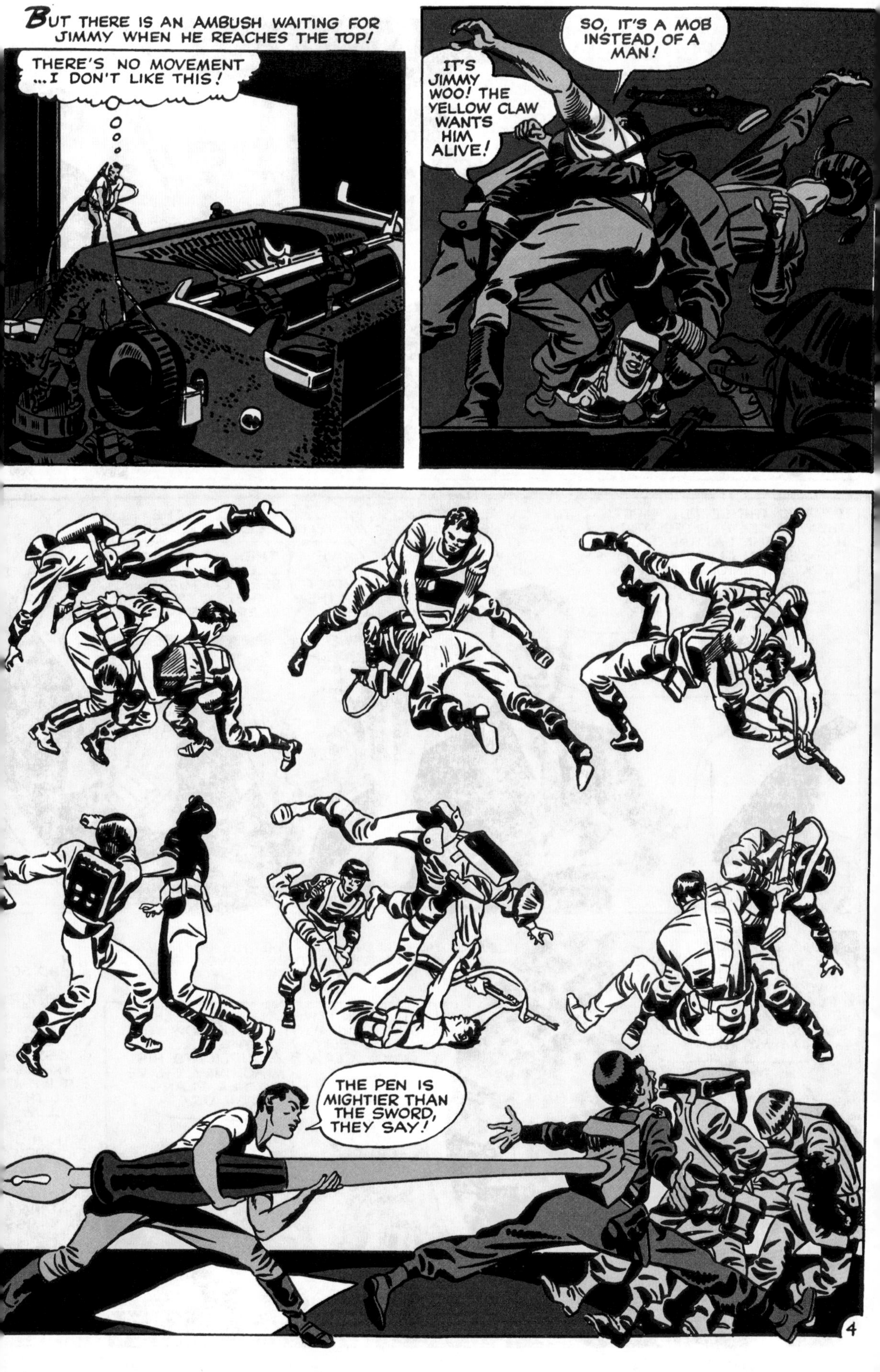

BUT THERE IS AN AMBUSH WAITING FOR JIMMY WHEN HE REACHES THE TOP!
THERE'S NO MOVEMENT ...I DON'T LIKE THIS!
IT'S JIMMY WOO! THE YELLOW CLAW WANTS HIM ALIVE!
SO, IT'S A MOB INSTEAD OF A MAN!
THE PEN IS MIGHTIER THAN THE SWORD, THEY SAY!

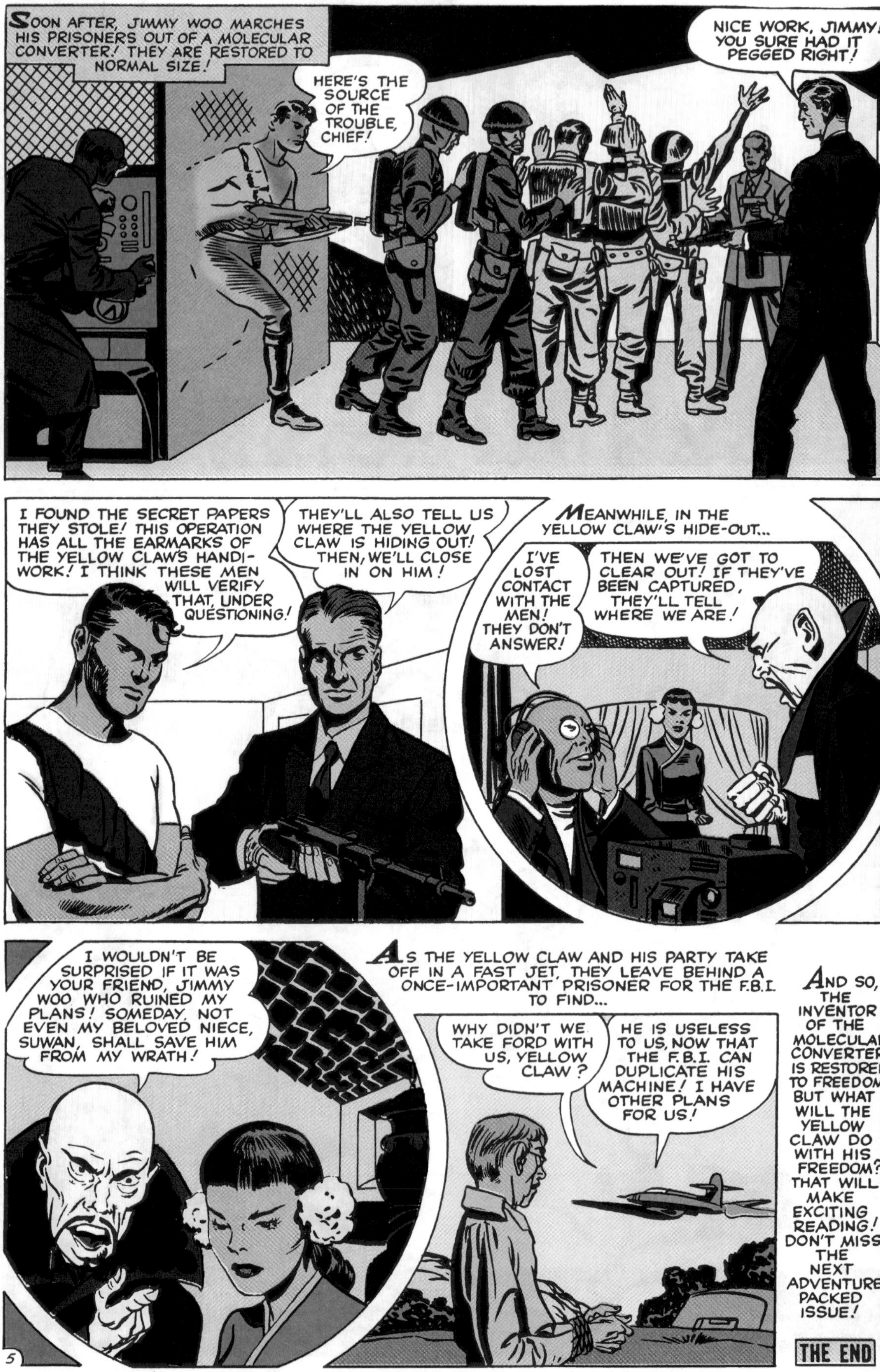
SOON AFTER, JIMMY WOO MARCHES HIS PRISONERS OUT OF A MOLECULAR CONVERTER! THEY ARE RESTORED TO NORMAL SIZE!
HERE'S THE SOURCE OF THE TROUBLE, CHIEF!
NICE WORK, JIMMY! YOU SURE HAD IT PEGGED RIGHT!
I FOUND THE SECRET PAPERS THEY STOLE! THIS OPERATION HAS ALL THE EARMARKS OF THE YELLOW CLAW'S HANDI-WORK! I THINK THESE MEN WILL VERIFY THAT, UNDER QUESTIONING!
THEY'LL ALSO TELL US WHERE THE YELLOW CLAW IS HIDING OUT! THEN, WE'LL CLOSE IN ON HIM!
MEANWHILE, IN THE YELLOW CLAW'S HIDE-OUT...
I'VE LOST CONTACT WITH THE MEN! THEY DON'T ANSWER!
THEN WE'VE GOT TO CLEAR OUT! IF THEY'VE BEEN CAPTURED, THEY'LL TELL WHERE WE ARE!
I WOULDN'T BE SURPRISED IF IT WAS YOUR FRIEND, JIMMY WOO WHO RUINED MY PLANS! SOMEDAY, NOT EVEN MY BELOVED NIECE, SUWAN, SHALL SAVE HIM FROM MY WRATH!
AS THE YELLOW CLAW AND HIS PARTY TAKE OFF IN A FAST JET, THEY LEAVE BEHIND A ONCE-IMPORTANT PRISONER FOR THE F.B.I. TO FIND...
WHY DIDN'T WE TAKE FORD WITH US, YELLOW CLAW?
HE IS USELESS TO US, NOW THAT THE F.B.I. CAN DUPLICATE HIS MACHINE! I HAVE OTHER PLANS FOR US!
AND SO, THE INVENTOR OF THE MOLECULAR CONVERTER IS RESTORED TO FREEDOM BUT WHAT WILL THE YELLOW CLAW DO WITH HIS FREEDOM? THAT WILL MAKE EXCITING READING! DON'T MISS THE NEXT ADVENTURE PACKED ISSUE!
THE END